The Quantified Process Approach to Neuropsychological Assessment

STUDIES ON NEUROPSYCHOLOGY, NEUROLOGY AND COGNITION

Series Editor:

Linas Bieliauskas, Ph.D.
University of Michigan, Ann Arbor, MI, USA

Other titles in this series:

Fundamentals of Functional Brain Imaging: A Guide to the Methods and their Applications to Psychology and Behavioral Neuroscience. Andrew C. Papanicolaou

Forensic Neuropsychology: Fundamentals and Practice. Edited by Jerry J. Sweet

Neuropsychological Differential Diagnosis. Konstantine K. Zakzanis, Larry Leach, and Edith Kaplan

Minority and Cross-Cultural Aspects of Neuropsychological Assessment. Edited by F. Richard Ferraro

Ethical Issues in Clinical Neuropsychology. Edited by Shane S. Bush and Michael L. Drexler

Practice of Child-Clinical Neuropsychology: An Introduction. Byron P. Rourke, Harry van der Vlugt, and Sean B. Rourke

The Practice of Clinical Neuropsychology. A Survey of Practice and Settings. Edited by Greg J. Lamberty, John C. Courtney, and Robert L. Heilbronner

Neuropsychological Rehabilitation: Theory and Practice. Edited by Barbara E. Wilson *Traumatic Brain Injury in Sports. An International Neuropsychological Perspective.* Edited by Mark R. Lovell, Ruben J. Echemendia, Jeffrey T. Barth, and Michael W. Collins

Methodological and Biostatistical Foundations of Clinical Neuropsychology and Medical and Health Disciplines. Edited by Domenic V. Cicchetti and Byron P. Rourke

A Casebook of Ethical Challenges in Neuropsychology. Edited by Shane S. Bush *Neurobehavioral Toxicology: Neurological and Neuropsychological Perspectives. Volume I Foundations and Methods.* Stanley Berent and James W. Albers

Neurobehavioral Toxicology: Neurological and Neuropsychological Perspectives. Volume II Peripheral Nervous System. James W. Albers and Stanley Berent

Geriatric Neuropsychology: Practice Essentials. Edited by Shane S. Bush and Thomas A. Martin

Brain Injury Treatment: Theories and Practices. Jose Leon-Carrion, Klaus R. H. Von Wild, and George Zitnay

The Quantified Process Approach to Neuropsychological Assessment

Edited by

Amir M. Poreh

Psychology Press
Taylor & Francis Group
New York London

First Published in 2006
by Psychology Press
Taylor & Francis Group
711 Third Avenue
New York, NY 10017

Published in Great Britain
by Psychology Press
Taylor & Francis Group
27 Church Road, Hove
East Sussex BN3 2FA

First issued in paperback 2014

Psychology Press is an imprint of the Taylor and Francis Group, an informa business

Typeset in Times by Macmillan India, Bangalore, India

Cover design by Jim Wilkie

Library of Congress Cataloging-in-Publication Data
The quantified process approach to neuropsychological assessment / edited by Amir Poreh. – 1st ed.
p. cm.
Includes bibliographical references and indexes.
ISBN 1-84169-456-8 (hardback : alk. paper)
1. Neuropsychological tests. I. Poreh, Amir.
RC386.6.N48Q36 2006
616.8′0475–dc22

2005035530

ISBN13: 978-1-84169-456-6 (hbk)
ISBN13: 978-1-138-00623-2 (hbk)

To my loving wife:

Eshet chayil mi yimtza v'rachok mip'ninim michrah

[An accomplished woman, who can find? Far beyond pearls is her value]

Contents

List of figures

List of tables

About the editor

Amir M. Poreh, Ph.D., is an Assistant Professor and Director of the Undergraduate Program in the Department of Psychology at Cleveland State University. He previously held a faculty position at Hebrew University in the Department of Psychology, and served for 9 years as the staff neuropsychologist in the Department of Neurosurgery at Sheba Medical Center. In this setting, he conducted evaluations during carotid artery amobarbital injections (Wada), intra-operative as well as pre- and post-surgical neuropsychological evaluations. During that period he also served as a forensic expert, and a consultant to the Israeli Social Security, Israeli Ministry of Defense – Department of Rehabilitation, Israeli Defense Industries (TAAS), and Israeli Aircraft Industries. Dr. Poreh is an active member of the International Neuropsychological Society, National Academy of Neuropsychology, and has published more than 30 articles and book chapters in the field of neuropsychology.

List of contributors

Daniel N. Allen, Ph.D., University of Nevada, Las Vegas, NV

Bradley N. Axelrod, Ph.D., John D. Dingell Department of Veterans Affairs Medical Center, Detroit, MI

W. Keith Berg, Ph.D., University of Florida, Gainesville, FL

L. Dana Byrd, Ph.D., Columbia University/New York Psychiatric Institute, New York, NY

Joshua E. Caron, M.A., University of Nevada, Las Vegas, NV

Gerald Goldstein, Ph.D., VA Pittsburgh Healthcare System, Pittsburgh, PA

Nancy Hebben, Ph.D., Harvard Medical School, Boston, MA

Anita M. Hubley, Ph.D., The University of British Columbia, Vancouver, BC, Canada

Amy J. Jak, Ph.D., Veterans Medical Research Foundation, VA San Diego Healthcare System, San Diego, CA

David S. Kreiner, Ph.D., Central Missouri State University, Warrensburg, MO

Greg J. Lamberty, Ph.D., Noran Neurological Clinic, Minneapolis, MN

David W. Loring, Ph.D., University of Florida, Gainesville, FL

Christine A. MacDonald, M.S., Temple University, Philadelphia, PA

Joseph P. H. McNamara, M.S., University of Florida, Gainesville, FL

William Milberg, Ph.D., GRECC, VA Boston Healthcare, Boston, MA

Morris Moscovitch, Ph.D., Baycrest Centre for Geriatric Care, and University of Toronto, Toronto, ON, Canada

Megan E. O'Connell, M.A., University of Victoria, Victoria, BC, Canada

Amir M. Poreh, Ph.D., Cleveland State University, Cleveland, OH

Joseph H. Ricker, Ph.D., University of Pittsburgh, Pittsburgh, PA

Joseph J. Ryan, Ph.D., Central Missouri State University, Warrensburg, MO

Maria T. Schultheis, Ph.D., Drexel University, Philadelphia, PA

Paula K. Shear, Ph.D., University of Cincinnati, Cincinnati, OH

Daniel J. Slick, Ph.D., BC's Children's Hospital, Vancouver, BC, Canada

Esther Strauss, Ph.D., University of Victoria, Victoria, BC, Canada

Angela K. Troyer, Ph.D., Baycrest Centre for Geriatric Care, Toronto, ON, Canada

Holly Tuokko, Ph.D., University of Victoria, Victoria, BC, Canada

Eli Vakil, Ph.D., Bar-Ilan University, Ramat-Gan, Israel

John L. Woodard, Ph.D., Rosalind Franklin University of Medicine and Science, North Chicago, IL

From the series editor

Quantified and quantifiable measurement is the bread and butter of clinical neuropsychological assessment. This new addition to our series, *The Quantified Process Approach to Neuropsychological Assessment*, edited by Amir M. Poreh, compiles the most current information on many of the tests and measures used in contemporary assessment. As pointed out in the preface by David W. Loring, this volume gives "insight by reliably demonstrating specific brain–behavior relationships in a systematic fashion."

In keeping with the focus of our series, Dr. Poreh has melded solid clinical applications looking at cognitive processes with up-to-date research foundations for the measures. The tests covered a range from quantification (and an outline of models for quantification) of the Boston Process Approach to derived Trail Making Test indices, to measures of suboptimal performance. This volume will encourage individual clinicians to look behind the numbers when interpreting their test data, to achieve a greater understanding of where the numbers come from, and how they relate to brain function. As such, the volume will prove valuable to all who strive to appreciate psychometrics and the limits as well as its promise of cognitive measurement.

Dr. Poreh provides a most welcome extension to our series and we trust it will find a valuable place on the bookshelf of students, practitioners, and scientists who seek to better understand and extend the sophistication of quantifying the assessment of behavior.

Linas A. Bieliauskas
Ann Arbor
February, 2006

Preface

David W. Loring

Understanding classic brain–behavior relationships and neurobehavioral syndromes was the primary attraction that led many of us to choose careers in neuropsychology. Patients with hemispatial neglect or confabulatory amnestic syndrome continue to amaze even seasoned neuropsychologists, but demonstrate just a portion of the visible spectrum of behavior change associated with neurological injury. These examples, of course, are well known and well described. In contrast, the discovery of a previously unknown relationship, particularly when it helps to clarify either an unusual clinical presentation or assists with patient management, continues to motivate our field to better understand the brain and the behavioral processes that it directs.

During recent years, however, much of the literature on neuropsychological assessment has tended to emphasize its sensitivity to a monolithic but poorly operationalized construct of "brain damage" following traumatic brain injury, and whether specific neuropsychological findings can be trusted to be valid and reflective of a patient's true abilities. Almost without exception, professional neuropsychological journals contain multiple papers in each issue reporting sensitivity of a particular test or test battery to either "brain damage," "malingering," or both. Similarly, malingering and forensic neuropsychology books are also top-selling texts in the field. Of course, since the majority of neuropsychologists, at least in North America, are involved from time to time in either disability determination or medico-legal consultation, these types of articles and books increase the skill of clinicians performing assessments in which large sums of money potentially lie in the balance.

It is against this backdrop that the volume on *The Quantified Process Approach to Neuropsychological Assessment*, edited by Amir M. Poreh, appears. The contents of this volume form a stark contrast with much of medico-legal application of neuropsychology, and remind the reader that neuropsychology emerged as a discipline to better understand how the brain works and the ways in which various brain injuries may selectively alter neuropsychological performance. Even Halstead's investigations with tests that subsequently became the Halstead–Reitan Battery, a battery that few would suggest lends itself to a process-oriented evaluation given its purported reliance on "blind interpretation," was originally developed to assess differential performances of frontal patients to those with nonfrontal lesions (Halstead, 1947).

The present volume describing the quantified process approach to neuropsychological assessment is a welcome addition to those neuropsychologists who want to take a peek behind neuropsychological numbers to better characterize a patient's performance when presented with specific neuropsychological tasks. Not only does it supply tools that will provide new insight into brain–behavior relationships, but more importantly, will provide this insight by reliably demonstrating specific behavior–behavior relationships in a systemic fashion. Thus, verification of an independent researcher will have the organizational structure to apply the same clinical methods to qualitative assessment.

Great diversity exists in the chapters, and in that diversity, there will be something of interest to benefit most practitioners of neuropsychology. The content ranges from historical, to statistical and mathematical, to measures that clarify test performances, to development of measures of inadequately assessed neuropsychological constructs.

The immediate clinical applicability of information in this volume will depend in part on the underlying usage rate of many of the primary procedures described. For example, it is probable that the Complex Figure is more widely used than the Hooper Visual Organization Test, and new approaches for analyzing the Complex Figure will have greater potential to be incorporated into the general neuropsychology community. Since patient responses for the Complex Figure are drawn rather than chosen as with the Hooper, there is a much greater opportunity to develop process-based systems to characterize performance. Block design also lends itself to process-oriented description of patient performance, and since this test forms part of most neuropsychological batteries, the techniques described in this book will be of potential value to many. Similarly, since verbal generative fluency tasks are common components to many neuropsychological assessments, the addition of switching and clustering measures, which can be derived from traditional assessment procedures, provide great potential, both for clinical and research applications. Thus, there is great potential for tests in current usage to be extended in a systematized fashion.

Other chapters are less "test" dependent. For example, although the method of scoring temporal order or Learning over Trials is described for the Rey Auditory Verbal Learning task, these specific methods can easily be generalized to other serial word-learning tasks. Because normative or reference information to guide interpretation will not be available, however, using these scoring approaches will limit their application to more research settings than immediate clinical evaluation.

On the opposite end of the spectrum are the approaches to scoring "clock drawing." Clock drawing is more of a procedure than a formal test, and is administered with multiple approaches using different times and scoring techniques. Information about the different approaches that have been used to quantify its qualitative features will hopefully spur clinicians who routinely evaluate elderly patients to consider adding this valuable measure to their assessment.

Of course, not everything that we can measure is important. Being able to measure constructs and derive new process measures by combining or developing information from existing procedures, however, is the necessary first step to evaluate their clinical and scientific merit. In this context, this volume is already a neuropsychological success.

Reference

Halstead, W. C. (1947). *Brain and intelligence*. Chicago: University of Chicago.

Part I

Fundamentals

The Quantified Process Approach is a novel methodological framework for improving traditional neuropsychological tests by quantitatively recording the process by which one solves traditional psychological tasks. Using this approach, an examiner can identify the contribution of various cognitive modules to the final test score. The tenets and paradigms of the Quantified Process Approach are discussed in Chapter 1. In Chapter 2, William Milberg and Nancy Hebben describe the historical antecedents and limitations of the Boston Process Approach, and provide the rationale for the paradigm shift and its advantages. The methodological hurdles of the Quantified Process Approach are discussed in Chapter 3.

1 A brief introduction to the Quantified Process Approach

Amir M. Poreh

Introduction

Neuropsychological assessment has been influenced and molded by different theoretical paradigms. As a result, a wide range of complimenting and conflicting assessment techniques have been developed throughout the years. Early on, many clinicians favored assessment techniques that use standardized "achievement" procedures, which employ nomothetic interpretation of test data (Halstead, 1947; Reitan, 1964). These techniques, incorporated in both fixed and flexible test batteries, were derived by psychologists trained predominantly in laboratories who emphasized classical test theory and related psychometric principles (see Franzen, 2000 for a review of this topic).

At the same time, some practicing neuropsychologists felt that the standardized assessment tools lack sufficient correlation brain functioning theories. These neuropsychologists developed a clinical approach to neuropsychological assessment that employed qualitative analysis of the processes and strategies by which examinees perform tests and solve problems (Goldstein, 1942; Luria, 1980; Luria & Majovski, 1977; Werner, 1937). This qualitative "process" approach relied heavily on single case studies, the use of nonstandardized measures, qualitative observations of patient performance, and employed ideographic interpretations of test data (Christensen, 1975; Luria, 1980).

Up until the early 1970s, the process approach was mainly employed in Europe. However, with the emergence of behavioral neurology and clinical/anatomical localization theories (Geschwind, 1965), it gained support in the United States, where it was further developed, albeit with some major alterations. First, American clinical researchers attempted to adapt this approach for traditional standardized neuropsychological assessment (Kaplan, 1983, 1990). Second, unlike the more traditional European process approach, attempts were made to operationally define the methods by which behavior was assessed (Milberg, Hebben, & Kaplan, 1996). Namely, procedures for testing clinical "limits" were defined, so as to enable repeated assessment. This development allowed for a more accurate evaluation of error patterns (Kaplan, 1988). As Edith Kaplan and her associates in the Boston metropolitan region conducted most of the seminal work on the process approach, this approach was termed the "Boston Process Approach".

As pointed out by Kaplan (1988):

> In general then, the (Boston) process approach to neuropsychological assessment differs from the fixed and flexible battery approaches in that the standardized and experimental tests are not scored in the standardized binary fashion (right or wrong), and in many cases are not administered in the standardized manner. It differs from the clinical investigative approach in that qualitative aspects of behavior are quantified and subjected to statistical analyses rather than just described, and that testing of clinical limits is operationally defined, repeatable, and quantifiable, as opposed to particularized for a given patient. (p. 130).

However, as noted by Erickson (1995), many of the insights and assertions of the proponents of the Boston Process Approach had not been subjected to either empirical inquiry or psychometric analyses. For example, although observations on the process and types of errors that characterize the performance of patients with lateralized brain-injury on the Block Design Test were reported in several book chapters in the past 30 years (Kaplan, 1988; Kaplan, Palmer, Weinstein, & Baker, 1981; Milberg et al., 1996), until recently they were not subjected to empirical systematic documentation or systematic research. Based on such examples, Erickson (1995) concluded, "more work is needed to undergrid many of the clinical assertions of the process approach."

Erickson's (1995) criticism echoes the debate among clinical psychologists regarding the relative merits of the clinical as opposed to the statistical method of inquiry. Whereas many clinicians assert that the qualitative process approach may improve the ecological validity of the traditional neuropsychological test battery, others, like Meehl (1954, 1957), have concluded that mechanical data collection, algorithmic combination, and statistical prediction are superior to the clinical collection, synthesis, and diagnostic method. Although this latter conclusion has often been criticized (i.e., Holt, 1988; Holt & Luborsky, 1958), by the 1980s a consensus regarding the merits of statistical prediction dominated the field (Dawes, 1994; Dawes, Faust, & Meehl, 1990; Richards & Wierzbicki, 1993; Turk & Salovey, 1989; Wiggins, 1981). As a result, the qualitative method of data collection and integration as advocated by supporters of the Boston Process Approach was criticized (Spreen & Strauss, 1998).

Given this, proponents of the Boston Process Approach started to develop new psychometrically sound measures based on advancements in cognitive information processing models. These new measures may be classified under the analytical approach to neuropsychological assessment (McKenna & Warrington, 1996). Examples of such measures include the California Verbal Learning Test (Delis, Kramer, Kaplan, & Ober, 1987) and the Revised Strategy Application Task (R-SAT) (Levin, Dawson, Boutet, Schwartz, & Stuss, 2000).

Parallel to the latter trend, researchers attempted to quantify the process by which subjects solve existing achievement tests. Although this trend represents a natural step in the evolution of the Boston Process Approach, it fundamentally departs from the traditional qualitative line of inquiry. In particular, such research strongly emphasizes standardized administration and scoring, allowing for the replicability of findings. Furthermore, this approach emphasizes both nomothetic data analysis as well as evaluation of the test results using robust criteria (Franzen, 2000; Hambleton, 1983; Stuss & Levin, 2002). Poreh (2000) suggested that the evolution in the study of the Boston Process Approach represents a paradigm shift in neuropsychological assessment and termed this collective body of new research the Quantified Process Approach.

The enterprise of quantifying the process approach (the Quantified Process Approach) is in its infancy, beginning only a decade ago. Much of the work in this area has been guided by the observations outlined in the teaching and publications of Edith Kaplan. Nevertheless, without a clear outline, researchers and clinicians have proceeded to quantify the process approach in a somewhat tangential way. Hence, from a theoretical perspective, it is very important to outline the basic methodologies that govern this process. Three such methodologies were outlined by Poreh (2000):

(1) *The "Satellite" Testing Paradigm* (Milberg et al., 1996): An approach by which new complimentary tasks are developed for the purpose of clarifying the test performance on an existing neuropsychological test.
(2) *The Composition Paradigm*: An approach by which data on a given test that have been largely overlooked are compiled and subsequently analyzed, resulting in new indices that are believed to reflect additional underlying constructs impacting test performance.
(3) *The Decomposition Paradigm*: An approach that investigates the relationship between test items of a given measure according to underlying facets, resulting in the development of new subscores.

Table 1.1 lists representative published additions and indexes classified by each of these three paradigms. A detailed discussion of the different paradigms follows.

The "Satellite" Testing Paradigm

The "Satellite" Testing Paradigm is characterized by the creation of complimentary tasks that aid clinicians in identifying, clarifying, and evaluating skills that underlie patient performance. Typical examples of this approach include the Wechsler Adult Intelligence Scale Revised as a Neuropsychological Instrument (WAIS-NI; Kaplan, Fein, Morris, & Delis, 1991) and the Wechsler Intelligence Scale for Children III as a Process Instrument (WISC-III PI; Kaplan, Fein, Kramer, Delis, & Morris, 1999). These test batteries were designed to supplement the Wechsler Intelligence Tests, and examine in a quantified fashion the qualitative aspects and problem-solving strategies

Table 1.1 A sample of Quantified Process Approach indexes and satellite tests

Methodology and tests	*References*
Satellite Tests	
Digit-Symbol Recognition	Collaer and Evans (1986)
Digit-Symbol Coding	Kelly and Britton (1996)
TMT Oral Version	Abraham, Axelrod, and Ricker (1996)
WMS-Russell's Revision	Russell (1975)
AVLT Incidental Learning	Vakil and Blachstein (1994)
ROCF Recognition	Meyer and Meyer (1995), Fastenau (1996)
Composition Paradigm	
Clock Drawing Scoring—6 Indexes	See Suhr, Grace, Allen, Nadler, and McKenna (1998) for a review
COWA Clustering & Switching	Troyer (1997)
ROCF Copying Strategy—10 Indexes	See Troyer and Wishart (1997) for a review
AVLT Gained and Lost Access Indexes	
Decomposition Paradigm	
WMS-Logical Prose Indexes	Vakil, Arbell, Gozlan, Hoofien, and Blachstein (1992), Kleinman and Waber (1994)
ROCF Global Local Indexes	Poreh and Shye (1998)
Category Test	Allen et al. (1999)

Note: TMT, Trail Making Test; WMS, Wechsler Memory Scale; AVLT, Rey Auditory Verbal Learning Test; ROCF, Rey–Osterrieth Complex Figure; COWA, Controlled Oral Word Association.

patients utilize on various subtests. The adaptation of the Digit-Symbol Subtest exemplifies this trend. Following Willoughby (1929) and Collaer and Evans (1986), Kaplan et al. (1991) added an optional Digit-Symbol-Incidental Learning portion in order to assess whether poor performance is due to a failure to learn or a failure to remember the Digit-Symbol combinations. A second optional procedure, the Digit-Symbol-Copy, requires the examinee to copy symbols without having to match them to numbers. Poor performance on this task purportedly reveals graphomotor deficits (Kelly & Britton, 1996; Wechsler, 1997).

Another satellite test is the Oral Paradigm of the Trail Making Test (TMT; Reitan, 1958). This test was designed to supplement the traditional TMT. Studies show that the Oral Paradigm of the TMT may be useful in controlling for motoric or visual spatial impairments, allowing for the clarification of errors on the original test (Abraham et al., 1996; Ricker & Axelrod, 1994; Ricker, Axelrod, & Houtler, 1996).

Additional examples of the Satellite Approach are Russell's (1975) revision of the Wechsler Memory Scale (WMS; Wechsler, 1945), which adds an evaluation of long-term recall to the test; Vakil and Blachstein's (1994) supplementary incidental learning task from the Rey Auditory Verbal Learning Test (AVLT; Rey, 1958); Meyer and Meyer's (1995) recognition task from the Rey–Osterrieth Complex Figure (ROCF; Osterrieth, 1944), and the Extended TMT (Stanczak, Lynch, McNeil, & Brown, 1998).

The Composition Paradigm

While the Satellite Testing Paradigm is characterized by the creation of new tasks that supplement existing tests, the Composition Paradigm allows for the generation of new indices for existing tests, by analyzing patterns of test-taking performance using previously collected data. The Controlled Oral Word Association Test (COWA; Spreen & Benton, 1969, 1977) and the AVLT will be used to exemplify the value of this general approach.

Since the early 1980s, studies of the COWA have been concerned with the use of categorical (semantic association) and phonemic (naming a word that starts with a certain letter) fluency indices. Early studies examined both of these indices for the purpose of differentiating between right and left hemisphere deficits (Milner, 1964; Parks et al., 1988; Perret, 1974). More recent studies have used the discrepancy between the above indices to distinguish between anterior as opposed to posterior damage to speech areas (Butters, Salmon, Granholm, Heindel, & Lyon, 1987; Gourovitch, Goldberg, & Weinberger, 1996; Monsch, Bondi, Butters, & Salmon, 1992). However, given the multiple factors that are involved in speech fluency, as affirmed by multiple brain imaging studies, no firm conclusions can be drawn from either of these methods.

To elucidate the contribution of different neurocognitive mechanisms to the COWA performance, Troyer et al. (1997) composed two new indices: clustering (i.e., the production of words within semantic or phonemic subcategories) and switching (i.e., the ability to shift between clusters). In a series of studies, they show that young adults generate more words and switch more often on the semantic fluency task than do older adults. On the phonemic fluency task, however, older participants produce larger clusters than younger participants. Additionally, they found that divided attention decreases both the number of words generated as well as switching ability on the phonemic fluency task only. Other researchers demonstrate the usefulness of Troyer et al.'s (1997) Composition Paradigm for both the understanding of the impact of acculturation on language functioning (Kempler, Teng, Dick, Taussig, & Davi, 1998) as well as the characteristics of language deficits of schizophrenic patients (Robert et al., 1998).

Woodard, Dunlosky, and Salthouse (1999) applied the composition paradigm to clarify trial-by-trial AVLT performance and thus rectify the test's inability to estimate encoding and consolidation deficits across adjacent test trials. To this end, they developed the "gained access" and "lost access" indices that provide the proportion of items recalled or not recalled (gained and lost items) on successive trials. Woodard et al. (1999) examined the validity of the above indices in a group of Alzheimer's patients and in a control group. They report that the former patients achieve both lower scores on the "gained access" index, suggesting that Alzheimer's disease impairs one's ability to produce a stable memory representation of new material in long-term memory, as well as higher scores on the "lost access" index, suggesting that they suffer from deficient memory consolidation, leading to rapid inter-trial forgetting, and, in turn, poor performance. Woodard et al. (1999) have thus concluded that this methodology may aid in uncovering cognitive processes that underlie Alzheimer's disease and may also be applicable for the evaluation of other impaired populations.

Many other researchers have developed new indices using the composition approach. These include, for example, the TMT indices (i.e., Lamberty, Putnam, Chatel, & Bieliauskas, 1994), copying strategy indices of the ROCF (Bennet-Levy, 1984; Binder, 1982; Bylsma, Carison, Schretlen, Zonderman, & Resnick, 1997; Hamby, Wilkins, & Barry, 1993; Osterrieth, 1944; Poreh, 2000; Stern et al., 1995; Visser, 1973; Waber & Holmes, 1986), hierarchical visual processing indexes for the Block Design Test (Fischer & Leavell, 1995; Kramer, Kaplan, Blusewicz, & Preston, 1991; Troyer, Cullum, Smernoff, & Kozora, 1994; Wilde, Boake, & Sherer, 2000; Zipf-Williams et al., 2000), Clock Drawing Test scoring indices (Freedman, Leach, Kaplan, & Winocur, 1994; Ishiai, Sugishita, Ichikawa, Gono, & Watabiki, 1993; Kozora & Cullum, 1996; Mendez, Ala, & Underwood, 1992; Nadler, Grace, White, Butters, & Malloy, 1996; Rouleau, Salmon, & Butters, 1996; Sunderland et al., 1989; Tuokko, Hadjistavropoulos, Miller, & Beattie, 1992, 2000; Watson, Arfken, & Birge, 1993), and the WMS-III supplemental thematic recall indices (Wechsler, 1997).

The Decomposition Paradigm

While the composition approach involves the creation of new indices, the Decomposition Paradigm develops new subscores that depict underlying facets and patterns of performance. Traditionally this has been accomplished using factor analytical methods. However, given that neuropsychological test scores are typically not normally distributed, such procedures are often not suitable. Thus, researchers have had to rely on the decomposition of existing scales based on theory-driven facet or nonparametric classification techniques. The use of this paradigm in the analysis of the Wechsler Memory Scale Logical Memory subtest (WMS-LP; Wechsler, 1981) and the ROCF (Osterrieth, 1944) will exemplify its value.

Vakil et al.'s (1992) application of the "depth of processing" theory of memory (Butters & Cermak, 1974) to the WMS-LP illustrates the use of a theoretically driven decomposition approach. Using a questionnaire, they distinguished between the most important, important, and least important units of the stories. They then sampled a group of closed head injured (CHI) patients and assessed their pattern of retrieving the stories. The results suggest that one can decompose the WMS-LP subtest sum score so as to more effectively evaluate the type of patient errors on this test.

Kleinman and Waber (1994) also decomposed the WMS-LP subtest sum score using theoretically based facets. Following Johnson, Bransford, Nyberg, and Cleary (1972), Sachs (1967), and Webster, Godlewski, Hanley, and Sowa (1992), they argue that the recollection of stories is guided by schemas which are activated when the story is heard or read. According to this model, subjects use the story's structure as a template for recall of the narrative. This template includes six structures: a setting, initiation event, internal response, attempt, direct consequence, and reaction. Using the above model, they proceeded to decompose the Anna Thompson story for the purpose of identifying the strategies used by children with and without leukemia to recall this logical prose subtest. Their ensuing analysis indicated that the control subjects relied on schemas to recall the story while the children with leukemia were unable to benefit from such strategies.

A similar strategy was employed to assess the multidimensional nature of the Category Test. Allen et al. (1999) factor analyzed the subtests. Similar to previous studies (Fischer & Dean, 1990), they demonstrated that subtests 1 and 2 tap into counting abilities, subtests 3 and 4 assess proportional reasoning, and subtests 5 and 6 require intact spatial reasoning, with subtest 7 loading on all factors.

Much like traditional factor analyses, the above studies illustrate that the decomposition of a test may produce multiple factor solutions and they should therefore be followed up by confirmatory studies. Addressing this need, Poreh and Shye (1998) examined several theoretically based decomposition models of the ROCF sum score, global and local as opposed to right-, left-, and middle-sided dimensions. Using Faceted Smallest Space Analysis, they evaluated the validity of these dimensions by examining the similarity of the ROCF elements in patients with well-documented structural brain lesions. In addition, using the more traditional Discriminant Function Analysis, they examined the diagnostic validity of the resulting ROCF indices. Both analyses suggested that the right-sided local elements of this figure are the most useful for discriminating between right- and left-hemisphere-damaged patients.

Conclusions

The proliferation of studies by different researchers in the last decade, which have quantitatively analyzed the processes by which individuals solve common neuropsychological tasks, confirm both the need and the value of the Quantitative Process Approach. The emergence of this approach is not coincidental. It compliments recent advances in functional brain imaging research, which allows us to observe the temporal activation of discrete brain regions during the performance of neurocognitive tasks. Using three patterns of analysis, important contributions toward the quantification of the Boston Process Approach have been made. However, it is noted that none of these studies have fully analyzed the process of performing a process task. This is not surprising, given that present day pencil and paper recording methods limit the ability to fully record such processes. Maximizing the recent advances of the Quantified Process Approach necessitates new complimentary technologies. Such technologies must be able to capture and digitize the process of performing neuropsychological tests in an ecologically valid manner. Examples include Poreh's (2004, 2005) recently developed software that employs a digital pen, voice recognition software, and online video cameras. Such technologies will not only improve the ability of neuropsychologists to observe how examinees solve neuropsychological tasks but may also allow them to apply complex algorithms that quantify such performance in real time. With the advent of such technologies and continual research, it is likely that this new approach will be integrated into mainstream neuropsychological assessment.

References

Abraham, E., Axelrod, B., & Ricker, J. (1996). Application of the Oral Trail Making Test. *Archives of Clinical Neuropsychology*, *11*, 697–701.

Allen, D. N., Goldstein, G., & Mariano, E. (1999). Is the Halstead Category Test a multidimensional instrument? *Journal of Clinical and Experimental Neuropsychology*, *21*(2), 237–244.

Bennet-Levy, J. (1984). Determinants of performance on the Rey–Osterrieth Complex Figure Test: An analysis and a new technique for single case assessment. *British Journal of Clinical Psychology*, *23*, 109–119.

Binder, L. M. (1982). Constructional strategies on complex figure drawings after unilateral brain damage. *Journal of Clinical Neuropsychology*, *4*, 51–88.

Butters, N., & Cermak, L. S. (1974). The role of cognitive factors in the memory disorders of alcoholic patients with the Korsakoff syndrome. *Annals of the New York Academy of Sciences*, *233*, 61–75.

Butters, N., Salmon, D. P., Granholm, E., Heindel, W., & Lyon, L. (1987). Neuropsychological differentiation of amnesic and dementing states. In S. M. Stahl & S. D. Iversen (Eds.), *Cognitive neurochemistry* (pp. 3–20). Oxford, UK: Oxford University Press.

Bylsma, F. W., Carison, M. C., Schretlen, D., Zonderman, A., & Resnick, S. (1997). Rey–Osterrieth Complex Figure Test (CFT) Q-Scores performance in 328 healthy adults ages 20 to 94. *Journal of the International Neuropsychological Society*, *3*, 70.

Christensen, A. (1975). *Luria's neuropsychological investigations*. New York: Spectrum.

Collaer, M. L., & Evans, J. R. (1986). A measure of short-term visual memory based on the WISC-R Coding subtest. *Journal of Clinical Psychology*, *38*, 641–644.

Dawes, R. M. (1994). Psychological measurement. *Psychological Review*, *101*, 278–281.

Dawes. R. M., Faust, D., & Meehl, P. E. (1990). Clinical versus actuarial judgment. *Science*, *243*, 1668–1674.

Delis, D. C., Kramer, J. H., Kaplan, E., & Ober, B. A. (1987). *California Verbal Learning Test: Adult research edition*. New York: The Psychological Corporation.

Erickson, R. C. (1995). A review and critique of the process approach in neuropsychological assessment. *Neuropsychology Review*, *5*(4), 223–243.

Fastenau, P. S. (1996). Development and preliminary standardization of the "Extended Complex Figure Test" (ECFT). *Journal of Clinical and Experimental Neuropsychology*, *18*(1), 63–76.

Fischer, R. S., & Leavell, C. A. (1995). Analysis of configural and detail errors on block design (abstract). *Journal of the International Neuropsychological Society*, *1U*, 178.

Fischer, W. E., & Dean, R. S. (1990). Factor structure of the Halstead Category Test by age and gender. *International Journal of Clinical Neuropsychology*, *12*, 180–183.

Franzen, M.D. (2000). *Reliability and validity in neuropsychological assessment* (2nd ed.). New York: Plenum/Kluwer Academic.

Freedman, M., Leach, L., Kaplan, E., & Winocur, G. (1994). *Clock drawing: A neuropsychological analysis*. New York: Oxford University Press.

Geschwind, N. (1965). Disconnection syndromes in animals and man. *Brain*, *88*, 237–294.

Goldstein, K. (1942). *After effects of brain injury in war*. New York: Grune and Stratton.

Gourovitch, M. L., Goldberg, T. E., & Weinberger, D. R. (1996). Verbal fluency deficits in patients with schizophrenia: Semantic fluency is differentially impaired as compared with phonologic fluency. *Neuropsychology*, *10*, 573–577.

Halstead, W. C. (1947). *Brain and intelligence: A quantitative study of the frontal lobes*. Chicago: University of Chicago Press.

Hambleton, R. K. (Ed.). (1983). *Applications of item response theory*. Vancouver, Canada: Educational Research Institute of British Columbia.

Hamby, S. L.,Wilkins, J. W., & Barry, N. S. (1993). Organizational quality on the Rey–Osterrieth and Taylor Complex Figure Tests: A new scoring system. *Psychological Assessment*, *5*, 27–33.

Holt, R. R. (1988). Clinical and statistical prediction: A retrospective and would-be integrative perspective. *Journal of Personality Assessment*, *50*, 376–386.

Holt, R. R., & Luborsky, L. (1958). *Personality patterns of psychiatrists. Vol. I. A study of methods for selecting residents*. New York: Basic Books.

Ishiai, S., Sugishita, M., Ichikawa, T., Gono, S., & Watabiki, S. (1993). Clock Drawing Test and unilateral spatial neglect. *Neurology*, *43*(1), 106–110.

Johnson, M. K., Bransford, J. D., Nyberg, S. E., & Cleary, J. J. (1972). Comprehension factors in interpreting memory for abstract and concrete sentences. *Journal of Verbal Learning and Verbal Behavior*, *11*, 451–454.

Kaplan, E. (1983). Process and achievement resisted. In S. Waper & B. Kaplan (Eds.), *Toward a holistic development of psychology* (pp. 143–156). Hillsdale, NJ: Erlbaum.

Kaplan, E. (1988). A process approach to neuropsychological assessment. In T. Boll & B. K. Bryant (Eds.), *Clinical neuropsychology and brain function: Research, measurement, and practice* (pp. 125–167). Washington, DC: American Psychological Association.

Kaplan, E. (1990). The process approach to neuropsychological assessment of psychiatric patients. *Journal of Neuropsychiatry and Clinical Neurosciences*, *2*, 72–87.

Kaplan, E., Fein, D., Kramer, J., Delis, D., & Morris, R. (1999). *WISC-III as a Process Instrument Test Manual*. San Antonio, TX: The Psychological Corporation.

Kaplan, E., Fein, D., Morris, R., & Delis, D. C. (1991). *The Wechsler Adult Intelligence Scale Revised as a Neuropsychological Instrument*. San Antonio, TX: The Psychological Corporation.

Kaplan, E., Palmer, E. P., Weinstein, C., & Baker, E. (1981). *Block design: A brain behavior based analysis*. Paper presented at the annual European meeting of the International Neuropsychological Society, Bergen, Norway.

Kelly, T. P., & Britton P. G. (1996). Sex differences on an adaptation of the Digit Symbol subtest of the Wechsler Intelligence Scale for Children-III. *Perceptual and Motor Skills*, *83*(3 Part 1), 843–847.

Kempler, D., Teng, E. L., Dick, M., Taussig, I. M., & Davi, D. (1998). The effects of age, education, ethnicity on verbal fluency. *Journal of the International Neuropsychological Society*, *4*, 531–538.

Kleinman, S. N., & Waber, D. P. (1994). Prose memory strategies of children treated for leukemia: A story grammar analysis of the Anna Thompson passage. *Neuropsychology*, *8*, 464–470.

Kozora, E., & Cullum, C. M. (1996). Qualitative features of clock drawings in normal aging and Alzheimer's disease. *Assessment*, *1*, 179–187.

Kramer, J. H., Kaplan, E., Blusewicz, M. J., & Preston, K. A. (1991). Visual hierarchical analysis of Block Design configural errors. *Journal of Clinical and Experimental Neuropsychology*, *13*(4), 455–465.

Lamberty, G. J., Putnam, S. H., Chatel, D. M., & Bieliauskas, L. A. (1994). Derived Trail Making Test indices: A preliminary report. *Neuropsychiatry, Neuropsychology, and Behavioral Neurology*, *7*, 230–234.

Levine, B., Dawson, D., Boutet, I., Schwartz, M. L., & Stuss, D. T. (2000). Assessment of strategic selfregulation in traumatic brain injury: Its relationship to injury severity and psychosocial outcome. *Neuropsychology*, *14*, 491–500.

Luria, A. R. (1980). *Higher cortical functions in man* (2nd ed.). New York: Oxford University Press.

Luria, A. R., & Majovski, L.V. (1977). Basic approach used in American and Soviet clinical neuropsychology. *American Psychologist*, (Nov.), 959–971.

McKenna, P., & Warrington, E. K. (1996). The analytical approach to neuropsychological assessment. In I. Grant & K. M. Adams (Eds.), *Neuropsychological assessment of neuropsychiatric disorders* (2nd ed., pp. 58–80). New York: Oxford University Press.

Meehl, P. E. (1954). *Clinical versus statistical prediction*. Minneapolis, MN: University of Minnesota Press.

Meehl, P. E. (1957). Wanted—A good cookbook. *American Psychologist*, *11*, 263–272.

Mendez, M. F., Ala, T., & Underwood, K. L. (1992). Development of scoring criteria for the clock drawing task in Alzheimer's disease. *Journal of the American Geriatrics Society*, *40*(11), 1095–1099. Related Articles, Links.

Meyer, J. E., & Meyer, K. R. (1995). *Rey Complex Figure Test and recognition trial: Professional manual*. Odessa, FL: Psychological Assessment Resources.

Milberg, W. P., Hebben, N., & Kaplan, E. (1996). The Boston Process Approach to neuropsychological assessment. In I. Grant & K. M. Adams (Eds.), *Neuropsychological assessment of neuropsychiatric disorders* (2nd ed., pp. 58–80). New York: Oxford University Press.

Milner, B. (1964). Effects of different brain lesions on card sorting. *Archives of Neuropsychology*, *9*, 90–100.

Monsch, A. U., Bondi, M. W., Butters, N., & Salmon, D. P. (1992). Comparisons of verbal fluency tasks in the detection of dementia of the Alzheimer type. *Archives of Neurology*, *49*, 1253–1258.

Nadler, J. D., Grace, J., White, D. A., Butters, M. A., & Malloy, P. F. (1996). Laterality difference in quantative and qualitative Hooper performance. *Archives of Clinical Neuropsychology*, *11*, 223–229.

Osterrieth, P. A. (1944). Le test de copie dune figure complexe: Contribution a l'etude de la perception et de la memoire. Test of copying a complex figure: Contribution to the study of perception and memory. *Archives de Psychologie*, *30*, 206–356.

Parks, R., Loewenstein, D., Dodrill, L., Barker, W., Yoshii, F., Chang, Y., Emran, A., Apicella, A., Sheramata, W., & Duara, R. (1988). Cerebral metabolic effects of a verbal fluency test: A PET scan study. *Journal of Clinical and Experimental Neuropsychology*, *10*, 565–575.

Perret, E. (1974). The left frontal lobe of man and the suppression of habitual responses in verbal categorical behavior. *Neuropsychologia*, *12*, 323–333.

Poreh, A., & Shye, S. (1998). Examination of the global and local features of the Rey–Osterrieth Complex Figure using faceted smallest space analysis. *Clinical Neuropsychologist*, *12*, 453–467.

Poreh, A. M. (2000). The quantified process approach: An emerging methodology to neuropsychological assessment. *Clinical Neuropsychologist*, *14*(2), 212–222.

Poreh, A. M. (2004). *The Clock Drawing Test*. Cleveland, OH: Quantified Process Scoring Systems Corporation.

Poreh, A. M. (2005) *The Poreh Complex Figure Test*. Cleveland, OH: Quantified Process Scoring Systems Corporation.

Reitan, R. M. (1958). The validity of the Trail Making Test as an indicator of organic brain injury. *Perceptual and Motor Skills*, *8*, 271–276.

Reitan, R. M. (1964). Psychological deficits resulting from cerebral lesions in man. In J. Warren, & K. Akert (Eds.), *The frontal granular cortex and behavior*. New York: McGraw-Hill.

Rey, A. (1958). *L'examen clinique en psychologie*. Paris: Presse Universitaire de France.

Richards, M. S., & Wierzbicki, M. (1993). Anchoring errors in clinical-like judgments. *Journal of Clinical Psychology*, *46*, 358–365.

Ricker, J. H., & Axelrod, B. N. (1994). Analysis of an oral paradigm for the Trail Making Test. *Assessment*, *1*, 47–51.

Ricker, J. H., Axelrod, B. N., & Houtler, B. D. (1996). Clinical validation of the Oral Trail Making Test. *Neuropsychiatry, Neuropsychology, and Behavioral Neurology*, *9*, 50–53.

Robert, P. H., LaFont, V., Medecin, I., Berthet, L., Thauby, S., Baudu, C., & Darcourt, G. (1998). Clustering and switching strategies in verbal fluency: Comparison between schizophrenics and healthy adults. *Journal of the International Neuropsychological Society*, *4*, 539–546.

Rouleau, I., Salmon, D. P., & Butters, N. (1996). Longitudinal analysis of clock drawing in Alzheimer's disease patients. *Brain & Cognition*, *31*, 17–34.

Russell, E. W. (1975). A multiple scoring method for the assessment of complex memory functions. *Journal of Consulting and Clinical Psychology*, *3*, 800–809.

Sachs, J. (1967). Recognition memory for syntactic and semantic aspects of a connected discourse. *Perception and Psychophysics*, *2*, 437–442.

Spreen, O., & Strauss, E. (1998). *A compendium of neuropsychological tests: Administration, norms and commentary*. Oxford, UK: Oxford University Press.

Spreen, O. F., & Benton, A. L. (1969, 1977). *Neurosensory Center Comprehensive Examination for Aphasia (NCCEA)*. Victoria: University of Victoria Neuropsychological Laboratory.

Stanczak, D. E., Lynch, M. D., McNeil, C. K., & Brown, B. (1998). The Expanded Trail Making Test: Rationale, development, and psychometric properties. *Archives of Clinical Neuropsychology*, *13*, 473–487.

Stern, R. A., Singer, E. A., Duke, L. M., Singer, N. G., Morey, C. E., Daughtrey, E. W., & Kaplan, E. (1995). The Boston Qualitative Scoring System for the Rey–Osterrieth Complex Figure: Description and interrater reliability. *Clinical Neuropsychologist*, *8*, 309–322.

Stuss, D. T., & Levin, B. (2002). Adult clinical neuropsychology—Lessons from studies of the frontal lobes. *Annual Review of Psychology*, *53*, 401–433.

Suhr, J., Grace, J., Allen, J., Nadler, J., & McKenna, M. (1998). Quantitative and qualitative performance of stroke versus normal elderly on six clock drawing systems. *Archives of Clinical Neuropsychology*, *13*, 495–502.

Sunderland, T., Hill, J. L., Mellow, A. M., Lawlor, B. A., Gundersheimer, J., Newhouse, P. A., & Grafman, J. H. (1989). Clock drawing in Alzheimer's disease. A novel measure of dementia severity. *Journal of the American Geriatric Society*, *37*(8), 725–729.

Troyer, A. K., Cullum, C. M., Smernoff, E. N., & Kozora, E. (1994). Age effects on Block Design: Qualitative performance features and extended time effects. *Neuropsychology*, *8*, 95–99.

Troyer, A. K., Moscovitch, M., & Winocur, G. (1997). Clustering and switching as two components of verbal fluency: Evidence from younger and older healthy adults. *Neuropsychology*, *11*, 138–146.

Troyer, A. K., & Wishart, H. A. (1997). A comparison of qualitative scoring systems for the Rey–Osterrieth Complex Figure Test. *Clinical Neuropsychologist*, *11*, 381–390.

Tuokko, H., Hadjistavropoulos, T., Miller, J. A., & Beattie, B. L. (1992). The Clock Test: A sensitive measure to differentiate normal elderly from those with Alzheimer disease. *Journal of the American Geriatrics Society*, *40*, 579–584.

Tuokko, H., Hadjistavropoulos, T., Rae, S., & O'Rourke, N. (2000). A comparison of alternative approaches to the scoring of clock drawing. *Archives of Clinical Neuropsychology*, *15*, 137–148.

Turk, D. C., & Salovey, P. (1989). Clinical judgment and decision-making. In C. R. Snyder, & F. R. Donelson (Eds.), *Handbook of social and clinical psychology*. New York: Pergamon Press.

Vakil, E., Arbell, N., Gozlan, M., Hoofien, D., & Blachstein, H. (1992). Relative importance of informational units and their role in long term recall by closed head injured patients and control groups. *Journal of Consulting and Clinical Psychology*, *60*, 802–803.

Vakil, E., & Blachstein, H. (1994). A supplementary measure in the Rey AVLT for assessing incidental learning of temporal order. *Journal of Clinical Psychology*, *50*, 240–245.

Visser, R. S. H. (1973). *Manual of the Complex Figure Test*. Amsterdam: Swets and Zeitlinger.

Waber, D. P., & Holmes, J. M. (1986). Assessing children's memory productions of the Rey–Osterrieth Complex Figure. *Journal of Clinical and Experimental Neuropsychology*, *8*, 563–580.

Watson, Y. I., Arfken, C. L., & Birge, S. J. (1993). Clock completion: An objective screening test for dementia. *Journal of the American Geriatrics Society*, *41*(11), 1235–1240.

Webster, J. S., Godlewski, M. C., Hanley, G. L., & Sowa, M.V. (1992). A scoring method for logical memory that is sensitive to right-hemispheric dysfunction. *Journal of Clinical and Experimental Neuropsychology*, *14*, 222–238.

Wechsler, D. A. (1945). A standardized memory scale for clinical use. *Journal of Psychology*, *19*, 87–95.

Wechsler, D. (1981). *Wechsler Adult Intelligence Scale-Revised*. San Antonio, TX: The Psychological Corporation.

Wechsler, D. A. (1997). *WAIS-III, WMS-III—Technical Manual*. San Antonio, TX: The Psychological Corporation.

Werner, H. (1937). Process and achievement: A basic problem of education and developmental psychology. *Harvard Educational Review*, *7*, 353–368.

Wiggins, J. S. (1981). Clinical and statistical prediction: Where are we and where do we go from here? *Clinical Psychology Review*, *1*, 3–18.

Wilde, M. C., Boake, C., & Sherer, M. (2000). Wechsler Adult Intelligence Scale-Revised Block Design broken configuration errors in nonpenetrating traumatic brain injury. *Applied Neuropsychology*, *7*(4), 208–214.

Willoughby, R. R. (1929). Incidental learning. *Journal of Educational Psychology*, *20*, 671–682.

Woodard, J., Dunlosky, J., & Salthouse, T. (1999). Task decomposition analysis of intertrial free recall performance on the Rey Auditory Verbal Learning Test in normal aging and Alzheimer's disease. *Journal of Clinical and Experimental Psychology*, *21*, 666–676.

Zipf-Williams, E. M., Shear, P. K., Strongin, D., Winegarden, B. J., & Morrell, M. J. (2000). Qualitative block design performance in epilepsy patients. *Archives in Clinical Neuropsychology*, *15*(2), 149–157.

2 The historical antecedents of the Boston Process Approach

William Milberg and Nancy Hebben

As this chapter is being written in the spring of 2004, it is probably safe to say that a majority of contemporary practicing clinical neuropsychologists use tests, observational techniques, or interpretive logic that were influenced by or directly derived from what is now called "The Boston Process Approach to Neuropsychological Assessment" (Milberg, Hebben, & Kaplan, 1986, 1996). Such tests as the California Verbal Learning Test (CVLT; Delis, Kramer, Kaplan, & Ober, 1987), the Wechsler Adult Intelligence Scale-Revised as a Neuropsychological Instrument (WAIS-R NI; Kaplan, Fein, Morris, & Delis, 1991), the Delis–Kaplan Executive Function System (Delis, Kaplan, & Kramer, 2001) and the Wechsler Intelligence Scale for Children – Fourth Edition (WISC-IV; Wechsler, 2003) were directly based on or influenced by the Boston Process Approach. The Boston Process Approach or Process Approach is sometimes discussed as if it is a test battery or a set of specific tests that have been modified to collect data relevant to the assessment of brain damage. Although there are indeed sets of tests and modifications of tests that are associated with this label (e.g., CVLT and WAIS-NI), it is probably more accurate to think of the Process Approach as a general paradigm for assessing the effects of brain damage: a paradigm that emphasizes the observation and analysis of problem-solving strategies used by patients in the course of test taking. The ultimate goal of this approach is the development of a portrait of the elemental cognitive strengths and weaknesses that a patient will bring to deal with the various problems and challenges of the real world. Instead of emphasizing empirical demonstrations of sensitivity to the presence of brain damage per se, the strength of the Process Approach is its ability to yield rich and intuitively appealing descriptions of a patient or client, and as such, has humanized the process of neuropsychology for many clinicians.

Although there are arguable weaknesses and limits to this approach, there is no question that in less than 20 years since the name "Boston Process Approach" first appeared in print (Milberg, Hebben, & Kaplan, 1986) this paradigm has become a central part of mainstream neuropsychological practice in North America, Europe, and other parts of the world. It is now taken for granted that the detailed analysis of cognitive function for the purpose of making inferences about the presence and nature of brain dysfunction is a primary goal of the practice of neuropsychology (Hebben & Milberg, 2002). This was not always the case. While in the 1940s, Ward Halstead developed adaptations of psychological assessment methods, the idea that clinical neuropsychologists could use the analysis of the building blocks of cognitive operations to help with the diagnosis and treatment of the consequences of brain dysfunction was largely unknown and even unacceptable as an approach, particularly in North America, even into the mid-1970s.

The creation and development of what we now call the Process Approach was largely the work of Edith Kaplan, who had been a highly energetic and curious research assistant at the Boston Veterans Administration Hospital in the late 1950s, while she continued to work as a graduate student in developmental psychology at Clark University. During the 1960s and early 1970s, Dr. Kaplan worked with Harold Goodglass developing what was to become the worldwide standard in the assessment of acquired language disorders, i.e., The Boston Diagnostic Aphasia Examination (BDAE) (described in Goodglass & Kaplan, 1983).

In 1968, Dr. Kaplan earned her Ph.D. in developmental psychology and in 1976 she joined the clinical staff of the Boston Veterans Administration (VA) Hospital. It was at this time that she began putting into general clinical practice the ideas and observations she had made during the previous two decades. Like many great acts of creativity in science and the arts, Dr. Kaplan connected a number of disparate ideas from different fields and seemingly unrelated scientific domains to advance a set of ideas that ultimately became known as the Boston Process Approach. An understanding of the historical context in which the Boston Process Approach was developed is not only important as it contributes to the understanding of the intellectual underpinnings of Dr. Kaplan's methods, but also as it provides a basis for why it should be regarded as a milestone in the history of clinical neuropsychology.

By the mid-1970s, the Halstead–Reitan Neuropsychological Battery (HRB) was virtually established as the benchmark method for assessing brain damage, and in many practitioners' minds the battery had become synonymous with clinical neuropsychology itself. The HRB was based largely on the work of Ward Halstead, who believed that the brain was organized by holistic, mass action principles (see Hebben & Milberg, 2002 for a more detailed review). Halstead had developed a battery of tests that, with few exceptions, were chosen primarily because they were demonstrated to be empirically sensitive to the presence of "brain damage." Other than the Category Test, which was developed by Halstead to be a measure of what he considered to be the most uniquely human, phylogenetically advanced function of "biological intelligence" (Halstead, 1947), the tests that comprised his battery were tirelessly culled from the hundreds of available psychological, vocational, and educational tests of his day.

In the early 1950s, his former graduate student, Ralph Reitan, modified and systematized Halstead's original battery to include observations of left- vs. right-sided motor performance, a sensory-perceptual examination, and an aphasia screening examination (Reitan, 1955). He also fleshed out the norms for the battery, and developed empirically derived indices that had some success in lesion localization. The resulting fixed battery of tests, widely known as the HRB, stimulated a remarkable body of research as Halstead's original methods were applied to different patient populations, such as patients with epilepsy and psychiatric illness, as well as to children.

There are a number of reasons why the HRB gained such widespread acceptance. First, at the time of the development of the HRB, clinical psychologists had very few tools for even the coarse detection of what were then known as "organic brain syndromes" or the various symptoms associated with the disquietingly terse category of "organicity." For example, clinical psychologists employed special scoring systems to detect "organicity" based on the Rorschach Inkblot Test (Piotrowski, 1957; Rorschach, 1921) and the Bender-Gestalt (Bender, 1938). These systems were often supported by poorly designed studies and the testimonials of its users, rather than by systematic and scientific data collection.

Second, the HRB became popular because other methods of determining the extent of brain damage were either ineffective (e.g., skull x-rays) or potentially dangerous (e.g., angiography, pneumoencephalography). In the days before computerized tomography (CT) and magnetic resonance imaging (MRI), the HRB with its demonstratable ability to identify at least some forms of brain damage, quickly gained popularity and acceptance as the gold standard for the assessment of what was known at the time as "organic brain syndromes." The fixed battery approach pioneered by Halstead and Reitan had the advantage of providing a standard set of measures by which different patients could be compared to each other.

By the 1960s and 1970s, empiricism and behaviorism had taken a solid foothold in American academic psychology. Most psychological research was focused on the study of observable behavior, rather than cognition, consciousness, and the mind. The latter areas had been the traditional foci of philosophy and academic psychology before the publication of John Watson's papers placed behavior at the center of scientific psychology (e.g., Watson, 1913). The HRB, as a purely behaviorally based clinical method and paradigm for studying the brain, fits perfectly into an academic environment focused on schedules of reinforcement and operant conditioning rather than topics such as consciousness, memory, language, and even morality, which had dominated psychology until the First World War.

It was against this intellectual backdrop that Edith Kaplan came to the Boston VA, where a critical mass of investigators had begun to work on the traditional problems of psychology by examining the effects of disease-based brain lesions on behavior. Researchers and clinicians interested in language, memory, perception, and other classic psychological issues coalesced largely around the charismatic leadership of Norman Geschwind, one of the great behavioral neurologists of the 20th century, and Harold Goodglass, a clinical psychologist who brought the study of aphasia into the realm of psychology.

While behaviorism was still the rule in the early 1970s in most American Universities, a quiet revolution was taking place gradually reclaiming the study of the mind and, in particular, cognition as the proper focus of scientific psychology. It is beyond the scope of this chapter to review all the forces that helped change the focus of psychology from stimulus–response theory to cognition, but among the quiet revolutionists one could include Donald Broadbent, Noam Chomsky, George Miller, and Ulric Neisser, and many others who showed how powerful the combination of theories of cognition and experimental methods could be when used to make detailed inferences about phenomena that were not directly observable as the literal behavioral measures favored by John Watson, B. F. Skinner, and much of academic psychology of the time. It was in Boston that psychology's emerging new focus on cognition had begun to revolutionize studies of the brain. Drs. Geschwind and Goodglass came from different disciplines, but both approached the task of studying the brain as a process of analysis and reduction to basic elements. This work was influenced by German neurology, theoretical linguistics, and cognitive psychology and was quite different in its experimental approach from that of the Halstead–Reitan tradition. Davis Howes, Jean Gleason, Howard Gardner, Edgar Zurif, and Sheila Blumstein joined Dr. Goodglass to adapt the methods of psychophysics, linguistics, and developmental psychology in redefining the study of aphasia. At the same time, Nelson Butters' and Laird Cermak's studies of memory and amnesia and Marlene Oscar-Berman's adaptations of animal learning paradigms to study human brain–behavior relationships helped bring the world of psychological studies of brain damage to the attention of mainstream experimental psychology.

In the 1970s, clinical neuropsychology had just begun to emerge as a specialty, and was, for the most part, populated by clinical psychologists. At that time, at least in the United States, training programs for clinical psychologists either followed the traditions of psychodynamic/psychoanalytic theory or the emerging ideas derived from behaviorism and learning theory. Formal training in clinical neuropsychology was virtually nonexistent, so most clinical neuropsychologists of that time learned their craft on the job, through brief training seminars, or, if they were lucky, through the tutelage of a mentor. Although the forces that began to shift the focus of experimental psychologists back toward the mind were in force, the theories and methods used to study human language, memory, visual perception, and reasoning had not made their way into the literature of clinical neuropsychology. Furthermore, for the most part, the study of psychopathology, personality, or psychotherapy, all areas that were the scientific core of clinical psychology in general, had not yet been studied as part of clinical neuropsychology. The vast majority of clinical neuropsychologists used the HRB as their main tool. As a graduate student in developmental psychology with Heinz Werner at Clark

University, Edith Kaplan came to neuropsychology without being entrenched within the partisan confines of either psychoanalysis or behavioral psychology.

Critically, Dr. Kaplan took her post at the Boston VA armed with what was then a radical challenge to the functionally oriented empirical approach to abilities testing of the time: the idea that the solution of a problem, or achievement, could occur through multiple routes, or processes. The distinction between process and achievement was the centerpiece of Heinz Werner's ideas about the changes that occurred with development, a distinction that was largely foreign to the practice of clinical neuropsychology. Werner wrote in a seminal paper in the *Harvard Educational Review* in 1937 (Werner, 1937) that cognitive development was characterized by changes in the means by which children solved problems. He began this paper with the rhetorical question: "Does the genesis of 'learning,' 'abstraction,' 'reasoning,' or whatever term one chooses to use, mean the development of a unitary function? Or does it mean the history of an accomplishment achieved by process-patterns, which are quite different at different levels?" His answer presaged the central tenet of modern cognitive psychology and neuroscience, fields that would not emerge for at least four more decades:

> … mental development, or training, does not consist so much of a quantitative increase in accomplishment, one based on a unitary function, as of a reorganization of processes conditioned either by the introduction of a new process, or by a change of dominance of function in a given process-pattern. Processes at different levels are involved in any improvement within a special field of mental activity, no matter whether this improvement is due to training or to a natural ripening of the mentality.

This core concept informed everything that Dr. Kaplan thought about when she was looking at a patient who suffered from the devastating symptoms of brain damage. Where experts in the HRB encouraged unbiased examination of test data under conditions that blinded the clinician to the clinical presentation and history of the patient (Reitan & Davison, 1974), Edith Kaplan was compelled to watch a patient's every move when performing standardized tests. Any hesitation, corrected miss-step or error was a potential source of hypotheses about the true problems underlying a patient's actual test performance. Although this observational approach drove Edith to become an acute observer of a patient's behavior, it is not clear whether this alone would have allowed her to make compelling inferences about brain–behavior relationships.

A second major force helped bring the idea of making process-based inferences from test behavior into the issues of brain–behavior relationships. This force came in the form of a 32-year-old neurologist, named Norman Geschwind, who joined the Boston VA Neurology Service in 1958, the same year that Edith Kaplan came to work for Harold Goodglass. The chief of neurology, Dr. Frederick Quadfasel, had induced Geschwind to come to the VA, where there was an already active program to study and treat patients with aphasia. In the years that followed, Norman Geschwind would go on to become the father of modern behavioral neurology, bringing together classical analyses of intercortical connectionism as formulated by Karl Wernicke and other 19th century neurologists with modern discoveries of neuroanatomy and neurophysiology. It is a matter of lore of how fellow Brooklynite Geschwind and Edith Kaplan first met, but apparently, they were part of a loose circle of friends growing up in New York, which included Dr. Goodglass and Dr. Kaplan's then-husband Bernard Kaplan, who was a psychologist at Clark.

By luck or coincidence, these three re-converged with a common interest in aphasia and the brain in 1958. The story is told that Dr. Kaplan approached Dr. Geschwind with a case of an aphasic patient who produced dysgraphic errors when writing with one hand, but not the other. She also had noticed that the patient solved a puzzle construction task called Block Design from the Wechsler Adult Intelligence Scale (WAIS) (Wechsler, 1955) differently when the task was placed to his right than when the task was placed to his left. The patient was later found to have a lesion of the corpus callosum. This case was published in 1962 (Geschwind & Kaplan, 1962) and was the seed that prompted Dr. Geschwind to formulate the ideas that would serve as the basis of his paper, "Disconnection syndromes in animal and man" (Geschwind, 1965). This case solidified for Dr. Kaplan the importance of making detailed observations about the conditions that affected a patient's ability to perform tasks, and critically, that these unique observations had potential neurobiological significance.

It is interesting that while the then inchoate profession of clinical neuropsychology was guided by the American scientific guideposts of empiricism and behaviorism, a Russian neuropsychologist named Alexander Luria had been developing ideas that in many ways paralleled those of Kaplan and Geschwind. Luria (1966) had developed an extensive theory of brain–behavior relationships that also had at its core the idea of a componential analysis of symptoms and task behavior, and the idea that brain function was based on the coordinated activity of multiple interacting neural structures. These methods were in many ways extensively developed by the time that Kaplan started combining the lessons of Heinz Werner with her keen powers of observation to the exciting new ideas of neural connectivity and the study of cognition that surrounded her at the Boston VA. Although there were attempts to standardize Luria's methods and make them accessible to most practicing neuropsychologists (e.g., Golden, Hammeke, & Purisch, 1978), the Boston Process Approach seemed to have captured the imagination of a wider audience of practitioners. This was in spite of the fact that many of Dr. Kaplan's observations have not been subjected to strict tests of diagnostic sensitivity and specificity that had originally brought the HRB to the forefront.

Luria's methods probably did not get wider acceptance because of the sheer complexity of its constituent tests and inferential structure. In contrast, the foundation of the Process Approach has been traditional psychological testing methods that are more familiar and accessible. Although there have been very successful tests that were based on the paradigm of the Process Approach (e.g., CVLT), the appeal of the Boston Process Approach is the promise of connecting the clinician directly with the patient, making the observations and interactions of two human beings the center of the diagnostic process. This inherent connection between clinician and patient, and the effect of joining clinical psychology to the larger movement centering the study of psychology on cognition accounts for a permanent place of the Process Approach in the history of modern clinical neuropsychology.

Conclusion: The limits and future of the Process Approach

Although the Boston Process Approach and its attendant features of using observational methods to supplement standard test administration data, the use of flexible test batteries that may be adapted to study the details of particular problems, and of its goal of uncovering the underlying cognitive processes involved in test performance have been responsible for its increasing popularity and movement into the mainstream of neuropsychological practice, these features come with a price and inherent dangers.

The first problem is the severe limits of data supporting the sensitivity and specificity of many of the qualitative features of test performance that are the center of the approach. Although some features such as "breaking configuration" have been claimed to be pathognomic of brain injury (Milberg, Hebben, & Kaplan, 1996), it is not clear how often such features appear in normals, or in nonbrain-damaged psychiatric populations. Without norms that take into account age, education, and other demographics there is a great danger that the presence of certain qualitative features may be used to incorrectly infer the presence of brain damage or other states. This problem is also true for making predictions about real-life functional, vocational, or academic performance. Although it would seem that providing information about the basic constituents of learning styles and abilities that may be relevant to rehabilitation or school achievement would be a central goal of neuropsychological assessment, the data that support the generalizability of test performance to real-life situations are almost nonexistent.

In addition to the basic empirical problem of test validation that characterizes many of the central features of the process approach, the complexities and skills needed to be an effective practitioner of this method have not yet been well standardized. Dr. Kaplan is a superb teacher and mentor who has trained many students, and as of this writing still actively presents workshops and seminars effectively exposing a large number of clinicians to her teachings. However, Dr. Kaplan's mastery and the mastery of some of her students of these techniques is no guarantee that everyone using this approach can be equally skilled at making the clinical observations and decisions needed to apply this approach successfully. Such issues as inter-rater reliability, and clinicians' own sensitivity and specificity in detecting the presence of qualitative features have not been addressed for many of the basic observations that comprise the main teachings of the Process Approach. One need only attend a single case conference held by Dr. Kaplan or read one of the detailed descriptions of her methods (e.g., Milberg, Hebben, & Kaplan, 1986, 1996) to understand the potential wealth of information inherent in these methods. However, the next steps of subjecting the central tenets of the Boston Process Approach to scientific psychometric scrutiny are critical as clinical neuropsychology advances as a scientific discipline and as a profession.

References

Bender, L. (1938). *A visual motor Gestalt Test and its clinical use.* Research Monograph No. 3. New York: American Orthopsychiatric Association.

Delis, D. C., Kaplan, E., & Kramer, J. H. (2001). *Delis–Kaplan executive function system.* San Antonio, TX: The Psychological Corporation.

Delis, D. C., Kramer, J. H., Kaplan, E., & Ober, B. A. (1987). *California Verbal Learning Test: Adult version manual.* San Antonio, TX: The Psychological Corporation.

Geschwind, N. (1965). Disconnection syndromes in animals and man (Parts I, II). *Brain, 88*, 237–294, 585–644.

Geschwind, N., & Kaplan, E. (1962). A human cerebral disconnection syndrome: A preliminary report. *Neurology, 12*, 675–683.

Golden, C. J., Hammeke, T. A., & Purisch, A. D. (1978). Diagnostic validity of a standardized neuropsychological battery derived from Luria's neuropsychological tests. *Journal of Consulting and Clinical Psychology, 46*, 1258–1265.

Goodglass, H., & Kaplan, E. (1983). *The assessment of aphasia and related disorders* (2nd ed.). Philadelphia: Lea & Febiger.

Halstead, W. C. (1947). *Brain and intelligence.* Chicago: University of Chicago Press.

Hebben, N., & Milberg, W. (2002). *Essentials of neuropsychological assessment.* New York: Wiley.

Kaplan, E., Fein, D., Morris, R., & Delis, D. C. (1991). *WAIS-R NI manual.* San Antonio, TX: The Psychological Corporation.

Luria, A. R. (1966). *Higher cortical functions in man.* New York: Basic Books, Inc.

Milberg, W. P., Hebben, N., & Kaplan, E. (1986). The Boston Process Approach to neuropsychological assessment. In I. Grant & K. M. Adams (Eds.), *Neuropsychological assessment of neuropsychiatric disorders* (pp. 65–86). New York: Oxford University Press.

Milberg, W. P., Hebben, N., & Kaplan, E. (1996). The Boston Process Approach to neuropsychological assessment. In I. Grant & K. M. Adams (Eds.), *Neuropsychological assessment of neuropsychiatric disorders* (2nd ed., pp. 58–80). New York: Oxford University Press.

Piotrowski, Z. A. (1957). *Perceptanalysis.* New York: Macmillan.

Reitan, R. M. (1955). The distribution according to age of a psychological measure dependent upon organic brain functions. *Journal of Gerontology, 10*, 338.

Reitan, R. M., & Davison, L. A. (Eds.). (1974). *Clinical neuropsychology: Current status and applications*. New York: Wiley.

Rorschach, H. (1921). *Psychodiagnostik*. Bern: Huber.

Watson, J. B. (1913). Psychology as the behaviorist views it. *Psychological Review*, *20*, 158–177.

Wechsler, D. (1955). *Manual for the Wechsler Adult Intelligence Scale*. New York: The Psychological Corporation.

Wechsler, D. (2003). *Wechsler Intelligence Scale for Children* (4th ed.). San Antonio, TX: The Psychological Corporation.

Werner, H. (1937). Process and achievement—a basic problem of education and developmental psychology. *Harvard Educational Review*, *7*, 353–368.

3 Methodological quandaries of the Quantified Process Approach

Amir M. Poreh

Introduction

The emergence of the Quantified Process Approach (QPA, Poreh, 2000) reflects a growing recognition that the qualitative observations and anecdotes of patient performance on standardized neuropsychological measures, as delineated by the Boston Process Approach (BPA), cannot be unified into a solid database. Furthermore, it is unclear as to whether the clinical predictions of the BPA can be empirically supported (Hebben & Milberg, 2002) given the absence of precise norms, clearly spelled out blueprint of how and when these procedures should be used, and tremendous variations in the interpretation of its findings. It should be stressed, however, that in spite of the shortcomings of the qualitative approach, its basic thesis, as outlined by Hans Werner and Edith Kaplan that different cognitive processes are used by different individuals to solve the same problem, remains valid and of paramount importance. Indeed, this thesis and the experience obtained using the BPA are important building blocks for development of the QPA. It is also recognized that in order to fully understand the nature and cause of a given patient's neurocognitive deficits, these processes must be discerned and associated with state-of-the-art functional brain imaging studies.

Bridging the qualitative and quantitative aspects of neuropsychological assessment is not a simple task. One of the stumbling blocks in this process is the existence of unresolved methodological problems. These problems are a function of both the complexity of the strategies utilized by patients to process cognitive tasks and the multiple directions such processes may take. The purpose of this chapter is to examine some of these problems and their relation to the three previously outlined methodologies for quantifying the process approach: the Satellite Test, the Composition, and the Decomposition methodologies. This examination will concentrate on the application of these methodologies and the need to ensure that they meet prevailing professional standards for psychological measures (Anastasi, 1996; Hunsley & Bailey, 1999), namely, the issues of norms, reliability, validity, and diagnostic verification. For illustrative purposes, the author will refer to ongoing lines of research in this area and critically evaluate the problems associated with each of these methodologies.

The Satellite Test Paradigm

Background

Following Edith Kaplan, test developers that adhere to the process approach commonly introduce a complimentary task (a Satellite Test) to evaluate the performance of an individual on a neuropsychological task and gaining insight into the source of the patient's difficulties. Such a task is supposed to contain all but one of the components that make up the original task.

The use of the Satellite Test Paradigm is exemplified well by examining the first Satellite Tests developed for the assessment of attention. As noted by van Zomeren and Brouwer (1994, p. 37), "A task only becomes an attention task when the effect of increased selection or concentration is assessed by comparing performance in the easy and difficult versions, or by comparing the performance across time such as the first 5 minutes with that in the 10th to 15th minute. Scores indicating an impairment of attention should be based on the difference between performance in the situation requiring the greatest attention and that requiring the least." This recognition explains why the Satellite Test Paradigm has often been used to enhance the validity of existing tests of divided attention. For example, the Trail Making Test and the Digit Symbol Test. Similarly, they have been introduced to enhance the utility of other tasks, such as verbal and nonverbal memory tests (Power, Logue, McCarty, Rosenstiel, & Ziesat, 1979), and executive function tasks, such as the Clock Drawing Test.

Clearly, the Satellite Test methodology provides the most systematized course for quantifying the BPA. It is noted, however, that initially the publication of some Satellite Tests was not accompanied by empirical data. Only after they were incorporated by test publishers into existing neuropsychological measures and gained popularity, were they complemented by high-quality psychometric studies. This process is exemplified by Russell's (1975) revision of the WMS (Wechsler, 1945) and its later incorporation into the WMS-R. Another example is the incorporation of Martha Storandt's (1976) Symbol Copy Test in the Wechsler Intelligence Scales.

Psychometric shortcomings

The use of difference scores is at the heart of quantitative Satellite Tests. This follows from the examiner's need to determine both the statistical significance of differences between examinee performance on the original and the Satellite tests, as well as to analyze the frequency of the difference in normal and clinical populations. Statistical differences between the two scores are tested by hypothesizing no actual difference between an examinee's scores on any two given tasks. If the difference between the standard scores on the two tasks is significant at a selected level of probability, then the examiner might conclude that a significant difference exists in the observed direction. The other method for interpreting the difference score is examining the frequency of the observed difference in a relevant comparison group. This allows us to assess the base rate of the difference in a given population.

One concern with interpreting difference scores, however, is that they tend to be unreliable and create a host of other problems (see Crocker & Algina, 1986 for a review of this topic). Classic reliability theory states that an observed score is composed of both a true score (T) and error (E). When using a difference score, E is expected to be larger because E of the difference is composed of error from both the scores used to create it. Furthermore, T is expected to be reduced because whatever is common to the two measures is being canceled out. As a result, the reliability of a difference score is expected to be lower than the reliability of either score on which it is based. Formula (3.1) is used to assess the reliability of a difference score:

$$r = \frac{\frac{1}{2}(r_{11} + r_{22}) - r_{12}}{1 - r_{12}} \tag{3.1}$$

where r_{11} and r_{22} are the reliabilities of the first and second measures, respectively, and r_{12} the correlation between the first and the second measures.

This formula shows that the greatest reliability of the difference score is obtained when using measures that are each highly reliable but are minimally correlated. Clearly, most psychological tests, particularly neuropsychological complimentary tasks, rarely achieve this “ideal” goal. Therefore, in such cases, the use of this simple subtraction method may be detrimental.

Early on, Payne and Jones (1957) introduced a correction formula for use when comparing between the WAIS Verbal and Performance Scale IQ scores. The following formula:

$$Z_D = \frac{Z_X - Z_Y}{\sqrt{2 - 2r_{xy}}} \tag{3.2}$$

may be used to estimate the abnormality of differences between an individual’s scores on two tests and attenuates for the intercorrelation between the two measures. Applications of the formula generally yield good approximations to empirically determined “abnormal” differences between Verbal and Performance IQs (Grossman, Herman, & Matarazzo, 1985; Silverstein, 1981) as well as a good estimation of the abnormality of discrepancies between memory indices (Mittenberg, Thompson, & Schwartz, 1991).

Payne and Jones’ formula calls for converting the individual’s raw scores on the two tests into Z scores (Z_X and Z_Y) based on the normative data. r_{xy} in this formula represents the correlation between the two tests. The limitation of Payne and Jones’ formula, particularly with regard to neuropsychological research, is that it assumes that scores reflect population parameters and that the two measures are normally distributed.

Crawford, David, Howell, and Garthwaite (1998) suggested that Payne and Jones’ formula systematically overestimates the abnormality of an individual’s difference score due to the use of population statistics. Following

Sokal and Rohlf (1995), they advocated the use of sample statistical parameters rather than population parameters for estimating the abnormality of test score differences. Crawford et al.'s formula

$$t = \frac{Z_{X_1} - Z_{Y_1}}{\sqrt{(2 - 2r_{xy})((N_2 + 1)/N_2)}} \tag{3.3}$$

assesses the difference using the t distribution and includes a correction for small sample size (N). Note, however, that when $N_2 \gg 1$ the two formulas give identical results. For example, for $N > 10$ the difference between t and Z_D is less than 5%.

Crawford and his associates applied the above formula to establish a quantified definition of classical dissociation on traditional neuropsychological tests. Adopted from behavioral neurology, the classical dissociation model suggests that when patients (group A) with localized damage in a particular area of the brain (a_1) exhibit deficits on task X yet perform within normal limits on task Y, and patients (group B) with localized damage in another area of the brain (b_1) exhibit deficits on task Y but not on task X, then a dissociation in cognitive functions of the two areas of the brain can be established. Thus, a statistically significant difference between the performance on tasks X and Y might reflect a quantifiable degree of such dissociation. Although current Satellite Tests were not designed to assess for classical dissociation, Crawford's work appears to suggest that the development of such tasks could be of great importance.

Several neuropsychologists have attempted to bypass the problems of difference scores by employing ratio scores. For example, Arbuthnott and Frank (2000) used test ratio scores for comparing the first and second parts of the Trail Making Test (TMT_b/TMT_a). O'Bryant, Hilsabeck, Fisher, and McCaffrey (2003) employed this methodology to assess effort on the TMT and illustrated that the above TMT ratio is significantly low in litigants suspected of malingering. Martin, Hoffman, and Donders (2003) and others have shown that TMT ratio scores fail to demonstrate sensitivity to degree of head injury severity and fail to reliably identify dissimulators. The use of ratio scores is also problematic from a statistical perspective, as ratio scores typically produce skewed distributions and false positives (see Cohen & Cohen, 1983). Nunnally (1978) also notes that, in some cases, difference scores may exhibit reliabilities higher than the threshold and are more reliable than the viable alternative, such as ratio scores.

Edwards (2001) suggests that the reliability of difference scores is ultimately an empirical matter. Hence, while at first glance the use of Satellite Tests appears to provide a straightforward approach to intra-test performance analysis, its proper development and use is complex and requires considerable statistical insight.

Validity and clinical utility

The incremental validity of many of the Satellite Tests remains unclear. This state of affairs reflects the lack of precise guidelines for their use and paucity of studies that show their incremental clinical advantage. Namely, failure to demonstrate that the administration of the test adds useful information, beyond that of the data obtained through traditional assessment strategies. The aforementioned Digit Symbol Recognition (DSR; Collaer & Evans, 1982) subtest, the most well-known Satellite Test, illustrates this issue. As mentioned earlier, this test was developed for the assessment of short-term memory and was later incorporated into the WAIS-NI and WISC-III PI. Like many other Satellite Tests, however, its construct validity was only partially examined (Crowe, Benedict, Enrico, Mancuso, Mathews, & Wallace, 1999) and its added value in the diagnosis of incidental memory deficits and the prediction of treatment outcome remains unclear. Hence, proposals for new Satellite Tests should also meet criterion-related validity standards, requiring the design of studies that assess the test's sensitivity and specificity, positive and negative predictive value, as well as hit rate.

Satellite Tests also need to be evaluated with respect to their clinical utility. Furthermore, it is imperative that studies should address the cost of administration in terms of professional time needed to administer, score, and interpret such measures given the growing pressure by managed health care to reduce the cost of neuropsychological evaluations. This pressure has resulted in a drive to shorten, rather than lengthen, the assessment process (Franzen, 2000; Lichtenberg, 1998; Randolph, 2002; Sweet, Westergaard, & Moberg, 1996). A reflection of this trend is found in the numerous articles that have introduced shortened versions of existing neuropsychological measures (i.e., Donders, 1996; Lansing, Ivnik, Cullum, & Randolph, 1999; Paolo, Axelrod, & Tröster, 1996; Vanderploeg, LaLone, Greblo, & Schinka, 1998; Woodard, Benedict, & Roberts, 1997).

Practice effects

Another issue that inhibits the use of many Satellite Tests is the possible effect of their administration on the psychometric properties of the core test. Spreen and Strauss (1998) address this issue and conclude that due to practice effects, the modifications of existing tests may limit the ability of clinicians to interpret their findings using the original published norms. Additionally, they noted that the modified test may measure a substantially different construct than the original test. While this issue is of potentially great concern, few studies have evaluated it empirically. The only two articles that have been published on this topic indicate that the administration of Satellite Tests does not induce practice effects. Specifically, Slick, Hopp, Strauss, Fox, Pinch, and Stickgold (1996) examined the optional modifications of the WAIS-NI on the subsequent re-administration of the WAIS-R.

They failed to show that the addition of Satellite Tests affects the test–retest reliability coefficients of WAIS-R subtests. However, they did stress that until normative studies demonstrate otherwise, it is misleading to refer to the two measures as equivalent and conclude that the WAIS-R NI requires its own comprehensive norms. Gaudette and Smith (1999) demonstrate that the process-oriented administration of the WAIS-R's Picture Arrangement subtest does not affect the final outcome, allowing for the preservation of the accumulated data of this subtest. Finally, while some Satellite Tests may be vulnerable to practice effects, others may not. These include, for example, the oral paradigm of the TMT, the recognition portion of the Rey–Osterrieth Complex Figure (ROCF), and the supplementary incidental learning portion of the AVLT.

The Composition Paradigm

Background

The Composition Paradigm involves the specification of measurable empirical indices that define and characterize the process or the strategies by which a patient successfully tackles complex tasks and that are associated with well-defined abilities/deficiencies. This approach possesses a theoretical edge over the Satellite one, as neither the task nor its administration procedure is modified, which suggests that one could achieve this goal with the help of the accumulated experience and knowledge gained by the traditional analysis and scoring of such tasks. However, as will be explained below, the contribution of clinical experience, while helpful, particularly for simple tasks, is insufficient for complex tasks.

The traditional scoring of performance has usually focused on the final results. When a task is successfully accomplished by only a small, fixed number of actions or steps, it might be possible to evaluate the process used to solve the task by grading these steps according to their efficiency or ability to accomplish the task. One may also evaluate objective characteristics of the process, such as speed. In such cases, the indices that characterize the process may be determined empirically by the performance data and the development may be defined as "data driven". However, when the number of possible actions or steps is large or when the final outcome of the task is not predetermined, identification of meaningful indices is often "theory driven". The problem is that in most cases, the theoretical hypotheses that attempt to score processes cannot be easily confirmed. At best, one may find a correlation between various processes and the traditional score on the final task.

Both the Tower of Hanoi and the Tower of London tests are good examples of tasks amenable to the development of "data-driven" indices. Both tasks are characterized by a finite number of permissible steps or operators. Each move toward the solution of the task is enumerated by applying an operator. For example, in the case of the Tower of Hanoi, in moving a piece from one peg to another, only two possible move operators can be applied. For such tests, neuropsychologists have typically developed data-driven indices.

When the number of permissible moves is large, failure to take all of them into consideration may result in a misinterpretation of the process. Consider, for example, Delis, Kaplan, and Kramer's (1997) revision of the Five Point Test (originally developed by Regard, Strauss, & Knapp, 1982; Regard, 1991). In this version, the patient is asked to draw as many configurations as possible within a set time period by connecting five points to form unique designs. The test includes parts with distractors and different arrangements of dots in space (see Figure 3.1). Analysis of Delis et al.'s test shows that the number of possible designs depends on the number of dots, permissible operators, and their configuration. One should thus score both the process and the final outcome of the test (number of lines drawn), taking all of these parameters into consideration. This may be calculated using basic set theory in mathematics.[1]

Developing indices for evaluating performance on the task of copying the ROCF, or any other complex figure, must be "theory driven" as numerous modes of copying are possible. The theory in this case is a hypothesis as to how a particular task "should" be optimally performed. The hypothesis is then supported by comparing the copying process with the final quality of the copied configuration as well as with the ability of the subject to recall the figure after a definite time. Bennet-Levy (1984), for example, proposed scores for copying the ROCF. The first and simpler scoring method gives points for drawing continuously straight lines. The second scoring method is based on the assumption that before one starts copying the figure they should recognize the symmetrical elements of the figure and in particular those that are symmetrical with respect to the horizontal and vertical axes. According to this hypothesis, one should first draw the large rectangular and then add its vertical and horizontal axes followed by the diagonals or vice versa, which together form the shape of the Union Jack (see Figure 3.2). Bennet-Levy also defined a combined Strategy Score that is equal to the sum of the Continuity and Symmetry Scores.

Thus, the Strategy Score for drawing the Union Jack is highest when drawing the large rectangular in a continuous fashion. Observations suggest,

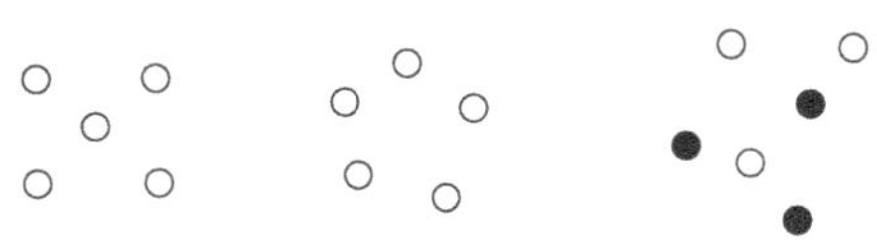

Figure 3.1 Variations on the Five Point Test.

[1] When the form includes Regard's original configuration, the number of possible permutations is calculated by the following formula:
$C8 + 2C8 + 3C8 + 4C8 + 5C8 + 6C8 + 7C8 + 8C8$ where $iCn = i!/(n!*(n - i)!)$

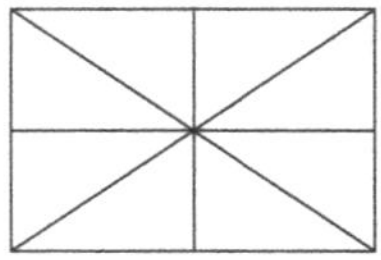

Figure 3.2 The shape of the Union Jack.

however, that professional right-handed draftsmen do not necessarily follow this "optimal" sequence and prefer to draw the upper and right lines of the large rectangle at first from left to right followed by the complimented L section of the rectangle, as they try to prevent obstruction of the drawing by the hand and to maintain eye contact with the edge of the pencil. Furthermore, Bennet-Levy does not give credit for drawing the diagonals before the axes of symmetry of the Union Jack, not taking into account that it ensures that the axes and the diagonals meet at the center of the rectangle.

It turns out, however, that some examinees copy the Union Jack configuration in a piecemeal fashion. For example, they might copy either the right, left, top, or bottom portion of the rectangle first. Then, they might insert some of the inner elements followed by the remaining outline of the symmetrical rectangle. Finally, they might add the inner elements of the remaining portion of the figure, as described in Figure 3.3. Bennet-Levy did not refer to three similar piecemeal copying methods, which are shown in Figure 3.4.

In sum, there are two important features that are common to the development of both data- and theory-driven indices. First, a detailed *cognitive task analysis* is required, so that the problem space is defined in order to develop a computational scoring model. Second, the researcher must identify the sequence of operators used by subjects (defined by Chi (1997) as a solution pass). Alternatively, one may assume that a particular path, such as continuity of line drawings used by Bennet-Levy (1984), reflects a particular construct. Hence, the goal of the analysis is to see whether there is a match between the path the solver takes and the sequence of operators that a simulation model generates.

Incremental validity

Another concern with regard to the Composition Method relates to its incremental validity. This issue is exemplified by Nadler, Grace, White, Malloy, and Butters' (1996) recommendation to utilize additional indices for identifying anomic deficits and for clarifying how they affect performance on the Hooper Visual Organization Test (HVOT; Hooper, 1958, 1983). While this recommendation may be useful under certain conditions, most neuropsychologists would pick up on language deficits by employing measures specifically designed for this purpose ("fixed" or "flexible" test battery). For example, by administering standard measures of language abilities such as

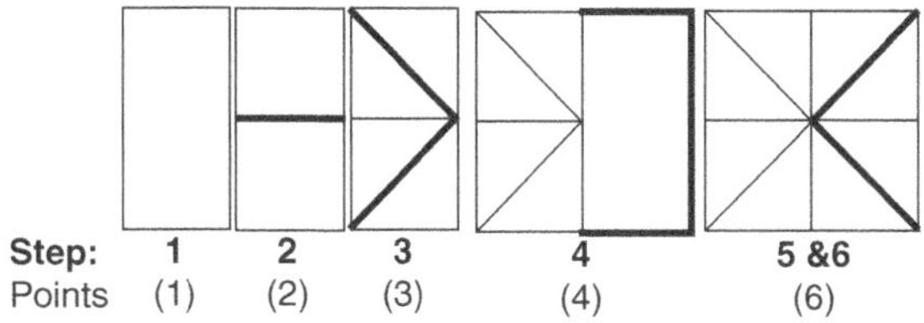

Figure 3.3 A piecemeal copying strategy. (The accumulated symmetry points assigned at each step appear in the parentheses.)

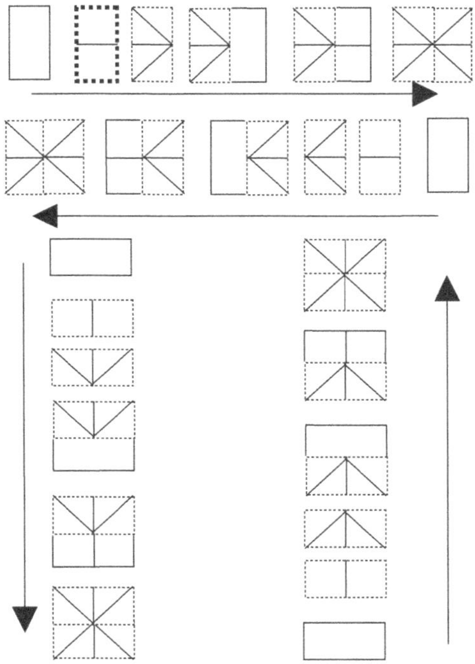

Figure 3.4 Four possible piecemeal copying ways of copying the Union Jack.

the Boston Naming Test (BNT; Kaplan, Goodglass, & Weintraub, 1978) together with visual spatial tests that do not require intact language abilities, such as the ROCF, one would both identify the language deficits and be able to gain additional insight into patients' visual–perceptual functions. Thus, the utilization of new indices for the understanding of the neurocognitive basis of test errors should be evaluated with regard to their ability to add useful information above and beyond that which is typically obtained in standard clinical practice. Furthermore, it is also useful to assess the incremental validity of existing indices using well-designed criteria. This is exemplified in the work of Angela Troyer and her associates (Troyer & Wishart, 1997), who compared the incremental validity of 10 organizational strategy indices for scoring the ROCF copy strategy. Systematic coding of the data and analyses allowed Troyer and her colleagues to identify the most reliable and valid organizational strategies for predicting memory impairment on the recall portion of this test.

Clinical utility

The inherit complexity of many of the neuropsychological tasks, particularly those that require the development of theory-driven indices, has led to the copious quantification of particular tasks. For example, 10 different indices have been developed for the assessment of the strategy of copying the ROCF (Troyer & Wishart, 1997) and at least six indices for the purpose of quantifying the Clock Drawing Test (Suhr, Grace, Allen, Nadler, & Mckenna, 1998). As such, considerable research is needed to evaluate their relative clinical utility.

The Decomposition Approach

Proponents of the BPA often suggest that individual test items within standardized neuropsychological measures might tap into particular cognitive constructs. Proposed correlations between given test items and a particular cognitive construct are usually based on clinical experience, the face validity of test items, and existing theoretical, cognitive science models. For example, Edith Kaplan (1988) suggested that certain items of the Block Design Test require global visual processing, whereas other items include specific stimuli and therefore assess local visual processing. This specific conclusion is based on data that emerged only in patients with localized brain-damaged patients, and only when the stimuli are presented in a particular fashion, in the left or right quadrant of the visual field. Therefore, it is not clear whether this conclusion is valid for other populations with nonlocalized brain injuries.

To address the multidimensional nature of psychological measures, clinical researchers often employ factor analytical techniques to decompose psychological measures and assess clinical hypotheses. These methods rely on parametric statistics and may have serious drawbacks. As Delis, Jacobson, Bondi, Hamilton, and Salmon (2003) recently noted, factor analytical techniques require a large pool of subjects. Otherwise, the resulting factor solutions may be highly unreliable. Furthermore, parametric statistical techniques require the use of normally distributed data, a prerequisite that is rarely met in clinical studies. Hence, clinical researchers often attempt to decompose common neuropsychological measures using large samples of normal subjects. While such statistical methods result in parsimonious solutions, they often lack a clear relationship with our understanding of the related neurocognitive constructs.

The masking of important constructs using factorial analysis was exemplified by Delis and his associates' factorial analyses of the California Verbal Learning Test. Another example is the numerous studies that have attempted to evaluate the construct of the Wechsler Intelligence Test. Such studies distinguish between verbal and nonverbal subtests, which were later related to the distinction between the right- and left-hemispheric processing. However, in every Introductory Neuropsychology textbook it is now recognized that such a distinction is not only oversimplified but may be misleading. In order to gain insight into the effect of brain injury or the particular deficits associated with particular WAIS-III tasks, one needs to apply new procedures to decompose the existing measures.

One method for decomposing data that has achieved a strong foothold in neuropsychological research during the past decade is the use of Multidimensional Scaling Techniques (MDS). This family of statistical procedures does not require that the test data be normally distributed nor do they require large numbers of subjects, and may therefore serve as a promising alternative to traditional factorial analysis.

The use of MDS in neuropsychological research may be traced to Chan and his colleagues (Chan, Butters, Paulson, Salmon, Swenson, & Maloney, 1993; Chan, Butters, Salmon, Johnson, Paulson, & Swenson, 1995). Using this procedure, they examined the representation of semantic memory in patients suffering from Alzheimer's and Huntington's disease. In doing so, they were able to map the spatial representation and degree of association between concepts of semantic memory. Subjects were provided with a triadic comparisons task in which they had to choose from among three concepts (animal names). Twelve animals were presented in every possible combination. This procedure produced a proximity score, which was then subjected to ADDTREE and MDS analysis.

Sylvester and Shimamura (2002) applied Chan and his colleagues' paradigm to evaluate the semantic representation of patients with frontal-lobe lesions. They examined 11 patients with unilateral dorsolateral frontal-lobe lesions and 10 control subjects. They then applied the resulting data to INDSCAL MDS and Pathfinder analyses. The resulting data showed no differences between the control and frontal-lobe participants. Similar findings were found in a second experiment that employed a slightly different paradigm. Sylvester and Shimamura (2002) concluded that frontal-lobe patients exhibit intact semantic knowledge yet suffer from marked deficits in strategic retrieval of such data.

The use of multidimensional techniques in psychological research is still in its infancy and remains controversial. Several studies (i.e., Milberg & McGlinchey, 2003; Rogers, 2003) have recently debated the use of MDS in the investigation of semantic memory. Their criticism focuses on the particular experimental paradigms that are employed for assessing degradation as opposed to retrieval deficits and has received considerable attention. Scant notice was given to the fact that the proximity matrixes generated by most MDS are mainly exploratory and subject to post-facto interpretation. Researchers are in need of statistical procedures that allow for the generation of competing hypotheses regarding how the data collected might decompose and then empirically assess such hypotheses. One of the few MDS techniques that achieve this goal is Faceted Smallest Space Analyses. Poreh and Shye (1998) applied this technique to evaluate Edith Kaplan's distinction between global/local elements of the ROCF. This in turn allowed them to decompose the copy and recall scores of the test.

Reliability and incremental validity

One of the serious limitations of the decomposition approach is the issue of reliability. Typically, when one employs such methodology, the resulting subscales produce fewer test items than the original measures. As noted in basic psychometric text books, this might result in the production of unreliable subscales. Moreover, because such subscales exhibit high inter-item homogeneity, the attenuation cannot be estimated using the published data (see Nunnally, 1978 for more details on this topic). As a result, there is a need to carry out a lengthy and expensive re-standardization process for many of these newly published indices.

Studies that investigate the construct validity of published indices using related measures are uncommon (Poreh & Shye, 1998; Woodward, Dunlosky, & Salthouse, 1999). Furthermore, even fewer studies have examined their diagnostic utility. Suhr et al.'s (1998) study of the six Clock Drawing scoring systems, for example, came up with disappointing conclusions. Although they were able to classify between stroke patients and normal controls, none of the indices adequately distinguished between various groups of stroke patients. According to their study, however, qualitative indices were helpful in lateralizing the lesion site and differentiating between cortical and subcortical groups.

Summary and conclusions

The material presented in this chapter reflects the emergence of a growing number of studies in the past decade that have emphasized the quantification of the process approach. These studies collectively facilitate the objective identification and analysis of cognitive and behavioral processes underlying common neuropsychological test performance as well as their relationship to underlying current models of neuroscience research. Clearly, the tremendous variation of processes and the complexity of each process make it difficult to achieve these goals. Nevertheless, considerable progress has already been made in advancing the QPA using three key methodologies. Each of these methodologies has its own advantages, shortcomings, and problems related to validity, reliability, and clinical utility. Some of these problems have been solved using newly developed statistical and analytical methods. However, considerable research is still required. During the upcoming years, as digital acquisition technology, such as voice recognition and graphic input devices mature, we will start moving ahead at a breakneck speed to improve the study of brain and behavior using modern and more traditional neuropsychological measures.

References

Anastasi, A. (1996). *Psychological testing* (7th ed.). New York: Macmillan.

Arbuthnott, K., & Frank, J. (2000). Trail Making Test, part B as a measure of executive control: Validation using a set-switching paradigm. *Journal of Clinical and Experimental Neuropsychology*, *22*(4), 518–528.

Bennet-Levy, J. (1984). Determinants of performance on the Rey–Osterrieth Complex Figure Test: An analysis and a new technique for single case assessment. *British Journal of Clinical Psychology*, *23*, 109–119.

Chan, A., Butters, N., Paulson, J., Salmon, D., Swenson, M., & Maloney, L. (1993). An assessment of the semantic network in patients with Alzheimer's disease. *Journal of Cognitive Neuroscience*, *5*, 254–261.

Chan, A., Butters, N., Salmon, D., Johnson, S., Paulson, J., & Swenson, M. (1995). A neuropsychological study of the semantic networks in demented and amnesic patients. *Neuropsychology*, *9*, 177–186.

Chi, M. T. (1997). Quantifying qualitative analyses of verbal data: A practical guide. *The Journal of Learning Sciences*, *6*(3), 271–315.

Cohen, J., & Cohen, P. (1983). *Applied multiple regression/correlation analysis for the behavioral sciences*. Hillsdale, NJ: Lawrence Erlbaum Associates, Inc.

Collaer, M. L., & Evans, J. R. (1982). A measure of short-term visual memory based on the WISC-R coding subtest. *Journal of Clinical Psychology*, *38*(3), 641–644.

Crawford, J. R., Howell, D. C., & Garthwaite, P. H. (1998). Payne and Jones revisited: Estimating the Abnormality of Test Score differences using a modified paired samples *t* test. *Journal of Clinical and Experimental Neuropsychology*, *20*(6), 898–905.

Crocker, L., & Algina, J. (1986). *Introduction to classical and modern test theory*. Forth Worth, TX: Harcourt Brace Jovanovich College Publishers.

Crowe, S. F., Benedict, T., Enrico, J., Mancuso, N., Matthews, C., & Wallace, J. (1999). Cognitive determinants of performance on the Digit Symbol-Coding Test, and the symbol search test of the WAIS-III, and the symbol digit modalities test: An analysis in a healthy sample. *Australian Psychologist*, *34*, 204–210.

Delis, D. C., Jacobson, M., Bondi, M. W., Hamilton, J. M., & Salmon, D. P. (2003). The myth of testing construct validity using factor analysis or correlations with normal or mixed clinical populations: Lessons from memory assessment. *Journal of the International Neuropsychological Society*, *9*(6), 936–946.

Delis, D. C., Kaplan, E., & Kramer, J. H. (1997). *Delis–Kaplan executive function system*. San Antonio, TX: The Psychological Corporation.

Donders, J. (1996). Validity of short forms of the intermediate Halstead Category Test in children with traumatic brain injury. *Archives of Clinical Neuropsychology*, *11*, 131–137.

Edwards, J. (2001). Ten difference score myths. *Organizational Research Methods*, *4*(3), 265–287.

Franzen, M. D. (2000). *Reliability and validity in neuropsychological assessment* (2nd ed.). New York: Plenum/Kluwer Academic.

Gaudette, M. D., & Smith, J. A. (1999). Process-oriented administration of the Picture Arrangement Test does not affect the quantitative outcome. *Applied Neuropsychology*, *5*, 154–158.

Grossman, F. M., Herman, D. O., & Matarazzo, J. D. (1985). Statistically inferred vs. empirically observed VIQ-PIQ differences in the WAIS-R. *Journal of Clinical Psychology*, *41*, 268–272.

Hebben, N., & Milberg, W. (2002). *Essentials of neuropsychological assessment*. New York: Wiley.

Hooper, E. (1958, 1983). *The Hooper Visual Organization Test*. Los Angeles: Western Psychological Services.

Hunsley, J., & Bailey, J. M. (1999). The clinical utility of the Rorschach: Unfulfilled promises and an uncertain future. *Psychological Assessment*, *11*(3), 266–277.

Kaplan, E. (1988). A process approach to neuropsychological assessment. In T. Boll & B. K. Bryant (Eds.), *Clinical neuropsychology and brain function: Research, measurement, and practice* (pp. 125–167). Washington, DC: American Psychological Association.

Kaplan, E., Goodglass, H., & Weintraub, S. (1978). *The Boston Naming Test: Experimental edition*. Philadelphia: Lea & Febiger.

Lansing, A. E., Ivnik, R. J., Cullum, C. M., & Randolph, C. (1999). An empirically derived short form of the Boston Naming Test. *Psychological Assessment*, *11*, 266–277.

Lichtenberg, P. A. (1998). Cost-effective geriatric neuropsychology. In P. E. Hartman-Stein (Ed.), *Innovative behavioral healthcare for older adults: A guidebook for changing times* (pp. 79–102). San Francisco, CA: Jossey-Bass.

Martin, T. A., Hoffman, N. M., & Donders, J. (2003). Clinical utility of the Trail Making Test Ratio Score. *Applied Neuropsychology*, *10*(3), 163–169.

Milberg, W., & McGlinchey, R. (2003). Taking the thumbs off the multidimensional scales in the debate on semantic memory and Alzhiemer's disease: A comment on Sorm et al. (2003). *Neuropsychology*, *17*(2), 312–314.

Mittenberg, W., Thompson, G. B., & Schwartz, J. A. (1991). Abnormal and reliable differences among Wechsler Memory Scale — Revised subtests. *Psychological Assessment*, *3*, 492–495.

Nadler, J. D., Grace, J., White, D. A., Butters, M. A., & Malloy, P. F. (1996). Laterality difference in quantative and qualitative Hooper performance. *Archives of Clinical Neuropsychology*, *11*, 223–229.

Nadler, J. D., Grace, J., White, D. A., Malloy, P. F., & Butters, M. (1996). Laterality differences in qualitative and quantitative Hooper Visual Organization Test performance. *Archives of Clinical Neuropsychology*, *11*, 223–229.

Nunnally, J. C. (1978). *Psychometric theory* (2nd ed.). New York: McGraw-Hill.

O'Bryant, S. E., Hilsabeck, R. C., Fisher, J. M., & McCaffrey, R. J. (2003). Utility of the Trail Making Test in the assessment of malingering in a sample of mild traumatic brain injury litigants. *The Clinical Neuropsychologist*, *17*(1), 69–74.

Paolo, A. M., Axelrod, B. N., & Tröster, A. I. (1996). Utility of a Wisconsin Card Sorting Test Short Form in persons with Alzheimer's and Parkinson's disease. *Journal of Clinical and Experimental Neuropsychology*, *18*, 892–897.

Payne, R. W., & Jones, G. (1957). Statistics for the investigation of individual cases. *Journal of Clinical Psychology*, *13*, 115–121.

Poreh, A. M. (2000). The quantified process approach. *Clinical Neuropsychology*, *14*(2), 212–222.

Poreh, A., & Shye, S. (1998). Examination of the global and local features of the Rey–Osterrieth Complex Figure using faceted smallest space analysis. *Clinical Neuropsychologist*, *12*(4), 453–467.

Power, D. G., Logue, P. E., McCarty, S. M., Rosenstiel, A. K., & Ziesat, H. A. (1979). Brief report: Inter-rater reliability of the Russell revision of the Wechsler Memory Scale: An attempt to clarify some ambiguities in scoring. *Journal of Clinical Neuropsychology*, *1*, 343–345.

Randolph, C. (2002). Neuropsychological testing: Evolution and emerging trends. *CNS Spectrums*, *7*(4), 307–312.
Regard, M. (1991). The perception and control of emotions: Hemispheric differences and the role of the frontal lobes. Habilitationsschrift, Zurich: University Hospital Department of Neurology.
Regard, M., Strauss, E., & Knapp, P. (1982). Children's production on verbal and nonverbal fluency tasks. *Perceptual and Motor Skills*, *55*, 839–844.
Rogers, T. T. (2003). Is there madness in the method? A comment on Storms et al. *Neuropsychology*, *17*(2), 289–301.
Russell, E. W. (1975). A multiple scoring method for the assessment of complex memory functions. *Journal of Consulting and Clinical Psychology*, *3*, 800–809.
Silverstein, A. B. (1981). Reliability and abnormality of test score differences. *Journal of Clinical Psychology*, *37*, 392–394.
Slick, D., Hopp, G., Strauss, E., Fox, D., Pinch, D., & Stickgold, K. (1996). Effects of prior testing with the WAIS-R NI on subsequent retest with the WAIS-R. *Archives of Neuropsychology*, *11*, 123–130.
Sokal, R. R., & Rohlf, J. F. (1995). *Biometry* (3rd ed.). San Francisco, CA: W. H. Freeman.
Spreen, O., & Strauss, E. (1998). *A compendium of neuropsychological tests: Administration, norms and commentary*. Oxford, UK: Oxford University Press.
Storandt, M. (1976). Speed and coding effects in relation to age and ability level. *Developmental Psychology*, *12*(2), 177–178.
Suhr, J., Grace, J., Allen, J., Nadler, J., & McKenna, M. (1998). Quantitative and qualitative performance of stroke versus normal elderly on six clock drawing systems. *Archives of Clinical Neuropsychology*, *13*(6), 495–502.
Sweet, J. H., Westergaard, C. K., & Moberg, P. J. (1996). Managed care experiences of clinical neuropsychologists. *Clinical Neuropsychologist*, *9*, 214–218.
Sylvester, C. Y., & Shimamura, A. P. (2002). Evidence for intact semantic representations in patients with frontal lobe lesions. *Neuropsychology*, *16*(2), 197–207.
Troyer, A. K., & Wishart, H. A. (1997). A comparison of qualitative scoring systems for the Rey–Osterrieth Complex Figure Test. *Clinical Neuropsychologist*, *11*, 381–390.
Vanderploeg, R. D., LaLone, L. V., Greblo, P., & Schinka, J. A. (1998). Odd–even short forms of the Judgment of Line Orientation Test. *Applied Neuropsychology*, *4*, 244–246.
van Zomeren, A. H., & Brouwer, W. H. (1994). Theories and concepts of attention. In *Clinical neuropsychology of attention* (Chapter 2). New York: Oxford University Press.
Wechsler, D. A. (1945). A standardized memory scale for clinical use. *Journal of Psychology*, *19*, 87–95.
Woodard, J. L., Benedict, R. H., & Roberts, V. J. (1997). Short-form alternatives to the Judgment of Line Orientation Test. *Journal of Clinical and Experimental Neuropsychology*, *18*, 898–904.
Woodward, J., Dunlosky, J., & Salthouse, T. (1999). Task decomposition analysis of intertrial free recall performance on the Rey Auditory Verbal Learning Test in normal aging and Alzheimer's disease. *Journal of Clinical and Experimental Psychology*, *21*, 666–676.

Part II

The Satellite Testing Paradigm

The "Satellite" Testing Paradigm is an approach by which new complimentary tasks are developed for the purpose of clarifying the test performance on an existing neuropsychological test. In Chapter 4, Bradley N. Axelrod and Greg J. Lamberty describe the development of the Oral Trail Making Test, a novel task for assessing an individual's ability to perform the set-shifting component of the TMT without visual and motor confounds. In Chapter 5, Joseph J. Ryan and David S. Kreiner describe the development of the Digit Symbol-Coding subtest, norms, psychometric properties, base rate data, and patterns of change in 30-s intervals. In Chapter 6, Eli Vakil describes the development of a supplementary temporal-order judgment measure for the Rey Auditory Verbal Learning Test (AVLT). The chapter also provides the necessary forms, norms, and validation data for this new measure. In Chapter 7, Maria T. Schultheis and Joseph H. Ricker describe the Hooper Object Naming Test and subsequent development of the Multiple-Choice adaptation of the HVOT (MC-HVOT).

4 The Oral Trail Making Test

Bradley N. Axelrod and Greg J. Lamberty

Introduction

The Trail Making Test (TMT; Reitan, 1955) is one of the most often used tasks of neuropsychological functioning. Survey studies consistently report TMT as one of the favored tasks for evaluation of executive functioning (e.g., Butler, Retzlaff, & Vanderploeg, 1991). The more difficult TMT-B requires cognitive set shifting, working memory, visual scanning, and motor skills. In its primary form, TMT is a strong indicator of brain dysfunction (e.g., Alekoumbidies, Charter, Adkins, & Seacat, 1987; Dodrill, 1978; O'Donnell, 1983) and one of the most sensitive to brain dysfunction in the Halstead Reitan Neuropsychological Test Battery (Reitan & Wolfson, 1985). TMT is sensitive to recovery of function in individuals evaluated longitudinally (Stuss, Stethem, Hughenholtz, & Richard, 1989). Finally, the measure has demonstrated predictive validity in vocational outcome in brain-injured individuals (Lewinsohn, 1973). The set-shifting aspect of TMT-B is assumed to tap executive functioning abilities, commonly considered to be mediated by anterior portions of the brain. Thus, patients who perform poorly on other measures of executive functioning typically also perform poorly on TMT-B (Jarvis & Barth, 1994).

In light of the clinical utility and sensitivity of TMT, its use with individuals who are visually or motorically compromised was considered. Namely, the authors who studied the Oral TMT attempted to first assess its use relative to the traditional TMT. As TMT performance includes the additional components of visual acuity and intact motor functioning, the time required to complete TMT might be lengthened by patients with peripheral, non-neurologic, deficiencies in these areas. For example, an individual with arthritis might perform the task slowly, although the ability to process the information cognitively is not compromised. Similarly, one with poor vision might not be able to perform the task at all. Eliminating this set-shifting task for non-neurologic reasons also removes the clinical information contributed by the measure. The introduction of a nonmotor and nonvisual version was initiated in response to retaining this task that otherwise provides important executive functioning data.

The purpose of this task is to assess an individual's ability to perform the set-shifting component of the TMT without visual and motor confounds. This procedure is of particular necessity when patients present with impairment in vision or motor skills, unrelated to a neurologic event.

Description

The TMT is composed of two parts: (1) TMT Part A and (2) TMT Part B. TMT Part A (TMT-A) requires the patient to perform a simple paper and pencil connect-the-dots task using numerals from 1 to 25. TMT Part B (TMT-B) requires the participant to sequentially alternate between numbers and letters. Ricker, Axelrod, and colleagues (Abraham, Axelrod, & Ricker, 1996; Ricker & Axelrod, 1994; Ricker, Axelrod, & Houtler, 1996) introduced an orally administered version of TMT. In Oral TMT-A, the participant simply counts forward from 1 to 25, simply to introduce the individual to the format of the task. For Oral TMT-B, the individual is asked to alternate between numbers and letters, sequentially, until they reach the number 13. Based on studies with nonpatient community dwelling adults, rehabilitation patients following stroke, and mixed clinical patients referred for neuropsychological evaluation, estimations of written TMT-A and TMT-B were developed.

Source

There is no commercial source for this variant administration of the TMT. Clinicians may design their own scoring sheet based on the description of the task.

Administration

In contrast with written TMT administration, there are no sample trials with the test materials. The verbal instructions appear below.

Oral TMT-A

"I'd like you to count from 1 to 25 as quickly as you can. 1, 2, 3, 4, and so on. Ready? Begin." If a mistake is made, the examiner stops the participant and points out the last correct item. Then, the participant continues with the series from the corrected number. The total time required to complete the series, including the time to offer corrections, is recorded.

Oral TMT-B

"Now, I'd like you to switch between numbers and letters when you count. 1, A, 2, B, 3, C, and so on until you reach the number 13." If the participant makes an error, the examiner identifies the last correct item and tells the participant to continue the series from that item. The total time required to complete the series, including the time to offer corrections, is recorded.

Approximate administration time

The completion of both tasks is typically under 5 min.

Scoring

The total time required to complete Oral TMT-A and Oral TMT-B are the primary scores of interest, with the more important score being the time for TMT-B. Based on existing studies with normal controls, multiplying Oral TMT-B time by 2.6 estimates the time to complete written TMT-B. The oral-to-written projected score can then be corrected for demographic information via existing databases (e.g., Heaton, Grant, & Matthews, 1991).

Comment

Limited research has demonstrated the sensitivity of Oral TMT in the detection of cognitive changes in comparison to nonpatient controls (Barncord, 2002), patients who otherwise do not demonstrate cognitive deficits (Ricker et al., 1996), and relative to other tasks within a patient population (e.g., Chiaravalloti & DeLuca, 2002). Although these studies offer external validation of Oral TMT, they do not allow one to use the Oral TMT with the existing knowledge base.

Perhaps, the more important application of Oral TMT pertains to its ability to predict written TMT performance. In that Oral TMT was intended to provide an estimation of TMT performance, with confounds of visual and motor skills accounted for, such predictions of written TMT performance is reasonable. The time taken to complete Oral TMT-A can generally be multiplied by 3.7 to estimate TMT-A performance (e.g., Ricker & Axelrod, 1994). However, the intent of TMT-A is to familiarize a patient with the visual–motor component of the task. TMT-A is not intended to be a complex task. When presented in the oral format, the task is simply addressing the individual's ability to count from 1 to 25. Perhaps it is for that reason that the correlation of TMT-A to Oral TMT-A in nonpatient samples ranges from being unrelated ($r = -0.10$; Oliveira-Souza et al., 2000) to mildly ($r = 0.29$; Mrazik, Yuspeh, Drane, Klingler, Huthwaite, & Dildine, 2001) or strongly ($r = 0.68$; Ricker & Axelrod, 1994) related.

In contrast, correlations of TMT-B to Oral TMT-B in nonclinical samples range from 0.59 to 0.72 (Mrazik et al., 2001; Oliveira-Souza et al., 2000; Ricker & Axelrod, 1994). The utility of TMT as a neuropsychological measure really lies in the complexity of TMT-B. Consequently, most research has addressed the sensitivity of Oral TMT-B as an estimate of TMT-B performance. Initial normative studies with community dwelling individuals found the ratio obtained by dividing TMT-B by Oral TMT-B to average 2.4 (Ricker & Axelrod, 1994). A subsequent study with 55 normal volunteers aged 18 to 73 revealed a similar ratio (ratio = 2.6) when TMT-B was divided by Oral TMT-B (Oliveira-Souza et al., 2000). Similar ratios were obtained when Oral TMT was assessed in a mixed clinical neuropsychological sample (ratio = 2.6). A general guideline of multiplying Oral TMT-B by 2.6 to estimate TMT-B is recommended (see Table 4.1).

With the introduction of demographically corrected normative data, the need to demographically correct this information for the Oral TMT is indicated. Converting the Oral TMT-B score into an estimated TMT-B score allows neuropsychologists the opportunity to estimate demographically corrected scores in comparison to scores from other tasks. In the original normative study, projected TMT-B scores were entered into the demographic normative database for demographic correction (Heaton et al., 1991). The T-scores for written TMT-B that were generated for the nonpatient sample averaged 52. Projected TMT-B scores that were demographically corrected resulted in an average T-score of 49. Clearly, these scores are comparable. This method was applied in the clinical setting with mixed clinical patients (Abraham et al., 1996) in which written TMT-B T-scores averaged 42.5 and

Table 4.1 Summary of Oral TMT-B and written-to-Oral TMT-B ratio scores

Study	*Mean age*	*Oral TMT-B*	*TMT-B/Oral TMT-B*	*Source*
Nonpatient adults	49.6 (19.6)	33.9 (17.6)	not available	Mrazik, Yuspeh, Drane, Klingler, Huthwaite, and Dildine (2001)
Nonpatient adults	38.0 (14.0)	25.0 (18.0)	2.6	Oliveira-Souza et al. (2000)
Nonpatient adults	18.9 (1.1)	24.1 (10.9)	2.3 (0.9)	Ricker and Axelrod (1994)
Nonpatient adults	31.9 (8.9)	22.8 (10.6)	2.6 (1.0)	
Nonpatient adults	83.5 (6.6)	40.2 (56)	2.7 (0.3)	
Mixed clinical patients	31.3 (5.6)	41.5 (24.4)	2.6 (1.2)	Abraham, Axelrod, and Ricker (1996)
Mixed clinical patients	48.5 (5.2)	52.0 (40.9)	2.6 (1.1)	
Mixed clinical patients	68.3 (5.2)	79.0 (55.7)	2.7 (1.4)	

projected TMT-B scores from Oral TMT-B averaged 38.2. Demographic correction of converted scores revealed comparable findings to Wisconsin Card Sorting Test scores in patients following strokes (Ricker et al., 1996).

Potential confounding factors

Demographic information and cognitive status is differentially related to the time required to complete Oral TMT-B. However, as appears to be the case with the ratio of TMT-A to TMT-B (see Chapter 10 in this volume), the introduction of a ratio between written and Oral TMT-B is not affected by such confounds.

Age

The Oral to written TMT-B ratio does not appear to be age-sensitive. Ricker and Axelrod (1994) found that the ratios did not differ across differing age groups, individuals averaging 19 (ratio = 2.3), 32 (ratio = 2.7), and 84 (ratio = 2.4) years of age-generated comparable ratio scores (Ricker & Axelrod, 1994) to each other. The lack of age effect on the ratio contrasts with the significant age effect observed in raw score performance on both TMT-B and Oral TMT-B. Studies with normal controls presented significantly slower speed with older adults when compared across age groups. Similarly, the correlations of Oral TMT-B with age are moderately high ($r = 0.69$) when the ages include the elderly (Mrazik et al., 2001; Ricker & Axelrod, 1994). Ruchinskas (2001) found that the incidence of being unable to perform the task was greater in older individuals. The age-related finding was also observed in a mixed clinical sample. Abraham et al. (1996) found patients referred for neuropsychological assessment, with mean ages of 31 and 48, had significantly faster TMT-B and Oral TMT-B than did a group of 68-year-old patients. As stated above, the written-to-Oral TMT-B ratio does not differ across ages. In the study with clinical patients, the youngest two groups each had ratio scores of 2.6 each while the older group's ratio was 2.7.

Education

The confounding effects of education and general cognitive functioning have been preliminarily studied with Oral TMT. Studies with nonpatients have found education to be related to poorer Oral TMT-B performance in less educated populations (Ruchinskas, 2001). A similar finding is observed relative to performance on Vocabulary, however the ratio of TMT-B to Oral TMT-B did not differ (Ricker & Axelrod, 1994).

Cognitive functioning

The consistency of the ratio score for Oral TMT-B with individuals who otherwise perform poorly on TMT-B was investigated. The mixed clinical sample presented by Abraham et al. (1996) was subdivided into four groups based on their T-score performance of TMT-B, using the demographic corrections (Heaton et al., 1991). The resulted groups were formulated based on T-scores less than 29, 30 to 39, 40 to 59, and more than 59. The four groups did not differ relative to age or education level. Raw TMT-B times for the groups were obviously faster for the groups with higher T-scores. Similarly, Oral TMT-B was faster for the T-score groups that had better performance. In contrast, the ratio score of written-to-Oral TMT-B did not differ across the groups.

References

Abraham, E., Axelrod, B. N., & Ricker, J. H. (1996). Application of the Oral Trail Making Test to a mixed clinical sample. *Archives of Clinical Neuropsychology*, *11*, 697–701.

Alekoumbides, A., Charter, R. A., Adkins, T. G., & Seacat, G. F. (1987). The diagnosis of brain damage by the WAIS, WMS, and Reitan Battery utilizing standardized scores corrected for age and education. *International Journal of Clinical Neuropsychology*, *9*, 11–28.

Barncord, S. W. (2002). An Oral Trail Making Test: A validity investigation. *Archives of Clinical Neuropsychology*, *17*, 827.

Butler, M., Retzlaff, P., & Vanderploeg, R. D. (1991). Neuropsychological test usage. *Professional Psychology: Research and Practice*, *22*, 510–521.

Chiaravalloti, N. D., & DeLuca, J. (2002). Self-generation as a means of maximizing learning in multiple sclerosis: An application of the generation effect. *Archives of Physical Medicine and Rehabilitation*, *83*, 1070–1079.

Dodrill, C. B. (1978). A neuropsychological battery for epilepsy. *Epilepsia*, *19*, 611–623.

Heaton, R. K., Grant, I., & Matthews, C. G. (1991). *Comprehensive norms for an expanded Halstead–Reitan Battery: Demographic corrections, research findings, and clinical applications*. Odessa, FL: Psychological Assessment Resources.

Jarvis, P. E., & Barth, J. T. (1994). *Halstead–Reitan Test Battery: A guide to interpretations and clinical applications*. Odessa, FL: Psychological Assessment Resources, Inc.

Lewinsohn, P. M. (1973). *Psychological assessment of patients with brain injury*. Unpublished manuscript. University of Oregon, Eugene, OR.

Mrazik, M., Yuspeh, R. L., Drane, D. L., Klingler, L., Huthwaite, J., & Dildine, D. (2001). The Oral Trail Making Test: Demographic influences and preliminary normative data. *Archives of Clinical Neuropsychology*, *16*, 835.

O'Donnell, J. P. (1983). Neuropsychological test findings for normal, learning disabled, and brain damaged young adults. *Journal of Consulting and Clinical Psychology*, *51*, 726–729.

Oliveira-Souza, R., Moll, J., Passman, L. J., Cunha, F. C., Paes, F., Adriano, M. V., Ignacio, F. A., & Marrocos, R. P. (2000). Trail making and cognitive set-shifting. *Arquivos de Neuro-Psiquiatria*, *58*, 826–829.

Reitan, R. M. (1955). The relationship of the Trail Making Test to organic brain damage. *Journal of General Psychology*, *53*, 97–107.

Reitan, R. M., & Wolfson, D. (1985). *The Halstead–Reitan Neuropsychological Test Battery: Theory and clinical interpretation*. Tucson, AZ: Neuropsychology Press.

Ricker, J. H., & Axelrod, B. N. (1994). Analysis of an oral paradigm for the Trail Making Test. *Assessment*, *1*, 47–51.

Ricker, J. H., Axelrod, B. N., & Houtler, B. D. (1996). Clinical validation of the Oral Trail Making Test. *Neuropsychiatry, Neuropsychology, and Behavioral Neurology*, *9*, 50–53.

Ruchinskas, R. (2001). The utility of the Oral Trail Making Test with older individuals. *Archives of Clinical Neuropsychology*, *16*, 839.

Stuss, D. T., Stethem, L., Hugenholtz, H., & Richard, M. T. (1989). Traumatic brain injury: A comparison of three clinical tests, and analysis of recovery. *The Clinical Neuropsychologist*, *3*, 145–156.

5 Clinical applications of the Digit Symbol-Coding subtest

Joseph J. Ryan and David S. Kreiner

History

Symbol substitution tests are among the oldest and most well established of all psychological measures. These tasks require a motor response (i.e., copying) and the ability to associate symbols with numbers or vice versa. The speed and accuracy with which an examinee completes the test is traditionally considered an indication of his or her intellectual ability. Such a test was incorporated into the Army Beta Examination, which was used to screen illiterate military recruits during World War I (Tulsky, Saklofske, & Zhu, 2003). Unlike the modern version of the test, it contained a symbol substitution test that was administered via pantomime and therefore did not require reading, writing, or the comprehension of spoken English.

David Wechsler adapted the Digit Symbol test to the Wechsler–Bellevue Intelligence Scale-Form I (WB-I; Wechsler, 1939). In his adaptation, the original 67 stimuli from the Army Beta subtest were utilized without alteration, but the completion time was reduced from 120 to 90 s. With the appearance of the Wechsler Adult Intelligence Scale (WAIS; Wechsler, 1955), the Digit Symbol subtest was expanded to 90 items and one or more of the symbols were changed. When the revised WAIS was published 26 years later (i.e., WAIS-R; Wechsler, 1981), the Digit Symbol subtest was increased to 93 items. In the 1997 revision (i.e., WAIS-III), the Digit Symbol subtest was redesigned to be more accommodating to left-handed examinees by providing more space between the key and the answer sheet. This improvement reduces the chance that left-handers will inadvertently obscure the key during task administration. Additional modifications included an increase in the number of items to be completed (i.e., from 93 to 133), setting the time limit at 120 s, renaming the task as the Digit Symbol-Coding subtest, and adding two Satellite Tests: the Digit Symbol-Incidental Learning and Digit Symbol-Copy. The latter procedures have been used by practitioners and researchers for over half a century, but they were never included as part of the standard Wechsler Scale until publication of the WAIS-III (e.g., Burik, 1950; Kaplan, Fein, Morris, & Delis, 1991; Murstein & Leipold, 1961). The Incidental Learning procedure was popularized by Hart, Kwentus, Wade, and Hamer

(1987), whereas the Copy procedure appears to have first been introduced into the literature by Storandt (1976). The purpose of this Satellite Test is to provide a rapid screening tool for detecting memory dysfunction and to help explain the reasons for poor performance on the Digit Symbol-Coding subtest (e.g., graphomotor slowing vs. impaired learning).

Description

Digit Symbol-Coding is printed on a single page and requires the examinee to copy symbols that are paired with numbers. The test stimuli are presented in a key that consists of nine individual boxes that contain a number (i.e., from 1 to 9) in the upper portion and a symbol in the lower portion. A different symbol appears under each number. The key is positioned at the top of the page and is followed by 3 in of blank space. Seven rows each of 20 boxes are positioned approximately one third of the way down the page. A total of 140 boxes with a number in the top portion and a blank space in the lower portion are provided. The first seven boxes are designated as sample or practice items. This is a multifaceted task that measures graphomotor speed and accuracy as well as the ability to quickly form associations between numbers and symbols. It requires mental flexibility, visual-motor coordination, attention-concentration, perceptual speed, short-term memory, and visual scanning and tracking (Joy, Fein, & Kaplan, 2003a; Sattler & Ryan, 2001a). Additional individual and situational factors that influence test behavior include planning, distractibility, reflectivity/impulsivity, verbal elaboration, visual elaboration, and the ability to perform under time pressures (McGrew & Flanagan, 1998).

Unlike subtests in the WAIS-III battery that have been designated as high in cultural content (i.e., Vocabulary, Similarities, and Information), Digit Symbol-Coding has been characterized as low in cultural content (McGrew & Flanagan, 1998). Thus, subtest performance should be relatively independent of the degree to which an examinee has assimilated the basics of mainstream United States culture during the mid-1990s. However, it needs to be kept in mind that degree of acculturation is not synonymous with gender, educational level, and/or race/ethnicity. Moreover, an examinee who is well acculturated to the United States might perform poorly on this subtest simply because he/she has little or no experience with paper-and-pencil types of tasks (Kaufman & Lichtenberger, 2002).

The Incidental Learning procedure consists of Pairing and Free Recall components. Pairing is composed of two rows of nine boxes each. The upper portion of each box contains a number from 1 to 9 and the lower portion is blank. The Free Recall component is a blank space at the bottom of the page. The Incidental Learning procedure is designed to measure paired associate learning (i.e., Pairing) and short-term memory for symbols independent of the numbers (i.e., Free Recall).

Digit Symbol-Copy in the WAIS-III version consists of 140 boxes arranged in seven rows. The upper part of each box contains a symbol and the lower portion is blank. This task features the same symbols found in the Digit Symbol-Coding subtest. The examinee is instructed to copy each symbol in the box below it. This task primarily measures perceptual and graphomotor speed.

Administration and scoring

Administration of the Digit Symbol-Coding subtest and its optional procedures, Digit Symbol-Incidental Learning and Digit Symbol-Copy, requires a stopwatch and two pencils without erasers. The subtest should not be administered to persons with obvious impairment of the dominant arm or hand or to someone with significant visual acuity problems or visual neglect. Based on a sample of 62 patients at a Veterans Affairs Medical Center, Ryan, Lopez, and Werth (1998) found that the average time required to administer Digit Symbol-Coding was 3 min, 37s (range = 2 min, 29 s to 6 min, 15 s). This is the least time-consuming subtest in the WAIS-III test battery. Average administration times for the optional Incidental Learning and Copy components were 3 min, 18 s (range = 1 min, 12 s to 10 min, 52 s) and 2 min, 5 s (range = 1 min, 43 s to 4 min, 25 s), respectively.

During administration of Digit Symbol-Coding, the examiner reads the instructions verbatim and completes three demonstration items while verbally and manually directing the examinee's attention to the key printed at the top of the page. The examinee then copies four practice symbols and, if they are reproduced correctly, is instructed to begin the subtest. The time limit is 120 s and the raw score is based on the total number of symbols correctly matched and copied within the time limit. Possible raw scores range from 0 to 133.

The *WAIS-III Administration and Scoring Manual* indicates that no one other than the examiner and examinee should be in the room during Scale administration. It is possible that a third-party observer might negatively, or positively, influence test performance by increasing an examinee's anxiety level, altering motivation, or possibly serving as a source of distraction (McSweeny, Becker, Naugle, Snow, Binder, & Thompson, 1998). The test manual also states that seating arrangement is crucial for efficient test administration and that the examiner should sit across the table, facing the examinee. This arrangement allows the examiner to observe important test-taking behaviors and enhances his/her appreciation of the examinee beyond what can be obtained from the test score alone. However, it is important to keep in mind that during administration of Digit Symbol-Coding and Digit Symbol-Copy, the examiner must be in a convenient position to unobtrusively mark the protocols if he/she wishes to keep track of an examinee's rate of transcription or plans on testing incidental recall and the examinee does not complete four rows of symbols before the time limit expires.

The influence of seating arrangement on WAIS Digit Symbol scores was evaluated by Delprato and Jackson (1975) using 80 college students (40 males,

40 females) and two seating arrangements, face-to-face and corner-to-corner (i.e., examinee sat on the side of the table adjacent to that on which the examiner sat). Results indicated that males scored reliably higher in the corner-to-corner than the face-to-face seating arrangement. Changes in seating arrangement did not affect the scores of female participants. This finding underscores the importance of adhering to standardized administration as recommended by Wechsler (1997a).

Some clinicians decompose the Digit-Symbol score by recording the examinee's progress at 30-, 60-, and 90-s intervals (Kaplan, Fein, Morris, & Delis, 1991). This maneuver allows one to determine overall visual-motor speed and whether the rate of transcription is characterized by variability or consistency over time. To administer the Incidental Learning components, which are discussed below, the examinee must complete at least four rows of symbols. On occasion, an individual will need more than 120 s to satisfy the four-row requirement. If this happens, the score for Digit Symbol-Coding is still the number of symbols copied within the 120 s time limit.

Scoring is accomplished by placing a cardboard template directly over the array of boxes to determine the number of accurately reproduced symbols. This appears to be a simple procedure, but it is not foolproof. Ryan and Schnakenberg-Ott (2003) found that when doctoral level psychologists and psychology graduate students scored two WAIS-III protocols, they sometimes experienced difficulty scoring the Digit Symbol-Coding subtest. Failure to subtract points for incorrectly reproduced symbols was the most common error.

Immediately following completion of the Digit Symbol-Coding subtest, the examinee is presented the Incidental Learning Satellite task of Pairing Satellite task and is instructed to fill in all the symbols that he/she can remember, across both rows. The raw score is based on the number of symbols that are correctly drawn and matched to an appropriate numeral. The total possible raw score points range from 0 to 18. Next, the completed number-symbol rows are covered with a blank sheet of paper and the examinee's attention is directed to the lower half of page 6. The examinee is instructed to write down all of the symbols he/she can remember, in any order. This is the Free Recall component of the task. The raw score ranges from 0 to 9 and is based on the number of symbols correctly drawn from memory. The Pairing and Free Recall tasks are not timed.

The Incidental Learning task is scored either by visual inspection of the two rows of boxes or by using a template, such as the one provided in the WAIS-III kit. Ryan and Schnakenberg-Ott (2003) found that this relatively simple scoring task was completed incorrectly by two of 38 study participants (one psychologist and one graduate student). The errors made by these individuals involved assignment of credit to an incorrect recollection, adding only the first row of correct Pairing responses, and failure to count any of the Free Recall responses.

In the Digit Symbol-Copy Satellite procedure, the examinee copies a few items and, if he/she reproduces each item correctly, is instructed to copy the remaining marks or symbols as quickly as he/she can. The time limit is 90 s and the raw score is determined by assigning one point for each correctly copied symbol. The maximum possible raw score is 133. Some practitioners follow along as the symbols are copied and place marks on the protocol every 30 s to assess rate of transcription across the three time intervals.

Examiners may either visually inspect the symbol reproductions for accuracy or use the scoring template provided in the WAIS-III kit. Even with this assistance, errors sometimes occur when scoring Digit Symbol-Copy. Ryan and Schnakenberg-Ott (2003) reported that two out of 38 examiners in their study made large addition errors (e.g., 43 symbols were copied within 90 s, but a score of 53 was recorded) during the scoring process. Also, five examiners made the same scoring error, which was due to a problem with the scoring template. In the second row of the Response Booklet, the symbol to be copied has three sides and is open to the left. Unfortunately, the scoring template for this item is a figure that is open at the top. When the template is used to score the item, a correctly copied symbol is scored as an error (Sattler & Ryan, 2001a).

The recording of pertinent behavioral observations is an essential part of subtest administration and often aids in score interpretation. A trained examiner will look for signs of neurological impairment (e.g., scanning difficulties), psychological problems (e.g., compulsive tendencies), education-related deficits (e.g., holding the pencil incorrectly), and/or situational variables (e.g., poor motivation) that may invalidate the subtest score. Table 5.1 provides examples of potentially relevant behavioral observations.

Norms

Digit Symbol-Coding

Raw scores on the subtest are converted into scaled scores (M = 10; SD = 3; range = 1–19) by using Tables A.1 and A.2 (p. 181–194) in the *WAIS-III Administration and Scoring Manual*. The scores in Table A.1 are based on 2450 individuals selected to be representative of the United States population during the mid-1990s. The sample was stratified on age (13 age groups that range from 16–17 to 85–89 years), gender (males and females at appropriate proportions for each age group), race/ethnicity (Euro American = 1925; African American = 279; Hispanic American = 181; Other = 65), education (five levels from ≤ 8 to ≥ 16 years), and geographic region (Northeast; North Central; South; West). Table A.2 provides supplemental norms based on a census-matched sample of 600 individuals in the age range from 20 to 34 years. These norms may be used to compare an older person's level of performance with that of a group of optimally functioning young adults.

Inspection of the Digit Symbol-Coding norms indicates that older adults are less proficient than younger adults on this subtest (Ryan, Sattler, & Lopez, 2000; Sattler & Ryan, 2001a). To highlight age changes in the allotment of

Table 5.1 Some noteworthy behavioral observations during Digit Symbol-Coding and possible implications

Observations	*Possible implications*
Referring to the key on every item	Memory problem (Kaufman & Lichtenberger, 1999)
Excessive time needed to locate the correct place in the key or find correct place on the protocol	Visual scanning problem (Kaplan et al., 1991)
Tends not to return to the leftmost box	Neglect (Kaplan et al., 1991)
Expansion of symbol beyond the box, micrographic reproductions, uneven/light pencil strokes, tremor	Visual-motor problem (Kaplan et al., 1991)
Overwriting individual symbols	Motor persistence (Kaplan, 1990)
Awkward grip on pencil/pencil strokes that are not fluid	Visual-motor coordination problem (Kaufman & Lichtenberger, 2002)
Distortion of reproduced symbols	Visual-perceptual problem (Kaufman & Lichtenberger, 2002)
Excessive number of incorrect number-symbol matches during Digit Symbol-Coding	Thought disorder, learning disability, or response bias (Joy, Fein, Kaplan, & Freedman, 2000)
Works meticulously to make precise symbols, ignores instructions to work quickly	Sacrifices speed for accuracy (Lacritz & Cullum, 2003)
Loses "set," forgets the nature of the task, finds difficulty in shifting back and forth from numbers to symbols, simply copies the digits	Impaired executive functions (Joy et al., 2003a; Kaplan et al., 1991)

age-corrected scaled-score points, the lower limit of the raw score range for Digit Symbol-Coding that equals a scaled score of 10 in the supplemental norms (Table A.2) was determined. Next, using this raw score, scaled scores from Table A.1 were obtained for each of the 13 age groups in the standardization sample. The number of points above or below the average for the supplemental norm group was determined by subtracting 10 from each of the scaled scores. Table 5.2 indicates that performance on Digit Symbol-Coding peaks in the age range from 18 to 24 years and begins to drop off at 45 years of age, with steady decline thereafter. As a further illustration of the age factor, consider the observation that a raw score of 76 produces a scaled score of 10 in the supplemental norm group. However, at ages 85–89 years the same raw score converts into an age-corrected scaled score of 18. The eight points awarded to elderly examinees for a raw score of 76 changes the percentile for the raw score from the 50th to the 99th.

Also provided in Table 5.2 are the raw score points (i.e., lower limits of raw score ranges from Table A.1) needed at each age level to obtain an average age-corrected scaled score. For instance, a Digit Symbol-Coding raw score of 79 yields an age-corrected scaled score of 10 for someone 18–19 years of age. However, in the age range from 85 to 89 years, a raw score of 33 is required to obtain an age-corrected scaled score of 10. This indicates that examinees in the oldest age range need 46 fewer raw-score points than someone from 18 to 19 years of age to achieve an average level of performance.

Analysis of the WAIS-III standardization sample indicates that, in addition to chronological age, Digit Symbol-Coding scores are influenced by educational level, gender, and ethnicity. Thus, Digit Symbol-Coding performance is highly correlated ($r = 0.37$) with years of education, the average scaled score of females is 0.5 of a standard deviation greater than the average scaled score of males, and Caucasian examinees, on average, outperform African American and Hispanic examinees (Kaufman & Lichtenberger, 2002). Because of these findings, demographically (i.e., by age, education, gender, and ethnicity) corrected norms have been developed using 2726 healthy persons (2450 from the standardization sample plus 276 individuals from the "education over-samples"). These norms are available only in WAIS-III scoring/interpretation/report writing software packages published by The Psychological Corporation (1999, 2001).

To illustrate the influence of demographic variables on Digit Symbol-Coding performance, consider the case of a hypothetical 45-year-old examinee with a raw score of 69. The norms contained in the *WAIS-III Administration and Scoring Manual* indicate that this value is at the 50th percentile. However, when The Psychological Corporation computer software with demographic corrections is used to score the subtest, and the examinee is further identified as a high-school educated white male, the raw score of 69 is at the 58th percentile. If the examinee is entered as a female instead of a male, the raw score converts into a percentile rank of 34.4. Table 5.3 provides additional examples of how different combinations of gender (i.e., male or

Table 5.2 Additional scaled score points by age awarded to Digit Symbol-Coding

	Age range												
	16–17	*18–19*	*20–24*	*25–29*	*30–34*	*35–44*	*45–54*	*55–64*	*65–69*	*70–74*	*75–79*	*80–84*	*85–89*
Additional Points	0	−1	−1	0	0	0	1	3	4	5	6	7	8
Minimum Raw Scores	75	79	78	76	75	73	68	59	52	49	45	40	33

Notes: 1. When the supplemental norms group receives a scaled score of 10 and minimum raw score points needed to obtain a scaled score of 10 at 13 age groups.
2. Negative entries reflect performance that exceeds the supplemental norms group of persons 24–34 years. Adapted from Ryan et al. (2000).

Table 5.3 Influence of demographic variables on Digit Symbol-Coding percentiles of a 45-year-old examinee with a raw score of 69

Years of education	*Male*			*Female*		
	Caucasian	*African American*	*Hispanic*	*Caucasian*	*African American*	*Hispanic*
< 8	94.5	91.9	88.4	86.4	78.8	69.1
12	57.9	81.5	65.5	34.4	61.7	38.2
16	38.2	65.5	42.0	18.4	42.0	18.4

female), education (i.e., < 8 or 12 years), and ethnicity (Caucasian, African American, or Hispanic) alter the meaning of Digit Symbol-Coding scores for the hypothetical 45-year-old. Table 5.4 presents similar data for a hypothetical 74-year-old examinee with a raw score of 69 on Digit Symbol-Coding (scaled score of 14). For instance, if the examinee is a Caucasian female college graduate this raw score is approximately at the 73rd percentile. Conversely, a Hispanic female with <8 years of education who earns the same raw score is placed at approximately the 98th percentile. To insure accurate interpretation of the subtest, practitioners need to internalize the fact that normal and impaired performance levels may be defined differently according to each examinee's unique combination of demographic characteristics.

Digit Symbol-Incidental Learning

Raw scores for the Pairing and Free Recall components are converted into cumulative percentages for the 13 age groups in the standardization sample using Table A.11 in Appendix A of the *WAIS-III Administration and Scoring Manual*. The norms for both tasks are based on the same neuropsychologically intact 2450 individuals who completed the Digit Symbol-Coding subtest. Inspection of these norms indicates that, as with the Digit Symbol-Coding subtest, older adults are less proficient than younger adults on both Pairing and Free Recall. Because of this observation, we conducted an analysis of the standardization data for these procedures and determined that education and age are potentially the most important factors in determining an examinee's scores. Therefore, Tables 5.5 and 5.6 are provided for the conversion of raw scores on Pairing and Free Recall into cumulative percentages/percentile ranks for three levels of education (<12 years, 12 years, and >12 years) across four age groupings (16–29, 30–54, 55–74, and 75–89 years). The cumulative percentage for a given score may change if the examinee's age and level of education are considered simultaneously. For example, if a 56-year-old examinee with less than 12 years of education earns a Pairing raw score of 4, this converts into a cumulative percentage/percentile rank of 5 according to Table A.11 in the *WAIS-III Administration and Scoring Manual*. However, if Table 5.5 is used, the raw score of four pairs recalled converts to a cumulative percentage/percentile rank of 25. Likewise, if the same 56-year-old examinee recalled five individual symbols, this converts into a cumulative percentage/percentile rank of 10 using Table A.11. If Table 5.6 is consulted, the recall of five symbols converts into a cumulative percentage/percentile rank of 25.

Digit Symbol-Copy

Raw scores are converted into cumulative percentages for the 13 age groups in the standardization sample using Table A.11 in Appendix A of the *WAIS-III Administration and Scoring Manual*. These norms are based on 2408

Table 5.4 Influence of demographic variables on Digit Symbol-Coding percentiles of a 74-year-old examinee with a raw score of 69

Years of education	*Male*			*Female*		
	Caucasian	*African American*	*Hispanic*	*Caucasian*	*African American*	*Hispanic*
< 8	99.9	99.9	99.7	99.3	99.5	98.2
12	94.5	99.6	97.7	86.4	98.2	90.3
16	86.4	98.9	90.3	72.5	95.5	75.8

Table 5.5 Incidental Learning-Pairing: Cumulative percentages associated with raw score by education level and age

	Education											
	Below 12				*12*				*Above 12*			
	Age											
Cumulative percentage	16–29	30–54	55–74	75-89	16–29	30–54	55–74	75–89	16–29	30–54	55–74	75–89
1	1	0	0	0	2	1	1	0	0	1	0	0
2	4	1	0	0	3	2	1	0	1	2	0	0
5	6	4	1	0	6	4	2	1	5	5	2	0
10	9	5	2	1	9	6	4	2	7	6	4	2
25	12	7	4	4	11	9	6	5	11	10	6	5
50	15	11	8	6	14	12	9	8	14	13	10	9

Note: A two-way between subjects ANOVA on pairing scores indicated a significant main effect of education, $F(2, 2322) = 11.61$, $p < 0.0001$, a significant main effect of age, $F(2, 2322) = 219.26$, $p < 0.0001$, and a significant interaction of education and age, $F(2, 2322) = 5.01$, $p < 0.0001$.

Table 5.6 Incidental Learning-Free Recall: Cumulative percentages associated with raw score by education level and age

	Education											
	Below 12				*12*				*Above 12*			
	Age											
Cumulative percentage	16–29	30–54	55–74	75–89	16–29	30–54	55–74	75–89	16–29	30–54	55–74	75–89
1	1	1	1	1	1	1	1	1	1	1	1	1
2	1	1	1	1	1	1	1	1	1	1	1	1
5	1	1	1	1	1	1	1	3	1	1	2	1
1	4	2	3	2	1	1	1	4	2	3	4	3
25	7	6	5	4	6	6	5	4	6	6	6	5
50	8	7	7	6	7	7	7	6	8	7	7	6

Note: A two-way between subjects ANOVA on Free Recall scores indicated a significant main effect of education, $F(2, 2322) = 3.24$, $p = 0.04$, a significant main effect of age, $F(2, 2322) = 18.62$, $p < 0.0001$, and a significant interaction of education and age, $F(2, 2322) = 3.89$, $p = 0.0007$.

neuropsychologically intact individuals. Inspection of these norms indicates that, as with the Digit Symbol-Coding subtest and the Incidental Learning component, older adults are less proficient than younger adults and therefore copy fewer symbols during the allotted 90 s. Because of this observation, we conducted an analysis of the standardization data for this procedure and found that education and age are the two most important factors in determining an examinee's score. Therefore, Table 5.7 is provided for the conversion of raw scores on Digit Symbol-Copy into cumulative percentages according to three levels of education (<12, 12, and >12 years) across four age groupings (16–29, 30–54, 55–74, and 75–89 years). The cumulative percentage for a given score may change if the examinee's age and level of education are considered simultaneously. For example, if a 70-year-old examinee with 14 years of education earns a Copy raw score of 61, this converts into a cumulative percentage of approximately 10 referring to Table A.11 in the *WAIS-III Administration and Scoring Manual*. However, if Table 5.7 is used, the raw score of 61 converts into a cumulative percentage of 2.

Psychometric properties

Stability information for the Digit Symbol-Coding subtest is reported in the *WAIS-III/WMS-III Technical Manual* (The Psychological Corporation, 1997). The WAIS-III was administered twice to a sample of 394 individuals aged 16–29 years (n = 100), 30–54 years (n = 102), 55–74 years (n = 104), and 75–89 years (n = 88). The mean test-retest interval was approximately 35 days, with a range from 14 to 84 days. In the total sample, the stability coefficient was a very respectable 0.86. For the separate age groups, stability coefficients were: 0.81 (16–19 years), 0.84 (30–54 years), 0.86 (55–74 years), and 0.91 (75–89 years). However, the mean practice effects of 1.1, 1.2, 0.8, and 0.6 were statistically significant for each of the four age groups, respectively (Sattler & Ryan, 2001b). The average Standard Error of Measurement (SEM) for the Digit Symbol-Coding subtest is 1.19. For the separate age groups, the SEMs are 1.31 (17–29 years), 1.20 (30–54 years), 1.12 (55–74 years), and 1.08 (75–89 years).

Based on the 2450 individuals in the WAIS-III standardization sample, the Digit Symbol-Coding subtest correlates 0.49, 0.50, and 0.53 with the WAIS-III Verbal Scale, Performance Scale, and Full Scale IQs, respectively. It is a fair measure of general intelligence, with a *g* loading of 0.59. Thus, 35% of the variance in Digit Symbol-Coding performance is attributable to general intelligence. On the other hand, subtest specificity is ample across all 13 age ranges in the standardization sample. Taken together, these statistical characteristics indicate that the Digit Symbol-Coding subtest possesses both reliable (i.e., not the result of measurement error) and distinctive variance that justifies interpretation of specific subtest functions (Sattler & Ryan, 2001b).

Reliability and stability data for the Digit Symbol-Incidental Learning procedure are unavailable. However, scores from the Incidental Learning

Table 5.7 Digit-Symbol Copy scores: Cumulative percentages associated with raw score by education level and age

	Education											
	Below 12				*12*				*Above 12*			
	Age											
Cumulative percentage	16–29	30–54	55–74	75–89	16–29	30–54	55–74	75–89	16–29	30–54	55–74	75–89
1	49	44	31	19	51	58	41	33	83	81	54	33
2	69	48	32	22	57	62	46	36	87	84	61	42
5	81	60	47	33	77	76	54	46	93	91	69	51
10	91	73	55	42	92	87	65	54	99	98	75	58
25	106	90	69	54	112	100	80	63	118	113	89	72
50	123	109	85	69	130	116	95	79	132	128	103	86

Note: A two-way between-subjects ANOVA on Copy scores indicated a significant main effect of education, $F(2, 2402) = 80.12$, $p < 0.0001$, a significant main effect of age, $F(2, 2402) = 468.265$, $p < 0.0001$, and a significant interaction of education and age, $F(2, 2402) = 3.28$, $p = 0.003$.

component correlate significantly, albeit moderately, with summary measures from the Wechsler Memory Scale-III (WMS-III; Wechsler, 1997b). Joy, Kaplan, and Fein (2003b) used participants (n = 1167) from the WAIS-III/WMS-III standardization sample and calculated average correlations across age groups of 0.40 and 0.45 between Pairing scores and the Auditory Immediate and Auditory Delayed memory indexes, respectively. Correlations between Free Recall scores and the Auditory Immediate and Auditory Delayed memory indexes were 0.38 and 0.41, respectively. The associations between Incidental Learning and WMS-III visual memory performance were less impressive, but still statistically significant. Between Pairing scores and Visual Immediate and Visual Delayed memory indexes, correlations were 0.32 and 0.34, respectively. Finally, Free Recall scores and Visual Immediate and Visual Delayed memory indexes correlate 0.30 and 0.32.

In a second investigation using a sample of 87 undergraduate college students, Joy et al. (2003a) reported correlations of 0.53 (Pairing) and 0.61 (Free Recall) between the Digit Symbol-Incidental Learning components and a composite measure of visual memory (i.e., WMS-Revised Visual Reproduction subtest and Rey–Osterrieth Complex Figure delayed recall). In a clinical sample of 228 veterans with a variety of diagnoses (i.e., psychiatric, neurological, or substance abuse disorders), the correlations between WMS-III Immediate Memory Index and the Pairing and Free Recall scores were 0.44 and 0.45. The General Memory Index correlated 0.41 with Pairing and 0.41 with Free Recall (Kreiner & Ryan, 2001).

The Digit Symbol-Copy task has not been investigated in terms of reliability or stability. However, in a group of college students Copy scores were highly correlated with specialized measures of graphomotor speed (r = 0.67) and saccadic eye movements (r = 0.50), but unrelated to tests of memory (Joy et al., 2003a).

Relevant studies

A wide variety of neurological and/or psychiatric disorders can result in depressed Digit Symbol-Coding performance. For example, it is typically among the lowest subtest scores in the Wechsler battery for patients with traumatic brain injury (Donders, Tulsky, & Zhu, 2001; Langeluddecke & Lucas, 2003), Alcoholic Korsakoff's syndrome (Butters & Cermak, 1980), and Alzheimer's disease (Drachman, O'Donnell, Lew, & Swearer, 1990; Hart, Kwentus, Wade, & Hamer, 1987) as well as among patients with anxiety, depression, or schizophrenia (Groth-Marnat, 2003; Hart et al., 1987; Kellerman & Burry, 1991; Zimmerman & Woo-Sam, 1973).

Performance on the Digit Symbol subtest also discriminates normal elderly from brain-injured elderly. Ryan, Brown, and Paolo (2005) examined WAIS-R performance differences between 54 healthy individuals (age M = 79.3 years, SD = 4.9) and a demographically matched sample of neurologically impaired seniors (age M = 79.6 years, SD = 4.5). The Digit Symbol scaled score was the most powerful of the 11 subtests for discriminating groups as evidenced by a correct classification rate of 79.6%. These authors acknowledged that the 50% base rate for brain damage in their study might have contributed to unrealistically high group discrimination. To evaluate this possibility, a supplemental analysis of Digit Symbol scaled score cutoffs (i.e., normal ≥ 4; brain damaged ≤ 3) was undertaken. An additional 172 healthy elderly taken from the Ryan, Paolo, and Brungardt (1990) normative sample were added to the control group (total $n = 225$), changing the base rate for brain injury to a more realistic 19.4%. Application of the Digit Symbol cutoffs resulted in an overall hit rate of 80.3% with sensitivity of 83.3% and specificity of 79.6%. These findings suggest that the original hit rate was not an artifact of an unrealistically high brain damage base rate.

Results of the Digit Symbol-Coding subtest are also frequently associated with the severity and prognosis of a disorder. For instance, Drachman et al. (1990) studied the predictive power of Digit Symbol performance in a sample of 42 persons with probable Alzheimer's disease. At initial assessment, the Digit Symbol scaled score mean was 2.5 points ($SD = 1.8$). At 3-year follow-up, 89% of the patients with an initial scaled score of 1 were dependent for Activities of Daily Living (ADL), 66% were incontinent, and 65% were institutionalized. The corresponding percentages for patients with scaled scores >1 were 50%, 41%, and 31%, respectively.

Kaplan (1990) proferred the view that test interpretations based exclusively on quantitative results are sometimes misleading and that the process used to complete a task may be as informative as the final score. Kaplan et al. (1991) noted that specific errors observed during administration of the Digit Symbol subtest might reflect diffuse cognitive impairment or even frontal systems dysfunction. This is an example of the Composition Paradigm in the Quantified Process Approach (QPA; Poreh, 2000) in which additional test data are used to clarify the constructs underlying test performance. Paolo and Ryan (1994a) responded to Kaplan et al. by providing base rate statistics for five types of qualitative errors made by elderly persons during completion of the WAIS-R Digit Symbol subtest. Table 5.8 provides brief descriptions of the qualitative errors and their hypothesized interpretations. Two hundred and twenty-five healthy individuals 75–96 years of age were used to develop base rates and a second sample of 42 elderly with confirmed brain damage/dysfunction were used for comparison. Only shape completion (5.8%) and wrong symbol/skipping a number (16.9%) occurred more than 5% of the time in the normal sample. Among brain-damaged patients, the frequencies of these error types were 19% for shape completion and 31% for wrong number/skipping a number. Tests for the significance of independent proportions revealed that brain-damaged individuals committed more shape completion errors than healthy controls. The groups did not differ with respect to the proportions of errors that involve wrong number or skipping a number.

The Digit Symbol-Coding Incidental Learning Satellite Test may be used to quickly screen examinees for impaired memory. In a study using healthy

Table 5.8 Description of qualitative errors and their hypothesized interpretations on Digit Symbol-Coding

Error	*Hypothesized interpretation*
Shape completion: Examinee makes the symbol more salient. For example, the symbol associated with the number 7 is drawn as an "A"	Frontal system and/or diffuse cognitive dysfunction (Kaplan et al., 1991)
Closing in: Examinee uses the edge of the box as part of the reproduced symbol	Same as above
Numbers: Examinee copies the numbers instead of the associated symbols	Same as above
Perseveration: Examinee draws the same symbol under two consecutive numbers	Same as above
Overwriting: Examinee draws a symbol and then retraces the reproduced symbol one or more times	Motor impersistence (Kaplan, 1990)
Other: Examinee associates the wrong symbol with number and/or skips a number	Failure to comprehend directions, inattention/visual scanning problems

Adapted from Paolo and Ryan (1994a).

elderly volunteers and patients with either major depression or mild Alzheimer's disease (Hart et al., 1987), the mean WAIS Digit Symbol raw score of controls ($M = 43.7$, $SD = 1.8$) was significantly higher than the mean raw scores of both patient groups (Depressed $M = 27.0$, $SD = 2.2$; Alzheimer's $M = 25.1$, $SD = 2.5$). Although depressed and dementia patients could not be differentiated on the basis of the traditional Digit Symbol raw scores, the Incidental Learning components successfully separated the groups. Depressed patients produced mean Pairing ($M = 4.3$, $SD = 0.6$) and Free Recall ($M = 6.1$, $SD = 0.5$) scores that were significantly higher than those of the dementia patients (Pairing $M = 0.7$, $SD = 0.2$; Free Recall $M = 1.7$, $SD = 0.5$). The controls ($M = 6.9$, $SD = 0.3$) and depressed patients had similar Free Recall means (6.9 vs. 6.1), but the average Pairing score of the latter group was significantly below that of the controls ($M = 6.4$, $SD = 0.4$).

Digit Symbol scaled scores are sometimes comparably reduced among patients with Alzheimer's disease and Parkinson's disease. However, the Incidental Learning procedures of Free Recall and Pairing are capable of differentiating the diagnostic groups. Demakis, Sawyer, Fritz, and Sweet (2001) reported mean Pairing and Free Recall scores of 1.4 ($SD = 1.8$) and 3.0 ($SD = 2.0$), and 3.1 ($SD = 2.3$) and 5.3 ($SD = 2.3$), respectively, for patients with either Alzheimer's or Parkinson's disease. A discriminant function analysis using only the Free Recall scores (selected because they had a larger effect size than Pairing) yielded a correct classification rate of 76%. Some individuals with Parkinson's disease score within the average range on both Digit Symbol-Coding and the Incidental Learning procedures (Peavy et al., 2001). Nevertheless, many of these patients can be differentiated from normal controls using qualitative information. For example, when controls made errors they tended to be rotations of the three-sided symbols, whereas Parkinson's patients showed a noteworthy tendency to rotate symbols other than the three-sided squares and to make frequent perseverations.

It can be safely assumed that the Digit Symbol-Coding scaled scores of patients with traumatic brain injury will be significantly below those of normal controls with similar demographic characteristics (Langeluddecke & Lucas, 2003). Highly significant differences between patients with brain injury and normal controls have also been reported for the Incidental Learning procedures. Mercer, Harrell, Miller, Childs, Rockers, and Deldotto (1998) utilized the WAIS-R and compared Pairing and Free Recall scores of 49 healthy adults with those of 45 individuals with a history of traumatic brain injury. The mean time since injury was 6.5 years. The brain-injured patients earned Pairing and Free recall mean scores of 2.73 ($SD = 2.32$) and 4.27 ($SD = 2.36$), whereas the controls had a mean Pairing score of 7.57 ($SD = 1.57$) and a mean Free Recall score of 8.12 ($SD = 1.11$). Mercer et al. (1998) concluded that scores on the Incidental Learning procedures are capable of differentiating individuals with brain injuries from healthy adults.

Base rate information can sometimes be used by practitioners to determine whether a given test response, pattern, or sign has diagnostic significance. The

WAIS-III Administration and Scoring Manual along with Tables 5.5 and 5.6 in this chapter provide normative data for the Digit Symbol-Incidental Learning procedures in the form of cumulative percentages associated with raw scores. These norms are used for level of performance interpretation of the Incidental Learning procedures. However, in order to identify potential relationships that may exist between recall patterns and a designation of "abnormality," the frequency with which each number–symbol pair and each individual symbol is remembered or forgotten by healthy adults, as well as selected clinical samples, must be determined. Tables 5.9 and 5.10 provide information on the frequencies with which the nine associated number–symbol pairs (i.e., Pairing) and nine individual symbols (i.e., Free Recall) are recalled by the WAIS-III standardization sample. The data are presented according to three levels of education (i.e., <12, 12, and >12 years) and four age ranges (i.e., 16–29, 30–54, 55–74, and 75–89 years). Inspection of the tables indicates that some of the number–symbol pairs and individual symbols are relatively easy to remember, whereas others appear to be more difficult. For instance, across the various age and education levels recall rates are highest for the 1st and 9th number–symbol pairs and tend to be the lowest for the 4th and 5th number–symbol pairs. With respect to Free Recall performance, the 9th symbol tends to be the most frequently recalled across the majority of age and education levels, whereas the 4th symbol tends to be the most frequently omitted. These results are similar to those reported by Cole and Glosser (1999) in a sample of patients with epilepsy.

Schnakenberg-Ott, Ryan, and Tree (2004) provided information on the frequencies with which the nine associated number–symbol pairs (i.e., Pairing) and nine individual symbols (i.e., Free Recall) are recalled by a group of college students (*M* age = 22.15 years, *SD* = 5.12 years) and a sample of patients with substance abuse disorders (*M* age = 45.95 years, *SD* = 9.43 years). Table 5.11 reports the percentages of individuals in each group who correctly paired each symbol with its associated number, while Table 5.12 provides the percentages in both groups who recalled each symbol correctly.

Inspection of the tables indicates that 99% of the student participants and 89% of patients successfully paired the appropriate symbol with the number 1. Conversely, only 43% of the students correctly paired the appropriate symbol with the number 3, while the lowest recall frequency for patients was 30% for the number 4 and its associated symbol. With respect to Free Recall performance, 98% of the students remembered the 1st symbol, but only 61% recalled the 3rd. Among patient participants, the most frequently recalled symbol was the 9th (97%) and the most infrequently recalled symbol was the 4th (50%).

The base rates provided in Tables 5.9, 5.10, 5.11, and 5.12 may be useful for detecting unusual recall patterns on the Pairing and Free Recall procedures. Perhaps failure to recall the 1st and 9th number–symbol pairs while remembering the 3rd, 4th, and 5th pairs reflects response bias or poor

Table 5.9 Incidental Learning-Pairing: Mean scores and percentage of individuals recalling each symbol by education level and age

			Symbol									
Education	*Age*	*N*	*1*	*2*	*3*	*4*	*5*	*6*	*7*	*8*	*9*	*Mean score*
Below 12	16–29	247	98	89	68	66	68	89	78	89	96	14.24
Below 12	30–54	74	91	82	47	46	39	78	49	70	91	10.92
Below 12	55–74	149	79	68	32	17	21	58	36	57	74	7.89
Below 12	75–89	160	77	55	28	15	14	49	38	48	69	6.81
12 years	16–29	235	96	90	61	60	61	87	72	89	94	13.52
12 years	30–54	212	93	88	52	42	48	79	62	81	94	12.02
12 years	55–74	221	86	75	39	28	29	59	46	62	83	9.09
12 years	75–89	145	87	70	32	17	17	43	46	47	71	7.78
Above 12	16–29	267	96	85	62	64	65	86	72	84	92	13.48
Above 12	30–54	322	95	87	58	49	54	83	68	84	94	12.58
Above 12	55–74	186	90	80	45	26	34	63	55	66	87	9.96
Above 12	75–89	116	79	70	34	22	27	58	48	57	83	8.61

Table 5.10 Incidental Learning-Free Recall: Mean scores and percentage of individuals recalling each symbol by education level and age

			Symbol									
Education	*Age*	*N*	*1*	*2*	*3*	*4*	*5*	*6*	*7*	*8*	*9*	*Mean score*
Below 12	16–29	247	86	80	72	64	72	87	72	83	99	7.14
Below 12	30–54	74	74	70	65	47	59	89	50	70	97	6.23
Below 12	55–74	149	74	70	62	46	56	85	58	75	93	6.19
Below 12	75–89	160	68	62	46	36	48	83	48	66	82	5.39
12 years	16–29	235	79	74	61	56	70	83	64	75	98	6.60
12 years	30–54	212	75	73	61	47	62	79	54	74	97	6.22
12 years	55–74	221	78	66	59	46	63	81	48	74	93	6.08
12 years	75–89	145	86	74	61	34	64	90	52	74	90	6.23
Above 12	16–29	267	81	76	63	64	73	84	67	79	97	6.84
Above 12	30–54	322	83	77	64	54	68	83	63	80	98	6.71
Above 12	55–74	186	83	81	68	48	65	89	59	78	94	6.64
Above 12	75–89	116	73	69	55	42	58	80	46	72	96	5.91

Table 5.11 Percentage of individuals obtaining correct symbols on Incidental Learning-Pairing

Symbol	*1*	*2*	*3*	*4*	*5*	*6*	*7*	*8*	*9*
Students (n = 104)	99	88	43	48	54	75	64	88	95
Patients (n = 73)	89	79	41	30	44	65	53	75	89

Adapted from Schnakenberg-Ott et al. (2004).

Table 5.12 Percentage of individuals obtaining correct symbols on Incidental Learning-Free Recall

Symbol	*1*	*2*	*3*	*4*	*5*	*6*	*7*	*8*	*9*
Students (n = 104)	98	90	61	62	83	94	63	90	98
Patients (n = 73)	89	83	72	50	65	95	61	95	97

Adapted from Schnakenberg-Ott et al. (2004).

motivation during the task. Research is needed to determine the meaning of various Pairing and Free Recall patterns and additional base rate tables should be developed for clinical (e.g., traumatic brain injury, dementia) and forensic (e.g., litigating traumatic brain injury cases, felons awaiting trial) samples.

In order to increase the clinical yield of the Digit Symbol-Coding subtest, Kaplan et al. (1991) recommend that examinee's progress be recorded at 30-s intervals in addition to the number recorded at 120 s. This Decomposition Approach (Poreh, 2000) allows one to track an examinee's progress and determine his/her rate of transcription. It also reflects the presence of consistency or variability in performance over time. Kaplan et al. (1991) offered a series of interpretative hypotheses for differing transcription patterns, a sample of which is presented in Table 5.13. Paolo and Ryan (1994) tested the hypothesis that elderly persons demonstrate a "warm-up" pattern that starts out slowly, but increases over each 30-s interval. Using a sample of 221 healthy persons 75 years and older (M = 80.5 years, SD = 4.85 years), these authors used cluster analysis on the WAIS-R Digit Symbol data and found that the predicted "warm-up" pattern did not emerge. It did appear, however, in the records of 7.2% of the sample when pattern groups were derived by visual inspection. According to the cluster analysis, approximately 61% of participants showed a slight drop during the middle 30-s interval followed by no change in the number of symbols copied during the final 30 s. When pattern groups were

Table 5.13 Interpretive hypotheses for Digit Symbol-Coding 30-, 60-, and 90-s intervals (Kaplan et al., 1991)

Pattern	*Interpretive hypothesis*
(1) Starts out slowly but increases over each 30-s interval	Warm up, characteristic of elderly *or* Incidental Learning, should check key less often as copy rate increases
(2) Copy rate slows over successive 30-s intervals	Undue susceptibility to fatigue
(3) Copy rate evenly slowed over all 30-s intervals	Slowness of depression *or* generalized activation defect

constituted using visual inspection, approximately 45% of the participants showed a decline during the second 30-s interval with subsequent improvement during the final 30-s interval. As mentioned previously, these data do not support the Kaplan et al. "warm-up" hypothesis for healthy elderly.

The only other published investigation we could locate concerning transcription patterns on the Digit Symbol-Coding subtest is that of Dumont, Farr, Willis, and Whelly (1998) using the Wechsler Intelligence Scale for Children-Third Edition (WISC-III; Wechsler, 1991). These authors hypothesized that school children should be able to produce a "learning" pattern on the Digit Symbol subtest. Thus, at each 30-s interval there will be an increase in the number of symbols copied because examinees are rapidly memorizing the number–symbol pairs and they no longer need to refer to the key in order to complete the task. Based on a sample of 351 children (age range from 8 years to 16 years) with suspected learning disabilities, Dumont et al. (1998) found that none of the participants demonstrated a pattern of consistent improvement across each 30-s interval. Conversely, the most frequent patterns of performance were, respectively, (a) decline during 30 to 90 s with improvement on the 90- to 120-s interval (17.9% of cases) and (b) decline during 30 to 60 s followed by improvement between 60 and 90 s, and decline from 90 to 120 s. The authors concluded that the "learning" pattern on Digit Symbol-Coding did not characterize the performance of children with suspected learning disabilities. Unfortunately, in the absence of a healthy control group for comparison, it cannot be determined whether the Dumont et al. (1998) findings are a reflection of school-identified learning disabilities or are typical for children in general. Additional research is needed to address this question.

Ryan, Schnakenberg-Ott, and Brown (2004) examined 103 college students with the WAIS-III Digit Symbol-Coding subtest and collected 30-s interval data as well as the total number of symbols copied after 120 s. It was hypothesized that healthy young adults, with their well-developed learning and visual-motor skills, would be likely to obtain average or above average scaled scores on Digit Symbol-Coding and also demonstrate a "learning" pattern with successive increases in symbols copied at each 30-s interval. The mean scaled score for the group was 11.88 ($SD = 2.48$), a value falling at approximately the 75th percentile. However, the expected "learning" pattern occurred in only 2.9% of the sample. The most frequently encountered transcription pattern was a decline in the 30- to 60-s interval followed by successive increases in symbols copied at 60 to 90 s and again at 90 to 120 s (18.4%). The second most frequent pattern involved a decline (30 to 60 s), an increase (60 to 90 s), and a decline (90 to 120 s). Seventeen (16.5%) participants produced this pattern. It was concluded that even among healthy college students with normal Digit Symbol-Coding performance, the Kaplan et al. (1991) proposed "learning" pattern was not typical. For all participants, Table 5.14 presents the numbers and percentages of individuals who

Table 5.14 Pattern of change relative to the first 30-s interval for subsequent 30-s intervals and change from first to last interval

Patterns of change			*Change from first to last interval*		
Pattern	*N*	*Of total*	*Raw score change*	*N*	*Of total*
decline, decline, decline	3	2.9	6	1	0.9
decline, decline, same	2	1.9	5	2	1.9
decline, same, same	1	0.9	4	1	0.9
decline, same, decline	3	2.9	3	3	2.9
decline, decline, improve	11	10.7	2	13	12.6
decline, improve, improve	19	18.4	1	15	14.6
decline, improve, same	9	8.7	0	15	14.6
decline, same, improve	10	9.7	−1	11	10.7
decline, improve, decline	17	16.5	−2	15	14.6
improve, decline, improve	6	5.8	−3	14	13.6
improve, improve, decline	9	8.7	−4	6	5.8
improve, same, decline	2	1.9	−5	4	3.9
improve, improve, improve	3	2.9	−6	2	1.9
improve, decline, same	1	0.9	−7	1	0.9
improve, decline, decline	1	0.9			
same, decline, improve	2	1.9			
same, same, improve	1	0.9			
same, same, same	1	0.9			
same, decline, same	1	0.9			
same, improve, same	1	0.9			

demonstrated "decline," improvement," or "no change," over each 30-s interval, regardless of the magnitude of the difference.

Interpretation

The Digit Symbol-Coding subtest is highly sensitive to cognitive dysfunction regardless of etiology (e.g., head trauma or dementia syndrome) or lesion localization. Scores on this subtest are also influenced by demographic variables and behavioral factors. In the former category are examinee's age, gender, ethnicity, and educational level, whereas in the latter category are anxiety, concern for accuracy and detail, persistence, and the capacity to work under externally imposed time pressures. Digit Symbol-Coding is used by many practitioners as a screening test because it is multifaceted and highly sensitive to most conditions that compromise brain functions and produce abnormalities in attention, visual motor skill, visual scanning, and/or mentation (Lezak, 1995). Conversely, the high level of sensitivity of this subtest renders it totally nonspecific. Thus, a low score on Digit Symbol-Coding, by itself, does not allow for the delineation of an examinee's problem.

The influence of demographic variables should be kept in mind whenever one interprets results of the Digit Symbol-Coding subtest (Kaufman & Lichtenberger, 2002). Analysis of the WAIS-III standardization sample indicates that age has a marked impact on subtest raw scores, but this variable is adequately controlled by converting raw scores into scaled scores using Table A.1 of the *WAIS-III Administration and Scoring Manual*. Years of education is significantly correlated ($r = 0.37$) with Digit Symbol-Coding performance, suggesting that a low score on the subtest may have a different meaning for individuals from varying educational backgrounds. The clinical implication is that if Digit Symbol-Coding is used to screen for cognitive impairment, the cutoff score for examinees with <12 years of education should be lower than that for examinees with a college diploma. Research is needed to determine the most appropriate cutoff scores for Digit Symbol-Coding performance at different levels of educational attainment. Similarly, cutoff scores that take into consideration examinee's gender and ethnicity are also needed. In the absence of validated, demographically adjusted cutoff scores, it seems appropriate to use the norms provided by The Psychological Corporation (1999, 2001). These norms allow one to estimate the adequacy of an individual's Digit Symbol-Coding performance relative to standardization participants who are similar in terms of age, gender, educational level, and ethnicity. When coupled with behavioral observations and follow-up assessment with measures of specific, relatively pure aspects of cognitive functioning, this approach should clarify the meaning of most Digit Symbol-Coding scores.

Using the Satellite Paradigm, the optional procedures are designed to help determine the reason for a deficient score on Digit Symbol-Coding. Using the norms provided in the *WAIS-III Administration and Scoring Manual*, consider a hypothetical examinee with a scaled score of 5 on Digit Symbol-Coding and cumulative percentages/percentile ranks for Incidental Learning-Pairing, Incidental Learning-Free Recall, and Copy of 2, 5, and 50, respectively. This pattern suggests that the relatively poor score on Digit Symbol-Coding was due, at least in part, to reduced recall of the test stimuli. Another pattern to watch for is poor performance on both Digit Symbol-Coding and Digit Symbol-Copy, but significantly better scores on Pairing and Free Recall. This pattern may suggest that impaired graphomotor speed was responsible for the low score on Digit Symbol-Coding. It is also possible that an examinee will earn low scores on Digit Symbol-Coding and both of the optional procedures.

In a sample of 228 patients at a VA Medical Center referred for neuropsychological assessment, the pattern of low Digit Symbol-Coding plus low Copy was more frequent than the pattern of low Digit Symbol-Coding plus low Incidental Learning. Thus, in this patient sample motor skill was more important than incidental memory in explaining Digit Symbol-Coding performance (Kreiner & Ryan, 2001). Because Digit Symbol-Coding is a highly complex subtest, it may be inaccurate in some cases to interpret a poor score as simply reflecting deficient graphomotor speed or impaired incidental memory, or a combination of the two. Instead, a Digit Symbol-Coding scaled score in the impaired range may result from visual scanning problems, reduced integrity of executive functions, and/or a perceptual speed deficit (Joy et al., 2003a). The reasons for a poor score on Digit Symbol-Coding may also differ for normal examinees vs. patients with identified neuropathologies such as right hemisphere brain damage or a substance abuse disorder (Glosser, Butters, & Kaplan, 1977). Behavioral observations during subtest administration (see Table 5.1), consideration of qualitative information (see Table 5.8), and follow-up testing with specialized measures (e.g., visual scanning tests) should help clarify the reason or reasons for a low score. Finally, in clinical practice the definition of a low-scaled score on Digit Symbol-Coding frequently differs from one examiner to the other. Nevertheless, we recommend that for examinees "in general" a score at or below the 5th percentile should be cause for concern, whereas higher standards may be applied for unusually accomplished individuals (e.g., advanced degrees, important literary or scientific accomplishments, etc.).

Joy et al. (2003b) offered clinical guidelines for interpretation of Pairing and Free Recall scores based on the analysis of the WAIS-III/WMS-III (Wechsler, 1997a, 1997b) standardization sample. Participants were divided according to age (i.e., younger = 16–49 years, older = 50–89 years) and memory status (i.e., with or without impairment). Memory impairment was operationally defined as a score <85 on at least one of four selected WMS-III Indexes (i.e., Auditory Immediate, Auditory Delayed, Visual Immediate, and/or Visual Delayed). The suggested Pairing cutoffs for younger and older examinees who are likely to have memory impairment are ≤ 6 (or three or fewer number–symbol pairs) and ≤ 4 (or two or fewer number–symbol pairs), respectively. The suggested cutoff score for possible memory impairment using Free Recall, regardless of age, is ≤ 4 symbols correctly reproduced. Table 5.15 contains information directly

Table 5.15 Diagnostic validity indices for recommended cutoff scores on Pairing and Free Recall

	Pairing		*Free Recall*	
	Younger ≤ 6	*Older* ≤ 4	*Younger* ≤ 4	*Older* ≤ 4
Sensitivity	0.13	0.35	0.04	0.19
Specificity	0.97	0.92	0.99	0.96
Positive predictive power	0.61	0.66	0.67	0.78
Negative predictive power	0.72	0.76	0.70	0.70

Adapted from Joy et al. (2003b).

relevant to the clinical utility of these cutoff scores and shows that for both measures sensitivity is low, but specificity is excellent, and positive and negative predictive power are high enough to justify their application.

Joy et al. (2003b) recommend supplementing interpretation of cutoff scores with inspection of Digit Symbol-Coding performance. Specifically, if Pairing and/or Free Recall are below the cutoffs and the Digit Symbol-Coding raw score is ≤49, the probability is very high that a clinically significant memory disorder has been detected and requires further evaluation. Additional interpretative observations suggest that older adults who recall eight or more pairs or earn a perfect score on Free Recall are unlikely to have memory impairment and that a similar conclusion pertains to adults under 50 years of age who earn Pairing scores of 17 or 18. Also, a Pairing and/or Free Recall score below the suggested cutoff, in combination with a low Digit Symbol-Coding raw score, is more predictive of impaired memory than is poor Incidental Learning in isolation.

Chronological age was the only demographic variable considered by Joy et al. (2003b) when they developed their cutoff scores. However, analysis of Incidental Learning data from the WAIS-III standardization sample indicated that education, as well as age, contributes to performance on Pairing and Free Recall. Therefore, prior to forming a final conclusion about the meaning of a Pairing or Free Recall score, the examiner may wish to consult Table 5.5 and/or Table 5.6. For example, a 75-year-old examinee with 10 years of education and a raw Pairing score of 4 (i.e., two or fewer number–symbol pairs) has achieved a value within the impaired range. However, inspection of Table 5.5 indicates that a raw score of 4 converts into a cumulative percentage of 25, suggesting that this is not an unusually poor performance when the influence of age and education are considered simultaneously. Additional aides to test interpretation frequently include behavioral observations (see Table 5.1), evaluation of qualitative evidence (see Table 5.8), the pattern of recalled and forgotten stimuli compared to base rates (Tables 5.9, 5.10, 5.11, and 5.12), and consideration of Digit Symbol-Copy results. Examination of the pattern of transcription over the four 30-s intervals during Digit Symbol-Coding (and possibly Digit Symbol-Copy) may also provide useful information. Although research is needed to clarify the meaning of variable transcription rates, when these 30-s interval scores are coupled with relevant behavioral observations they may support clinically sensible interpretations. For example, an examinee who performs equally poorly across all four intervals, displays a lackadaisical attitude, and comments about the "silly" nature of the test likely demonstrates poor motivation.

Much of the material in this chapter has not been previously published. Further empirical research is needed to determine, for example, the meaning of Digit Symbol-Incidental Learning performance that does not conform to base rates in terms of recall and forgetting patterns. Could an unusual recall and forgetting pattern reflect response bias or formal thought disorder or an as yet unidentified disorder? Likewise, effort should be directed toward investigating further the interpretive hypotheses offered by advocates of the process approach to neuropsychological assessment (e.g., Kaplan et al., 1991). Also, basic assumptions about Digit Symbol-Coding performance may need to be reconsidered. For instance, it makes sense to conclude that examinees who learn the number–symbol pairs during Digit Symbol-Coding will earn better scores on the subtest than persons who do not assimilate the associated pairs (Kaufman & Lichtenberger, 2002). However, Joy et al. (2003a), after considering the amount of time required for memory scanning of learned associations vs. visual scanning of the key, noted that a memorization strategy might lead to poorer Digit Symbol-Coding performance than would scanning the key for every item. With the above caveats in mind, it is hoped that the present chapter will simultaneously prove useful to assessment practitioners and serve as a modest impetus for future research.

References

Burik, T. (1950). Relative roles of learning and motor factors involved in the digit symbol test. *Journal of Psychology*, *30*, 33–42.

Butters, N., & Cermak, L. S. (1980). *Alcoholic Korsakoff's syndrome: An information-processing approach to amnesia*. New York: Academic Press.

Cole, L. C., & Glosser, G. (1999). Use of the WAIS-R Digit Symbol Incidental Recall test as a measure of memory in temporal lobe epilepsy patients. *Journal of the International Neuropsychological Society*, *5*, 142.

Delprato, D. J., & Jackson, D. E. (1975). The effects of seating arrangement upon WAIS Digit Span and Digit Symbol performance. *Journal of Clinical Psychology*, *31*, 88–89.

Demakis, G. J., Sawyer, T. P., Fritz, D., & Sweet, J. J. (2001). Incidental recall on WAIS-R Digit Symbol discriminates Alzheimer's and Parkinson's diseases. *Journal of Clinical Psychology*, *57*, 387–394.

Donders, J., Tulsky, D. S., & Zhu, J. (2001). Criterion validity of new WAIS-III subtest scores after traumatic brain injury. *Journal of the International Neuropsychological Society*, *7*, 892–898.

Drachman, D. A., O'Donnell, B. F., Lew, R. A., & Swearer, J. M. (1990). The prognosis in Alzheimer's disease: 'How far' rather than 'How fast' best predicts the course. *Archives of Neurology*, *47*, 851–856.

Dumont, R., Farr, L. P., Willis, J. O., & Whelley, P. (1998). 30-second interval performance on the Coding subtest of the WISC-III: Further evidence of WISC folklore? *Psychology in the Schools*, *35*, 111–117.

Glosser, G., Butters, N., & Kaplan, E. (1977). Visuoperceptual processes in brain damaged patients on the Digit Symbol substitution test. *International Journal of Neuroscience*, *7*, 59–66.

Groth-Marnat, G. (2003). *Handbook of psychological assessment* (4th ed.). New York: Wiley.

Hart, R. P., Kwentus, J. A., Wade, J. B., & Hamer, R. M. (1987). Digit Symbol performance in mild dementia and depression. *Journal of Consulting and Clinical Psychology*, *55*, 236–238.

Joy, S., Fein, D., & Kaplan, E. (2003a). Decoding Digit Symbol: Speed, memory, and visual scanning. *Assessment*, *10*, 56–65.

Joy, S., Fein, D., Kaplan, E., & Freedman, M. (2000). Speed and memory in WAIS-R-NI Digit Symbol performance among healthy older adults. *Journal of the International Neuropsychological Society*, *6*, 770–780.

Joy, S., Kaplan, E., & Fein, D. (2003b). Digit Symbol-Incidental Learning in the WAIS-III: Construct validity and clinical significance. *The Clinical Neuropsychologist*, *17*, 182–194.

Kaplan, E. (1990). The process approach to neuropsychological assessment of psychiatric patients. *Journal of Neuropsychiatry*, *2*, 72–87.

Kaplan, E., Fein, D., Morris, R., & Delis, D. (1991). *WAIS-R as a neuropsychological instrument (WAIS-R-NI)*. San Antonio, TX: The Psychological Corporation.

Kaufman, A. S., & Lichtenberger, E. O. (1999). *Essentials of WAIS-III assessment*. New York: Wiley.

Kaufman, A. S., & Lichtenberger, E. O. (2002). *Assessing adolescent and adult intelligence* (2nd ed.). Boston: Allyn and Bacon.

Kellerman, H., & Burry, A. (1991). *Handbook of psychodiagnostic testing: The analysis of personality in the psychological report* (2nd ed.). Boston: Allyn and Bacon.

Kreiner, D. S., & Ryan, J. J. (2001). Memory and motor skill components of the WAIS-III Digit Symbol-Coding subtest. *The Clinical Neuropsychologist*, *15*, 109–113.

Lacritz, L. H., & Cullum, C. M. (2003). The WAIS-III and WMS-III: Practical issues and frequently asked questions. In D. S. Tulsky, D. H. Saklofske, G. J. Chelune, R. K. Heaton, R. J. Ivnik, R. Bornstein, A. Prifitera, & M. F. Ledbetter (Eds.), *Clinical interpretation of the WAIS-III and WMS-III*. New York: Academic Press.

Langeluddecke, P. M., & Lucas, S. K. (2003). Wechsler Adult Intelligence Scale-Third Edition findings in relation to severity of brain injury in litigants. *The Clinical Neuropsychologist*, *17*, 273–284.

Lezak, M. D. (1995). *Neuropsychological assessment* (3rd ed.). New York: Oxford University Press.

McGrew, K. S., & Flanagan, D. P. (1998). *The intelligence test desk reference (ITDR): Gf-Gc cross-battery assessment*. Boston: Allyn and Bacon.

McSweeny, A. J., Becker, B. C., Naugle, R. I., Snow, W. G., Binder, L. M., & Thompson, L. L. (1998). Ethical issues related to the presence of third party observers in clinical neuropsychological evaluations. *The Clinical Neuropsychologist*, *12*, 552–559.

Mercer, W. N., Harrell, E. H., Miller, D. C., Childs, H. W., Rockers, D. M., & Deldotto, J. E. (1998). Performance of healthy adults versus individuals with brain injuries on the supplemental measures of the WAIS-R NI. *Brain Injury*, *12*, 753–758.

Murstein, B. I., & Leipold, W. D. (1961). The role of learning and motor abilities in the Wechsler Bellevue Digit-Symbol subtest. *Educational and Psychological Measurement*, *21*, 103–112.

Paolo, A. M., & Ryan, J. J. (1994a). Base rates of WAIS-R qualitative information for persons 75 years and older. *Assessment*, *1*, 83–88.

Paolo, A. M., & Ryan, J. J. (1994b). WAIS-R Digit Symbol patterns for persons 75 years and older. *Journal of Psychoeducational Assessment*, *12*, 67–75.

Peavy, G. M., Salmon, D. P., Bear, I., Paulsen, J. S., Cahn, D. A., Hofstetter, C. R., Kaplan, E., Delis, D. C., & Shults, C. W. (2001). Detection of mild cognitive deficits in Parkinson's disease patients with the WAIS-R NI. *Journal of the International Neuropsychological Society*, *7*, 535–543.

Poreh, A. M. (2000). The Quantified Process Approach: An emerging methodology to neuropsychological assessment. *The Clinical Neuropsychologist*, *14*, 212–222.

Ryan, J. J., Brown, K. I., & Paolo, A. M. (2005). Discrimination of healthy and brain damaged elderly using the WAIS-R. *International Journal of Neuroscience*, *23*, 140–145.

Ryan, J. J., Lopez, S. J., & Werth, T. R. (1998). Administration time estimates for WAIS-III subtests, scales, and short forms in a clinical sample. *Journal of Psychoeducational Assessment*, *16*, 315–323.

Ryan, J. J., Paolo, A. M., & Brungardt, T. M. (1990). Standardization of the WAIS-R for persons 75 years and older. *Psychological Assessment: A Journal of Consulting and Clinical Psychology*, *2*, 404–411.

Ryan, J. J., Sattler, J. M., & Lopez, S. J. (2000). Age effects on Wechsler Adult Intelligence Scale-III subtests. *Archives of Clinical Neuropsychology*, *15*, 311–317.

Ryan, J. J., & Schnakenberg-Ott, S. D. (2003). Scoring reliability on the Wechsler Adult Intelligence Scale-Third Edition (WAIS-III). *Assessment*, *10*, 151–159.

Ryan, J. J., Schnakenberg-Ott, S. D., & Brown, K. I. (2004). *WAIS-III Digit Symbol-Coding patterns among healthy young adults.* Manuscript submitted for editorial review.

Sattler, J. M., & Ryan, J. J. (2001a). WAIS-III subtests and interpreting the WAIS-III. In J. M. Sattler (Ed.), *Assessment of children: Cognitive applications* (4th ed., pp. 415–454). San Diego, CA: Author.

Sattler, J. M., & Ryan, J. J. (2001b). Wechsler Adult Intelligence Scale-III (WAIS-III): Description. In J. M. Sattler (Ed.), *Assessment of children: Cognitive applications* (4th ed., pp. 375–414). San Diego, CA: Author.

Schnakenberg-Ott, S., Ryan, J. J., & Tree, H. A. (2004). WAIS-III Digit Symbol-Incidental Learning base rates: Findings for college student and patient samples. *Perceptual and Motor Skills*, *99*, 903–908.

Storandt, M. (1976). Speed and coding effects in relation to age and ability level. *Developmental Psychology*, *12*, 177–178.

The Psychological Corporation. (2001). *WAIS-III/WMS-III/WIAT-II Writer*. San Antonio, TX: Author.

The Psychological Corporation. (1999). *WAIS-III/WMS-III/WIAT-II Scoring Assistant.* San Antonio, TX: Author.

The Psychological Corporation. (1997). *WAIS-III/WMS-III technical manual*. San Antonio, TX: Author.

Tulsky, D. S., Saklofske, D. H., & Zhu, J. (2003). Revising a standard: An evaluation of the origin and development of the WAIS-III. In D. S. Tulsky, D. H. Saklofske, G. J. Chelune, R. K. Heaton, R. J. Ivnik, R. Bornstein, A. Prifitera, & M. F. Leadbetter (Eds.), *Clinical interpretation of the WAIS-III and WMS-III.* New York: Academic Press.

Wechsler, D. (1939). *The measurement of adult intelligence.* Baltimore, MD: Williams & Wilkins.

Wechsler, D. (1955). *Manual for the Wechsler Adult Intelligence Scale.* New York: The Psychological Corporation.

Wechsler, D. (1981). *Manual for the Wechsler Adult Intelligence Scale-Revised.* New York: The Psychological Corporation.

Wechsler, D. (1991). *Manual for the Wechsler Intelligence Scale for Children-Third Edition.* San Antonio, TX: The Psychological Corporation.

Wechsler, D. (1997a). *WAIS-III administration and scoring manual.* San Antonio, TX: The Psychological Corporation.

Wechsler, D. (1997b). *Wechsler Memory Scale-Third Edition (WMS-III).* San Antonio, TX: The Psychological Corporation.

Zimmerman, I. L., & Woo-Sam, J. M. (1973). *Clinical interpretation of the WAIS.* New York: Grune & Stratton.

6 The added value of a temporal-order judgment measure to the Rey Auditory Verbal Learning Test (AVLT)

Eli Vakil

Introduction

Memory for temporal order has been studied extensively in healthy individuals as well as in different patient groups. These studies have made a significant theoretical contribution to the understanding of normal and abnormal human memory. Hasher and Zacks (1979) claimed that temporal order, along with frequency of occurrence and spatial location, are encoded automatically. As such, they are unaffected by either person variables (e.g., age, intelligence, or mood) or task variables (e.g., instructions, strategy, or practice). Some studies have supported Hasher and Zacks' claim by demonstrating invariance in performance over age or instructional conditions (Audy, Sullivan, & Gross, 1988; Azary, Audy, & Gross, 1989). By contrast, other studies have reported results that are at odds with Hasher and Zacks' claim (Kausler, Lichty, & Davis, 1985; Kausler, Salthouse, & Saults, 1988; McCormack, 1981; Naveh-Benjamin, 1990; Vakil & Tweedy, 1994; Vakil et al., 1997).

The main contention of the "temporal-order deficit hypothesis" of amnesia is that impaired memory for temporal order is the source of the memory deficit in amnesia (Huppert & Piercy, 1976). Other researchers have extended this theory, suggesting the "contextual-memory deficit hypothesis" of amnesia (Hirst, 1982; Hirst & Volpe, 1982; Mayes, MacDonald, Donlan, Pears, & Meudel, 1992; Pickering, Mayes, & Fairbairn, 1989). According to the latter hypothesis, amnesia is a result of poor memory for contextual information. Memory for temporal order is a specific example of contextual information that is impaired in amnesic patients.

Schacter, Harbluk, and McLachlan (1984) introduced the distinction between item (or fact) and source memory. Source memory refers to the background information of an item or event, such as its temporal order, spatial location, or modality of presentation (i.e., visual vs. auditory). Several studies have found impaired source memory in patients with frontal-lobe lesions (Janowsky, Shimamura, & Squire, 1989). Contrary to the "contextual-memory deficit hypothesis," Shimamura and Squire (1987, 1991) found that the degree of source amnesia was unrelated to item memory impairment.

Memory for temporal order, one of the most studied source memory tasks, was found impaired in patients with frontal-lobe damage, while memory for items was intact (Butters, Kaszniak, Glisky, Eslinger, & Schacter, 1994; Eslinger & Grattan, 1994; McAndrews & Milner, 1991; Shimamura, Janowsky, & Squire, 1990). Impaired memory for temporal order was also reported in studies with other patient groups with diseases or injuries involving the frontal lobes, such as Korsakoff's syndrome (Huppert & Piercy, 1976). Frontal lobes were found to be the most vulnerable cortical areas following closed-head injury (CHI) (Adams, 1975). Patients with CHI were shown to have impaired memory for temporal order when measured directly (Vakil & Tweedy, 1994; Vakil, Gordon, Birnstok, Aberbuch, & Groswasser, 2001), but showed preserved temporal order when measured indirectly (Vakil, Sherf, Hoffman, & Stern, 1998). A similar pattern of findings was reported with older adults (Vakil, Weise, & Enbar, 1997). That is, the direct but not the indirect measures of temporal order were related to age.

A supplementary measure of temporal order in the Rey Auditory Verbal Learning Test

It is quite surprising that memory for temporal order, despite its theoretical importance and its sensitivity to a variety of brain injuries as reviewed above, is barely included in memory assessment batteries. The Rey Auditory Verbal Learning Test (AVLT) is a test widely used for clinical and research purposes (Lezak, 1995). One of the reasons for its popularity is that many memory measures can be extracted from it, such as immediate and delayed recall, learning rate, recognition, proactive and retroactive interference, and primacy and recency effects (Lezak, 1995; Wiens, McMinn, & Crossen, 1988).

The Rey AVLT consists of 15 common nouns, which are read to the participants in five consecutive trials in a fixed order. Following each trial, participants are asked to recall the words read previously, without mentioning the importance of temporal order. Vakil and Blachstein (1994) took advantage of this fact by adding a trial to the test that measures memory for temporal order. In Trial 10, following the recognition trial, participants are given the 15 words of the first list written in an order different from that in which they had originally heard them. Participants are asked to rewrite the words in their original order (see Appendix A). It is important to ensure that *all* of the 15 words are rearranged, even if a person is not sure of the exact position of a particular word that he or she is asked to guess. The temporal-order score could not be accurately calculated in the case of missing words.

Three alternative scores were proposed as temporal-order measures. The advantages and disadvantages of each will be discussed below. The three measures are:

Hits—the number of words placed exactly in their original serial position. Thus, scores range from 0 to 15.

Absolute deviations—the sum of the absolute deviation (i.e., ignoring the direction of the deviation whether it is positive or negative) of each word from its original position (Vakil & Tweedy, 1994). For each word, the score ranged from 0 to 14. Accordingly, the lower the score, the more accurate the performance.

Correlations—Pearson Product Moment correlations are calculated for each person, between the recalled order and the original order of presentation (Tzeng, Lee, & Wetzel, 1979). The correlation scores range from 0 (i.e., random relation between the original and judged temporal order) to a score of 1 (i.e., perfect performance). A negative score is treated as the reflected random performance (i.e., score of 0). Thus, the scores for a perfect performance would be: hits = 15, absolute deviation = 0, and correlation = 1. Appendix B presents an example of temporal-order judgment and the three temporal-order scores.

Although hit rate is the simplest to score, the disadvantage of this score is that it dichotomizes performance to correct or incorrect. Consider, for example, the case in which a person has shifted the words only one position from the original position. Even if the order between most of the words is preserved, this performance will be scored as zero. By contrast, absolute deviations and correlations evaluate performance as a continuum that reflects the proximity to the original temporal order of the word list. On the one hand, the advantage of the correlation score over the absolute deviation score is that the former is a known score and, as such, is easily understood and interpretable. On the other hand, the advantage of the absolute deviation score over the correlation score is that it is easier to calculate manually. Therefore, our recommendation is to use the correlation score in research when the correlation formula can be applied in the analysis of group performance. However, for purposes of individual assessment, the absolute deviation score is recommended. Norms are provided for all three scoring systems in Table 6.1 for adults (taken from Vakil & Blachstein, 1997) and in Table 6.2 for children (taken from Vakil, Blachstein, & Sheinman, 1998). All three measures of temporal order were found to be sensitive to age in the adults' standardization sample. However, in the children's study, only the correlation and the absolute deviation scores, but not the hits score, were sensitive to age. This finding further confirms our claim that the hit score is a less sensitive measure and is therefore less recommended as a temporal-order score.

Findings with the temporal-order measure of the Rey AVLT

On the basis of factor analysis studies with adult participants, scores extracted from the Rey AVLT reflect different aspects of verbal memory (Ryan, Rosenberg, & Mittenberg, 1984). Vakil and Blachstein (1993) submitted different scores generated from the Rey AVLT to factor analysis, including the temporal-order measure. The basic factors that were identified were "acquisition" and "retention." The latter could be further subdivided into "storage" and "retrieval," thus yielding a total of three factors. Temporal-order score loaded on the "retrieval" factor. This finding was interpreted by

Table 6.1 Means and SD of the three temporal-order scores for males and females in each age group

	Age group (years)					
	Males					
Measure	*20–29 (n = 57)*	*30–39 (n = 39)*	*40–49 (n = 42)*	*50–59 (n = 27)*	*60–69 (n = 48)*	*70–91 (n = 44)*
Absolute deviation	26.32 (15.62)	27.00 (17.49)	34.33 (17.87)	35.15 (15.19)	39.94 (14.34)	45.73 (14.47)
Correlation	0.79 (0.18)	0.77 (0.22)	0.69 (0.25)	0.66 (0.20)	0.60 (0.20)	0.53 (0.23)
Hits	6.16 (3.69)	5.82 (3.28)	4.50 (3.01)	4.22 (3.08)	3.56 (2.78)	3.16 (1.74)
	Females					
Measure	*20–29 (n = 60)*	*30–39 (n = 24)*	*40–49 (n = 44)*	*50–59 (n = 28)*	*60–69 (n = 67)*	*70–91 (n = 48)*
Absolute deviation	22.17 (16.04)	23.67 (14.80)	34.68 (17.88)	31.29 (10.98)	40.30 (18.79)	44.46 (14.84)
Correlation	0.83 (0.19)	0.82 (0.19)	0.67 (0. 26)	0.73 (0.15)	0.61 (0.25)	0.55 (0.23)
Hits	7.05 (3.60)	6.08 (3.15)	4.55 (3.24)	4.82 (2.42)	3.85 (2.78)	3.48 (2.09)

the authors to indicate that retrieval is related to the internal organization of information as reflected by the temporal-order measure.

As reported earlier, patients with CHI were shown to have impaired memory for temporal order when measured directly (Vakil et al., 2001; Vakil & Tweedy, 1994), but showed preserved temporal order when measured indirectly (Vakil, Sherf, Hoffman, & Stern, 1998). The temporal-order measure, added to the Rey AVLT, could be viewed as a direct measure because it requires intentional retrieval of the temporal order. In the learning trials of the Rey AVLT (1–5), participants are asked to recall the words read previously, without mentioning the importance of temporal order. Vakil, Blachstein, and Hoofien (1991) have suggested viewing the order in which the words are spontaneously recalled as an incidental retrieval measure of temporal order when compared to the original order of presentation. Thus, temporal order can be evaluated under the intentional retrieval condition (i.e., Trial 10) and under the incidental retrieval condition (Trial 5).

Vakil et al. (1991) compared the performance of 35 patients with severe CHI (mean age 29) to that of 35 matched control individuals, on the incidental and

Table 6.2 Means and SD of the three temporal-order scores for boys and girls in each age group

	Age group (years)									
	Boys									
Measure	*8* (n = *51*)	*9* (n = *51*)	*10* (n = *56*)	*11* (n = *55*)	*12* (n = *45*)	*13* (n = *42*)	*14* (n = *42*)	*15* (n = *61*)	*16* (n = *47*)	*17* (n = *37*)
Absolute deviation	37.17 (18.59)	32.92 (15.27)	29.71 (16.50)	28.40 (17.48)	26.18 (16.22)	28.86 (17.44)	27.56 (15.44)	28.51 (14.97)	31.37 (14.98)	28.69 (14.25)
Correlation	0.63 (0.27)	0.70 (0.21)	0.77 (0.16)	0.75 (0.23)	0.78 (0.20)	0.75 (0.23)	0.77 (0.19)	0.76 (0.17)	0.73 (0.21)	0.75 (0.19)
Hits	4.39 (2.47)	4.88 (2.97)	4.93 (2.76)	5.47 (2.91)	5.98 (3.12)	5.43 (3.25)	5.90 (2.89)	5.48 (2.84)	5.09 (2.16)	5.62 (2.56)
	Girls									
Measure	*8* (n = *49*)	*9* (n = *49*)	*10* (n = *54*)	*11* (n = *48*)	*12* (n = *45*)	*13* (n = *41*)	*14* (n = *45*)	*15* (n = *43*)	*16* (n = *43*)	*17* (n = *39*)
Absolute deviation	31.23 (16.10)	26.96 (12.67)	27.04 (14.06)	24.65 (15.10)	23.12 (15.76)	30.52 (16.27)	24.66 (10.20)	28.79 (18.00)	30.37 (16.76)	26.21 (11.64)
Correlation	0.72 (0.20)	0.79 (0.17)	0.79 (0.18)	0.80 (0.21)	0.79 (0.21)	0.73 (0.22)	0.81 (0.12)	0.76 (0.22)	0.72 (0.23)	0.79 (0.15)
Hits	5.16 (2.37)	5.43 (2.23)	5.69 (2.55)	5.92 (2.65)	6.22 (3.23)	5.39 (2.97)	5.39 (1.99)	5.44 (3.50)	5.58 (2.77)	5.41 (2.90)

intentional retrieval of temporal-order measures. Patients with CHI ($M = 0.52$) and the matched control individuals ($M = 0.62$) did not differ significantly on the incidental measure of temporal order as measured with the correlation score. However, the control participants were significantly more accurate in their intentional memory of temporal order ($M = 0.78$) than the patient group ($M = 0.48$). Furthermore, for both groups, the intentional but not the incidental measure of temporal order was significantly correlated with several of the other memory measures derived from the Rey AVLT. Interestingly, for the control group, intentional but not incidental measure of temporal order was significantly correlated to age and education. In the patient group, however, neither of the temporal-order scores was correlated with age or education. The authors noticed that the correlation scores in the two retrieval conditions were significantly above chance for most of the control participants and for about half of the patients with CHI.

A similar study by Vakil, Blachstein, Rochberg, and Vardi (2004) with 25 children (mean age 14.84) who sustained CHI and a matched control group yielded a similar pattern of results: The patient ($M = 0.54$) and control groups ($M = 0.47$) did not differ significantly on incidental temporal-order performance. However, the control participants were significantly more accurate in their intentional memory of temporal order ($M = 0.84$) than the patient group ($M = 0.62$).

Thus, the poor intentional temporal-order judgment of the group of patients with CHI provides an additional indication of frontal-lobe dysfunction in this patient group (Adams, 1975). The dissociation between intentional and incidental retrieval of temporal order (with the former being impaired and the latter preserved) is consistent with the previous reports on adults who sustained CHI (Vakil et al., 1998, 2001; Vakil & Tweedy, 1994). The latter dissociation may be explained in light of the previous findings, which demonstrate that, just as in patients with amnesia, memory is impaired in patients with CHI when tested directly (i.e., intentional retrieval is required). However, when tested indirectly, the performance of patients with CHI falls within the normal range.

The finding that performance under incidental retrieval of temporal order was not significantly different between patients (adults and children) who sustained CHI and matched controls should be interpreted cautiously. It is possible that the controls, either adults or children, preferred a retrieval strategy such as clustering, rather than temporal order. This would be consistent with Delis, Freeland, Kramer, and Kaplan (1988), who identify two learning strategies in the process of learning a list of words: semantic clustering (categorization) and serial clustering (temporal order). They also found trade-off relations between these two strategies, so when one is used the other is not. With the test they used, the California Verbal Learning Test (CVLT), they found that semantic clustering was the more effective learning strategy. Note, however, that the word list in the CVLT consists of 16 words, 4 words from each of 4 categories, unlike the list in the Rey AVLT, which consists of 15 unrelated words. Thus, it is possible that in the case of the Rey AVLT, although semantic clustering is always possible, it requires much more effort to be effective, so that participants would prefer the serial clustering strategy. Further research is essential in order to clarify this matter.

In sum, memory for temporal order has been studied from different theoretical perspectives (i.e., automatic processes, contextual information, and source memory). In spite of its theoretical significance, temporal order is not adequately represented in standard memory batteries. The supplementary measure of temporal order in the Rey AVLT rectifies this situation to some degree. Several studies with children and adults that used this measure found it to be sensitive to age and to CHI. Thus, this measure enhances the sensitivity of Rey AVLT as a diagnostic tool.

References

Adams, J. H. (1975). The neuropathology of head injury. In P. J. Binken & G. W. Bruyn (Eds.), *Handbook of clinical neurology* (pp. 35–65). New York: Elsevier.

Audy, B. C., Sullivan, C., & Gross, H. A. (1988). The effect of constrained rehearsal of judgement of temporal order. *Bulletin of the Psychonomic Society*, *26*, 548–551.

Azary, N. P., Audy, B. C., & Gross, H. A. (1989). Effects of instructions on memory for temporal order. *Bulletin of the Psychonomic Society*, *27*, 203–205.

Butters, M. A., Kaszniak, A. W., Glisky, E. L., Eslinger, P. J., & Schacter, D. L. (1994). Recency discrimination deficit in frontal lobe patients. *Neuropsychology*, *8*, 343–353.

Delis, D. C., Freeland, J., Kramer, J. H., & Kaplan, E. (1988). Integrating clinical assessment with cognitive neuroscience: Construct validation of the California Verbal Learning Test. *Journal of Consulting and Clinical Psychology*, *56*, 123–130.

Eslinger, P. J., & Grattan, L. M. (1994). Altered serial position learning after frontal lobe lesion. *Neuropsychologia*, *32*, 729–739.

Hasher, L., & Zacks, R. T. (1979). Automatic and effortful processes in memory. *Journal of Experimental Psychology: General*, *108*, 356–388.

Hirst, W. (1982). The amnesic syndrome: Description and explanation. *Psychological Bulletin*, *91*, 435–460.

Hirst, W., & Volpe, B. T. (1982). Temporal order judgment with amnesia. *Brain and Cognition*, *1*, 294–306.

Huppert, F. A., & Piercy, M. (1976). Recognition memory in amnesic patients: Effect of temporal, context and familiarity of material. *Cortex*, *12*, 3–20.

Janowsky, J. S., Shimamura, A. P., & Squire, L. R. (1989). Source memory impairment in patients with frontal lobe lesions. *Neuropsychologia*, *27*, 1043–1056.

Kausler, D. H., Lichty, W., & Davis, T. M. (1985). Temporal memory for performed activities: Intentionality and adult age differences. *Developmental Psychology*, *21*, 1132–1138.

Kausler, D. H., Salthouse, T. A., & Saults, J. S. (1988). Temporal memory over the adult life-span. *American Journal of Psychology*, *101*, 207–215.

Lezak, M. D. (1995). *Neuropsychological assessment* (3rd ed.). New York: Oxford University Press.

Mayes, A. R., MacDonald, C., Donlan, L., Pears, J., & Meudel, P. R. (1992). Amnesics have a disproportionately severe memory deficit for interactive context. *The Quarterly Journal of Experimental Psychology, 45A*, 265–297.

McAndrews, M. P., & Milner, B. (1991). The frontal cortex and memory for temporal order. *Neuropsychologia, 29*, 840–859.

McCormack, P. D. (1981). Temporal coding by young and elderly adults: A test of the Hasher–Zacks model. *Developmental Psychology, 17*, 509–515.

Naveh-Benjamin, M. (1990). Coding of temporal order information: An automatic process? *Journal of Experimental Psychology: Learning, Memory, and Cognition, 16*, 117–126.

Pickering, A. D., Mayes, A. R., & Fairbairn, A. F. (1989). Amnesia and memory for modality information. *Neuropsychologia, 27*, 1249–1259.

Ryan, J. J., Rosenberg, S. J., & Mittenberg, W. (1984). Factor analysis of the Rey Auditory-Verbal Learning Test. *The International Journal of Clinical Neuropsychology, 6*, 239–341.

Schacter, D. L., Harbluk, J. L., & McLachlan, D. R. (1984). Retrieval without recollection: An experimental analysis of source amnesia. *Journal of Verbal Learning and Verbal Behavior, 23*, 593–611.

Shimamura, A. P., Janowsky, J. S., & Squire, L. R. (1990). Memory for the temporal order of events in patients with frontal lobe lesions and amnesic patients. *Neuropsychologia, 28*, 803–813.

Shimamura, A. P., & Squire, L. R. (1987). A neuropsychological study of fact memory and source amnesia. *Journal of Experimental Psychology: Learning, Memory, and Cognition, 13*, 464–473.

Shimamura, A. P., & Squire, L. R. (1991). The relationship between fact and source memory: Findings from amnesic patients and normal subjects. *Psychology, 19*, 1–10.

Tzeng, O. J. L., Lee, A. T., & Wetzel, C. D. (1979). Temporal coding in verbal information processing. *Journal of Experimental Psychology: Human Learning and Memory, 5*, 52–64.

Vakil, E., & Blachstein, H. (1993). Rey Auditory-Verbal Learning Test: Structure analysis. *Journal of Clinical Psychology, 49*, 883–890.

Vakil, E., & Blachstein, H. (1994). A supplementary measure in the Rey AVLT for assessing incidental learning of temporal order. *Journal of Clinical Psychology, 50*, 240–245.

Vakil, E., & Blachstein, H. (1997). Rey AVLT: Developmental norms for adults and the sensitivity of different memory measures to age. *Clinical Neuropsychologist, 11*, 356–369.

Vakil, E., Blachstein, H., & Hoofien, D. (1991). Automatic temporal order judgment: The effect of intentionality of retrieval on closed-head-injured patients. *Journal of Clinical and Experimental Neuropsychology, 13*, 291–298.

Vakil, E., Blachstein, H., Rochberg, J., & Vardi, M. (2004). Characterization of memory impairment following closed-head injury in children using the Rey Auditory Verbal Learning Test (AVLT). *Child Neuropsychology, 10*, 57–66.

Vakil, E., Blachstein, H., & Sheinman, M. (1998). Rey AVLT: Developmental norms for children and the sensitivity of different memory measures to age. *Child Neuropsychology, 4*, 161–177.

Vakil, E., Gordon, Y., Birnstok, S., Aberbuch, S., & Groswasser, Z. (2001). Declarative and nondeclarative sequence learning tasks: Closed-head injured patients versus control participants. *Journal of Clinical and Experimental Neuropsychology*, *23*, 207–214.

Vakil, E., Sherf, R., Hoffman, M., & Stern, M. (1998). Direct and indirect memory measures of temporal order and spatial location: Control versus closed-head injury participants. *Neuropsychiatry, Neuropsychology, and Behavioral Neurology*, *11*, 212–217.

Vakil, E., & Tweedy, J. R. (1994). Memory for temporal order and spatial position information: Tests of the automatic effortful distinction. *Neuropsychiatry, Neuropsychology, and Behavioral Neurology*, *7*, 281–288.

Vakil, E., Weise, M., & Enbar, S. (1997). Direct and indirect memory measures of temporal order: Younger versus older adults. *International Journal of Aging and Human Development*, *45*, 195–206.

Wiens, A. N., McMinn, M. R., & Crossen, J. R. (1988). Rey Auditory Verbal Learning Test: Development of norms for healthy young adults. *Clinical Neuropsychologist*, *2*, 67–87.

Appendix

Appendix A Trial 10: The 15 words of the first list are presented in the left column. Please rewrite these words, in the right column, in the original order that they were read to you

Farmer	1
Color	2
Drum	3
Moon	4
Parent	5
River	6
Bell	7
Coffee	8
Nose	9
Garden	10
Curtain	11
School	12
Turkey	13
House	14
Hat	15

Appendix B An example of temporal-order judgment and the three temporal-order scores

Original order	*Arranged order*	*Hits*	*Absolute deviation*	*Correlation*[a]
1. Drum	Drum	1	0	
2. Curtain	Curtain	1	0	
3. Bell	Bell	1	0	
4. Coffee	Turkey	0	8	
5. School	Garden	0	3	
6. Parent	Nose	0	5	
7. Moon	Coffee	0	3	
8. Garden	River	0	7	
9. Hat	Color	0	4	
10. Farmer	Moon	0	3	
11. Nose	Hat	0	2	
12. Turkey	Farmer	0	2	
13. Color	Parent	0	7	
14. House	House	1	0	
15. River	School	0	10	
	Total	4	54	$r = 0.396$

[a]Pearson Product Moment correlation.

7 Adaptation of the Hooper Visual Organization Test

Maria T. Schultheis and Joseph H. Ricker

Introduction and limitations of the original HVOT

The Hooper Visual Organization Test (HVOT; Hooper, 1958, 1983) is a measure of visual organization and integration frequently used by neuropsychological practitioners (Camara, Nathan, & Puente, 2000; Lundin & DeFilippis, 1999). The standard administration presents examinees with common objects (e.g., hammer, apple, shoe) that have been visually segmented and rotated, requiring examinees to mentally reassemble the component pieces and to verbally identify (i.e., name) the object.

In the earlier neuropsychological assessment literature there was an ongoing debate pertaining to the HVOT's utility in assessing global and localized brain dysfunction. For example, Wang (1977) reported no differences in the performance of left as compared to right brain-damaged patients. Boyd (1981) found the HVOT to correctly classify 74% of a sample into brain-damaged and nonbrain-damaged groups. However, it should be noted, that "brain damage" as a unitary concept has been harshly criticized and is no longer considered to be specific enough (Rathbaum & Smith, 1982).

In the 1990s, a growing number of neuropsychological studies concentrated on demonstrating the HVOT's utility in assessing specific types of cerebral impairment. Investigators have reported reduced HVOT performance in patients with focal nondominant parietal lobe damage (Fitz, Conrad, & Sarff, 1992) as well as in patients with dementing processes involving the parietal lobes (Ricker, Keenan, & Jacobson, 1994). The HVOT has also been used to assess visuoperceptual functioning in a variety of clinical populations. Gomez-Tortosa, Barroso, and Garcia Ruiz (1996) demonstrated that the HVOT was somewhat sensitive in identifying early symptomatic from asymptomatic Huntington's disease carriers. York and Cermak (1995) reported that patients with a right hemisphere cerebral vascular accident (CVA) performed more poorly than patients with a left hemisphere CVA. Finally, Wang (1977) and Fitz et al. (1992) examined the performance of brain-injured patients on this task. They reported that HVOT scores, when adjusted for age and education, were significantly lower in patients with lesions involving the right parietal lobe. In addition, developmental trends in HVOT performance have been demonstrated in children (Kirk, 1992; Seidel, 1994).

Intuitively, it would seem that performance on this measure might be affected by factors other than visual integration, much in the same way that visual memory is affected by visual or perceptual process (Ricker et al., 1994). Specifically, it would seem possible that object naming might impact performance given the nature of the visual naming response required on the HVOT. This limitation reflects the growing recognition among clinical neuropsychologists that the sum scores on most cognitive measures are too simplistic to capture the complex structures and processes that underlie the performance of most cognitive tasks.

Alternative measures of visual-spatial perception

An obvious "work-around" solution for this limitation as described above is simply to use visuospatial tests that have no naming or other verbal response component. In practice, however, this is not so simple. Most abstract or "naming-free" visuospatial tests still require graphomotor output, e.g., the Rey–Osterrieth Complex Figure (Rey & Osterrieth, 1993), the Beery Visual-Motor Integration Test (Beery, Buktenica, & Beery, 2004), or figure copying from the Benton Visual Retention Test (Sivan, 1991).

Inferences from other tests

Another possible strategy is to attempt to gauge the effects of confrontation naming on the HVOT by "comparing" performance from naming tests such as the Boston Naming Test (Goodglass, Kaplan, & Barresi, 2000) or the Visual Naming Test (VNT; Benton & Hamsher, 1989). Such tests, however, are designed to test for difficulties in object naming and not visuospatial perception *per se*. In addition, the objects in such tests are rarely the same items as in the HVOT, thus there is no way to directly compare ability to name an object against ability to perceive the object. This was the primary rationale for the development of an experimental object-naming test derived from the HVOT stimulus items.

Development of the Hooper Object Naming Test

Initially, the issue of HVOT and naming was formally addressed in a two-part study (Ricker & Axelrod, 1995). The first part of the study evaluated the relationship between the general construct of object-naming ability and performance on the HVOT. The second part of the study directly investigated whether confrontation naming of each specific HVOT item influenced performance on the HVOT.

In the first part of the study, 50 male veterans (mean age = 52.9 years, *SD* = 14.2 years; mean education = 11.4 years, *SD* = 2.17 years) were examined using the regular administration of the spiral-bound HVOT, the Wechsler Adult Intelligence Scale-Revised (WAIS-R; Wechsler, 1991), and the VNT from the Multilingual Aphasia Exam (Benton & Hamsher, 1989).

Hierarchical multiple regression analyses were conducted on standardized HVOT scores corrected for age and education. On the first step of the regression, the three WAIS-R factor scores (i.e., Verbal Comprehension, Perceptual Organization, and Freedom from Distractibility) were simultaneously entered to determine the effects of general cognitive status on the HVOT. This first regression entry accounted for 48% of the variance in HVOT scores, $R = 0.70$, $F(3, 46) = 14.3$, $p < 0.0001$, with Perceptual Organization emerging as the only statistically significant WAIS-R factor score ($p = 0.0002$). Raw scores from the VNT were entered on the second step of the regression, which accounted for 11% of additional variance (F change $= 12.4$, $p = 0.0001$), suggesting a significant contribution of general naming ability to HVOT performance. The entire model accounted for 59% of total variance in HVOT performance, $R = 0.77$, $F(4, 45) = 16.5$, $p < 0.0001$. In order to ensure that relationships between factor scores and confrontation-naming skills had not been overlooked, the order of entry was reversed in a second regression equation, with comparable results, $R = 0.74$, $F(4, 45) = 13.3$, $p < 0.0001$. Again, Perceptual Organization emerged as the only significant factor.

The results from that first study supported the role of the primary contribution of perceptual organizational ability to HVOT performance, a finding that was maintained in a later study conducted by a different group of investigators (Paolo, Cluff, & Ryan, 1996). These data also underscore the relationship between object-naming ability and quantitative performance on this measure. This latter finding offered support to the idea that examiners might consider an individual's object-naming ability when interpreting HVOT scores. The findings did not address, however, whether examinees have a task-specific naming impairment that might attenuate HVOT performance. Thus, a second investigation was designed that sought to determine if an individual's ability to name the *specific* objects presented in the HVOT would be related to overall performance.

In the second phase of the investigation, a different sample of 50 consecutively referred patients was examined. Fifty men (mean age = 56.4 years, $SD = 15.86$ years; range = 27 to 57 years; mean years of education = 11.2, $SD = 2.1$ years, range = 6 to 17 years; 19 African Americans and 31 Caucasians) comprised the sample. Each stimulus card from the HVOT was redrawn to scale by a professional artist, thus producing a completed figure without segmentation lines. The new stimulus cards were photoreproduced on heavy card stock and bound in the original order of administration. This process yielded an object-naming test with the HVOT visual stimuli as the objects to be identified verbally (hence, the "Hooper Object Naming Test" or "HONT"). As in the first study, each subject also completed the HVOT, the WAIS-R, and the VNT, according to standard administration. The visual naming adaptation of the HVOT (HONT) was administered immediately following the administration of the standard HVOT.

To ensure that the results from the first sample were generalizable to the second sample, the original multiple regressions were repeated and the pattern of results was comparable. As in Study 1, the first step of the regression analysis accounted for much of the variance in HVOT performance, $R^2 = 46\%$; $F(3, 46) = 13.0$, $p < 0.001$, and general naming ability made significant secondary contributions, R^2 change = 0.05; F change = 4.74, $p = 0.04$; overall $F(4, 45) = 9.6$, $p < 0.0001$. As with the first study, the order of variable entry into the regression equation was reversed and comparable results were obtained. The VNT and HONT were directly compared to evaluate their equivalence as measures of naming ability. Using the raw scores from the VNT and HONT, an intraclass correlation coefficient (ICC) was derived between the two tests (Shrout & Fleiss, 1979). The resulting coefficient (ICC $r = 0.08$) fell in the "poor" range, indicating that there was no significant relationship between the two measures.

A hierarchical multiple regression was conducted in two steps on HVOT scores using adjustments for age and education from the HVOT technical manual (Hooper, 1983). On the first step, the Perceptual Organization factor from the WAIS-R was entered, which accounted for 44% of the variance in HVOT performance, $R = 0.67$; $F(1, 48) = 38.1$, $p < 0.0001$. The number of correct responses from the HONT was entered in the second step of the regression. The HONT did not account for a significant amount of variance in HVOT performance (R^2 change = 0.01, F change = 0.6, $p = 0.46$). The results of the second study again strongly suggest that perceptual organizational ability accounts for most of the variance in HVOT performance. This finding has been further supported by a more recent investigation, which demonstrated that Perceptual Organization accounted for 45% of the variance in HVOT performance in a stroke population (Greve, Lindberg, Bianchini, & Adams, 2000).

Additionally, the ability of an individual to name the HVOT stimuli appears unrelated to actual test performance. Thus, it appears that even if a patient's object-naming ability is generally impaired, this factor is not likely to significantly attenuate HVOT performance. In other words, the degree of object-naming ability required on the HVOT does not appear to be of sufficient difficulty or complexity to impair performance. Of course, while patients with pronounced aphasia might be able to visually organize the HVOT stimulus items, they may still be unable to communicate the information verbally. To address this likely common scenario, we have more recently developed and examined a multiple-choice version of the HVOT (Schultheis, Caplan, Ricker, & Woessner, 2000).

Development of the Multiple-Choice adaptation of the HVOT

The Multiple-Choice HVOT (MC-HVOT) was developed by photoreproducing each stimulus item from the HVOT onto an 8.5 × 11 in sheet of paper. The MC-HVOT consists of 30 stimulus items, each a photoreproduction of the original stimuli from the HVOT. As with the HVOT, each MC-HVOT stimulus is a black ink line drawing of a common object, which has been sectioned into two or more parts that are presented in a scattered and rotated array. The MC-HVOT stimulus is presented on an 8.5 × 11 in card (horizontally), with the drawing on the top of the page and four response choices printed directly below the stimulus item.

For each item, four response choices were generated. The choices included (1) the correct answer; (2) an "isolate" response; (3) a "poor global integration response;" and (4) a foil. The "isolate" response indicator was included because of commonly reported clinical observations, namely, that some patients identify an isolated detail of the stimulus rather than naming the integrated whole (e.g., "pipe" on item 22; see Lezak et al., 2004). The "poor global integration" response indicator was developed to capture responses reflecting poor visual integration resulting from incomplete visual synthesis. The foils were selected from incorrect answers provided in the HVOT manual and from past patient protocols. To further ensure correct classification of response choices in the MC-HVOT, four doctoral-level neuropsychologists independently categorized response choices into one of the four categories (i.e., "correct," "isolate," "poor global," and "foil"). All four respondents correctly categorized items with 95% agreement. Items that were inconsistently categorized were not included in the final version of the MC-HVOT.

Individual administration of the MC-HVOT is accomplished by placing the test binder in front of the respondent and stating: "This is a test of your ability to recognize picture of objects, when the pictures have been cut up and rearranged. On each page, you will see one cut up picture and four choices of what that picture might be. Look at the each picture and decide what it might be if the pieces were put together and then select the choice you think names the object. Select one of the choices even if it is a guess." After these instructions, each item is administered individually with no time limit or discontinuation rule. The time required to administer the entire test is approximately 15 to 20 min.

In a preliminary study of the MC-HVOT (Schultheis et al., 2000), we examined 14 individuals referred for neuropsychological evaluation as part of an inpatient treatment plan. Participants were recruited from two rehabilitation centers located in two different states. Each participant had sustained a single focal brain insult from either a stroke or a lateralized traumatic cerebral contusion. Each was examined within the first 90 days after onset (mean number of days postinjury = 18.5; SD = 12.3). Participants had a mean age of 35.1 years and a mean years of education of 10.9 (ranging from 5 to 12 years). Each individual was administered the HVOT following standardized procedures. Those achieving scores on the HVOT consistent with a "moderate probability of impairment" (i.e., < 20 correct; Hooper, 1983) were administered the Boston Naming Test (BNT) to determine degree of confrontation-naming impairment. Individuals obtaining BNT scores below the 10th percentile were subsequently administered the MC-HVOT approximately 24 h following administration of the HVOT (in order to reduce effects of exposure to stimulus items). Paired sample t-tests demonstrated that dysnomic individuals achieved a significantly greater number of correct responses on the MC-HVOT than on the standard administration of the HVOT, $t = -8.3$, df(13); $p < 0.03$. To examine differences in clinical classification based on the traditional HVOT administration as compared to the MC-HVOT, each performance level was assigned a clinical descriptor in accordance with the HVOT test manual. The four possible ratings of clinical impairment were: performance within normal limits = 0; mild impairment = 1; moderate impairment = 2; and severe impairment = 3. As anticipated, given the observed improvement in the total number correct between the MC-HVOT and the HVOT, a Wilcoxon signed-rank test revealed a significant change in clinical description of level of impairment ($z = -3.72$, $p < 0.001$). Specifically, the vast majority of individuals (93%) demonstrated higher clinical ratings using scores from the MC-HVOT, with individual ratings improving from moderately impaired (mean ranking = 2.3; SEM = 0.13) to slightly below mildly impaired (mean ranking = 0.93; SEM = 0.22).

Based on CT reports, participants were classified into two groups: primarily left hemisphere (LH; $n = 8$) vs. primarily right hemisphere (RH; $n = 6$) involvement. A *t*-test demonstrated no significant differences on MC-HVOT performance between the LH and RH groups, t (12) $= -1.69$; $p = 0.116$. To examine the degree of difference between the HVOT and the MC-HVOT at an individual level, a difference score was calculated (i.e., *MC-HVOT total raw score* minus *HVOT total raw score*). A *t*-test comparing difference scores revealed no significant difference between RH and LH groups, t (12) $= -1.28$; $p = 0.224$. Specifically, the RH group performed approximately 8 points higher on the MC-HVOT, while the LH group improved by an average of 10.9 points. Additional analysis of individual cases, however, demonstrated that only 16% of the RH group obtained a performance that was within normal limits on the MC-HVOT, while 50% of the LH group demonstrated performance that was within normal limits. Error analysis revealed that the RH group made a significantly greater number of "poor global integration" errors than the LH group, t (12) $= 3.18$; $p < 0.01$. No other significant differences in error types were noted between groups.

The findings from the MC-HVOT study suggest that the object-naming requirement of the HVOT has a significant impact on the performance of truly dysnomic individuals. This was evidenced by the overall higher levels of HVOT performance that were achieved when the task was presented in a multiple-choice format. These findings suggest that reducing (or eliminating) the actual demand characteristic of object naming on the HVOT may provide clinicians with a clearer assessment of visual synthesis skills.

Administration and scoring considerations

The development of both the HONT and MC-HVOT was for the purposes of research, and neither has been standardized nor marketed for use as a clinical assessment instrument. Nonetheless, these test adaptations could prove to be useful adjuncts in clinical applications and interpretation of visuospatial test performance.

Interpretive strategies with particular syndromes

The findings of empirical studies with HONT have demonstrated that the impact of confrontation-naming deficits (i.e., dysnomia) is minimal. The lack of a significant direct relationship between object-naming ability and HVOT performance in a mixed clinical sample is not surprising, however, given the development of the HVOT. Object-naming tests are explicitly developed as measures of confrontation-naming ability. They contain items of varying levels of difficulty and are standardized using samples of individuals with confrontation-naming problems. In contrast, the HVOT was developed in relation to difficulty level of perceptual integration rather than object-naming ability. This is not to say that there is no effect whatsoever in individuals with language disorders. The findings from the MC-HVOT among individuals with actual dysnomia and lateralized cerebral dysfunction suggest that dysnomia does have an impact on clinical interpretation.

Future directions

The HONT and MC-HVOT may be clinically useful additions to the administration of the HVOT for individuals who perform poorly on the HVOT (e.g., <20 correct). Qualitatively, these adaptations could assist in determining if poor performance results from an overall expressive deficit rather than impaired visual integration.

In order to fully elaborate on the various adaptations of the HVOT and similar measures, additional studies will need to be conducted in populations that have sustained very focal cerebral lesions, as well as in those with more diffuse involvement. Many, if not most, clinical populations have multifocal or diffuse cerebral involvement, such as is encountered in most persons with traumatic brain injury, multiple sclerosis, or neurodegenerative conditions such as Huntington's disease or Alzheimer's disease.

Additional studies will need to be conducted in order to demonstrate recovery of function. The practice effects of the HVOT are also problematic. In general, once an individual is able to determine the object presented, they tend to retain that knowledge and thus performance will be "contaminated" for future use. To our knowledge, there are no parallel or alternative forms of HVOT. In order to truly assess HVOT recovery in performance, an alternate form of equivalent item difficulty and equivalent overall test difficulty will need to be developed.

All of the studies and adaptations of the HVOT discussed to this point have been psychometric and behavioral. Cerebral substrates thought to subsume or mediate the cognitive processes required for test performance are, at best, inferred or correlated. A very promising line of research for assessing the

HVOT (and for that matter, other neuropsychological tests) is the application of functional neuroimaging technologies in conjunction with detailed testing. In fact, there is already one study of the HVOT that capitalizes on behavioral and imaging data (Moritz, Johnson, McMillan, Haughton, & Meyerand, 2004). In this study, a group of healthy individuals were presented with the stimulus items from the HVOT while undergoing blood oxygen level dependent (BOLD), functional magnetic resonance imaging (FMRI). In that study, 19 healthy individuals (11 men and 8 women, average age of 22.9 years) performed the HVOT, visually projected for use in the FMRI scanning environment. The findings demonstrated bilateral activity in posterior brain regions, predominantly in superior parietal lobes, ventral temporo-occipital cortex, and in posterior visual association areas. Additionally, there were activations noted in the frontal eye fields bilaterally, and to some degree in the left dorsolateral prefrontal cortex. The investigators interpreted these findings as suggesting that the information processing required of the HVOT predominantly utilizes posterior and inferior brain regions that are classically associated with visuospatial performance. In addition, there is involvement of the visual gaze center and some level of executive control. This latter finding is not surprising, however, given that there is a certain degree of executive control processing required in order to mentally assemble and organize information into a meaningful whole and to integrate the Gestalt into some symbol of a familiar object. This groundbreaking functional imaging study of the HVOT is very exciting and promising. It is still clear, however, that additional replication is necessary and that studies will need to be conducted in clinical populations. In particular, it would be of interest to see which parts of the brain are involved (or not involved) in HVOT performance among individuals with focal or diffuse brain injury, and at different levels of behavioral performance. For example, an individual with infarction involving the right parietal lobe may have difficulty accessing information processing resources mediated by that brain area. Clearly, if they are unable to perform the HVOT, one might say that this parietal lesion led to the deficit. If, however, that same individual demonstrated improvement over the course of their recovery, functional neuroimaging might assist in demonstrating brain reorganization or allocation of other intact brain resources. Only future research with appropriate paradigms and test–retest designs would allow for such inferences.

Summary

The HVOT has been demonstrated to be a clinically useful test in the assessment of visuospatial abilities. Although it requires participants to name objects, its linguistic demands are not such that it precludes successful performance in clinical populations. Research to date suggests that it is primarily a measure of perceptual-organizational ability and is likely a good index of functional integrity of those cerebral structures involved in complex visual information processing. Additional research that investigates alternate forms and cerebral processing correlates in clinical populations will serve to further our understanding of this instrument's clinical utility.

Acknowledgments

Copyright reproduction privileges for research purposes were obtained from Western Psychological Corporation, Los Angeles, CA.

This work was supported in part by an NSERC grant to E. Strauss.

References

Beery, K. E., Buktenica, N. A., & Beery, N. A. (2004). *Beery–Buktenica developmental test of visual-motor integration* (5th ed.). Lutz, FL: Psychological Assessment Resources.

Benton, A. L., & Hamsher, K. de. S. (1989). *Multilingual aphasia examination* (2nd ed.). Iowa City, IA: AJA Associates.

Boyd, J. (1981). A validity study of the Hooper Visual Organization Test. *Journal of Consulting and Clinical Psychology*, *49*, 15–19.

Camara, W. J., Nathan J. S., & Puente, A. E. (2000). Psychological test usage: Implications in professional psychology. *Professional Psychology: Research and Practice*, *31*(2), 141–154.

Fitz, A., Conrad, D., & Sarff, P. (1992). Hooper Visual Organization Test performance in lateralized brain injury. *Archives of Clinical Neuropsychology*, *7*, 243–250.

Gomez-Tortosa, E., Barroso, T., & Garcia Ruiz, P. (1996). Visual processing disorders in patients with Huntington's disease and asymptomatic carriers. *Journal of Neurology*, *243*, 286–292.

Goodglass, H., Kaplan, E., & Barresi, B. (2000). *Boston diagnostic aphasia examination* (3rd ed.). San Antonio, TX: The Psychological Corporation.

Greve, K. W., Lindberg, R. F., Bianchini, K. J., & Adams, D. (2000). Construct validity and predictive value of the Hooper Visual Organization Test in stroke rehabilitation. *Applied Neuropsychology*, *7*, 215–222.

Hooper, E. (1983). *Hooper Visual Organization Test*. Los Angeles: Western Psychological Services.

Hooper, H. E. (1958). *The Hooper Visual Organization Test Manual*. Los Angeles: Western Psychological Services.

Kirk, U. (1992). Evidence for early acquisition of visual organization ability: A developmental study. *The Clinical Neuropsychologist*, *6*, 171–177.

Lezak, M. D., Howieson, D. B., & Loring, D. W. (2004). *Neuropsychological assessment* (4th ed.). New York: Oxford University Press.

Lundin, K. A., & DeFilippis, N. A. (1999). Proposed schedule of usual and customary test administration times. *The Clinical Neuropsychologist*, *13*(4), 433–436.

Moritz, C. H., Johnson, S. C., McMillan, K. M., Haughton, V. M., & Meyerand, E. (2004). Functional MRI neuroanatomic correlates of the Hooper Visual Organization Test. *Journal of the International Neuropsychological Society*, *10*(7), 939–947.

Paolo, A., Cluff, R., & Ryan, J. (1996). Influence of perceptual organization and naming abilities on the Hooper Visual Organization Test. *Neuropsychiatry, Neuropsychology and Behavioral Neurology*, *9*, 254–257.

Rathbaum, J., & Smith, A. (1982). Comment on the validity of Boyd's validation study of the Hooper Visual Organization Test. *Journal of Consulting and Clinical Psychology*, *50*, 281–283.

Rey, A., & Osterrieth, P. (1993). Translations of excerpts from Rey's 'Psychological Examination of Traumatic Encephalopathy' and Osterrieth's 'The Complex Figure Test.' *The Clinical Neuropsychologist*, *7*, 2–21.

Ricker, J. H., & Axelrod, B. N. (1995). Hooper Visual Organization Test: Effects of object naming ability. *The Clinical Neuropsychologist*, *9*, 57–62.

Ricker, J. H., Keenan, P. A., & Jacobson, M. W. (1994). Visuoperceptual-spatial ability and visual memory in vascular dementia and dementia of the Alzheimer's type. *Neuropsychologia*, *32*, 1287–1296.

Schultheis, M. T., Caplan, B., Ricker, J. H., & Woessner, R. (2000). Fractioning the Hooper: A multiple-choice response format. *The Clinical Neuropsychologist*, *14*(2), 196–201.

Seidel, W. (1994). Applicability of the Hooper Visual Organization Test to pediatric populations: Preliminary findings. *The Clinical Neuropsychologist*, *8*, 59–68.

Shrout, P. E., & Fleiss, J. L. (1979). Intraclass correlations: Uses in assessing rater reliability. *Psychological Bulletin*, *2*, 420–428.

Sivan, A. (1991). *Benton Visual Retention Test* (5th ed.). San Antonio, TX: The Psychological Corporation.

Wang, P. (1977). Visual organization ability in brain damaged adults. *Perceptual and Motor Skills*, *45*, 723–728.

Wechsler, D. (1981). *Manual for the Wechsler Adult Intelligence Scale—Revised*. San Antonio, TX: The Psychological Corporation.

York, C., & Cermak, S. (1995). Visual perception and praxis in adults after stroke. *The American Journal of Occupational Therapy*, *49*, 543–550.

Part III

The Composition Paradigm

The Composition Paradigm is an approach by which new indices for existing tests are composed using previously collected, but not analyzed, data. Using this approach, the contribution of different neurocognitive mechanisms are elucidated, allowing for an increase in the resolution of the existing tests. In Chapter 8, John L. Woodard describes the development of new memory performance indexes for the Rey Auditory Verbal Learning Test. In Chapter 9, Angela K. Troyer and Morris Moscovitch describe the development, scoring roles, norms, and psychometric properties of the clustering and switching indexes for verbal fluency tests. In Chapter 10, Greg J. Lamberty and Bradley N. Axelrod describe the limitations, benefits, norms, and psychometric properties of various Trail Making Test indices. In Chapter 11, Holly Tuokko and Megan E. O'Connell review scoring guidelines, norms, and psychometric properties of indices that have been developed for quantifying the clock drawing.

In Chapter 12, Paula K. Shear and Amy J. Jak describe new indexes for quantifying the Block Design Test. Finally, in Chapter 13, W. Keith Berg, Dana L. Byrd, Joseph P. H. McNamara, and Christine A. MacDonald describe the development of new indices of planning abilities for the Tower of London task.

8 Memory performance indexes for the Rey Auditory Verbal Learning Test

John L. Woodard

Introduction

Learning a list of items and recalling this list at a later point in time are nearly universal, common everyday occurrences. It is perhaps for this reason that word list learning tasks have an extremely long history of use in neuropsychology and have become a central tool in the neuropsychologist's armamentarium for evaluation of human memory functioning. In addition to having good ecological validity, word list learning tasks lend themselves nicely to the study of a number of aspects of memory functioning, including learning, retention, recall, and recognition. Numerous performance indexes have been derived and developed in cognitive psychology and clinical neuropsychology to evaluate each of these components of memory functioning.

Although a number of multi-trial list learning procedures have been developed and used clinically, the technique described by André Rey that has come to be known as the Auditory Verbal Learning Test (AVLT; Rey, 1958) represents a memory assessment procedure that may have the longest history of continuous use (Boake, 2000). Since its original publication nearly 50 years ago, the test has been translated into a number of different languages, and approximately 20 different administration procedures have been reported in the clinical and experimental literature (Schmidt, 1996).

The purpose of this chapter is to review a variety of memory performance indexes for the AVLT that have been presented in the literature as they relate to the Quantified Process Approach. As it is easily administered and relatively simple to score, the AVLT generates a rich source of neuropsychological data. It can provide a considerable amount of information with respect to attention, rate of learning, primacy and recency effects, susceptibility to proactive and retroactive interference, immediate and delayed recall, delayed recognition, and subjective organization. After reviewing its historical background and general procedure, the major performance indexes from the AVLT will be reviewed, along with descriptions of their clinical utility taken from the literature.

Historical background

The use of multi-trial list learning tasks dates back at least to the work of Ebbinghaus (1885, 1964), who demonstrated the effects of the number of repetitions on retention as well as how retention varies as a function of time. In 1919, a single-trial list learning task was developed by the Swiss psychologist, Édouard Claparède. The Test de Mémoire des Mots (Test of Memory for Words) as originally published consisted of three 15-word lists (Series A, B, and C) that were reported to be of equal difficulty (Boake, 2000). A given word list was read aloud to an individual at the rate of 2 s per word, and 10 s after the last word had been presented, the examinee was asked to write down as many words as he or she could remember. Subsequently, André Rey, a student of Claparède, used these same word lists to develop a relatively simple multi-trial list learning task using repeated presentations of the 15 unrelated words to assess immediate learning and subsequent recognition of the list words embedded within a short story. Rey's procedure was published using the same three word lists from the Test of Memory for Words, in addition to a fourth list of 15 words of unknown origin (see Table 8.1), in his book, *L'examen clinique en psychologie* (*The Clinical Examination in Psychology*; Rey, 1958). This procedure, originally titled, *Mémorisation d'une série de 15*

Table 8.1 Original AVLT word lists (Rey, 1958)

List A	*List B*	*List C*	*List D*
Tambour (Drum)	Pupitre (Desk)	Orange (Orange)	Violon (Violin)
Rideau (Curtain)	Berger (Shepherd)	Fauteuil (Armchair)	Arbre (Tree)
Ceinture (Belt)	Moineau (Sparrow)	Crapaud (Toad)	Cravate (Necktie)
Café (Coffee)	Soulier (Shoe)	Bouchon (Cork)	Jambon (Ham)
Ecole (School)	Fourneau (Stove)	Voiture (Car)	Valise (Suitcase)
Parent (Parent)	Montagne (Mountain)	Menton (Chin)	Cousin (Cousin)
Soleil (Sun)	Lunette (Glasses)	Rivage (Shore)	Oreille (Ear)
Jardin (Garden)	Eponge (Sponge)	Savon (Soap)	Couteau (Knife)
Casquette (Cap)	Image (Picture)	Hotel (Hotel)	Escalier (Stairs)
Paysan (Farmer)	Bateau (Boat)	Cheval (Horse)	Chien (Dog)
Moustache (Mustache)	Mouton (Sheep)	Insecte (Insect)	Banane (Banana)
Dindon (Turkey)	Fusil (Rifle)	Toilette (Toilet)	Outil (Tool)
Couleur (Color)	Crayon (Pencil)	Marmite (Cooking pot)	Chasseur (Hunter)
Maison (House)	Eglise (Church)	Soldat (Soldier)	Seau (Bucket)
Riviere (River)	Poisson (Fish)	Serrure (Lock)	Campagne (Country)

Note: English translations by author in parentheses.

mots en 5 répétitions (*Memorization of a Series of 15 Words over Five Trials*) has come to be known as the Auditory Verbal Learning Test (AVLT).

In its original form, the procedure described by Rey (1958) involved the verbal presentation of 15 words to the examinee. The instructions provided considerable encouragement and feedback to the examinee. A 1-s interval separated the presentation of each word. Following presentation of this word list, the examinee was asked to recall as many words as possible, without respect to order. The examiner recorded correct words, words that were repeated without hesitation or an indication that they had been previously reported, words that were repeated with hesitation or some indication that they have been previously reported, and intrusion errors or incorrect words. After a fixed recall period of 60 s, the examiner indicated how many words from the list were correctly reported, and the 15 words were again presented, using the same study-test format for Trials 2–5. However, in contrast to the first trial, a fixed 90-s recall period was allotted for each of these trials, regardless of whether or not the examinee indicated that he or she was unable to recall any additional words.

The fixed recall period ensures that each presentation of the list is given at consistent intervals to every examinee, helping to control or hold constant the rate at which list items are presented to the examinee. Rey recommended making note of the number of words recalled in each 15-s block of each recall period, in order to facilitate analysis of the recall rhythm. Following the fifth and final study-test recall trial, Rey read a story to the examinee that had list words embedded within it and directed the examinee to make a verbal response whenever a word from the list was presented in the story. This recognition testing procedure was performed after all recall trials had been completed. No interference trial or delayed recall testing was described in the original procedure.

In the original description of the procedure (Rey, 1958), normative data for the task were presented for children from 5 to 15 years of age, as well as for adults with a variety of occupational backgrounds. In addition, detailed clinical interpretive information was also presented not only for the basic scores (number correct on each trial, perseverations, and intrusions) but also for the processes and learning styles exhibited by the examinee. He also presented case examples from a variety of clinical groups, including persons with mental retardation, learning disability, epilepsy, psychopathy, traumatic brain injury, dementia, and other neurological conditions.

Subsequently, in 1959, Edith Taylor translated the list words into English and developed an administration procedure for use of the AVLT with children (Taylor, 1959). Taylor advocated the use of an interference list, a new list of 15 words that was presented after the fifth study-test trial (often referred to as "List B"). Following the recall of the new (interference) list, the examinee was asked to recall the word list that had been presented five times. Although the addition of the interference list to the standard AVLT procedure is often attributed to Taylor (1959), Rey had reportedly described an AVLT procedure in conjunction with an interference list in a paper he presented at a 1940 conference in Geneva, Switzerland (Boake, 2000). However, in this paper, he did not present the word lists or ascribe a name to his procedure.

Taylor's (1959) translated word lists contained slight differences from the original words. The nature of the translations could account for performance differences between the original and translated lists, particularly with respect to word frequency differences across languages. For example, for List A, moon was substituted for soleil (sun), hat was substituted for casquette (cap), and nose was substituted for moustache (mustache). There were also the following alterations in List B translations: ranger was substituted for berger (shepherd), bird was substituted for moineau (sparrow), towel was substituted for éponge (sponge), cloud was substituted for image (picture), lamb was substituted for mouton (sheep), and gun was substituted for fusil (rifle). It is also important to note that the original French items from each of the three word lists in the Test of Memory for Words were purposely selected to be unrelated, bisyllabic nouns. Each of the items from each of the original French word lists has exactly two syllables. In contrast, the translated English version of the AVLT consists of a varying number of monosyllabic (7 from List A and 10 from List B) and bisyllabic (8 from List A and 5 from List B) items. The effect of this structural difference is largely unknown, although word length is known to affect learning and retention. Slight variations in the word list composition for the English word lists have also been observed over the years across other studies, ranging from substitution of related words to completely new word lists.

Description of procedure

Although over 20 different administration procedures have been described for the AVLT over the years (Schmidt, 1996), Muriel Lezak has perhaps been the most instrumental in introducing a relatively uniform AVLT administration technique to clinical neuropsychology (Lezak, 1976, 1983, 1995). In contrast to the original instructions, her AVLT instructions tend to minimize the amount of feedback and structure provided to the examinee. Lezak's instructions also require the presentation of words at a rate of one per second, which results in a faster presentation rate than that used in the original implementation of this procedure (1-s interval between words). The overall time required to administer the AVLT is approximately 10–15 min. The following procedural description is based on Lezak (1995) and is perhaps the most commonly used approach in clinical neuropsychology.

The AVLT involves five sequential presentations of a 15-word list (List A, Trials 1–5). Each word is presented at the rate of one word per second. Following the first presentation of all 15 words, the examinee is asked to recall verbally as many words as possible. The examiner records the words in the order that they are recalled by the examinee, including intrusion errors (recall of words not on the list) and perseveration errors (repetition of words already recalled without an indication that the examinee may have already recalled them). Subsequent presentations of List A words begin when the examinee is unable to recall any more words. It is important to stress to the examinee that he/she is to recall as many words as possible, including new words not previously recalled as well as words that were recalled on preceding trials. After the fifth attempt to recall List A words, a new 15-word list (List B) is presented to the examinee. The purpose of this list is to produce interference with respect to learning a new list as well as subsequently recalling an old list. After the examinee has recalled as many words as possible from List B (interference list recall trial, or Trial 6), he or she is asked to again recall as many words as possible from List A (postinterference recall trial, or Trial 7).

After approximately 30 min, the examinee is again asked to recall as many words from List A as possible (delayed recall trial). Finally, if the examinee generates only 13 words or less following the delayed recall trial, a recognition trial ensues in which the 15 words from List A are interspersed with List B words and 20 distractor words that were not on either List A or List B. The examinee is asked to indicate whether the word presented was from List A. As noted earlier, there are a number of administration modifications that have been reported for the AVLT, which use various combinations of recognition testing formats, as well as inclusion or exclusion of the interference list or delayed recall (Schmidt, 1996). Normative data can be found in several excellent sources as well (Mitrushina, Boone, & D'Elia, 1998; Schmidt, 1996; Spreen & Strauss, 1998).

A sample form for recording an examinee's responses for the recall trials is presented in Figure 8.1. In order to facilitate the analysis of recall order, it is recommended that the order in which words are recalled be indicated for each trial. By noting the order of word recall in this fashion, recall data can easily

List A (1 Word/Sec)	*1*	*2*	*3*	*4*	*5*	Σ	*List B*	*B*	*List A Recall (6) (Do Not Read)*			*20-min Delay*
Drum							Desk		Drum		Drum	
Curtain							Ranger		Curtain		Curtain	
Bell							Bird		Bell		Bell	
Coffee							Shoe		Coffee		Coffee	
School							Stove		School		School	
Parent							Mountain		Parent		Parent	
Moon							Glasses		Moon		Moon	
Garden							Towel		Garden		Garden	
Hat							Cloud		Hat		Hat	
Farmer							Boat		Farmer		Farmer	
Nose							Lamb		Nose		Nose	
Turkey							Gun		Turkey		Turkey	
Color							Pencil		Color		Color	
House							Church		House		House	
River							Fish		River		River	
							LOT		*Proactive I*		*Retroactive I*	
Scores	*1*	*2*	*3*	*4*	*5*		*Tr5-(5*Tr1)*	*B*	*Tr1/B*	*6*	*Tr6/Tr5*	*Delay*
Correct												
Intrusions												
Perseveration												

Figure 8.1 Rey Auditory Verbal Learning Test: Number words as they are recalled on each trial, add perseverations and intrusions.

be submitted to a computer program for analysis of serial or subjective organization. In addition, intrusion errors (recall of words that were not on a given list) and perseverative errors (recall of words that were previously recalled without an indication that the word had been named previously) should be noted in the spaces below each list of words.

Performance indexes

Rey was predominantly interested in analyzing patterns associated with the memory curve generated across learning trials. From his description of methods of analyzing different learning styles, it is apparent that he was keenly interested in interpreting basic memory processes that could be diagnostic of specific types of memory disorders. However, specific quantitative indexes associated with memory performance had not been developed or normed, and a number of his interpretations were primarily descriptive in nature.

A number of recent investigations have developed and quantified novel performance indexes based on the numeric data that can be generated from the AVLT to evaluate a variety of aspects involved in learning and memory. Given the large number of variations in administration procedures for the AVLT, it is important to keep such variations in mind when interpreting the performance indexes reviewed below. Poreh (2000) presented three paradigms that are associated with the Quantified Process Approach. Of these three approaches, virtually all quantified performance indexes for the AVLT have emerged from the Composition Paradigm, in which novel indexes are created from existing data to evaluate component processes relevant to task performance. Relatively few indexes have emerged from the Decomposition Paradigm, as most indexes of performance for the AVLT do not lend themselves well to factor analytic strategies.

The Satellite Testing Paradigm (discussed in greater detail in Chapter 6, this volume) has yielded significant procedural modifications for the AVLT and has led to the creation of important process descriptors for this task. For example, the addition of the interference list (List B; cf. Taylor, 1959), the delayed recall of List A, the evaluation of temporal order incidental recall (Vakil & Blachstein, 1994), and the various recognition approaches that have been used (substitution of yes–no recognition for recognition of list words embedded within a story), have modified the administration of the task from its original form. Moreover, the process indexes for the AVLT derived from the Satellite Testing Paradigm have illuminated important new dimensions on which to evaluate integrity of memory functioning.

Trial 1—attention

The number of words recalled on the first trial is often believed to reflect simple attention span. In order to facilitate its interpretation, one of the first performance index comparisons emerged from the Satellite Testing

Paradigm. In this approach, the number of words recalled on Trial 1 is compared to an individual's forward digit span in order to determine the extent to which fluctuations in attention may interfere with list recall after the first presentation. Persons who demonstrate much lower performance on Trial 1 of the AVLT relative to forward digit span may be overwhelmed by the presentation of 15 items on the first trial. Such patients may attend better if the number of items presented is titrated gradually to their maximum digit span, as is done when administering the digit span procedure. However, the data regarding the clinical utility of such a measure appear to be mixed.

Mungas (1983) compared the performance of patients from five clinical groups (amnesia, head trauma, schizophrenia, attention deficit disorder, and nonpsychotic psychiatric patients) on a variety of performance indexes from the AVLT. Neither absolute performance on Trial 1 nor the comparison between Trial 1 and forward digit span was effective in differentiating among the groups. However, age appeared to moderate the relationship between Trial 1 recall and forward digit span. Whereas forward digit span is relatively constant across age, the number of words recalled on Trial 1 has been reported to decline with age (Geffen, Moar, O'Hanlon, Clark, & Geffen, 1990). Therefore, the ratio of the number of words recalled on Trial 1 divided by the maximum forward digit span would be expected to > 1 for younger subjects but would be less < 1 for older subjects. However, this performance index has not been normed, and few studies have examined this hypothesis directly.

Lezak (1995) has commented that the immediate forward digit span and the number of words correctly recalled on Trial 1 should typically be within one or two points of each other, although forward digit span might be expected to exceed Trial 1 recall in patients who are susceptible to stimulus overload. When Trial 1 recall exceeds forward digit span, Lezak notes that fluctuations in motivation, inattention, or psychological factors such as anxiety may underlie this pattern. When recall performance on Trial 1 is low (but still within normal limits) relative to the recall performance for List B, Lezak (1995) has suggested this pattern may reflect difficulty with cognitive flexibility and shifting from one task to another. Quantification of these clinical observations would be extremely helpful for generating interpretive guidelines for this performance pattern. The Trial 1 recall to forward digit span ratio and the Trial 1 recall to List B ratio are potentially valuable indexes of attentional deployment processes that could benefit from further research and generation of normative data.

In contrast to the absence of clinical group differences reported by Mungas (1983), the absolute number of words recalled on Trial 1 has been shown to differ significantly between head-injured participants (M = 4.6), learning-disabled participants (M = 5.6), and nondisabled participants (M = 7.4) (O'Donnell, Radtke, Leicht, & Caesar, 1988). Among the learning-disabled participants, there were no differences in the number of recalled words on Trial 1 for learning-disabled participants with or without an elevated Halstead Impairment Index (HII). When persons diagnosed with dementia are compared to age-matched controls, significant group differences favoring controls with respect to the absolute number of words recalled on Trial 1 have been reported (Kraiuhin, Gordon, Stanfield, Meares, & Howson, 1986).

Similar findings were reported when contrasting patients with Alzheimer's disease (AD) with healthy age-matched control participants, and this initial performance difference can potentially lead to a scale-dependent interaction (Loftus, 1978) when comparing the subsequent learning curves for these two groups (Woodard, Dunlosky, & Salthouse, 1999). Healthy control participants have also been shown to demonstrate significantly better performance on Trial 1 than patients diagnosed with either schizophrenia or depression (Moritz, Heeren, Andresen, & Krausz, 2001).

IQ, age, and gender are important moderator variables that should be taken into consideration. IQ has been shown to be significantly related to Trial 1 performance among healthy participants (Geffen et al., 1990). The number of words recalled on Trial 1 declines significantly with increasing age (Mitrushina, Satz, Chervinsky, & D'Elia, 1991). Davis and colleagues (2003) reported similar findings, noting that Trial 1 recall declines with increasing age. Gender is an important moderator variable that should also be considered, as women typically outperform men across every trial of the AVLT. Based on studies reporting Trial 1 recall data for healthy participants, a reasonable expectation for Trial 1 performance is between five and nine words, with persons over 70 years of age performing at a slightly lower level.

Trial 5—best learning

In contrast to Trial 1 performance, recall performance following Trial 5 reflects the examinee's ability to profit from repeated exposure to the list in order to facilitate learning. Mungas (1983) observed dramatic group differences with respect to Trial 5 performance: amnestic patients demonstrated significantly poorer performance than the nonpsychotic psychiatric, attention deficit disorder, schizophrenia, and head trauma groups. In addition, the head trauma group demonstrated poorer performance than the nonpsychotic psychiatric group. There were no significant differences among the schizophrenia, attention deficit disorder, and nonpsychotic psychiatric groups.

The number of words recalled on Trial 5 has also been reported to differ significantly between participants who have sustained a head injury, learning-disabled participants with an elevated HII, learning-disabled participants with a low HII, and nondisabled participants (O'Donnell et al., 1988). Patients diagnosed with schizophrenia have been shown to perform similar to patients diagnosed with depression on Trial 5 recall, although both patient groups have been shown to perform at a lower level than healthy control participants (Moritz et al., 2001). However, in a study comparing individuals who have sustained a mild traumatic brain injury (MTBI) with matched controls, no significant group differences with respect to the number of words recalled on Trial 5 were observed (Guilmette & Rasile, 1995). In this study, significant performance variability was noted within the MTBI group relative to controls. The number of words recalled on Trial 5 has also been reported to be significantly better in age-matched controls than in AD patients (Woodard et al., 1999). Trial 5 performance has also been used as a component of a neuropsychological screening battery designed to detect cognitive impairment (Drebing, van Gorp, Stuck, Mitrushina, & Beck, 1994). Cutoff scores of <10, <8, and <6 words recalled on Trial 5 (corresponding to -1, -2, and -3 *SD* below age-appropriate means) were used. However, Trial 5 recall demonstrated the lowest accuracy of any measure of the battery when cutoff scores of -1 and -2 *SD* were used. Furthermore, when -3 *SD* was used as a cutoff, diagnostic accuracy was only 62%.

The literature indicates that age is also inversely related to the number of words recalled on Trial 5 (Mitrushina et al., 1991). Davis and colleagues (2003) reported similar findings, noting that Trial 5 recall declines with increasing age. Additionally, gender appears to be another important moderator of Trial 5 learning (Drebing et al., 1994), with females tending to outperform males.

Overall learning

Quantified process approaches to characterizing overall learning have largely emerged from the Composition Paradigm, in which relative performance across trials is compared. One of the earliest performance indexes that was developed for the AVLT involves a comparison between the number of words recalled on Trial 5 vs. the number of words recalled on Trial 1 (Query & Berger, 1980). This comparison is used to determine the extent to which the examinee can profit from repeated exposure to the word list. Moritz et al. (2001) reported equivalent performance for healthy controls, patients diagnosed with schizophrenia, and patients diagnosed with depression with respect to the difference between the number of words recalled on Trials 5 and 1. In a study comparing persons who had sustained a traumatic brain injury within 1 year of testing (early recovery group) or longer than 1 year of testing (late recovery group) with age-matched control participants, the ratio of the number of words recalled at Trial 5 to Trial 1 recall did not differ significantly across groups despite significant group differences in the total number of words recalled across all trials (Shum, Harris, & O'Gorman, 2000). Taken together, these findings suggest that comparisons between the number of words recalled at Trials 5 and 1 may have limited diagnostic utility.

In a sample of healthy participants, the difference between the number of words recalled at Trials 5 and Trial 1 demonstrated no significant effects of age or gender, suggesting that the rate of acquisition of words over trials is relatively invariant across age and gender (Geffen et al., 1990). Despite the fact that the number of words recalled at Trials 1 and 5 were shown to be inversely related to age, the overall difference between number of words recalled at Trials 5 and 1 showed no significant differences across four age groups that ranged between 57 and 85 years of age (Mitrushina et al., 1991).

The apparent absence of clinical and demographic differences for comparisons between Trials 5 and 1 suggests that trial-to-trial increases in learning may be relatively invariant across these dimensions.

Because the number of words recalled on Trial 5 may not necessarily exceed the number of words recalled on any other trial, the comparison of the maximum number of words recalled on any of Trials 2–5 vs. the number of words recalled at Trial 1 has also been proposed (Query & Megran, 1983). This second comparison contrasts initial learning with maximum learning capacity and may be helpful in cases where fatigue or lack of cooperation on later trials may be problematic. Unfortunately aside from this initial study, there has been relatively little systematic research into the diagnostic utility of this measure.

Given individual variability in learning performance, other studies have contrasted a pooling of the first two trials with the last two trials to form a learning efficiency index. Learning efficiency (defined here as the difference between the pooled recall for Trials 4 and 5 and the pooled recall for Trials 1 and 2) has been reported to be equivalent between healthy participants in their early 70s and those in their early 80s. However, Alzheimer's patients demonstrated significantly poorer learning efficiency relative to these two healthy aging groups (Antonelli, Capparella, Gemma, Marra, & Carbonin, 1995). Using the same learning efficiency index, Gainotti and Marra (1994) reported similar findings, with age-matched controls performing significantly better than either patients with AD or depressive pseudodementia patients.

Another index that has sometimes been used to quantify overall learning is simply the sum of the number of words correctly recalled from Trials 1–5. Patients with relatively circumscribed and well-defined frontal-lobe lesions have been shown to exhibit diminished recall across all learning trials relative to control participants; this apparently reduced learning capacity in patients with frontal-lobe lesions has been attributed to impaired subjective organization strategies (Eslinger & Grattan, 1994; Janowsky, Shimamura, & Squire, 1989). When patients with dementia are compared to age-matched controls, clear differences favoring controls with respect to the total number of words recalled across all trials are observed (Kraiuhin et al., 1986). In this study, female patients performed better than male patients, and female controls performed better than male controls, again demonstrating that gender is an important moderator variable. Significant differences have also been reported with respect to total number of words recalled between age-matched controls, depressive pseudodementia patients, and AD patients (Gainotti & Marra, 1994) and when contrasting AD patients with age-matched controls (Woodard et al., 1999).

Another study noted that among younger individuals, 90% of a sample of nondisabled young adults demonstrated total recall scores greater than or equal to 49, whereas 95% of the head-injured participants showed total recall scores less than or equal to 48 (O'Donnell et al., 1988). O'Donnell et al. also noted that 50% of the learning-disabled participants with a high HII and 65%

of those with a low HII demonstrated total recall scores greater than 48. However, these authors cautioned that group differences in Full Scale IQ were confounded with total recall scores, raising some degree of ambiguity with respect to these findings. In another study comparing head-injured patients with age-matched controls, the patients demonstrated a significantly lower number of words recalled across all trials relative to control participants, although there were no significant differences in performance between patients who had been injured within 1 year vs. more than 1 year prior to testing (Shum et al., 2000). An earlier study noted similar findings, with MTBI patients demonstrating a lower total number of words recalled across all trials relative to control participants (Guilmette & Rasile, 1995).

Among healthy participants, the total number of words recalled decreased with increasing age (Geffen et al., 1990), as persons over 70 years of age recalled at least 10 fewer words than participants aged between 16 and 59 years. Persons between the ages of 16 and 69 recalled at least eight fewer words than participants under 40 years of age. Another study of memory functioning in 161 healthy older participants between the ages of 62 and 100 years demonstrated that the total number of words recalled across all trials of the AVLT decreased significantly with age and was also positively related to education (Petersen, Smith, Kokmen, Ivnik, & Tangalos, 1992). Using a novel alternative form of the AVLT, it has been suggested that the sum of the number of words correctly recalled from Trials 1–5 shows the best test–retest reliability of any of the AVLT scores ($r = 0.77$; Geffen, Butterworth, & Geffen, 1994).

A final strategy for quantifying the overall ability to profit from repeated presentations of the word list has emerged from the Mayo Older American Normative Studies (MOANS) group (Ivnik et al., 1992a, 1992b; Ivnik, Malec, Tangalos, Petersen, Kokmen, & Kurland, 1990; Smith, Ivnik, Malec, Kokmen, Tangalos, & Kurland, 1992; Smith, Ivnik, Malec, & Tangalos, 1993). This index, referred to as Learning Over Trials (LOT), is computed by taking the sum of correctly recalled words across Trials 1–5 and subtracting five times the number of words recalled on Trial 1 (LOT = [sum of Trials 1–5] − 5*[sum of Trial 1]). This measure was proposed to reflect verbal learning efficiency. In conjunction with other measures of immediate learning from the Wechsler Memory Scale-Revised (WMS-R), LOT is used in the computation of the Learning factor score for the Mayo Cognitive Factor Scales (Smith, Ivnik, Malec, Petersen, Kokmen, & Tangalos, 1994). LOT has been shown to differentiate among patients with different degrees of dementia (Tierney, Nores, Snow, Fisher, Zorzitto, & Reid, 1994). Healthy control participants demonstrate the greatest LOT, followed by patients with moderate AD and Parkinson's dementia. Inpatients with severe AD demonstrated the lowest LOT.

Delayed recall

As noted earlier, all of the delayed recall performance indexes can be considered to have emerged from the Satellite Testing Paradigm, as Rey's original procedure did not involve a delayed recall period. Two measures are commonly used to assess delayed recall performance: (1) the absolute number of words recalled on the delayed recall trial; and (2) the relative number or proportion of words recalled on the delayed recall trial compared with the number of words recalled on Trial 5 or on the postinterference recall trial. Because the delayed recall period often varies across normative studies, it is important to use the exact delay interval specified when comparing an examinee's performance with a normative database. In addition, a number of studies in the literature have not given the interference trial. The absence of the interference trial (List B or Trial 6) and the postinterference List A recall trial (Trial 7) may lead to a higher savings score, decreased forgetting, or greater absolute number of words recalled during the delayed recall trial relative to studies that did include these additional recall trials.

In a group of healthy adults, Geffen et al. (1990) reported no significant differences between the number of words recalled on the delayed recall trial and the number of words recalled on the postinterference recall trial (Trial 7), suggesting no evidence of forgetting over a 20-min period. In addition, there was no differential influence of age or gender on the number of words recalled at each of these two trials; however, females and younger participants demonstrated better overall performance relative to males and older participants (Geffen et al., 1990). When contrasting healthy controls with AD patients, the presence of floor effects for AD patients on delayed recall trials may impact the results and subsequent interpretation (Woodard et al., 1999).

Vakil and Agmon-Ashkenazi (1997) reported similar findings when comparing the delayed recall trial with Trial 5. Older participants recalled fewer words overall than younger participants. However, a significant age by trial interaction was observed, reflecting a somewhat steeper forgetting rate for the older group relative to the younger group (Vakil & Agmon-Ashkenazi, 1997).

With respect to the absolute number of words recalled after 30 min, there were no significant differences between MTBI patients and controls, although somewhat more variability in performance was noted for the MTBI patients (Guilmette & Rasile, 1995). However, a significant difference was observed when the raw scores were converted into standard scores using age-corrected normative data published by Geffen et al. (1990). Therefore, age appears to influence absolute number of words recalled on the delayed recall trials. Gainotti and Marra (1994) reported absolute recall scores after 15 min of 7.68, 4.57, and 2.38 in healthy controls, depressive pseudodementia patients, and AD patients, respectively; these group differences are all significant.

Mungas (1983) reported that the proportion of words recalled on Trial 5 but not recalled on the delayed recall trial demonstrated a relationship with the degree of learning deficit. That is, patients with schizophrenia, attention-deficit disorder, and nonpsychotic psychiatric diagnoses demonstrated relatively little change between Trial 5 and the delayed recall trial. However, patients in the amnestic and head trauma groups recalled fewer words during the delayed recall trial relative to the number of words recalled on Trial 5.

When Trial 5 recall is compared to List A recall after a 15-min delay, patients with AD show a substantial degree of forgetting. Antonelli et al. (1995) reported that AD patients forgot over 71% of initially learned words after 15 min compared to forgetting rates of 26% and 42% for persons in their early 70s and early 80s, respectively. Similar findings were reported by Woodard et al. (1999) in which healthy controls with a mean age of 71.2 years demonstrated a savings score of 0.74, whereas AD patients had a savings score of 0.12. The absolute scores for the delayed recall trial parallel these forgetting rates: AD patients obtained a delayed recall score of 2.0 compared to delayed recall scores of 6.3 and 4.8 for examinees in their early 70s and early 80s, respectively. This study suggests that delayed recall declines with healthy aging, although the degree of delayed recall impairment seen in AD is substantially greater than would be expected due to age. In fact, the absolute number of words recalled after 30 min has been shown to be predictive (in combination with the Mental Control subtest from the Wechsler Memory Scale) of those individuals who would go on to develop AD among 123 initially nondemented memory-impaired patients (Tierney et al., 1996). Estevez-Gonzalez, Kulisevsky, Boltes, Otermin, and Garcia-Sanchez (2003) reported similar findings in 116 unselected patients with subjective memory complaints. Over a 2-year period, patients who demonstrated a score of zero on the delayed recall trial or who showed a 75% or greater "forgetting" rate (difference between Trial 5 recall and delayed recall trial, without presentation of the interference list or postinterference recall trial) tended to go on to develop AD (Estevez-Gonzalez et al., 2003).

The absolute number of words recalled on the delayed recall trial has been shown to be diminished in patients with schizophrenia and depression relative to healthy control participants (Moritz et al., 2001). Significant forgetting rates have also been reported in depressive pseudodementia patients relative to age-matched controls, although these patients show better savings than AD patients (Gainotti & Marra, 1994). When the absolute difference between the number of words recalled on the delayed recall trial and the number of words recalled on Trial 5 is used to quantify delayed recall ability, this difference was shown to increase ($p < 0.06$) with age, but was unrelated to education (Petersen et al., 1992).

A related approach to evaluating the ability to retain information over time was proposed by Ivnik and coworkers and was referred to as Long Term Percent Retention (LTPR; Ivnik et al., 1990). Expressed as a percentage, this measure is computed by taking the number of words recalled on the delayed recall trial divided by the number of words recalled on Trial 5 (LTPR = 100 × [Sum Delayed Recall]/Sum Trial 5). This percentage reflects the proportion of words retained across the delay period relative to the number of words learned following five repetitions of the word list. This measure has been proposed to reflect forgetting of previously learned information. However, this index can also be potentially misleading. For example, if only four words were learned across the five learning trials, and the same four words were recalled after the delay, the LTPR would be 100%. However, in an absolute sense, the overall level of performance reflects significantly impaired memory functioning. Therefore, it is important to consider both the absolute number of words recalled after the delay in conjunction with the LTPR measure. Nevertheless, LTPR has been shown to be sensitive to mild memory dysfunction as often seen with mild cognitive impairment (Woodard, Dorsett, Hermann, Cooper, & Sager, 2005). In addition, LTPR loads on a "retention" factor together with percent retention scores from the WMS-R in the MOANS standardization sample (Smith et al., 1992) and in a clinical sample (Smith et al., 1993) as evaluated with confirmatory factor analysis. In conjunction with percent retention measures from Logical Memory and Visual Reproduction from the WMS-R, LTPR is used in the computation of the Retention factor score for the Mayo Cognitive Factor Scales (Smith et al., 1994).

In order to investigate delayed recall independently of the effects of interference, some studies have compared the number of words recalled after the delay with the number of words recalled during the postinterference recall trial. No differences were observed between controls and head injury patients who were tested within 1 year (early recovery) or more than 1 year (late recovery) following their injury with respect to the ratio of words recalled on the delayed recall trial to the number of words recalled during the postinterference recall (Shum et al., 2000).

Temporal order

Vakil and Blachstein (1994) proposed an additional measure to assess incidental learning of temporal order in the AVLT. The authors used a Hebrew version of the AVLT in conjunction with a procedure similar to that described above. Following a delayed recognition trial that utilized a combination of the 15 words from List A, the 15 words from List B, and 20 words that were not previously presented, Vakil and Blachstein presented the List A words only in a different order than their original presentation. Examinees were asked to place the words from this list in their correct order of presentation. Based on responses from 190 participants without prior neurologic or psychiatric history, three measures of temporal order retrieval were proposed. The first measure simply reflected the number of words placed in their correct original positions (Hits). The second measure correlated the original order of words with the examinee's listed order (Correlation). The third measure summed the absolute deviation of each word listed by the subject from its original position (Absolute Deviation). Females tended to score better than males with respect to temporal order, and younger subjects tended to score better than older subjects with respect to these measures. Weak-to-modest correlations were observed between the measure of temporal order and other AVLT performance indexes (sum of words recalled on Trial 1, sum of words recalled across Trials 1–5, sum of words recalled on the delayed recall trial, sum of correct recognitions, and retroactive interference). No significant correlations were observed with respect to sum of words recalled on Trial 5 minus sum of words recalled on Trial 1 (Learning Increment), or proactive interference. The authors suggested that because of the weak correlations, the measure of temporal order may reflect a unique source of variance.

Primacy/recency

The order in which words are recalled on each trial may often reflect primacy and recency effects. Indexes reflecting primacy and recency effects have largely emerged from the Composition Paradigm. The latest and earliest presented words are typically recalled more frequently and consistently than words presented in the middle of the list. By attending to patterns of word recall from the early, middle, and later portions of the word list, clues regarding various types of memory pathology may be provided. In general, patients with encoding deficits and susceptibility to interference effects typically recall only those words from the latter portion of the list, whereas persons who are susceptible to stimulus overload may recall words predominately from the early portion of the word list. It is unusual to observe a greater proportion of words recalled from the middle portion of the word list relative to the early and later portions.

Mungas (1983) reported that the primacy effect was attenuated in amnesic patients, but their recency effect was unchanged relative to other diagnostic groups. Head trauma patients demonstrated less impairment than amnestic patients with respect to the primacy effect, while their recency effect was again unchanged. Mungas interpreted this impaired primacy effect in amnestic patients and head trauma patients as reflecting their increased susceptibility to interference.

O'Donnell et al. (1988) divided the 15 words from the word list into five blocks of three adjacent words and examined serial position effects on Trial 1 in a sample of learning-disabled, head-injured, and nondisabled participants. Overall, nondisabled participants demonstrated greater recall than learning-disabled and head-injured participants at each serial position block except for the fifth block (i.e., serial positions 13–15). There were no group differences with respect to the recency serial position component.

Among healthy participants between the ages of 16 and 86, primacy and recency serial position effects have been demonstrated, with younger participants and females tending to recall more words at any given serial position (Geffen et al., 1990). In a sample of older participants between the ages of 57 and 85, similar primacy and recency serial position effects were demonstrated, with younger participants again tending to recall more words at any given serial position than older participants (Mitrushina et al., 1991).

Comparison between primacy and recency effects for a group of AD patients, a group of participants in their early 70s, and a group of participants in their early 80s revealed the presence of a primacy and recency effect for both healthy groups, although the older participants demonstrated a slightly attenuated primacy effect, and the AD group demonstrated a substantially attenuated primacy effect (Antonelli et al., 1995). In the same study, all 3 groups demonstrated evidence of a recency effect. In addition, recall of words from the middle part of the list across the five trials was significantly diminished in the AD group compared to either of the two healthy older control groups.

Tierney et al. (1994) reported that patients with moderate and severe AD showed a greater recency effect than primacy effect, whereas controls and patients with Parkinson's disease demonstrated a similar proportion of words recalled in the primacy and recency portions of the serial position curve. Gainotti and Marra (1994) reported a markedly diminished primacy effect in AD patients compared to either age-matched controls or depressive pseudodementia patients. Two-thirds of their AD patients demonstrated a "Recency minus Primacy" score greater than three, compared to mean scores of −0.28 and 0.57 for the controls and depressive pseudodementia patients, respectively. Woodard et al. (1999) defined the primacy segment as serial positions 1–3, the middle segment or asymptote as serial positions 5–11, and the recency segment as serial positions 13–15. Averaged across trials, AD patients showed a smaller difference in proportion of words recalled between the asymptote and primacy segments relative to age-matched controls. The age-matched controls demonstrated a prototypic primacy and recency effect relative to asymptote, whereas the AD patients demonstrated a relatively large recency effect, while the proportion of words recalled from the primacy and asymptote segments was much smaller than the proportion of words recalled from the recency segment.

Patients with anterior communicating artery aneurysms demonstrated primacy and recency serial position effects, although these effects were at a lower level relative to controls (Stefanova, Kostic, Ziropadja, Markovic, & Ocic, 2002). These preserved primacy and recency effects were noteworthy given that the patients demonstrated significant memory impairment and executive functioning deficits. Persons who sustained either focal frontal or focal nonfrontal brain lesions both demonstrated preserved serial position effects during single trial learning (Trial 1; Eslinger & Grattan, 1994). However, on subsequent trials where the word list order was the same on every trial, persons with frontal-lobe lesions demonstrated no significant differences in the number of words recalled from the initial, middle, and final portions of the list, whereas persons with nonfrontal lesions demonstrated significantly better recall of words from the initial and final portions of the list relative to the middle portion of the list.

The preceding studies have identified the utility of evaluation of primacy and recency effects for characterizing differences between a variety of diagnostic groups. However, one study reported no significant differences in primacy or recency effects between patients with anterior brain damage, posterior brain damage, and psychiatric inpatients with no known brain lesion (Crockett, Hadjistavropoulos, & Hurwitz, 1992). It is possible that heterogeneity in the nature and location of brain injury may have obscured possible group differences in this study.

Gained access and lost access

Component analyses of multi-trial list learning tasks have demonstrated gains of new words across adjacent trials as well as the omission of previously recalled words on subsequent trials (Tulving, 1964). Examination of the number of new words recalled on a given trial that were not recalled on the immediately preceding trial reflects gained access. Gained access reflects the ability to profit from repeated presentations of the word list and is an important aspect of the learning curve. The number of words recalled on a given trial that were not recalled on the immediately succeeding trial reflects lost access or intertrial forgetting, and reflects another aspect of the learning curve. Blachstein, Vakil, and Hoofien (1993) first used the concepts of gained and lost access to analyze differences in the acquisition process in persons with closed head injury relative to healthy controls. Healthy controls demonstrated a greater number of words recalled across Trials 1–5, together with a steeper learning curve relative to closed head injury patients. Examination of gained and lost access revealed that the controls' better performance could be accounted for by significantly greater gained access and significantly less lost access from trial to trial relative to the closed head injury group (Blachstein et al., 1993).

Dunlosky and Salthouse (1996) investigated gained and lost access across the age span. Relative to younger participants, these authors found that there were no significant differences between older and younger participants with respect to lost access. However, older participants demonstrated significantly less gained access than younger participants. These findings suggest that age-related declines in trial-to-trial acquisition may affect list learning more than trial-to-trial forgetting over the age span (Dunlosky & Salthouse, 1996). Woodard, Dunlosky, and Salthouse (1996) compared gained and lost access components in AD patients and in a group of healthy controls, matched on age, education, and gender. The component analyses revealed significantly decreased gained access and significantly greater lost access from trial to trial in the AD patients relative to matched controls (Woodard et al., 1999). These two performance indexes appear to reflect intertrial acquisition and forgetting, respectively. Woodard et al. reported that the memory deficit in AD is associated with impairment in both of these domains. More importantly, Woodard et al. noted that gained access and lost access were uncorrelated, suggesting that these two performance indexes are independent and separable. The concept of gained and lost access was investigated more recently (Moulin, James, Freeman, & Jones, 2004), and the results of Woodard et al. (1999) were replicated in a larger sample of AD, Mild Cognitive Impairment (MCI), and healthy elderly participants using the CERAD Word List Learning measure. Finally, Davis et al. (2003) investigated gained and lost access scores in four age groups, using healthy participants. Increasing age was associated with increases in lost access. In contrast to the findings presented by Dunlosky and Salthouse (1996), gained access was observed to be the greatest between Trials 1 and 2, whereas Dunlosky and Salthouse (1996) demonstrated the lowest gained access between Trials 1 and 2. Nevertheless, age differences were minimal for measures of gained access. It should be noted, however, that there were some methodological differences in the two studies. Davis et al.'s (2003) study presented words at the rate of one word every 2 s, and they presented the words in a different order on each trial while Dunlosky and Salthouse (1996) presented words at the rate of one word each second, and the words did not differ in order across trials.

Another index that is closely related to the concept of gained and lost access has been proposed by Woodard, Dorsett, Hermann, and Sager (2005). This index investigates trial-to-trial performance increases. This "learning increment" is computed for each adjacent trial and simply identifies the percent increase in recall on one trial relative to the immediately preceding trial. For example, when comparing the number of words recalled for Trials 1 and 2, the learning increment would be computed as follows: (Trial 2 recall – Trial 1 recall)/Trial 1 recall. Therefore, this index reflects the percent increase in recall on Trial $n + 1$ relative to recall on Trial n.

Table 8.2 Trial-to-trial learning increments within five age decades

		Mean proportion increase in words recalled between adjacent trials			
Age (years)		*t12*	*t23*	*t34*	*t45*
40–49	*M*	0.54	0.20	0.10	0.05
	SD	0.37	0.21	0.15	0.11
	N	103	103	103	103
50–59	*M*	0.54	0.22	0.09	0.07
	SD	0.42	0.19	0.14	0.12
	N	188	188	188	188
60–69	*M*	0.50	0.24	0.12	0.07
	SD	0.39	0.24	0.19	0.15
	N	95	95	95	95
70–79	*M*	0.46	0.22	0.14	0.06
	SD	0.42	0.24	0.19	0.15
	N	86	86	86	86
80–89	*M*	0.46	0.21	0.15	0.06
	SD	0.33	0.24	0.22	0.15
	N	40	40	40	40
Total	*M*	0.51	0.22	0.11	0.06
	SD	0.40	0.22	0.17	0.13
	N	512	512	512	512

Note: $t_{n,\,n+1}$, percent increase in recall for Trial $n+1$ relative to Trial n.

When simple trial-to-trial percent increases are examined, the expected increases in recall performance due to repeated presentations are remarkably stable across age groups (Woodard et al., 2005). A total of 512 healthy individuals between the ages of 40 and 89 were administered the AVLT as part of a larger neuropsychological battery. Table 8.2 demonstrates the percent increases from trial to trial across five age decades. As can be seen in the table, there are no significant age group differences for any of the learning increment indexes across the age span. Results of a mixed design analysis of variance revealed no significant age or age by trial effects. Clearly, the biggest percent gain occurs between Trials 1 and 2, regardless of age. There were also no significant effects of gender. However, the absolute number of words recalled was significantly different, particularly for the oldest group studied. We hypothesize that failure to show such an increment may be associated with fluctuations in attention and concentration. Moreover, relatively small learning increments may be another way to document acquisition impairment.

Table 8.3 demonstrates the correlation between learning increment between adjacent trials and other performance indexes from the AVLT. The learning increment between Trials 1 and 2 was significantly positively associated with the sum of words recalled across Trials 1–5, LOT, and delayed recall raw score, suggesting that the ability to profit from a second repetition of the word list is an important determinant of overall acquisition and retention performance. In addition, greater learning increments on later trials (particularly between

Table 8.3 Correlations between trial-to-trial learning increments and recall performance indexes

		Correlations		
		Pearson correlation	*Sig(2-tailed)*	*N*
Sum of Trials (1–5)	*t*12	0.094	0.027	551
	*t*23	−0.068	0.112	551
	*t*34	−0.264	0.000	551
	*t*45	−0.177	0.000	551
LOT	*t*12	0.768	0.000	551
	*t*23	0.120	0.005	551
	*t*34	−0.111	0.009	551
	*t*45	−0.068	0.113	551
Delayed	*t*12	0.159	0.000	551
	*t*23	0.038	0.371	551
	*t*34	−0.186	0.000	551
	*t*45	−0.083	0.051	551

Note: $t_{n, n+1}$, percent increase in recall for Trial $n+1$ relative to Trial n; LOT, learning over trials.

Trials 3 and 4) become significantly negatively associated with acquisition and retention performance. That is, persons who demonstrate greater trial-to-trial gains on later trials may be manifesting greater acquisition difficulty, which in turn may affect their retention ability.

Gainotti and Marra (1994) compared trial-to-trial learning effects in healthy controls, depressive pseudodementia patients, and AD patients using absolute number of words recalled. Significant increments in absolute number of words recalled were observed between every adjacent trial for healthy controls. However, depressive pseudodementia patients demonstrated significant increases only between Trials 1–2 and Trials 2–3, whereas AD patients showed significant learning only between Trials 1 and 2. Given these findings, trial-to-trial learning increments may be of potential diagnostic utility. Future research investigating the reliability, validity, and clinical utility of the learning increment from trial to trial is encouraged.

Subjective organization

The tendency for individuals to impose greater organization of word lists across successive study-test trials was first described by Tulving and was referred to as subjective organization (Tulving, 1962). In healthy young adults, increasing subjective organization has been shown to be associated with better recall (Tulving & Donaldson, 1972). A variety of indexes of subjective organization have been proposed (Sternberg & Tulving, 1977; Woodard, 1991). Essentially, these indexes quantify the number of word pairs or the number of "tuples" or word groupings of a particular size (irrespective of order) that are recalled across adjacent trials.

The application of subjective organization scoring indexes to the AVLT emerged from the *Composition Paradigm*. For example, Mungas (1983) initially observed that nonpsychotic psychiatric patients showed increases in sequential organization across trials, whereas four other clinical groups (amnesia, head trauma, schizophrenia, and attention deficit disorder) demonstrated either no improvement or a decrease in sequential organization across trials. Measures of subjective organization may have potential clinical utility given that they have been shown to be related to recall proficiency in unimpaired participants (Pellegrino & Battig, 1972, 1974).

Age-related subjective organization differences have not been well investigated using the AVLT. One study developed a 30-item list that was presented over six trials, and measures of free recall and subjective organization were computed (Witte, Freund, & Sebby, 1990). Younger adults demonstrated greater subjective organization and free recall relative to older adults. Similar findings have been reported by Hultsch (1974), but other studies have failed to find evidence of age-related differences in subjective organization (Jackson & Schneider, 1982; Laurence, 1966).

Davis et al. (2003) investigated age-related differences in subjective organization across the five learning trials of the AVLT. They specifically examined the unidirectional subjective organization (SO) index that is computed across all trials as well as the bidirectional intertrial repetition or paired frequency (PF) index that is computed across each adjacent pair of trials (Sternberg & Tulving, 1977). Age was moderately negatively correlated with SO ($r = -0.28$). Modest correlations between number of words recalled and SO were reported for each of the four age groups studied ($r = 0.22$ to 0.51). In addition, participants in the youngest age group (30–45 years) exhibited the largest degree of SO; SO scores for this group were significantly greater than both the 61–75- and 76–90-year age groups. For the PF index, later trials demonstrated significant age-related correlations: Trials 3–4 ($r = -0.43$) and Trials 4–5 ($r = -0.38$). Therefore, it appears that SO tends to build with increasing repetitions of the list. Davis and colleagues also noted that young adults between ages 30 and 45 years demonstrated greater PF than adults who were 46 through 90 years of age. PF demonstrated somewhat stronger correlations with number of words recalled for each of the four age groups ($r = 0.22$ to 0.51). However, in interpreting these findings, it is important to note that the AVLT procedure in this study was markedly different from most other implementations of the AVLT. For example, words were presented at the rate of one word per 2 s, the list order was different for every presentation trial, the interference list was given at the very end of the procedure (following delayed recognition testing), delayed recall testing was performed at either 20 min or one day following the five learning trials, and delayed recognition testing using a 30-word list (15 targets and 15 distractors of unknown origin) followed the delayed recall testing.

O'Donnell et al. (1988) used the Pair Frequency Index (Sternberg & Tulving, 1977) to compare SO in a sample of nondisabled, learning-disabled, and head-injured participants. Across the immediate learning trials, the nondisabled participants demonstrated significantly greater SO than learning-disabled or head-injured participants. In each of the groups, a gradual increase in SO was seen across adjacent trials. However, there was no significant group by trial interaction. Subjective organization was also compared across Trial 5 and the postinterference recall trial. This comparison was expected to illustrate the maintenance of SO in memory following interference. Learning-disabled participants with an elevated HII and head-injured participants showed a significant decline in SO following interference relative to nondisabled participants and learning-disabled participants with a low HII.

Several research studies have investigated the influence of frontal-lobe lesions on the ability to implement SO strategies (Eslinger & Grattan, 1994; Gershberg & Shimamura, 1995; Janowsky et al., 1989) on the California Verbal Learning Test (CVLT; Alexander, Stuss, & Fansabedian, 2003). Because the AVLT consists of unrelated word lists, the demand for imposing an organizational strategy on the list to facilitate its recall is greater than for the CVLT, which contains words from each of four semantic categories. In general, these studies have pointed to a fairly consistent deficit in the use of subjective organization strategies by patients with frontal-lobe lesions.

Dorsolateral frontal lesions have been reported to compromise SO more than orbital frontal and nonfrontal lesions (Eslinger & Grattan, 1994).

Given the relative lack of information on SO for the AVLT across the age span, future research focusing on evaluating potential age and diagnostic differences in SO would be beneficial.

Susceptibility to proactive and retroactive interference

Proactive inhibition

A tendency for earlier learning to interfere with later learning is referred to as proactive inhibition. As noted earlier, the ability to evaluate proactive inhibition with the AVLT emerged from the Satellite Testing Paradigm, as an interference list (List B) was not part of the original AVLT. The susceptibility to proactive inhibition can be measured on the AVLT by comparing the number of words recalled on Trial 1 and the number words recalled from the interference list. Proactive inhibition would be demonstrated if the number of words recalled on Trial 1 was greater than the recall performance for the interference list (List B) by two or three words (Lezak, 1995). In pronounced cases, List A words may be generated during the attempt to recall List B words. In a sample of healthy participants, one study reported that approximately one more word was recalled on Trial 1 than on the interference trial, but this modest interference effect was not moderated by gender or age (Geffen et al., 1990). Main effects of gender and age, with performance favoring females and younger participants, were observed, however. In contrast, Woodard and colleagues (2005) have observed that women over the age of 65 demonstrate susceptibility to proactive interference relative to men. Women showed a one-word decrement between Trial 1 and List B, whereas men demonstrated virtually no difference between number of words recalled on either list. Patients with Parkinson's disease have been shown to exhibit greater susceptibility to proactive interference than patients with AD (Tierney et al., 1994). In another study, while the absolute number of words recalled following presentation of List B is diminished in patients with schizophrenia and depression relative to healthy controls, there were no significant group differences with respect to the proactive inhibition measure (Moritz et al., 2001). Similar findings have been reported when contrasting schizophrenic patients with healthy controls (Torres, Flashman, O'Leary, & Andreasen, 2001), with no significant group differences observed with respect to susceptibility to proactive interference.

Retroactive interference

The AVLT measure of retroactive interference emerges from the Satellite Testing Paradigm, because its computation requires the administration of the interference list (List B), which was not a component of the original AVLT. Retroactive interference reflects the tendency for later learning to interfere with recall of information learned earlier. This interference effect can be evaluated with the AVLT by comparing the number of words recalled on Trial 5 with the number of List A words recalled on the postinterference recall trial. Evidence of retroactive interference would be demonstrated if the number of original list words recalled following the presentation of the interference list was less than the number of words recalled on Trial 5. Among healthy participants, an average of one more word was recalled on Trial 5 than on the postinterference trial, and again, this modest interference effect was not moderated by gender or age (Geffen et al., 1990). Main effects of gender and age, with performance favoring females and younger participants, were again observed. Moritz et al. (2001) reported that controls outperformed patients with schizophrenia and depression with respect to the absolute number of words recalled during the postinterference recall trial. However, there were no significant group differences with respect to the retroactive interference measure. In contrast, Torres et al. (2001) reported that schizophrenic participants demonstrated increased susceptibility to retroactive interference but not to proactive interference relative to control participants. They noted that male patients in their sample clearly demonstrated increased susceptibility to retroactive interference, while female patients demonstrated somewhat more variable and less pronounced susceptibility to retroactive interference. In addition, Torres et al. (2001) reported that retroactive interference, but not proactive interference, was related to measures of executive functioning; therefore, schizophrenic participants who were deficient on measures of executive functioning would be expected to demonstrate greater susceptibility to retroactive interference but not proactive interference. Guilmette and Rasile (1995) reported no significant differences between MTBI patients and controls with respect to the absolute number of words recalled during the postinterference recall trial. However, when these raw scores were converted into age-corrected standard scores using normative data published by Geffen et al. (1990), significant group differences emerged. In contrast, Shum et al. (2000) reported that the ratio of words recalled on the postinterference recall trial to the number of words recalled on Trial 5 was significantly lower in head-injury patients who sustained their injury within 1 year of testing relative to control participants (early recovery). However, patients who sustained their injury more than 1 year prior to testing did not differ from control participants or the early recovery group on this index. It is possible that this index may be a better marker of acute memory deficits in persons who have sustained traumatic brain injury.

Recognition testing

In its original format, the AVLT used a short story containing the words on the list that was read aloud to the examinee. Whenever the examinee recognized a word from the list, he or she was directed to make a verbal indication. Several other recognition formats have emerged from the Satellite Testing

Approach since the original description of the AVLT, including the presentation of a written story, requiring the examinee to circle words from the list, as well as yes–no recognition in which the examinee is asked to indicate whether or not a word presented from a 30-, 45-, or 50-item list was from the original 15-word list. Typically, delayed recognition performance is much better than delayed recall performance.

In a sample of healthy adults (Geffen et al., 1990), when the number of words recalled after a 20-min delay was compared to delayed recognition performance (retrieval efficiency), the recall-recognition disparity was greater for males than for females, given the females' better recall performance overall. The recall-recognition disparity also appears to be greater for older participants than for younger participants, suggesting decreased retrieval efficiency with increasing age.

Among another group of healthy older adults, neither the number of words correctly recognized nor the number of false positives differed across age groups (Mitrushina et al., 1991). It is possible that the use of a restricted range of ages in this study may have attenuated the ability to identify significant age-related differences in recognition performance.

A number of prior studies have reported that patients with AD exhibit a tendency to commit numerous false-positive errors during recognition testing. These types of recognition errors have been reported to be rare for healthy controls or depressive pseudodementia patients, but they are frequent in AD patients (Gainotti & Marra, 1994).

The discriminability index, computed by summing the number of true positives and false positives and dividing by the total number of targets and distractors has been shown to differentiate between patients with Parkinson's disease and AD. Patients with Parkinson's disease have shown a greater discriminability index relative to patients with AD (Tierney et al., 1994). The Controlled Oral Word Association Test and an AVLT recognition measure (the percent of true positives and negatives recognized on a 30-item list) were reported to be the best measures from a larger neuropsychological battery for differentiating probable AD patients from patients with probable subcortical ischemic vascular dementia (Tierney et al., 2001).

Normative data

Given the relatively widespread clinical use of the AVLT, it is somewhat surprising that a consensually adopted normative database has not gained acceptance in the clinical community. Perhaps one of the earliest attempts at developing a framework within which to interpret AVLT performance scores was put forth by Query and Berger (1980) who administered the AVLT to 232 hospital patients who varied on age and diagnosis. Patients with acute brain syndrome and chronic brain syndrome were contrasted with nonbrain-injured hospital patients. The authors reported that irrespective of diagnosis, increasing age was associated with poorer learning (defined as the difference between the best recall performance on Trials 2–5 and Trial 1), and on the recognition trial. Recognition performance was also positively associated with IQ and education. Delayed recall was not influenced by age, education, or IQ.

Query and Megran (1983) subsequently published normative data for the AVLT using a sample of 677 male inpatients in a general hospital setting who ranged in age from 19 to 81. None of the patients was diagnosed as psychotic, brain injured, or suffering from Major Depression. A clear age-related decline in recall of words from Trial 1, Trial 5, recognition, and learning (defined as the difference between the best recall performance on Trials 2–5 and Trial 1) was evident. Recognition and learning performance were positively related with IQ. Age was observed to affect delayed recall much more than learning ability.

Until the late 1980s, the only normative data that existed for the AVLT were derived from male VA patients. The effect of gender and healthy cognitive status on AVLT performance was largely untested. Bleecker, Bolla-Wilson, Agnew, and Meyers (1988) studied 196 healthy men and women aged between 40 and 89 years. Performance by decade and gender was reported for Trials 1–5 and for the recognition trial. Using a regression analysis, this group demonstrated that age and gender accounted for a significant proportion of variance on each recall trial. Recognition performance was not affected by age, gender, or vocabulary score. No significant gender differences were observed for Trial 1. In general, men tended to have lower scores overall relative to women (Bleecker et al., 1988), a finding that has emerged from virtually every study of the AVLT that has examined gender differences.

Wiens, McMinn, and Crossen (1988) presented another attempt to develop a large-scale comprehensive set of normative data for the AVLT. Participants included 222 job applicants who were administered the Wechsler Adult Intelligence Scale-Revised (WAIS-R), the Rey–Osterrieth Complex Figure Test, the State-Trait Anxiety Inventory, and a modification of the Stroop Color Naming Test, in addition to the AVLT. The participants were applicants for civil-service positions and ranged in age from 20 to 49. However, there were relatively few women in the sample as a whole (13%). Normative data for the AVLT were presented according to WAIS-R Full Scale IQ, age, and education (Wiens et al., 1988). Age showed a significant negative correlation with the difference between the number of words recalled on Trials 5 and 1, as well as the number of words recalled on Trials 3 and 5. Number of years of education was positively related to the number of words recalled only on Trials 4 and 5. WAIS-R Full Scale IQ was significantly positively related to number of words recalled across each of the learning trials, as well as the difference in the number of words recalled on Trials 5 and 1. WAIS-R Full Scale IQ was unrelated to recognition performance. State and trait anxiety, as measured by the State-Trait Anxiety Inventory, were both unrelated to recall or recognition performance.

Up until this point, relatively little normative data had been developed for a broad range of ages, and performance differences between men and women had not been examined separately. Geffen et al. (1990) developed normative data for the AVLT for 153 adults (51% female) between the ages of 16 and 86. These data were grouped by gender and age. Across the learning trials, females tended to recall more words than males, and younger participants tended to recall more words than older participants. In addition, a variety of performance index measures and ratios were compared for men and women over a large age span, and this study provided a great deal of information regarding the nature of age-related changes in word list memory performance.

At approximately the same time that the Geffen et al.'s (1990) normative data were published, a significant initiative was underway to provide adequate normative data for persons who were 55 years of age or older for the AVLT (Ivnik et al., 1990). This large-scale study provided a complement to the Wiens et al. (1988) study, which examined AVLT performance in persons under age 50. A sample of 394 cognitively intact persons aged 55 years or older were administered the AVLT in addition to the WAIS-R and the Visual Spatial Learning Test. Although data for trial-by-trial performance were presented, two "learning" and two "memory" scores were recommended. With respect to the "learning" measures, Total Learning (sum of words recalled across the five learning trials) and LOT (Total Learning minus [5 × Trial 1]) were recommended, with the latter measure being recommended for illustrating the ability to show improved recall performance with repeated presentations of the list relative to the initial recall attempt. The "memory" measures were both reflective of "percent retention." Short-Term Percent Retention (STPR) reflects the number of words recalled during the postinterference trial relative to the number of words recalled on Trial 5 and Long-Term Percent Retention (LTPR) reflects the number of words recalled after a 30-min delay relative to the number of words recalled on Trial 5. Each of these four summary measures showed significant age-related declines. In addition to reporting age-appropriate percentile rankings for the four summary measures, this study also reported age-appropriate percentile rankings for trial-by-trial performance.

Schmidt (1996) has compiled an excellent summary of research on the AVLT, together with normative data from these studies, as well as metanormative data for children through older adults. The metanorms were computed by taking a pooled (weighted average) mean and standard deviation for the basic AVLT measures, including sum of words recalled on each trial, including Trials 1–5, List B, Trial 6, Delayed Recall, Recognition Memory, as well as the total number of words recalled across Trials 1–5. The advantage of the metanorms is that they capitalize on pooling data across samples, thereby increasing the sample size in each age category as well as the stability of the point estimates. However, Schmidt's (1996) handbook is nearly 10 years old, and because of this fact, it does not incorporate some of the recent developments in the literature that have taken place for the AVLT. Woodard and colleagues are in the process of computing AVLT normative data based on 551 healthy, community-dwelling individuals between the ages of 40 and 89.

Although age, gender, and education have been well studied and incorporated into many normative databases, it is somewhat surprising that few studies have directly investigated the influence of culture and ethnicity on AVLT performance. For example, differences across languages in word frequencies and cultural relevance of list words may have a large impact on list learning performance, particularly for non-English word lists. In addition, the extent to which normative data applied to performance indexes may be influenced by cultural group or degree of acculturation should also be carefully evaluated. One study compared 11 African-American and 32 Caucasian participants with mild-to-moderate AD using a brief neuropsychological battery that included an eight-item implementation of the AVLT (Ripich, Carpenter, & Ziol, 1997). After adjusting for education and Mini-Mental State Examination score, no significant group differences with respect to recall or recognition on the abbreviated AVLT were observed. Kennepohl, Shore, Nabors, and Hanks (2004) reported that lower performance on a number of neuropsychological measures, including the AVLT sum of words recalled for Trials 1–5, was associated with decreased levels of acculturation in a sample of African-American traumatic brain injury patients. Clearly, future studies using the Quantified Process Approach with the AVLT should investigate further how performance indexes may be influenced by ethnicity, culture, and degree of acculturation.

Alternate forms

List A is typically used for the learning trials and List B is generally used for the interference trial. A variety of other word lists have been used as alternative forms, some of which were originally derived from List C of Rey (1958), while other alternative forms do not seem to have stemmed from the original lists (e.g., Lezak, 1976, 1983, List C words). One study compared Lists A and C in a sample of 85 predominantly male hospital inpatients with a variety of psychiatric and neurological diagnoses (Ryan, Geisser, Randall, & Georgemiller, 1986). The average test–retest interval was approximately 2 h. The test–retest correlations were largely in the low to mid-0.6s, with a correlation of 0.71 observed for the fifth recall trial and 0.77 for the sum of words recalled across Trials 1–5. Although recall differences between List A and List C of less than one word were observed across each trial, these differences were significant on Trials 4 and 5, the postinterference trial, and for the sum of words recalled across Trials 1–5, suggesting that List A may be slightly easier than List C. Nevertheless, using a procedure described by Horton (1980), none of these differences were judged to be clinically significant.

Uchiyama et al. (1995) reported an investigation of alternate forms and longitudinal reliability between two forms of the AVLT in 2059 bisexual and homosexual HIV seronegative males. Participants were predominantly between the ages of 20 and 50, although the authors reported an additional group of participants who were 50 years of age and older. Although there were no significant performance differences between forms at either of these two assessment points, significant practice effects were noted longitudinally. This study used the conventional Lists A and B words presented in Lezak (1983) for the first version of the AVLT, whereas the second version of the AVLT used the Lists C and B words, also from Lezak (1983). It is important to note that the interference list was the same for both administrations. When testing was separated by 1 year, the test–retest reliability for the sum of words recalled across Trials 1–5 was 0.60 (Lists A–B) and 0.66 (Lists C–B), while the test–retest reliability for delayed recall was 0.66 (Lists A–B), and 0.81 (Lists C–B). The sum of words recalled on Trial 1 demonstrated a test–retest reliability of 0.3 (Lists A–B) and 0.52 (Lists C–B).

Interpretive strategy

Because the performance indexes reviewed in this chapter reflect cognitive processes underlying the overall learning process, it is important to keep in mind that an individual index should not be interpreted by itself. Indeed, it is important to evaluate a given performance index in the context of other performance indexes in order to understand strengths and weaknesses associated with a patient's verbal learning performance. Therefore, it is clear that an interpretive framework would be helpful for placing each of these indexes into a context when evaluating an examinee's performance on this measure. Figure 8.2 displays one possible framework, with performance on Trial 1 reflecting a starting point in the interpretive process. An examinee's level of performance on the first trial can provide some indication of whether the examinee's subsequent performance across trials may be affected by a tendency to be overwhelmed by the task, anxiety, inattention, or difficulty "warming up" to the task. Next, assuming that the preceding factors do not invalidate the examinee's performance on later trials, interpretation of the level of performance for the sum of words recalled over the five trials (or LOT) would follow. Determination of whether the examinee's overall performance is consistent or inconsistent with his/her same age peers using normative data provides a solid benchmark comparison. Investigation of within and across trial factors that may further characterize overall learning would follow. Identification of whether the expected primacy and recency effects are present, quantification of the relative proportions of gained and lost access across trials, determining whether the expected trial-to-trial learning increments are present, and evaluating the extent to which either serial organization, subjective organization, or no organization is used can all facilitate interpretation of overall learning. That is, each of these factors can shed additional light on cognitive strategies and processes underlying an examinee's overall performance. As noted earlier, each of these performance indexes can provide diagnostic information as well.

Evaluating the nature and extent of susceptibility to proactive and retroactive interference can be helpful in the interpretation of both overall learning

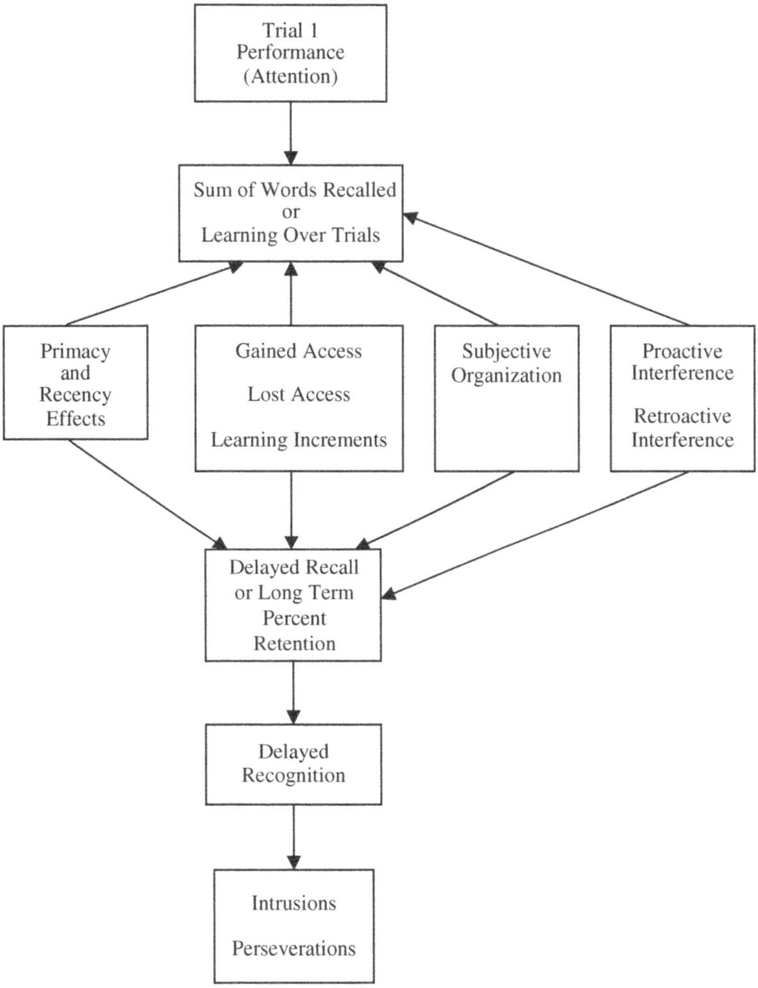

Figure 8.2 An interpretive strategy for evaluating performance on the Auditory Verbal Learning Test.

and delayed recall performance. For instance, a marked plateau on the last two or three trials that is preceded by normal performance on the first two trials may reflect an examinee's susceptibility to retroactive interference. As Rey (1958) noted, as the number of newly recalled words increases, it becomes more difficult to recall previously learned words (retroactive inhibition), and this effect increases over subsequent trials. Rey predicted that examinees who attempted to organize and structure their recall attempts (e.g., greater SO) would show less susceptibility to retroactive interference, while persons showing little ability to impose organization on the list would tend to exhibit greater susceptibility to retroactive interference. In any event, examinees who are especially sensitive to the effects of retroactive interference may show a more marked deceleration of their learning curve. Similarly, susceptibility to interference effects may underlie diminished performance during the delayed recall trial. Formal comparisons of List B recall to Trial 1 recall (proactive interference) and Trial 6 recall (postinterference recall trial) to Trial 5 recall (retroactive interference) using normative data can facilitate identification of these effects.

Performance on the delayed recognition trial relative to delayed recall can highlight possible encoding deficits that may underlie amnestic disorders (i.e., poor performance on both recall and recognition), whereas better performance on recognition relative to recall might suggest retrieval deficits.

Finally, the presence of intrusion errors and perseveration errors are relatively pathognomonic if they are somewhat frequent. With respect to intrusion errors, Rey (1958) differentiated between those errors that were derivatives of, synonymous, or associated with list words vs. errors that had no clear associative link to list words. Intrusion errors with an associative link to list words that appear early and subsequently are not repeated tend to suggest that the examinee can recognize such errors on later list presentations. However, persistent intrusion errors suggest a failure to recognize the presence of such errors from subsequent presentations of the list and may be associated with rapid development of an associative (but incorrect) complex. When such intrusion errors peak toward the final trials, fatigue, loss of control, decreased motivation, or self-consciousness regarding performance may be present. Rey considered intrusion errors without associative links to list words to be more serious. If such errors appear early and often, a clear inability to differentiate list words from extra-list words, a tendency to say as many words as possible to increase one's score, or an attempt to please the examiner might be suggested. If they occur infrequently or toward the final trials, fluctuations in attention might be suggested.

Perseverations rarely appear on Trial 1. However, if the number of perseverations increases in proportion to the number of words recalled, Rey suggested that impulsivity, decreased associative or organizational ability, difficulty differentiating words that have already been given from those that have not yet been given, an unconscious tendency to speak aloud one's thoughts, and a fear of having omitted a word may be operating. Perseverations that appear early and subsequently disappear is a sign of good adaptation to and understanding of the task. Rey noted that perseverations that appear on later trials tend to be associated with fatigue, a tendency to be overwhelmed by the task, a breakdown of organizational and associative ability when immediate memory capacity has been exceeded, or a reduction of effort in the presence of perceived increase in difficulty or when the examinee's maximum effort level has been surpassed. Perseverations given with some recognition that the word may have already been given is frequently observed, although Rey commented that examinees producing elevated levels of errors of this type may be attempting to diminish efforts related to self-control (i.e., giving up control of their performance to the examiner), looking for help, demonstrating a need for security or reassurance, or the behavior may be a strategy for reducing overall effort on the task.

Although interpretation can be performed at a variety of levels, Rey (1958) characterized a number of performance abnormalities drawn from his clinical experience with the AVLT. Integration of the abnormalities in overall learning capacity and the processes associated with the pattern of acquisition described by Rey with the performance indexes described above may provide one potentially useful interpretive framework.

Overall learning capacity

The total number of words acquired over the five learning trials may reflect the examinee's overall ability to learn verbal information that is frequently repeated. Although one may be tempted to equate learning ability with level of intellectual functioning, Rey was careful to point out that the ability to memorize is not necessarily synonymous with level of intellectual functioning. Individuals with an average level of intellectual functioning may perform at ceiling on the AVLT, whereas individuals with a superior level of intellectual functioning may only exhibit average to high average memory performance.

Although a simple total of words recalled over the five trials may provide a basic index of learning capacity, the individual's ability to profit from list repetitions is best assessed by comparing performance on Trial 5 to Trial 1, or better yet, using the age and education corrected MOANS index of LOT. Diminished ability to learn new words over repeated trials would suggest impairment in processes related to acquisition.

Pattern of acquisition

Performance on Trial 1 is typically expected to range between five and nine words for individuals between the ages of 6 and 70 years. Persons who are 70 years of age or older might be expected to recall between three and seven words on the first trial. Rey noted that diminished recall on the first trial was often associated with difficulty "warming up" to the task, emotionality, reactivity to the perceived difficulty of the task, a feeling of being overwhelmed by the number of words to learn, and anxiety. He noted the importance of comparing the first trial performance with performance on Trial 2. If diminished performance also occurs on Trial 2, but performance returns to normal levels on Trial 3 and beyond, these emotional factors and reactions are more likely. In contrast, if diminished performance continues beyond Trial 2, acquisition difficulty is likely to explain this diminished performance.

Rey also characterized various fluctuations in performance across trials that were associated with specific clinical features. For example, persons achieving a plateau on the last two or three trials after initially showing normal progress were characterized as demonstrating diminished dissociative and organizational ability, diminished effort, excessive fatigue, diminished motivation, and elevated susceptibility to retroactive interference. In contrast, persons showing a sudden drop in performance relative to earlier trials were associated with susceptibility to fatigue or impersistence in the ability to adapt to increasing memory load.

Summary

Clinical neuropsychology and cognitive psychology have contributed a number of methodologies for evaluating verbal memory performance using the AVLT. As has been suggested in the preceding review of studies, the AVLT can provide a rich source of clinical data that can assist with diagnosis as well as with characterizing islands of strength and shortcoming in an individual's memory performance. Because memory functioning is not a unitary phenomenon, a variety of aspects of memory performance must be considered in order to provide clues regarding the factors underlying memory impairment.

Strengths

The AVLT generates a considerable amount of data using a relatively challenging memory paradigm. A considerable amount of normative data is available for a number of summary measures for the instrument. Because the words on each list are unrelated, subjective organization strategies may be imposed in order to facilitate list recall. Whether or to what extent an examinee utilizes these strategies can be identified. This feature contrasts with other commonly used memory tests such as the CVLT-II and the HVLT-R, which feature words belonging to several semantic categories. In these latter tests, it is also of interest to determine whether or not the examinee utilizes semantic organization to facilitate recall, given that the pull to do so is relatively strong.

The AVLT can provide an index of attentional deployment through examination of recall performance on Trial 1, and one may evaluate the ability to profit from repeated exposure to the to-be-learned material. Aspects of proactive and retroactive interference may be evaluated, together with delayed recall performance and delayed recognition performance. Serial position effects may also be evaluated through examination of recall patterns on the AVLT. Different recognition testing strategies can be employed in order to determine whether the individual can identify list words embedded within a story vs. simply recognizing individually presented words.

The AVLT has been in existence for over 50 years, and a considerable amount of research has been performed with the instrument within the last 20 years. It remains a clinically useful measure for characterizing overall memory performance and for facilitating diagnosis of specific aspects of memory impairment.

Weaknesses

Although the AVLT possesses a number of strengths, there are some shortcomings to the measure as well. These limitations revolve principally around the psychometric characteristics of the instrument. The test–retest reliability of a number of summary measures is somewhat lower than would typically be desirable. It is possible that aspects of the word list may contribute to some of this unreliability. For example, the inclusion of both monosyllabic and bisyllabic words, together with a failure to control for word frequency may contribute to variability in resulting summary measures. Efforts directed at enhancing the reliability of scorers from the AVLT by consideration of alternative words and controlling for factors such as word length, concreteness, imageability, and word frequency may help to reduce some error variance and increase the overall reliability of summary scores.

Another minor limitation of the AVLT relates to the relative lack of parallel forms of the instrument. This limitation makes it somewhat difficult to perform serial testing with this measure. A wider range of forms that control for the stimulus characteristics mentioned above would be extremely helpful. A number of the summary measures discussed in this chapter, such as subjective organization, gained and lost access, and the evaluation of primacy and recency effects are somewhat cumbersome to calculate by hand. This issue may be related to the fact that many of the summary measures have not been examined frequently in the literature. The availability of computer scoring software that may quickly score an individual's recall performance across a number of parameters would be helpful not only for evaluating memory performance within that examinee, but it would also contribute to the eventual establishment of normative data for these more complicated summary measures. Finally, the AVLT represents a reasonably challenging assessment of memory for most individuals. However, for individuals with more significant memory impairment, or for those individuals with diminished intellectual functioning, the standard AVLT may be quite overwhelming. Efforts directed at creating short forms of this instrument should be considered in order to facilitate the evaluation of individuals with a greater degree of memory impairment. The short forms would be particularly useful for tracking dementia progression, as well as for evaluating the effectiveness of various pharmacological interventions.

References

Alexander, M. P., Stuss, D. T., & Fansabedian, N. (2003). California Verbal Learning Test: Performance by patients with focal frontal and non-frontal lesions. *Brain*, *126*(Pt 6), 1493–1503.

Antonelli, I. R., Capparella, O., Gemma, A., Marra, C., & Carbonin, P. U. (1995). Effects of aging and of Alzheimer's disease on verbal memory. *Journal of Clinical and Experimental Neuropsychology*, *17*(4), 580–589.

Blachstein, H., Vakil, E., & Hoofien, D. (1993). Impaired learning in patients with closed-head injuries: An analysis of components of the acquisition process. *Neuropsychology*, *7*(4), 530–535.

Bleecker, M. L., Bolla-Wilson, K., Agnew, J., & Meyers, D. A. (1988). Age-related sex differences in verbal memory. *Journal of Clinical Psychology*, *44*(3), 403–411.

Boake, C. (2000). Edouard Claparède and the Auditory Verbal Learning Test. *Journal of Clinical and Experimental Neuropsychology*, *22*(2), 286–292.

Crockett, D. J., Hadjistavropoulos, T., & Hurwitz, T. (1992). Primacy and recency effects in the assessment of memory using the Rey Auditory Verbal Learning Test. *Archives of Clinical Neuropsychology*, *7*(1), 97–107.

Davis, H. P., Small, S. A., Stern, Y., Mayeux, R., Feldstein, S. N., & Keller, F. R. (2003). Acquisition, recall, and forgetting of verbal information in long-term memory by young, middle-aged, and elderly individuals. *Cortex*, *39*, 1063–1091.

Drebing, C. E., van Gorp, W. G., Stuck, A. E., Mitrushina, M., & Beck, J. (1994). Early detection of cognitive decline in higher cognitively functioning older adults: Sensitivity and specificity of a neuropsychological screening battery. *Neuropsychology*, *8*(1), 31–37.

Dunlosky, J., & Salthouse, T. A. (1996). A decomposition of age-related differences in multi-trial free recall. *Aging, Neuropsychology, & Cognition*, *3*, 2–14.

Ebbinghaus, H. (1885). *Über das Gedächtnis*. Leipzig: Duncker & Humblot.

Ebbinghaus, H. (1964). *Memory: A contribution to experimental psychology*. New York: Dover.

Eslinger, P. J., & Grattan, L. M. (1994). Altered serial position learning after frontal lobe lesion. *Neuropsychologia*, *32*(6), 729–739.

Estevez-Gonzalez, A., Kulisevsky, J., Boltes, A., Otermin, P., & Garcia-Sanchez, C. (2003). Rey Verbal Learning Test is a useful tool for differential diagnosis in the preclinical phase of Alzheimer's disease: Comparison with mild cognitive impairment and normal aging. *International Journal of Geriatric Psychiatry*, *18*(11), 1021–1028.

Gainotti, G., & Marra, C. (1994). Some aspects of memory disorders clearly distinguish dementia of the Alzheimer's type from depressive pseudo-dementia. *Journal of Clinical and Experimental Neuropsychology*, *16*(1), 65–78.

Geffen, G., Moar, K. J., O'Hanlon, A. P., Clark, C. R., & Geffen, L. B. (1990). Performance measures of 16- to 86-year old males and females on the Auditory Verbal Learning Test. *The Clinical Neuropsychologist*, *4*(1), 45–63.

Geffen, G. M., Butterworth, P., & Geffen, L. B. (1994). Test–retest reliability of a new form of the Auditory Verbal Learning Test (AVLT). *Archives of Clinical Neuropsychology*, *9*(4), 303–316.

Gershberg, F. B., & Shimamura, A. P. (1995). Impaired use of organizational strategies in free recall following frontal lobe damage. *Neuropsychologia*, *33*(10), 1305–1333.

Guilmette, T. J., & Rasile, D. (1995). Sensitivity, specificity, and diagnostic accuracy of three verbal memory measures in the assessment of mild brain injury. *Neuropsychology*, *9*(3), 338–344.

Horton, A. M., Jr. (1980). Estimation of clinical significance: A brief note. *Psychological Reports*, *47*, 141–142.

Hultsch, D. F. (1974). Learning to learn in adulthood. *Journal of Gerontology*, *29*(3), 302–308.

Ivnik, R., Malec, J., Smith, G., Tangalos, E., Petersen, R., Kokmen, E., & Kurland, L. (1992a). Mayo's older Americans normative studies: Updated AVLT norms for ages 56 to 97. *The Clinical Neuropsychologist*, *6*(Suppl.), 83–104.

Ivnik, R., Malec, J., Smith, G., Tangalos, E., Petersen, R., Kokmen, E., & Kurland, L. (1992b). Mayo's older Americans normative studies: WMS-R norms for ages 56 to 94. *The Clinical Neuropsychologist*, *6*(Suppl.), 49–82.

Ivnik, R. J., Malec, J. F., Tangalos, E. G., Petersen, R. C., Kokmen, E., & Kurland, L. T. (1990). The Auditory-Verbal Learning Test (AVLT): Norms for ages 55 years and older. *Psychological Assessessment*, *2*(3), 304–312.

Jackson, D. K., & Schneider, H. G. (1982). Age differences in organization and recall: An analysis of rehearsal processes. *Psychological Reports*, *50*, 919–924.

Janowsky, J. S., Shimamura, A. P., & Squire, L. R. (1989). Memory and metamemory: Comparisons between patients with frontal lobe lesions and amnesic patients. *Psychobiology*, *17*, 3–11.

Kennepohl, S., Shore, D., Nabors, N., & Hanks, R. (2004). African American acculturation and neuropsychological test performance following traumatic brain injury. *Journal of the International Neuropsychological Society*, *10*, 566–577.

Kraiuhin, C., Gordon, E., Stanfield, P., Meares, R., & Howson, A. (1986). P300 and the effects of aging: Relevance to the diagnosis of dementia. *Experimental Aging Research*, *12*(4), 187–192.

Laurence, M. W. (1966). Age differences in performance and subjective organization in the free-recall learning of pictorial material. *Canadian Journal of Psychology*, *20*(4), 388–399.

Lezak, M. D. (1976). *Neuropsychological assessment*. New York: Oxford University Press.

Lezak, M. D. (1983). *Neuropsychological assessment* (2nd ed.). New York: Oxford University Press.

Lezak, M. D. (1995). *Neuropsychological assessment* (3rd ed.). New York: Oxford University Press.

Loftus, G. R. (1978). On interpretation of interactions. *Memory & Cognition*, *6*, 312–319.

Mitrushina, M., Satz, P., Chervinsky, A., & D'Elia, L. (1991). Performance of four age groups of normal elderly on the Rey Auditory-Verbal Learning Test. *Journal of Clinical Psychology*, *47*(3), 351–357.

Mitrushina, M. N., Boone, K. B., & D'Elia, L. F. (1998). *Handbook of normative data for neuropsychological assessment*. New York: Oxford University Press.

Moritz, S., Heeren, D., Andresen, B., & Krausz, M. (2001). An analysis of the specificity and the syndromal correlates of verbal memory impairments in schizophrenia. *Psychiatry Research*, *101*(1), 23–31.

Moulin, C. J. A., James, N., Freeman, J. E., & Jones, R. W. (2004). Deficient acquisition and consolidation: Intertrial free recall performance in Alzheimer's disease and mild cognitive impairment. *Journal of Clinical and Experimental Neuropsychology*, *26*(1), 1–10.

Mungas, D. (1983). Differential clinical sensitivity of specific parameters of the Rey Auditory-Verbal Learning Test. *Journal of Consulting Clinical Psychology*, *51*(6), 848–855.

O'Donnell, J. P., Radtke, R. C., Leicht, D. J., & Caesar, R. (1988). Encoding and retrieval processes in learning-disabled, head-injured, and nondisabled young adults. *Journal of General Psychology*, *115*(4), 355–368.

Pellegrino, J. W., & Battig, W. F. (1972). Effects of semantic list structure differences in free recall. *Psychonomic Science*, *29*(2), 65–67.

Pellegrino, J. W., & Battig, W. F. (1974). Relationships among higher order organizational measures and free recall. *Journal of Experimental Psychology*, *102*(3), 463–472.

Petersen, R., Smith, G., Kokmen, E., Ivnik, R., & Tangalos, E. (1992). Memory function in normal aging. *Neurology*, *42*, 396–401.

Poreh, A. M. (2000). The Quantified Process Approach: An emerging methodology to neuropsychological assessment. *The Clinical Neuropsychologist*, *14*, 212–222.

Query, W. T., & Berger, R. A. (1980). AVLT memory scores as a function of age among general medical, neurologic and alcoholic patients. *Journal of Clinical Psychology*, *36*(4), 1009–1012.

Query, W. T., & Megran, J. (1983). Age-related norms for AVLT in a male patient population. *Journal of Clinical Psychology*, *39*(1), 136–138.

Rey, A. (1958). *L'examen clinique en psychologie*. Paris: Presses Universitaires de France.

Ripich, D. N., Carpenter, B., & Ziol, E. (1997). Comparison of African-American and white persons with Alzheimer's disease on language measures. *Neurology*, *48*(3), 781–783.

Ryan, J. J., Geisser, M. E., Randall, D. M., & Georgemiller, R. J. (1986). Alternate form reliability and equivalency of the Rey Auditory Verbal Learning Test. *Journal of Clinical and Experimental Neuropsychology*, *8*(5), 611–616.

Schmidt, M. (1996). *Rey Auditory and Verbal Learning Test: A handbook*. Los Angeles: Western Psychological Services.

Shum, D. H., Harris, D., & O'Gorman, J. G. (2000). Effects of severe traumatic brain injury on visual memory. *Journal of Clinical and Experimental Neuropsychology*, *22*(1), 25–39.

Smith, G. E., Ivnik, R. J., Malec, J. F., Kokmen, E., Tangalos, E. G., & Kurland, L. T. (1992). Mayo's Older Americans Normative Studies (MOANS): Factor structure of a core battery. *Psychological Assessment*, *4*(3), 382–390.

Smith, G. E., Ivnik, R. J., Malec, J. F., Petersen, R. C., Kokmen, E., & Tangalos, E. G. (1994). Mayo cognitive factor scales: Derivation of a short battery and norms for factor scores. *Neuropsychology*, *8*(2), 194–202.

Smith, G. E., Ivnik, R. J., Malec, J. F., & Tangalos, E. G. (1993). Factor structure of the Mayo Older Americans Normative Sample (MOANS) core battery: Replication in a clinical sample. *Psychological Assessment*, *5*(1), 121–124.

Spreen, O., & Strauss, E. (1998). *A compendium of neuropsychological tests: Administration, norms, and commentary* (2nd ed.). New York: Oxford University Press.

Stefanova, E., Kostic, V. S., Ziropadja, L., Markovic, M., & Ocic, G. (2002). Serial position learning effects in patients with aneurysms of the anterior communicating artery. *Journal of Clinical and Experimental Neuropsychology*, *24*(5), 687–694.

Sternberg, R. J., & Tulving, E. (1977). The measurement of subjective organization in free recall. *Psychological Bulletin*, *84*, 539–556.

Taylor, E. M. (1959). *Psychological appraisal of children with cerebral defects*. Cambridge, MA: Harvard University Press.

Tierney, M. C., Black, S. E., Szalai, J. P., Snow, W. G., Fisher, R. H., Nadon, G., & Chui, H. C. (2001). Recognition memory and verbal fluency differentiate probable Alzheimer disease from subcortical ischemic vascular dementia. *Archives of Neurology*, *58*(10), 1654–1659.

Tierney, M. C., Nores, A., Snow, W. G., Fisher, R. H., Zorzitto, M. L., & Reid, D. W. (1994). Use of the Rey Auditory Verbal Learning Test in differentiating normal aging from Alzheimer's and Parkinson's dementia. *Psychological Assessment*, *6*, 129–134.

Tierney, M. C., Szalai, J. P., Snow, W. G., Fisher, R. H., Nores, A., Nadon, G., Dunn, E., & St. George-Hyslop, P. H. (1996). Prediction of probable Alzheimer's disease in memory-impaired patients: A prospective longitudinal study. *Neurology*, *46*(3), 661–665.

Torres, I. J., Flashman, L. A., O'Leary, D. S., & Andreasen, N. C. (2001). Effects of retroactive and proactive interference on word list recall in schizophrenia. *Journal of International Neuropsychological Society*, *7*(4), 481–490.

Tulving, E. (1962). Subjective organization in free recall of "unrelated" words. *Psychological Review*, *69*, 344–354.

Tulving, E. (1964). Intratrial and intertrial retention: Notes towards a theory of free recall verbal learning. *Psychology Review*, *71*, 219–237.

Uchiyama, C. L., D'Elia, L. F., Dellinger, A. M., Becker, J. T., Selnes, O. A., Wesch, J. E., Chen, B. B., Satz, P., van Gorp, W., & Miller, E. N. (1995). Alternate forms of the Auditory-Verbal Learning Test: Issues of test comparability, longitudinal reliability, and moderating demographic variables. *Archives of Clinical Neuropsychology*, *10*(2), 133–145.

Vakil, E., & Agmon-Ashkenazi, D. (1997). Baseline performance and learning rate of procedural and declarative memory tasks: Younger versus older adults. *Journal of Gerontology Series B: Psychological Sciences and Social Sciences*, *52*(5), P229–P234.

Vakil, E., & Blachstein, H. (1994). A supplementary measure in the Rey AVLT for assessing incidental learning of temporal order. *Journal of Clinical Psychology*, *50*, 240–245.

Wiens, A. N., McMinn, M. R., & Crossen, J. R. (1988). Rey Auditory-Verbal Learning Test: Development of norms for healthy young adults. *Clinical Neuropsychology*, *2*(1), 67–87.

Witte, K. L., Freund, J. S., & Sebby, R. A. (1990). Age differences in free recall and subjective organization. *Psychology and Aging*, *5*(2), 307–309.

Woodard, J. L. (1991). *The dual nature of secondary organization in the selective and restricted reminding tasks: An application of the search of associative memory model.* Wayne State U, MI, US.

Woodard, J. L., Dorsett, E. S. W., Hermann, B. P., Cooper, J. G., & Sager, M. A. (2005). Development of a brief cognitive screen for mild cognitive impairment and neurocognitive disorder. *Aging, Neuropsychology, and Cognition*, *12*(4), 299–315.

Woodard, J. L., Dorsett, E. S. W., Hermann, B. P., & Sager, M. A. (2005). Older adult normative data for the Rey Auditory Verbal Learning Test. *Manuscript in preparation.*

Woodard, J. L., Dunlosky, J. A., & Salthouse, T. A. (1999). Task decomposition analysis of intertrial free recall performance on the Rey Auditory Verbal Learning Test in normal aging and Alzheimer's disease. *Journal of Clinical and Experimental Neuropsychology*, *21*(5), 666–676.

9 Cognitive processes of verbal fluency tasks

Angela K. Troyer and Morris Moscovitch

Introduction

Verbal fluency or word generation tasks are among the most common tests used in clinical neuropsychological evaluation. Administration of fluency tasks involves allowing a limited amount of time for an individual to name as many words as possible according to specified rules. On phonemic fluency, words are generated that begin with a given letter such as "F," and on semantic fluency, words are generated that belong to a given category such as "animals." Traditionally, the score of interest is the total number of words generated within the allotted time period. However, as reviewed below, fluency tasks are multifactorial, involving a number of cognitive processes. As such, the traditional total score calculated does not fully capture the important aspects of any given individual's performance.

Fluency performance is thought to require multiple cognitive processes in part because multiple brain regions are critically involved. For example, fluency performance can be disrupted following lesions of the temporal lobes (e.g., Corcoran & Upton, 1993; Martin, Loring, Meador, & Lee, 1990) or the frontal lobes (e.g., Crowe, 1992; Miceli, Caltagirone, Gainotti, Masullo, & Silveri, 1981; Perret, 1974; Stuss et al., 1998). Similarly, functional brain imaging studies during fluency performance show activation of specific brain regions within both the temporal lobes (e.g., left parahippocampal gyrus; Frith, Friston, Liddle, & Frackowiak, 1991; left inferior temporal lobe; Klein, Milner, Zatorre, Meyer, & Evans, 1995) and the frontal lobes (e.g., left dorsolateral prefrontal gyrus; Cuenod, Bookheimer, Hertz-Pannier, Zefiro, Theodore, & Le Bihan, 1995; Frith et al., 1991).

Clustering and switching

The specific cognitive processes involved in fluency tasks have been identified in studies utilizing temporal and semantic analyses of word generation over extended time periods. The production of words on fluency tasks has been found to be unevenly distributed over time. That is, words tend to be produced in "spurts," or temporal clusters, with a short time interval between words in a cluster and a longer pause between clusters (e.g., Bousfield & Sedgewick, 1944).

On semantic fluency tasks, the words comprising these temporal clusters tend to be semantically related (Gruenewald & Lockhead, 1980; Pollio, 1964; Rosen & Engle, 1997). These findings led to the suggestion that performance on semantic fluency involves two processes: (1) a search for and production of words within semantic subcategories during the spurts and (2) a search for new semantic subcategories during the pauses between spurts (Gruenewald & Lockhead, 1980; Wixted & Rohrer, 1994). In other words, to perform a fluency task, the individual typically will generate words within a subcategory and, when this subcategory is exhausted, he or she will switch to a new one.

We have operationalized these cognitive components as clustering and switching (Troyer, Moscovitch, & Winocur, 1997). Clustering involves phonemic analysis on phonemic fluency (e.g., according to beginning phonemes, rhymes) and semantic categorization on semantic fluency (e.g., subgroups within the category). Clustering is thought to require temporal-lobe processes such as verbal memory and word storage, and it tends to be decreased in patient groups with neuropathology affecting temporal regions (reviewed subsequently). Switching, on the other hand, involves frontal-lobe processes such as strategic search processes and cognitive flexibility in shifting from one subcategory to another. Switching is decreased in patients with frontal-lobe involvement (reviewed subsequently). Clustering is thought to be relatively automatic whereas switching is thought to be an effortful process. This is supported by studies examining fluency performance by healthy adults under conditions of divided attention (Rende, Ramsberger, & Miyake, 2002; Troyer et al., 1997) showing that clustering is unaffected by an attention-demanding secondary task whereas switching is decreased by a secondary task.

In this chapter, we describe how to score clustering and switching based on traditional administration and recording procedures for phonemic and semantic fluency tests (Spreen & Strauss, 1998). We provide psychometric and normative data to allow clinicians to use these indices with individual patients. Finally, we describe the clinical usefulness of these indices by reviewing the literature on clustering and switching in research and patient populations.

Calculation of clustering and switching indexes

Fluency tasks

The normative data (Troyer, 2000) provided in this chapter are based on two versions of phonemic fluency, each with three trials (i.e., the letters F, A, and S, or the letters C, F, and L) and two trials of semantic fluency (i.e., animals and supermarket). To administer these tasks, consistent with standard instructions (e.g., Spreen & Strauss, 1998), participants are allotted 60 s for each trial. On phonemic fluency, they are asked to generate as many words as possible that began with each letter, excluding proper names and repetitions of the same word with different endings. On semantic fluency, participants are instructed to name as many different animals as possible (Spreen & Strauss,

1998) and as many items as possible that one can find or buy in a supermarket (Mattis, 1988). All responses are recorded by the examiner, regardless of whether they are correct or incorrect (e.g., intrusions or repetitions), in the order in which they are generated by the participant.

Three scores are obtained from each fluency task. These include the mean cluster size, the raw number of switches, and the total number of words generated. Instructions for determining these scores are provided subsequently. Detailed scoring rules are provided in the Appendix and a sample scored protocol is shown in Figure 9.1.

Clustering scores

On phonemic fluency, clusters are defined as successively generated words that begin with the same first two letters, differ only by a vowel sound, rhyme, or are homonyms. On animal fluency, clusters are defined as successively generated words belonging to the same semantic subcategories, such as African animals, Australian animals, North American wild animals, pets, and individual zoological categories, such as birds, canines, insects, primates, and so forth. On supermarket fluency, clusters include fruits, vegetables, dairy products, meats, and so forth. These categories were determined based on the naturally occurring clusters in our original participants' protocols (Troyer et al., 1997). The clusters used for supermarket fluency are also consistent with a previous scoring system (Tröster, Salmon, McCullough, & Butters, 1989). On phonemic fluency, only phonemic clusters are counted, and on semantic fluency,

F	A	S	Animals	Supermarket
far	apple	silly	dog	apples
fat	arm	Samuel X	cat	bananas
field	amplify	selfish	horse	grapes
few	artist	sarcasm	cow	celery
friend	acorn	sift	goat	carrots
frost	accept	seal	chicken	noodles
fright	astronaut	sell	turkey	milk
fight	arm X	sale	eagle	meat X
fall	army	start	zebra	steak
film		soon	whale	sausages
fair		sullen	fish	chicken
fare		swift	giraffe	soap
fiddle		surprise	hippo	cheese
full			elephant	cream
fortune			shark	milk X
fort			bird X	potatoes
			canary	bread
			robin	muffins
			monkey	rolls
total = 16 cluster = 6/11 = 0.54 switch =10	total = 8 cluster = 2/7 = 0.29 switch = 6	total = 12 cluster = 2/11 = 0.18 switch = 10	total = 18 cluster = 12/9 = 1.33 switch = 8	total = 17 cluster = 10/9 = 1.11 switch = 8
Phonemic fluency total = 36 cluster = 0.34 switch = 26			**Semantic fluency** total = 35 cluster = 1.22 switch = 16	

Figure 9.1 Sample scored protocol ("×" indicates an incorrectly generated word that does not count toward the "total" score; square brackets indicate clusters).

only semantic clusters are counted. This approach was taken because previous research (Raskin & Rearick, 1996), as well as initial examination of our own data, had shown that participants produce both very few phonemic clusters on semantic fluency and very few semantic clusters on phonemic fluency. (It should be noted, however, that others have argued that these latter types of clusters should also be considered; e.g., Abwender, Swan, Bowerman, & Connolly, 2001.) The size of the cluster is counted beginning with the second word in each cluster. The mean cluster size is then calculated by summing the size of each cluster and dividing by the number of clusters.

Switching scores

Switches are calculated as the number of transitions between clusters, including single words. The number of switches, therefore, is the same as the number of clusters minus the number of trials administered (e.g., three trials on phonemic fluency and two trials on semantic fluency).

For several reasons, the raw number of switches is used as the switching index rather than the number of switches adjusted for number of words generated. Conceptually, the raw number of switches is the behavior of interest, as it indicates the number of times an individual can generate a new cluster of responses. This is similar to the raw index used for the number of words generated. Knowing the percent of the words generated that were correct does not provide as much information as knowing the raw number of words generated (e.g., 90% could indicate 9 out of 10 or 36 out of 40). Furthermore, because switching is thought to determine, in part, the number of words generated (Troyer et al., 1997), adjusting switches according to the total words generated would be akin to correcting a cause for its effect. Consistent with these theoretical reasons for using a raw switching score, previous experience has indicated that only the raw score (and not an adjusted switching score) produces meaningful information. We have re-examined our data from patients with Alzheimer's and Parkinson's diseases (Troyer, Moscovitch, Winocur, Leach, & Freedman, 1998b) and found that no patient groups were impaired in comparison to controls on an adjusted switching score, despite large group impairments on other fluency measures. Similar findings were obtained by others (Epker, Lacritz, & Cullum, 1999; Tröster et al., 1998), indicating that an adjusted score does not capture important group differences in fluency performance.

Errors

A crucial aspect of the way that clustering and switching are calculated is that repetitions and intrusions are included in these scores (but excluded from the total score). This is done for two reasons. First, the errors provide information about the ongoing strategy used by the participant regardless of whether the responses are considered to be "correct." It is helpful to know, for example, that a participant was using a clustering strategy, even if it resulted in increased repetitions. Second, errors are included because both clustering and switching would otherwise be under-reported in patient populations in which perseverations are frequent.

In contrast, repetitions and intrusions are excluded from the number of correct words generated, consistent with standard scoring rules (Spreen & Strauss, 1998). On phonemic fluency, proper names and repetitions of the same word with a different ending are also excluded. On animal fluency, no credit is given for subcategory labels (e.g., bird) if specific exemplars are also given (e.g., robin, canary). In addition, sex- and age-specific names of the same animal species are considered to be the same animal (e.g., hen and rooster, cat and kitten). Similarly, on supermarket fluency, no credit is given for subcategory labels (e.g., fruits) if specific exemplars are also given (e.g., apple, banana).

On phonemic fluency, scores from the three trials (i.e., F, A, and S, or C, F, and L) are combined into a single score for each participant. Similarly, on semantic fluency, scores on the two trials (i.e., animals and supermarket) are combined into a single variable. The benefit of these combined scores is that they are based on a higher number of responses and are thus presumed to be more valid and reliable measures of fluency ability.

Normative data

The normative data provided in Table 9.1 are based on a sample of 411 healthy, community-dwelling adults (reported in Troyer, 2000). Ages ranged from 18 to 91 years (M = 59.8, SD = 20.7), and level of education ranged from 5 to 21 years (M = 13.9, SD = 2.9). Seventy percent of participants were women. Participants were fluent in English and testing was conducted in English. All participants were screened via interview for neurologic and psychiatric disorders that could affect cognitive function, and participants aged 60 and older were given brief cognitive tests to screen for cognitive decline (Anderson, Craik, & Naveh-Benjamin, 1998; Folstein, Folstein, & McHugh, 1975).

Relation to demographic variables

Sex is unrelated to clustering and switching scores, both in this normative sample (Troyer, 2000) and in a younger, independent sample (Ross, 2003). Age has a minimal effect on clustering, although older adults tend to produce slightly larger cluster sizes than young adults on phonemic fluency (Hughes & Bryan, 2002; Troyer, 2000). With advancing age, switching, on the other hand, decreases significantly (Hughes & Bryan, 2002; Troyer, 2000). Higher levels of education are associated with larger clustering and switching scores on phonemic but not semantic fluency (Troyer, 2000).

Calculation of normative data

Slightly different scores were obtained on the two versions of phonemic fluency in our normative sample (i.e., FAS and CFL; Troyer, 2000). Based on this finding, as well as the previously reported relations to demographic variables, the calculation of normative data involved performing regression analyses that

Table 9.1 Corrections, demographically corrected descriptive data, and percentiles for fluency scores

	Phonemic			*Semantic*		
	Cluster	*Switches*	*Total*	*Cluster*	*Switches*	*Total*
Age (years)	−0.001	+0.05	+0.04	−0.001	+0.11	+0.23
Education (years)	−0.015	−0.38	−1.06	−0.012	−0.25	−0.74
Form (FAS)	+0.094	−2.67	−2.18	na	na	na
Mean	0.24	23.9	28.6	0.94	23.4	46.9
SD	0.23	8.2	11.1	0.47	4.4	7.9
1st percentile	−0.16	6.6	4.3	0.24	13.4	28.3
5th percentile	−0.06	10.2	11.4	0.40	16.2	34.4
16th percentile	0.01	15.6	17.0	0.60	18.9	39.4
25th percentile	0.08	18.7	20.6	0.66	20.5	40.7
50th percentile	0.19	23.3	28.7	0.91	22.7	46.3
75th percentile	0.35	29.7	36.6	1.18	26.5	52.5
84th percentile	0.44	32.3	39.3	1.44	27.5	56.6
95th percentile	0.73	37.6	47.6	2.02	31.3	60.7
99th percentile	0.97	43.2	57.4	2.37	34.0	62.4

Adapted from A. K. Troyer (2000). Normative data for clustering and switching on verbal fluency tasks. *Journal of Clinical and Experimental Neuropsychology*, *22*, 374, published by Swets & Zeitlinger.

included age, education, and fluency version. Corrections were then determined by the B's from the regression analyses, and these corrections were applied to the original scores in order to calculate normative test data. The corrections are presented at the top of Table 9.1. Age and education corrections were applied for each year of age or formal education, respectively, and version corrections were applied for FAS. Percentiles were then calculated based on the actual distribution of the corrected scores (e.g., 16% of participants in our sample obtained scores at the 16th percentile or less). This method of determining percentiles was chosen because some score distributions (i.e., cluster size) were slightly skewed. Means, standard deviations, and percentiles for the corrected scores are presented in Table 9.1. Percentiles for individual raw scores can be obtained by adding the appropriate corrections and looking up the corresponding corrected score. We have provided examples of how to obtain percentiles for several hypothetical individuals (Troyer, 2000).

Critiques

Our method of calculating clustering and switching scores has faced some criticism. Mayr (2002) argued that, because fluency tasks have a strong time constraint, it is not possible to separate generalized slowing and decreased switching ability based on our switching measure. That is, slowed retrieval of words either within clusters or between clusters (i.e., switches) would result in decreased switching scores. To tease these out, Mayr suggests that it is necessary to perform detailed analyses of the time intervals between each word generated, comparing retrieval times for words generated within clusters and between clusters. This argument, that generalized slowing can account for decreased switching, may be somewhat mitigated by findings that measures of processing speed are unrelated to clustering and switching scores among healthy younger and older adults (Hughes & Byran, 2002). Moreover, the critique cannot account for the dissociation between deficits in switching and in clustering among patients who would seem to be impaired equally in slowing (i.e., those with Alzheimer's, Parkinson's, and Huntington's diseases), as reviewed subsequently.

Another criticism concerns our method of quantifying switches. Abwender et al. (2001) have suggested that there are different types of switches, as opposed to the single switch score that we calculate. They classified switches according to whether they occur between multi-word clusters (the so-called cluster switches, which reflect mental flexibility in switching between established clusters) or between single-word clusters (which may simply reflect lack of ability to cluster). Indeed, they found that cluster switching was highly related to another test of flexibility (i.e., Ruff Figural Fluency), whereas our method of measuring switching was not. Thus, there may be added benefit to even further decompositions of fluency performance.

Psychometric information

Psychometric information available for clustering and switching include inter-rater reliabilities, test–retest reliability, and construct validity.

Inter-rater reliabilities

Across several studies, the ability of independent raters to score clustering and switching in a similar way (i.e., inter-rater reliability) is high. We (Troyer et al., 1997) obtained inter-rater reliability scores, calculated as Pearson correlation coefficients, ranging from 0.94 to 0.96 based on ratings made by two independent raters on protocols produced by 42 healthy adults. Others have obtained similarly high inter-rater reliabilities when calculated using patient groups (0.91–0.99; Tröster et al., 1998), multiple raters (0.98–0.99; Ross, 2003), and larger sample sizes (0.89–0.99; Abwender et al., 2001; Ross, 2003).

Test–retest reliability

This has been examined in a single study. Ross (2003) administered a phonemic fluency task (i.e., CFL) to 55 healthy younger adults on two occasions over a 30-day period. Test–retest reliability was low, with reliability coefficients of 0.43 for cluster size, 0.58 for switches, and 0.70 for total words generated. All scores improved with repeated testing, showing a practice effect. Although the temporal stability of these scores is less than ideal, such low scores are not unusual for tests of executive ability, for which task novelty is crucial (reviewed in Ross, 2003; Spreen & Strauss, 1998). Additional information about test–retest reliability would clearly be useful, particularly for semantic fluency and in other populations such as normal aging and clinical patients.

Given the consistent practice effect (Ross, 2003), it may be preferable to perform repeated testing using different versions of a fluency task. As such, information about alternate-version reliability (e.g., fluency component scores obtained on FAS and CFL by the same individuals) would also be useful.

Construct validity

This has been examined primarily with two methods: examination of group differences and correlational methods. Studies examining differences between groups on measures of clustering and switching have provided evidence for the dissociability of clustering and switching and have provided information regarding brain regions involved in these components. That is, as reviewed in the final section of this chapter, a number of studies show that clustering is sensitive to changes in the temporal lobes, whereas switching is sensitive to changes in the frontal lobes (e.g., Lafont et al., 1998; Troyer, Moscovitch, Winocur, Alexander, & Stuss, 1998a; Troyer et al., 1998b; York, Levin, Grossman, Lai, & Krauss, 2003).

A few studies have examined the validity of the clustering and switching constructs by calculating correlations between the fluency measures and tests of executive function. Fluency switching was found to be correlated with mental set shifting on a card sorting test among patients with depression (Fossati, Guillaume, Ergis, & Allialaire, 2003). In contrast, among healthy young and older adults, neither clustering nor switching were correlated with Stroop interference scores, categories or perseverations on the Wisconsin Card Sorting Test, or errors on a self-ordered pointing task (Hughes & Bryan, 2002). Also, neither clustering nor switching were correlated with the Ruff Figural Fluency Test total patterns, or the California Verbal Learning Test clustering score (Abwender et al., 2001). Among patients with Parkinson's disease undergoing pallidotomy, clustering was not related to any composite cognitive score (i.e., tests of attention, language, executive ability, and memory) whereas switching was related to all composite scores (Demakis, Mercury, Sweet, Rezak, Eller, & Vergenz, 2003). Clearly, construct validity of the clustering and switching scores appears to be weak in these studies. Although examining correlations between similar tests is a common approach to validity testing, its relevance to tests of executive functioning is less clear, given that executive functions consist of various components, each mediated by different brain regions, and correlations among them are not necessarily expected. It would be interesting to examine correlations between switching scores on verbal fluency tasks and switching scores on other types of cognitive tasks (e.g., switching on attention tasks; Meiran, 1996).

Optimizing fluency performance

Clustering and switching can be thought of as strategies that an individual adopts. In other words, when an individual is requested to generate a large number of words in a limited amount of time, he or she may consciously decide to adopt a strategy of generating words within related clusters or, in contrast, to switch rapidly between clusters in order to maximize his or her performance. The question has arisen regarding what the optimal strategy might be. The research reviewed previously (Troyer et al., 1997) indicates a positive, linear relationship between cluster size and total number of words generated, suggesting that the optimal strategy may be to produce very large clusters in order to maximize the number of words produced. However, this linear finding may reflect a restricted range of cluster size, as most of our participants adopted highly successful strategies and did not use extremely large clusters. Thus, there may be an optimal range of clustering, wherein extremely small *or* extremely large clusters result in a smaller number of words generated in comparison to clusters within the optimal range. To answer the question of optimal strategy, we conducted a study that increased the range of cluster size by requiring participants to generate words within clusters of specified sizes ranging from very small to very large, and we examined the relationship between cluster size and words produced.

Participants were 41 community-dwelling older adults ranging in age from 60 to 71 years ($M = 65.4$, $SD = 3.5$). Level of education ranged from 8 to 18 years ($M = 13.8$, $SD = 2.3$). Participants were screened via interview for neurologic and psychiatric problems and scored at least 25/30 on the Mini Mental Status Examination (Folstein et al., 1975). The mean age-corrected scaled score on the Vocabulary subtest of the Wechsler Adult Intelligence Scale—Revised (Wechsler, 1981) was 12.3 ($SD = 1.9$), indicating above-average verbal intellectual abilities. All participants were fluent in English.

Seven phonemic fluency tasks (i.e., B, C, L, M, P, R, and T) and four semantic fluency tasks (i.e., animals, articles of clothing, occupations, and subjects of study) were administered to each participant. Pilot data showed that the mean number of words generated and the mean cluster size among the seven phonemic tasks and among the four semantic tasks were approximately equivalent (i.e., within 1 standard deviation). A time interval of 60 s was alloted for each fluency task. The first phonemic and semantic trials were administered to each participant according to standard administration procedures. On subsequent trials, participants were instructed to generate words within subgroups of specified sizes containing phonetically related or semantically related words for the phonemic and semantic fluency tasks, respectively (e.g., "F-words" in subgroups of three: far, fame, fall / fly, flower, flop / fee, free, flea / family, fair, fabulous / future, fur, furniture; "plants" in subgroups of four: maple, pine, elm, spruce / tulip, rose, daffodil, carnation / ivy, fern, spider plant, cactus / fir, willow, oak, cedar). Participants were told that they were allowed to repeat subcategories, although not successively, and that they should try to avoid repeating words. Before conducting these trials, sample responses and untimed practice trials were given. Cluster sizes of 0, 1, 2, 3, 4, and 5 were used for the phonemic and semantic tasks. Because there were more phonemic tasks than semantic tasks, in order to have a similar number of data points in each cluster size for each task, 28 participants performed all fluency trials, and 13 additional participants performed only the semantic trials.

Trend analysis (Winer, Brown, & Michels, 1991) was used to test for a quadratic relation and, by contrast, a linear relation between cluster size and number of correct words generated on the phonemic and semantic fluency tests. Figure 9.2 shows the number of words produced under each cluster-size condition. For phonemic fluency, the quadratic function was significant, $F(1, 27) = 7.24$, $p = 0.012$, and the linear function was not significant, $F(1, 27) < 1$. Similarly, for semantic fluency, the quadratic function was significant, $F(1, 40) = 29.45$, $p < 0.001$, and the linear function was not significant, $F(1, 40) < 1$.

There are two interesting implications regarding optimal fluency strategies suggested by these data: (1) Because clustering and switching are negatively correlated (Troyer et al., 1997), the best approach may be to balance clustering and switching rather than to focus on either alone. There is a clear cost to switching, and one would not want to switch too frequently. However, this cost is outweighed by time spent in a category without getting new items. (2) For both phonemic and semantic fluency, the best strategy was to produce clusters that were intermediate in size, about three to four items. It is possible that the optimal size of the cluster is determined by space in working memory. After that space (three to four items) is filled, the individual may have to start over, even in the same category, which means that it is no more efficient to continue clustering rather than to switch.

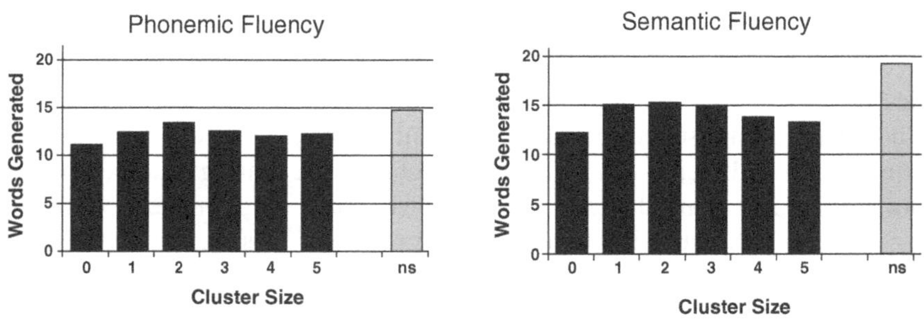

Figure 9.2 Number of words generated for each cluster size when participants were instructed to produce clusters of specified sizes ("ns" indicates that the cluster size was not specified, i.e., standard instructions were used).

Clinical applications

Clustering and switching have been shown to be dissociable components of verbal fluency performance. That is, as reviewed subsequently, clustering and switching show distinct relationships with overall fluency performance, and they are differentially affected by experimental manipulations and by neurological diseases and disorders. These differences suggest that an examination of clustering vs. switching may be useful in determining cognitive strengths and weaknesses and in making differential diagnoses in individual neuropsychological assessments.

Clustering and switching appear to play different roles in the performance of phonemic vs. semantic fluency among healthy adults. On phonemic fluency, switching was more highly correlated than clustering with total number of words generated. In contrast, on semantic fluency, clustering and switching were equally highly correlated with total number of words generated (Beatty, Testa, English, & Winn, 1997; Robert et al., 1998; Troyer et al., 1997). This pattern indicates that switching drives the number of words generated on phonemic fluency, whereas both clustering and switching are important on semantic fluency.

Patient studies

Following the initial identification and description of the clustering and switching components of verbal fluency tasks, numerous studies examining these variables in various populations have been conducted. As previously reviewed, clustering is thought to reflect temporal-lobe-based processes and should thus be decreased in patient populations with temporal-lobe involvement, whereas switching is thought to reflect frontal-lobe processes and should be decreased in populations with frontal involvement.

Regarding clustering, as expected, patients with left temporal lobectomy show decreased clustering on semantic fluency relative to patients with right temporal lobectomy (Troyer et al., 1998a). Early Alzheimer's disease, known to affect temporal regions preferentially early in the disease, is associated with decreased clustering on both phonemic and semantic fluency (Troyer et al., 1998b). Studies on patients with more severe Alzheimer's dementia have found global fluency impairments, affecting both clustering and switching (Epker et al., 1999; Tröster et al., 1998). Thus, it appears that a dissociation between clustering and switching is obtained only during the early stages of Alzheimer's disease, when the neuropathological changes in the brain are presumably more circumscribed.

Switching has been found to be affected by a number of experimental manipulations and conditions, supporting the role of the frontal lobes in this fluency component. Divided attention paradigms have been used as models of frontal-lobe dysfunction, such that under conditions of divided attention, healthy adults often show cognitive patterns similar to those of patients with frontal-lobe lesions (Moscovitch, 1994). On fluency tasks, divided attention results in decreased switching by healthy adults whereas clustering is generally unaffected (Rende et al., 2002; Troyer et al., 1997). Normal aging is also associated with decreased switching and intact clustering (Troyer, 2000; but see Hughes & Bryan, 2002, who obtained no age differences). Given prevalent theories that brain changes associated with normal aging predominate in the frontal lobes (e.g., Raz, 1996; West, 1996), this finding further supports the role of the frontal lobes in switching. More direct evidence of a relationship between switching and frontal lobe functioning comes from studies of patients with focal brain lesions. We found that patients with left-dorsolateral or superior-medial frontal lesions switched less frequently and produced normal cluster sizes in comparison to age-matched controls (Troyer et al., 1998a). Similarly, in a single case study of a patient with a focal left-hemisphere basal-ganglia lesion (presumably disrupting left frontal functioning), switching but not clustering was lower than expected (Troyer, Black, Armilio, & Moscovitch, 2004). Likewise, lesions of the globus pallidus (from pallidotomy performed for Parkinson's disease) result in decreased switching but not clustering (Demakis et al., 2003; Tröster, Woods, Fields, Hanisch, & Beatty, 2002; York et al., 2003). Neurodegenerative disorders that disrupt frontal/subcortical functioning are also associated with decreased switching. Several studies show the general pattern of greater deficits in switching than clustering by patients with Parkinson's disease with dementia (Epker et al., 1999; Tröster et al., 1998; Troyer et al., 1998b), Huntington's disease (Ho, Sahakian, Robbins, Barker, Rosser, & Hodges, 2002; Rich, Troyer, Bylsma, & Brandt, 1999; but see Tröster et al., 1998, who obtained global impairments), and multiple sclerosis (Tröster et al., 1998). Patients with Parkinson's disease with no dementia are generally unimpaired on all fluency measures (Tröster et al., 1998; Troyer et al., 1998b) although some studies have found specific deficits on switching (Donovan, Siegert, McDowall, & Abernathy, 1999) or both clustering and switching (Epker et al., 1999). Psychiatric disorders associated with decreased frontal lobe functioning, including schizophrenia and depression, also show general patterns of decreased fluency switching and intact clustering (Fossati et al., 2003; Lafont et al., 1998; Robert et al., 1998; Zakzanis, Troyer, Rich, & Heinrichs, 2000).

In conclusion, the qualitative measures of verbal fluency performance, clustering and switching, have proven to be of interest to clinical and experimental neuropsychologists. There are a number of different ways to conceptualize these constructs. Our conceptualization and definition of these fluency components have spawned independent studies that support our findings (e.g., Ho et al., 2002; Rende et al., 2002) and some that find discrepancies and suggest alternative methods (e.g., Abwender et al., 2001; Mayr, 2002). The normative data, psychometric information, and clinical findings reported here should help clinicians determine the usefulness of this type of information for individual neuropsychological evaluation.

References

Abwender, D. A., Swan, J. G., Bowerman, J. T., & Connolly, S. W. (2001). Qualitative analysis of verbal fluency output: Review and comparison of several scoring methods. *Assessment*, *8*, 323–338.

Anderson, N. D., Craik, F. I. M., & Naveh-Benjamin, M. (1998). The attentional demands of encoding and retrieval in younger and older adults: Evidence from divided attention costs. *Psychology and Aging*, *13*, 405–423.

Beatty, W. W., Testa, J. A., English, S., & Winn, P. (1997). Influences of clustering and switching on the verbal fluency performance of patients with Alzheimer's disease. *Aging, Neuropsychology, and Cognition*, *4*, 273–279.

Bousfield, W. A., & Sedgewick, C. H. W. (1944). An analysis of restricted associative responses. *Journal of General Psychology*, *30*, 149–165.

Corcoran, R., & Upton, D. (1993). A role for the hippocampus in card sorting? *Cortex*, *29*, 293–304.

Crowe, S. F. (1992). Dissociation of two frontal lobe syndromes by a test of verbal fluency. *Journal of Clinical and Experimental Neuropsychology*, *14*, 327–339.

Cuenod, C. A., Bookheimer, S. Y., Hertz-Pannier, L., Zefiro, T. A., Theodore, W. H., & Le Bihan, D. (1995). Functional MRI during word generation, using conventional equipment: A potential tool for language localization in the clinical environment. *Neurology*, *45*, 1821–1827.

Demakis, G. J., Mercury, M. G., Sweet, J. J., Rezak, M., Eller, T., & Vergenz, S. (2003). Qualitative analysis of verbal fluency before and after unilateral pallidotomy. *Clinical Neuropsychologist*, *17*, 322–330.

Donovan, K., Siegert, R., McDowall, J., & Abernathy, D. (1999). Clustering and switching in verbal fluency in Parkinson's disease. *New Zealand Journal of Psychology*, *28*, 61–66.

Epker, M. O., Lacritz, L. H., & Cullum, C. M. (1999). Comparative analysis of qualitative verbal fluency performance in normal elderly and demented populations. *Journal of Clinical and Experimental Neuropsychology*, *21*, 425–434.

Folstein, M. F., Folstein, S. E., & McHugh, P. R. (1975). Mini-Mental State: A practical method for grading the cognitive state of patients for the clinician. *Journal of Psychiatric Research*, *12*, 189–198.

Fossati, P., Guillaume, Le B., Ergis, A.-M., & Allialaire, J.-F. (2003). Qualitative analysis of verbal fluency in depression. *Psychiatry Research*, *117*, 17–24.

Frith, C. D., Friston, K. J., Liddle, P. F., & Frackowiak, R. S. J. (1991). A PET study of word finding. *Neuropsychologia*, *29*, 1137–1148.

Gruenewald, P. J., & Lockhead, G. R. (1980). The free recall of category examples. *Journal of Experimental Psychology: Human Learning and Memory*, *6*, 225–240.

Ho, A. K., Sahakian, B. J., Robbins, T. W., Barker, R. A., Rosser, A. E., & Hodges, J. R. (2002). Verbal fluency in Huntington's disease: A longitudinal analysis of phonemic and semantic clustering and switching. *Neuropsychologia*, *40*, 1277–1284.

Hughes, D. L., & Bryan, J. (2002). Adult age differences in strategy use during verbal fluency performance. *Journal of Clinical and Experimental Neuropsychology*, *24*, 642–654.

Klein, D., Milner, B., Zatorre, R. J., Meyer, E., & Evans, A. C. (1995). The neural substrates underlying word generation: A bilingual functional-imaging study. *Proceedings of the National Academy of Sciences*, *92*, 2899–2903.

Lafont, V., Medecin, I., Robert, P. H., Beaulieu, F. E., Kazes, M., Danion, J. M., Prignuey, D., & Darcourt, G. (1998). Initiation and supervisory processes in schizophrenia and depression. *Schizophrenia Research*, *34*, 49–57.

Martin, R. C., Loring, D. W., Meador, K. J., & Lee, G. P. (1990). The effects of lateralized temporal lobe dysfunction on formal and semantic word fluency. *Neuropsychologia*, *28*, 823–829.

Mattis, S. (1988). *Dementia rating scale*. Odessa, FL: Psychological Assessment Resources.

Mayr, U. (2002). On the dissociation between clustering and switching in verbal fluency: Comment on Troyer, Moscovitch, Winocur, Alexander, and Stuss. *Neuropsychologia*, *40*, 562–566.

Meiran, N. (1996). The reconfiguration of processing mode prior to task performance. *Journal of Experimental Psychology: Memory, Learning, and Cognition*, *22*, 1423–1442.

Miceli, G., Caltagirone, C., Gainotti, G., Masullo, C., & Silveri, M. C. (1981). Neuropsychological correlates of localized cerebral lesions in non-aphasic brain-damaged patients. *Journal of Clinical Neuropsychology*, *3*, 53–63.

Moscovitch, M. (1994). Cognitive resources and dual-task interference effects at retrieval in normal people: The role of the frontal lobes and medial temporal cortex. *Neuropsychology*, *8*, 524–534.

Perret, E. (1974). The left frontal lobe of man and the suppression of habitual responses in verbal categorical behaviour. *Neuropsychologia*, *12*, 323–330.

Pollio, H. R. (1964). Composition of associative clusters. *Journal of Experimental Psychology*, *67*, 199–208.

Raskin, S. A., & Rearick, E. (1996). Verbal fluency in individuals with mild traumatic brain injury. *Neuropsychology*, *10*, 416–422.

Raz, N. (1996). Neuroanatomy of the aging brain observed in vivo: A review of structural MRI findings. In E. D. Bigler (Ed.), *Neuroimaging II: Clinical applications* (pp. 153–184). New York: Plenum.

Rende, B., Ramsberger, G., & Miyake, A. (2002). Commonalities and differences in the working memory components underlying letter and category fluency tasks: A dual-task investigation. *Neuropsychology*, *16*, 309–321.

Rich, J. B., Troyer, A. K., Bylsma, F. W., & Brandt, J. (1999). Phonemic clustering and switching during word list generation in Huntington's disease: Relationship to other neuropsychological measures and disease progression. *Neuropsychology*, *13*, 525–531.

Robert, P. H., Lafont, V., Medecin, I., Berthet, L., Thauby, S., Baudu, C., & Darcourt, G. (1998). Clustering and switching strategies in verbal fluency tasks: Comparison between schizophrenic and healthy subjects. *Journal of the International Neuropsychological Society*, *4*, 539–546.

Rosen, V. M., & Engle, R. W. (1997). The role of working memory capacity in retrieval. *Journal of Experimental Psychology: General*, *126*, 211–227.

Ross, T. P. (2003). The reliability of cluster and switch scores for the Controlled Oral Word Association Test. *Archives of Clinical Neuropsychology*, *18*, 153–164.

Spreen, O., & Strauss, E. (1998). *A compendium of neuropsychological tests: Administration, norms, and commentary* (2nd ed.). New York: Oxford University Press.

Stuss, D. T., Alexander, M. P., Hamer, L., Palumbo, C., Dempster, R., Binns, M., Levine, B., & Izukawa, D. (1998). The effects of focal anterior and posterior brain lesions on verbal fluency. *Journal of the International Neuropsychological Society*, *4*, 265–278.

Tröster, A. I., Fields, J. A., Testa, J. A., Paul, R. H., Blanco, C. R., Hames, K. A., Salmon, D. P., & Beatty, W. W. (1998). Cortical and subcortical influences on clustering and switching in the performance of verbal fluency tasks. *Neuropsychologia*, *36*, 295–304.

Tröster, A. I., Salmon, D. P., McCullough, D., & Butters, N. (1989). A comparison of the category fluency deficits associated with Alzheimer's and Huntington's disease. *Brain and Language*, *37*, 500–513.

Tröster, A. I., Woods, S. P., Fields, J. A., Hanisch, C., & Beatty, W. W. (2002). Declines in switching underlie verbal fluency changes after unilateral pallidal surgery in Parkinson's disease. *Brain and Cognition*, *50*, 207–217.

Troyer, A. K. (2000). Normative data for clustering and switching on verbal fluency tests. *Journal of Clinical and Experimental Neuropsychology*, *22*, 370–378.

Troyer, A. K., Black, S. E., Armilio, M. L., & Moscovitch, M. (2004). Cognitive and motor functioning in a patient with selective infarction of the left basal ganglia: Evidence for decreased non-routine response selection and performance. *Neuropsychologia*, *42*, 902–911.

Troyer, A. K., Moscovitch, M., & Winocur, G. (1997). Clustering and switching as two components of verbal fluency: Evidence from younger and older healthy adults. *Neuropsychology*, *11*, 138–146.

Troyer, A. K., Moscovitch, M., Winocur, G., Alexander, M., & Stuss, D. (1998). Clustering and switching on verbal fluency: The effect of focal frontal- and temporal-lobe lesions. *Neuropsychologia*, *36*, 499–504.

Troyer, A. K., Moscovitch, M., Winocur, G., Leach, L., & Freedman, M. (1998). Clustering and switching on verbal fluency tests in Alzheimer's and Parkinson's disease. *Journal of the International Neuropsychological Society*, *4*, 137–143.

Wechsler, D. (1981). *The Wechsler Adult Intelligence Scale—Revised.* New York: The Psychological Corporation.

West, R. L. (1996). An application of prefrontal cortex function theory to cognitive aging. *Psychological Bulletin*, *120*, 272–292.

Winer, B. J., Brown, D. R., & Michels, K. M. (1991). *Statistical principles in experimental design* (3rd ed.). New York: McGraw-Hill.

Wixted, J. T., & Rohrer, D. (1994). Analyzing the dynamics of free recall: An integrative review of the empirical literature. *Psychonomic Bulletin and Review*, *1*, 89–106.

York, M. K., Levin, H. S., Grossman, R. G., Lai, E. C., & Krauss, J. K. (2003). Clustering and switching in phonemic fluency following pallidotomy for the treatment of Parkinson's disease. *Journal of Clinical and Experimental Neuropsychology*, *25*, 110–121.

Zakzanis, K. K., Troyer, A. K., Rich, J. B., & Heinrichs, R. W. (2000). Component analysis of verbal fluency in patients with schizophrenia. *Neuropsychiatry, Neuropsychology, and Behavioral Neurology*, *13*, 239–245.

Appendix[1]

Scoring rules for clustering and switching

Total number of correct words generated

This was calculated as the sum of all words produced, excluding errors and repetitions.

Mean cluster size

Cluster size was counted starting with the second word in a cluster. That is, a single word was given a cluster size of 0, two words had a cluster size of 1, three words had a cluster size of 2, and so forth. Errors and repetitions were included. The mean cluster size was computed for the three phonemic trials and for the two semantic trials.

Number of switches

This was calculated as the total number of transitions between clusters, including single words, for the three phonemic trials combined and for the two semantic trials combined. Errors and repetitions were included.

Phonemic fluency

Clusters on phonemic fluency trials consisted of successively generated words that shared any of the following phonemic characteristics:

First letters: words beginning with same first two letters, such as "arm" and "art"
Rhymes: words that rhyme, such as "sand" and "stand"
First and last sounds: words differing only by a vowel sound, regardless of the actual spelling, such as "sat," "seat," "soot," "sight," and "sought"
Homonyms: words with two or more different spellings, such as "some" and "sum," as indicated by the participant

Semantic fluency

Clusters on semantic fluency trials consisted of successively generated words belonging to the same subcategories, as specified below. Commonly generated examples are listed for each subcategory, although listings are not exhaustive.

[1]Adapted with permission from Troyer, A. K., Moscovitch, M., & Winocur, G. (1997). Clustering and switching as two components of verbal fluency: Evidence from younger and older healthy adults. *Neuropsychology*, *11*, 145–146, published by American Psychological Association.

Animals

African animals: aardvark, antelope, buffalo, camel, chameleon, cheetah, chimpanzee, cobra, eland, elephant, gazelle, giraffe, gnu, gorilla, hippopotamus, hyena, impala, jackal, lemur, leopard, lion, manatee, mongoose, monkey, ostrich, panther, rhinoceros, tiger, wildebeest, warthog, zebra

Australian animals: emu, kangaroo, kiwi, opossum, platypus, Tasmanian devil, wallaby, wombat

Arctic/Far North animals: auk, caribou, musk ox, penguin, polar bear, reindeer, seal

Farm animals: chicken, cow, donkey, ferret, goat, horse, mule, pig, sheep, turkey

North America animals: badger, bear, beaver, bobcat, caribou, chipmunk, cougar, deer, elk, fox, moose, mountain lion, puma, rabbit, raccoon, skunk, squirrel, wolf

Water animals: alligator, auk, beaver, crocodile, dolphin, fish, frog, lobster, manatee, muskrat, newt, octopus, otter, oyster, penguin, platypus, salamander, sea lion, seal, shark, toad, turtle, whale

Beasts of burden: camel, donkey, horse, llama, ox

Animals used for their fur: beaver, chinchilla, fox, mink, rabbit

Pets: budgie, canary, cat, dog, gerbil, golden retriever, guinea pig, hamster, parrot, rabbit

Birds: budgie, condor, eagle, finch, kiwi, macaw, parakeet, parrot, pelican, penguin, robin, toucan, woodpecker

Bovine: bison, buffalo, cow, musk ox, yak

Canine: coyote, dog, fox, hyena, jackal, wolf

Deers: antelope, caribou, eland, elk, gazelle, gnu, impala, moose, reindeer, wildebeest

Feline: bobcat, cat, cheetah, cougar, jaguar, leopard, lion, lynx, mountain lion, ocelot, panther, puma, tiger

Fish: bass, guppy, salmon, trout

Insects: ant, beetle, cockroach, flea, fly, praying mantis

Insectivores: aardvark, anteater, hedgehog, mole, shrew

Primates: ape, baboon, chimpanzee, gibbon, gorilla, human, lemur, marmoset, monkey, orangutan, shrew

Rabbits: coney, hare, pika, rabbit

Reptiles/amphibians: alligator, chameleon, crocodile, frog, gecko, iguana, lizard, newt, salamander, snake, toad, tortoise, turtle

Rodents: beaver, chinchilla, chipmunk, gerbil, gopher, groundhog, guinea pig, hamster, hedgehog, marmot, mole, mouse, muskrat, porcupine, rat, squirrel, woodchuck

Weasels: badger, ferret, marten, mink, mongoose, otter, polecat, skunk

Supermarket items

Fruits: applesauce, bananas, cranberries, juice, mango, nectarines, peaches, raisins

Vegetables: avocado, beans, carrots, eggplant, olives, pickles, tomatoes, zucchini

Dairy case items: cheese, cream, cream cheese, eggs, milk, sour cream, yogurt

Meats: bacon, chicken, fish, hamburger, hot dogs, pork, salmon, sausage, tuna

Beverages: coffee, juice, lemonade, milk, orange juice, pop, tea, water, wine

Condiments: jelly, ketchup, marmalade, mayonnaise, pickles, relish, salad dressing

Flavourings: chives, cinnamon, parsley, pepper, sage, salt, vanilla, vinegar

Sweets and snacks: candy, cake, crackers, donuts, gum, ice cream, pie, popcorn, pudding, torte

Grain products: barley, bread, cereal, corn meal, flour, macaroni, meal, muffins, oats, rice

Baking supplies: baking powder, cornstarch, eggs, flour, salt, shortening, spices, vanilla

Specific meals/dishes: coffee, eggs, syrup, waffles, spaghetti, tomato sauce, lettuce, onions, radishes, salad dressing; pork, beans

Household goods: ammonia, detergent, disinfectant, gift wrap, Kleenex, magazines, mop, pans, paper bags, paper towels, stamps, tin foil, toilet paper, wax paper

Personal toiletries: aspirin, comb, deodorant, medicine, mouthwash, toothpaste, vitamins

Infrastructure: aisles, basket, butcher, cash register, cashier, grocery bags, pharmacy, price tags, shelves, shopping cart

General scoring rules

In the case where two categories overlapped, with some items belonging to both categories, some items belonging exclusively to the first category, and some items belonging exclusively to the second category, the overlapping items were assigned to both categories. For example, for "dog, cat, tiger, lion," the first two items were scored as pets, and the last three items were scored as feline. "Cat" was included in both the pet category and the feline category.

In the case where smaller clusters were embedded within larger ones, or two categories overlapped, but all items could correctly be assigned to a single category, only the larger, common category was used. For example, for "sly, slit, slim, slam" all begin with "sl," but an additional cluster was not scored for the last two words, which differ only by a vowel sound.

10 Derived adult Trail Making Test indices

Greg J. Lamberty and Bradley N. Axelrod

Purpose

The Trail Making Test (TMT) is a measure of psychomotor speed and efficiency. It includes elements of attention, visuomotor tracking/scanning, and cognitive set-shifting ability. There are diverse opinions regarding the issue of whether the TMT is a measure of "executive function," though it is frequently described in this way in the neuropsychological literature (Arbuthnott & Frank, 2000; Lezak, Howieson, & Loring, 2004; Mitrushina, Boone, & D'Elia, 1999; Spreen & Strauss, 1998). Reitan and Wolfson (1985) described the TMT as "one of the best measures of general brain functions" because of the complex combination of different skills needed for successful completion of the task. The TMT remains one of the most commonly used neuropsychological test measures (Camara, Nathan, & Puente, 2000).

Existing studies have evaluated the contribution of age, education, and gender on TMT performance (e.g., Heaton, Miller, Taylor, & Grant, 2003). Several studies have looked specifically at various derived TMT indices, presumably as a means of divining information not readily available through raw scores alone (Arbuthnott & Frank, 2000; Corrigan & Hinkeldey, 1987; Drane, Yuspeh, Huthwaite, & Klinger, 2002; Hester, Kinsella, Ong, & McGregor, 2005; Horton & Roberts, 2001; Lamberty, Putnam, Chatel, Bieliauskas, & Adams, 1994; Lange, Iverson, Sakrewski, Ethel-King, & Franzen, 2005; Martin, Hoffman, & Donders, 2003). Typically, indices have been examined to minimize the substantial effect of demographic factors or to characterize a more pure aspect of cognitive functioning by using a patient as his/her own "control." The considerable demands of motor skill and speed are frequent confounds when comparing an individual's time-to-completion performance to a broad normative sample (see Chapter 4 in this book regarding the use of the Oral TMT as another method to control for motor confounds). In contrast, comparing an individual's own TMT-A and TMT-B scores effectively allows these confounding variables to be minimized. Whatever it is that differs between TMT-A and TMT-B should be more accurately reflected in such derived scores.

Source

The TMT is available from Reitan Neuropsychology Laboratory. It is also reported by some to be in the public domain (e.g., Horton & Roberts, 2003; Lezak et al., 2004). The advent of the currently used form of the TMT is not fully clear, despite efforts to track this down by earnest neuropsychological historians (e.g., Boake, 2002; Horton, 1979). Most sources describe the TMT as having its origins in the Army Individual Test Battery (1944), while crediting Reitan with popularizing the test and making it commercially available as the TMT, as a component of the Halstead Reitan Neuropsychological Test Battery (e.g., Lezak et al., 2004; Mitrushina, Boone, & D'Elia, 1999; Spreen & Strauss, 1998).

Boake (2002) talks briefly about the TMT history in his article covering the history of some modern intelligence measures. He and others have also shared their collected wisdom regarding the genesis of today's TMT in other forums and in personal communications. The original description of a measure that is reminiscent of the currently used TMT is given in an article by Brown and Partington (1942). In this article, a measure referred to as the "Distributed Attention Test" is described as "a modification of the Taylor Number Series." Subjects completed three different tasks, tracing first by numbers, then by letters, then in an alternating fashion (similar to TMT, Part B). The Army Individual Test Battery had a subtest referred to as the "Trailmaking Test," which was described in an article by Armitage (1946) who later published work based on this battery of tests with Reitan. Following the war, the TMT was republished in the Leiter–Partington Adult Performance Scale and subsequently the Leiter Adult Intelligence Scale. The measure was called the "Pathways" subtest (Partington & Leiter, 1949) and was said to differ from the version of Trail Making that eventually emerged as part of the Halstead Reitan Battery (HRB). Thus, there remain some questions regarding the claim of whether the current clinically used form of the TMT is in the public domain. To date there has not been a clear exposition of this specific question.

Description

The TMT consists of two parts. TMT Part A (TMT-A) is printed on two sides of a single sheet of paper. The front side consists of a sample test. There are eight numbered circles in a small rectangular array that comprises the sample. The subject is first given instructions for the sample for Trail A, after which they receive instructions for the full version on the opposite side of the page.

The same sequence is repeated for TMT Part B (TMT-B). The principal difference between Trails A and B is that Trail B contains both numbered and lettered circles, requiring the subject to shift between numbers and letters when connecting the circles (i.e., 1 – A – 2 – B – 3 – C … L – 13). This set-shifting component of Trail B is typically cited as the element that makes this a measure of cognitive flexibility or executive functioning.

Administration

Spreen and Strauss (1998, pp. 533–535) provide a thorough exposition of examiner instructions for TMT-A and TMT-B in their *Compendium*. These instructions will not be repeated here, except to highlight basic aspects of a typical administration. Spreen and Strauss' (1998) recommended instructions are essentially the same as those recommended by Reitan (1992), as well as by other general sources (Lezak et al., 2004; Mitrushina, Boone, & D'Elia, 1999).

Briefly, the subject is first presented with the sample portion of TMT-A. He is instructed to connect numbered circles as quickly as possible, going from 1 to 25 (which is marked with the word "END"), while not lifting the pencil from the paper. Any mistakes made on the TMT-A sample are identified and corrective feedback is given. The subject is then given the actual TMT-A form and is instructed to complete it in the same manner as the sample. The examiner points out any errors and the subject is directed to continue at the point where an error is made. Timing continues as errors are identified and corrected. The examiner records time to completion in seconds and may also note the number of errors.

A similar pattern is followed for TMT-B. That is, the subject is first given a sample test, which now consists of the same 8 circle array as seen in the TMT-A sample. However, the circles now contain the first four Arabic numerals (1–4) and the first four English alphabet letters (A–D). On the sample for TMT-B, the correct sequence is the same spatially as that for the TMT-A sample. That is, the actual path for successful completion of TMT-A and TMT-B sample items is the same. Once subjects successfully complete the TMT-B sample, they are instructed to complete the main TMT-B test sheet. Again, instead of simply connecting consecutively numbered circles, the subject is instructed to connect circles in an alternating fashion, starting with the first number ("1") and subsequently the first letter ("A"). Time to completion is recorded, as with TMT-A. Errors are identified and the subject is directed to correct the mistake and continue to the circle marked "13," which is labeled with the word "END."

Approximate administration time

Administration time for both parts of the TMT is typically between 5 and 10 min. Lezak et al. (2004) note that continuing beyond 4 or 5 min on TMT-B is probably not necessary with some individuals. Some degree of clinical judgment is appropriate in deciding to discontinue measures that are too difficult for a given patient, particularly when their performance has extended beyond well-established norms for significant impairment. In such cases, derived indices are rendered useless.

Scoring

The total time to completion (in seconds) is recorded for Parts A and B of the TMT. Historically, it has been recommended that errors be recorded as well

(Lezak et al., 2004), although it has generally not been the case that this information has been helpful in distinguishing clinical groups. A couple of recent reports indicated that errors were useful in distinguishing between patients with Alzheimer's disease and controls (Amieva et al., 1998; Rasmusson, Zonderman, Kawas, & Resnick, 1998). Yet other studies have indicated that there is little utility in examining the number of errors or error types in brain-damaged patients (Klusman, Cripe, & Dodrill, 1989; Lange et al., 2005; Ruffolo, Guilmette, & Willis, 2000). On balance, the use of error scores has not shown near the clinical utility in distinguishing groups as the basic time to completion data.

Both portions of the TMT have been shown to be sensitive to a range of disorders and varying levels of impairment. However, it has also been shown that typical time to completion data are substantially influenced by the demographic factors of age and education, both within normative and clinical samples (Bornstein, 1985; Horton & Roberts, 2001; Lamberty et al., 1994; Stuss, Stethem, & Poirer, 1987). Further, it has been noted by authors of major normative compendia (Lezak et al., 2004; Mitrushina et al., 1999) that there is often considerable variability across normative studies, thus highlighting the importance of selecting datasets based on specific clinical needs.

Considering demographic factors in normative datasets is a well-established practice in clinical neuropsychology (Heaton et al., 2003; Lamberty, 2002). In their *Revised Comprehensive Norms*, Heaton et al. (2003) illustrate how adherence to a given normative dataset (e.g., Russell, Neuringer, & Goldstein, 1970) can result in significant misclassifications where various demographic factors are concerned. In this context, using derived indices that minimize the effects of demographics on test scores is a clinically sensible practice. Many studies have shown that derived TMT indices do indeed minimize the influence of age and education, while presumably continuing to measure abilities that make the test sensitive to general cognitive impairment (Arbuthnott & Frank, 2000; Hester et al., 2005; Horton & Roberts, 2001; Lamberty et al., 1994).

While several different derived TMT indices and transformations have been proposed and examined, the two that have received the most attention in the literature are the difference (TMT-B minus TMT-A) and ratio (TMT-B divided by TMT-A) scores. The rationale for using these measures stems from the fact that TMT-A and TMT-B share elements of visual tracking/scanning, basic sequencing, and motor speed, while TMT-B has the added element of set-shifting or cognitive flexibility. Presumably, by subtracting or dividing the effects of TMT-A scores from TMT-B scores, the more basic demands of the simpler task (TMT-A) are held constant and a score that is reflective of the unique aspects of TMT-B emerges. A recent study by Arbuthnott and Frank (2000) showed that the B/A ratio was, in fact, the best indicator of executive functioning as indicated by similarity to a set-switching task with little or no motor demands.

Comment

Table 10.1 summarizes data from several normative and clinical studies referenced in this chapter. Time to completion data, difference, and ratio scores are presented as available from the original sources.

Difference score

The value of a derived index is measured by its ability to provide the clinician with unique information as compared to the usual test data. Lezak et al. (2004) describe the difference measure as a technique that "essentially removes the speed element from the test evaluation" (p. 372), while Heaton, Nelson, Thompson, Burks, and Franklin (1985) reasoned that the difference score was a "more pure measure of cognitive efficiency." The basic idea of subtracting from TMT-B the elements it shares with TMT-A is intuitively pleasing. However, it would seem that the difference measure is not likely to provide much unique information in situations where a patient's performance is close to the normative range for both portions (A and B). In such a case, the difference score will remain relatively small. Similarly, as the overall time to completion score increases, the difference score would likely increase, although it is not necessarily reflective of greater difficulty with the additional cognitive demands of TMT-B. As such, it would seem that the difference score would provide a greater level of information in situations where performances were in the lower end of the normative range, but not markedly or severely impaired. This is likely why the difference score has not shown itself to add much to typical time to completion data (Heilbronner, Henry, Buck, Adams, & Fogle, 1991; Horton & Roberts, 2001; Lamberty et al., 1994). Yet, even under circumstances where a derived index is not as effective as usual data in distinguishing between groups, it may be the case that it is less affected by confounds known to influence standard time to completion data, like age, education, and gender.

Reitan and Tarshes (1959) suggested that the TMT difference score was differentially sensitive to left hemisphere lesions, while most other studies have indicated poor discriminative ability, or merely trends toward being able to distinguish between different clinical groups (Corrigan & Hinkeldey, 1987; Heilbronner et al., 1991). Heaton et al. (1985) found that the difference score discriminated between normal individuals and those with multiple sclerosis (MS), although the difference between groups is likely from the shared motor speed in the MS sample. Lamberty et al. (1994) showed that the difference score was significantly different in three different clinical samples as compared to a small normative sample. However, the difference score was significantly correlated with age in all clinical groups, and with education in mild traumatic brain injury (TBI) and neuropsychiatric samples. Horton and Roberts (2001) found that the difference score was significantly affected by all demographic factors that were systematically assessed (i.e., age, education, race, and gender). Thus,

Table 10.1 Summary of data from several normative and clinical studies referenced in this chapter

		TMT-A	*TMT-B*	*B–A*	*B÷A*
Normative samples					
Drane et al. (2002)					
<20	(n = 18)	23.22 (6.56)	52.94 (20.10)	29.72 (16.21)	2.31 (0.58)
20–29	(n = 39)	26.12 (9.78)	60.92 (33.17)	35.31 (27.72)	2.36 (0.78)
30–39	(n = 53)	28.02 (8.78)	72.30 (28.55)	44.13 (26.72)	2.72 (1.21)
40–49	(n = 46)	31.00 (11.21)	81.26 (23.69)	50.04 (20.28)	2.80 (0.93)
50–59	(n = 38)	36.29 (16.41)	103.42 (50.26)	67.24 (39.35)	2.94 (0.88)
60–69	(n = 36)	39.60 (12.14)	105.23 (41.15)	65.60 (33.84)	2.70 (0.77)
70–79	(n = 36)	45.58 (18.91)	152.59 (88.42)	109.14 (73.87)	3.49 (1.76)
>80	(n = 19)	56.37 (20.20)	170.21 (84.68)	113.84 (70.73)	3.05 (1.05)
Hester et al. (2005)					
60–69	(n = 130)	40.1 (16.1)	92.4 (33.4)	52.3 (26.9)	2.43 (0.80)
70–74	(n = 106)	43.9 (16.9)	104.0 (48.2)	60.7 (39.9)	2.49 (1.01)
75–79	(n = 79)	50.4 (21.9)	118.5 (39.4)	68.2 (30.0)	2.47 (0.70)
80–89	(n = 48)	57.9 (33.4)	131.4 (52.5)	73.4 (41.5)	2.43 (0.73)
Lamberty et al. (2005)					
Normal	(n = 64)	26.6 (11.1)	56.6 (19.9)	30.0 (13.3)	2.24 (0.6)
Clinical samples					
Lange et al. (2005)					
Uncomplicated mild	(n = 328)	31.0 (12.8)	82.4 (44.6)	51.4 (38.5)	2.8 (1.1)
Mild with skull fracture	(n = 86)	34.4 (15.9)	94.4 (51.1)	60.0 (46.8)	2.9 (1.4)
Complicated mild	(n = 117)	36.8 (15.0)	104.9 (48.9)	68.2 (41.3)	3.0 (1.2)

Moderate to severe	(n = 40)	50.8 (28.4)	154.7 (68.8)	103.9 (70.9)	3.3 (2.0)
Lamberty et al. (1994)					
Alzheimer's disease	(n = 58)	61.9 (29.3)	214.3 (103.0)	152.3 (87.2)	3.73 (1.7)
Mild TBI	(n = 176)	43.4 (28.7)	111.9 (85.9)	68.5 (69.6)	2.67 (1.3)
Psychiatric	(n = 128)	43.3 (24.4)	103.6 (58.9)	60.3 (13.3)	2.50 (0.9)
Martin et al. (2003)					
Moderate to severe injury	(n = 41)	33.61 (10.28)	84.73 (34.39)		2.57 (0.81)
Mild injury	(n = 59)	29.93 (7.83)	69.34 (23.68)		2.36 (0.72)
Complicated history	(n = 48)	37.50 (19.67)	92.42 (69.53)		2.55 (1.25)
Horton and Roberts (2001) (substance abusers)					
18–20	(n = 241)			37.9 (20.9)	2.44 (0.97)
21–25	(n = 1100)			38.8 (19.8)	2.50 (0.90)
26–30	(n = 1884)			39.3 (19.1)	2.44 (0.86)
31–35	(n = 2022)			41.3 (21.1)	2.47 (0.90)
36–44	(n = 1994)			41.8 (20.7)	2.41 (0.86)
44+	(n = 448)			42.9 (20.5)	2.35 (0.90)

despite the fact that the difference score can discriminate between various clinical groups, it has never done so more effectively than the usual time to completion data, and significant demographic confounds persist, albeit not to as great an extent as with the usual clinically employed scores.

Ratio score

Examination of the ratio between TMT-B and TMT-A performances has been suggested as a means of determining a specific cognitive deficit. For instance, Golden, Osmon, Moses, and Berg (1981) simply suggested that ratio scores of < 2 indicate greater impairment on TMT-A, whereas ratio scores > 3 suggest greater impairment on TMT-B. Expanding on this relationship conceptually, Lezak et al. (1995, 2004) have suggested that a higher B/A ratio is suggestive of difficulties with conceptual tracking. Ratios < 2 are a bit more problematic in that it is difficult to imagine what manner of impairment would result in normatively better performance on the more difficult TMT-B as compared to TMT-A. Lamberty et al. (1994) proposed that this finding might suggest some basic motivational deficits. Namely, it would be difficult for a patient who is inclined to dissimulate to know how much longer it should take them to complete TMT-B than TMT-A. Although this result has not turned out to be the case when examined in a more systematic fashion (Martin et al., 2003). Another admittedly more speculative possibility for smaller ratio scores might be a "warming up" kind of effect wherein the patient performs slowly initially, but subsequently becomes more familiar or comfortable with the nature of the task and does correspondingly better on the second portion (i.e., TMT-B). The most consistent finding regarding the ratio score has been its relative resistance to the substantial influence of demographic factors (Horton & Roberts, 2001; Lamberty et al., 1994).

Corrigan and Hinkeldey (1987) examined the ratio score in a large mixed sample (cerebro vascular accident (CVA), TBI, various etiologies) of patients seen in a rehabilitation hospital setting. They found that both the ratio and difference scores were only marginally able to distinguish lesion laterality. More recent reports have found that the ratio measure is not particularly effective in distinguishing various groups based on head injury severity. Martin et al. (2003) found that the ratio score did not help to distinguish severity-based TBI groups, nor did it reliably identify individuals who were thought to have been malingering or dissimulating. Lange et al. (2005) determined that various derived TMT indices added little to the prediction of head injury severity, though it was the case that the ratio score was least strongly correlated with TMT-B performance, suggesting the possibility that it adds something different interpretively. Lamberty et al. (1994) examined the ratio in several different clinical samples and found that the ratio could distinguish between groups reasonably well, but not as well as usual time to completion data. Axelrod et al. (2000) found that the ratio distinguished between hospital patients and normal comparison subjects on a Hebrew version of the

TMT. Finally, Horton and Roberts (2001) reported results from a huge cohort of drug abusers that essentially verified the pervasive influence of various demographic factors on most TMT regular measures and derived measures—except the ratio score. There was a modestly significant effect of age on the ratio score, but this was in a sample of over 7000 subjects. There are thus mixed findings with regard to the utility of the TMT ratio as a measure to distinguish between various clinical groups and levels of injury severity. As with the difference measure it has typically been the case that the ratio score is not able to better discriminate between clinical groups than the usual clinical time to completion data.

A few recent normative studies have more systematically examined the ratio in normal and normal aging subjects. Drane et al. (2002) provided a normative sample that looked at the derived indices across a broad range of ages. Their findings suggested that both the difference and ratio measures were significantly associated with age, but that the age effect for the ratio was based on elevated ratio scores in the group of patients aged 70 to 79. That is, the 70–79-year-old group ratio score was significantly elevated relative to the three youngest groups. Interestingly, the ratio in this portion of the sample was the highest, while the standard deviations for both difference and ratio scores in this age group were the highest. Drane et al. (2002) also showed that very high levels of false-positive errors would have been made using the ratio cutoff score of 3.0 suggested in the Lamberty et al. (1994) paper. False-positive percentages ranged from 17 to 58, and very highest in the two oldest age groups. In direct contrast to these findings, a recent normative study with older Australian subjects showed very different results with respect to the ratio measure. Hester et al. (2005) found that while the difference score was significantly associated with both age and education, the ratio score was affected by education, but not age. In no case did the group normative data show average ratio scores that exceeded 2.5. The Hester et al. (2005) study had much larger sample sizes in the older age ranges, and even when they broke the sample into greater than and less than 12 grades, the average ratio scores did not approach the mean ratio scores reported by Drane et al. (2002). These findings underscore the point made by Lezak et al. (2004) regarding the use of specific normative samples. It is also the case that further normative work with large samples should present data for the derived indices so that a determination about their utility can be more thoroughly made.

References

Amieva, H., Lafont, S., Auriacombe, S., Rainville, C., Orgogozo, J. M., Dartigues, J. F., & Fabrigoule, C. (1998). Analysis of error types in the Trail Making Test evidences an inhibitory deficit in dementia of the Alzheimer type. *Journal of Clinical and Experimental Neuropsychology*, *20*, 280–285.

Arbuthnott, K., & Frank, J. (2000). Trail Making Test, part B as a measure of executive control: Validation using a set-switching paradigm. *Journal of Clinical and Experimental Neuropsychology*, *22*, 518–528.

Armitage, S. G. (1946). An analysis of the use of certain psychological tests for the evaluation of brain injury. *Psychological Monographs* (Whole No. 60).

Axelrod, B. N., Aharon-Peretz, J., Tomer, R., & Fisher, T. (2000). Creating interpretation guidelines for the Hebrew Trail Making Test. *Applied Neuropsychology*, *7*, 186–188.

Boake, C. (2002). From the Binet–Simon to the Wechsler–Bellevue: Tracing the history of intelligence testing. *Journal of Clinical & Experimental Neuropsychology*, *24*, 383–405.

Bornstein, R. A. (1985). Normative data on selected neuropsychological measures from a nonclinical sample. *Journal of Clinical Psychology*, *41*, 651–659.

Brown, R. R. & Partington, J. E. (1942). A psychometric comparison of narcotic addicts with hospital attendants. *Journal of General Psychology*, *27*, 71–79.

Butler, M., Retzlaff, P. D., & Vanderploeg, R. (1991). Neuropsychological test usage. *Professional Psychology: Research & Practice*, *22*, 510–512.

Camara, W., Nathan, J., & Puente, A. (2000). Psychological test usage: Implications in professional psychology. *Professional Psychology: Research and Practice*, *31*, 141–154.

Corrigan, J. D., & Hinkeldey, N. S. (1987). Relationships between parts A and B of the Trail Making Test. *Journal of Clinical Psychology*, *43*, 402–409.

Drane, D. L., Yuspeh, R. L., Huthwaite, J. S., & Klinger, L. K. (2002). Demographic characteristics and normative observations for derived Trail Making Test indices. *Neuropsychiatry, Neuropsychology, and Behavioral Neurology*, *15*, 39–43.

Golden, C. J., Osmon, D. C., Moses, J. A., & Berg, R. A. (1981). *Interpretation of the Halstead–Reitan Neuropsychological Test Battery*. New York: Grune & Stratton.

Heaton, R. K., Miller, S. W., Taylor, M. J., & Grant, I. (2003). *Revised comprehensive norms for an expanded Halstead–Reitan battery: Demographically adjusted neuropsychological norms for African American and Caucasian adults*. Lutz, FL: Psychological Assessment Resources.

Heaton, R. K., Nelson, L. M., Thompson, D. S., Burks, J. S., & Franklin, G. M. (1985). Neuropsychological findings in relapsing-remitting and chronic-progressive multiple sclerosis. *Journal of Consulting and Clinical Psychology*, *53*, 103–110.

Heilbronner, R. L., Henry, G. K., Buck, P., Adams, R. L., & Fogle, T. (1991). Lateralized brain damage and performance on Trail Making Test A and B, digit span forward and backward, and TPT memory and location. *Archives of Clinical Neuropsychology*, *6*, 251–258.

Hester, R., Kinsella, G. J., Ong, B., & McGregor, J. (2005). Demographic influences on baseline and derived scores from the Trail Making Test in healthy older Australian adults. *The Clinical Neuropsychologist*, *19*, 45–54.

Horton, A. M. (1979). Some suggestions regarding the clinical interpretation of the Trail Making Test. *Clinical Neuropsychology*, *1*, 20–23.

Horton, A. M., Jr., & Roberts, C. (2001). Derived Trail Making Test indices in a sample of substance abusers: Demographic effects. *International Journal of Neuroscience*, *111*, 147–156.

Horton, A. M., & Roberts, C. (2003). Demographic effects on the Trail Making Test in a drug abuse treatment sample. *Archives of Clinical Neuropsychology*, *18*, 49–56.

Klusman, L. E., Cripe, L. I., & Dodrill, C. B. (1989). Analysis of errors on the Trail Making Test. *Perceptual and Motor Skills*, *68*, 1199–1204.

Lamberty, G. J. (2002). Traditions and trends in neuropsychological assessment. In R. Ferraro (Ed.), *Minority and cross-cultural aspects of neuropsychological assessment*. Lisse, The Netherlands: Swets & Zeitlinger.

Lamberty, G. J., Putnam, S. H., Chatel, D. M., Bieliauskas, L. A., & Adams, K. M. (1994). Derived Trail-Making Test indices: A preliminary report. *Neuropsychiatry, Neuropsychology, & Behavioral Neurology*, *7*, 230–234.

Lange, R. T., Iverson, G. L., Sakrewski, M. J., Ethel-King, P. E., & Franzen, M. D. (2005). Interpreting the Trail Making Test following traumatic brain injury: Comparison of traditional time scores and derived indices. *Journal of Clinical and Experimental Neuropsychology*, *27*, 897–906.

Lezak, M. D. (1995). *Neuropsychological assessment* (3rd ed.). New York: Oxford University Press.

Lezak, M. D., Howieson, D. B., & Loring, D. W. (2004). *Neuropsychological assessment* (4th ed.). New York: Oxford University Press.

Martin, T. A., Hoffman, N. M., & Donders, J. (2003). Clinical utility of the Trail Making Test ratio score. *Applied Neuropsychology*, *10*, 163–169.

Mitrushina, M. N., Boone, K. B., & D'Elia, L. F. (1999). *Handbook of normative data for neuropsychological assessment*. New York: Oxford University Press.

Partington, J. E., & Leiter, R. G. (1949). Partington's pathway test. *The Psychological Service Center Bulletin*, *1*, 9–20.

Rasmusson, D. X., Zonderman, A. B., Kawas, C., & Resnick, S. M. (1998). Effects of age and dementia on the Trail Making Test. *The Clinical Neuropsychologist*, *12*, 169–178.

Reitan, R. M. (1992). *Trail Making Test: Manual for administration and scoring*. Reitan Neuropsychological Laboratory, South Tucson, AZ.

Reitan, R. M., & Tarshes, E. L. (1959). Differential effects of lateralizing lesions on the Trail Making Test. *Journal of Nervous and Mental Disease*, *129*, 257–262.

Reitan, R. M., & Wolfson, D. (1985). *The Halstead–Reitan Neuropsychological Test Battery: Theory and clinical interpretation*. Tucson, AZ: Neuropsychology Press.

Ruffolo, L. F., Guilmette, T. J., & Willis, W. J. (2000). Comparison of time and error rates on the Trail Making Test among patients with head injuries, experimental malingerers, patients with suspected effort on testing, and normal controls. *The Clinical Neuropsychologist*, *14*, 223–230.

Russell, E. W., Neuringer, C., & Goldstein, G. (1970). *Assessment of brain damage: A neuropsychological key approach*. New York: Wiley.

Spreen, O., & Strauss, E. (1998). *A compendium of neuropsychological tests: Administration, norms, and commentary* (2nd ed.). New York: Oxford University Press.

Stuss, D. T., Bisschop, S. M., Alexander, M. P., Levine, B., Katz, D., & Izukawa, D. (2001). The Trail Making Test: A study in focal lesion patients. *Psychological Assessment*, *13*, 230–239.

Stuss, D. T., Stethem, L. L., & Poirer, C. A. (1987). Comparison of three tests of attention and rapid information processing across six age groups. *Clinical Neuropsychologist*, *1*, 139–152.

11 A review of quantified approaches to the qualitative assessment of clock drawing

Holly Tuokko and Megan E. O'Connell

Introduction

Clock drawing has been used for decades in the assessment of neurological and neuropsychiatric conditions. Like many other drawing tasks, clock drawing is sensitive to damage in various brain regions, e.g., parietal lobes (Critchley, 1953; Goodglass & Kaplan, 1972) and frontotemporal regions (Mesulam, 1985; Moore & Wyke, 1984) and this has led clinicians and researchers to examine clock drawing for specific abnormalities. For example, clock drawings have been examined in patients with various lesions sites (e.g., left vs. right hemisphere, cortical vs. subcortical, anterior vs. posterior) and disorders (e.g., mood disorders, schizophrenia, etc.). Most recently, clock drawing has become popular as a screening tool for cognitive impairment emerging in later life. Dementia patients, regardless of etiology, may exhibit diffuse clock-drawing abnormalities. Pan, Stern, Sano, and Mayeux (1989) and Shulman (2000) have argued that clock drawing is an ideal screening tool as it is quick to administer, is well tolerated by even moderately to severely impaired patients, and assesses a wide range of cognitive abilities.

Although clock drawing may appear to be a simple task, multiple cognitive domains are required for accurate execution. The person asked to "draw a clock" must understand the instructions for the task, be able to retrieve clock-related information with different types of memory processes, translate this knowledge through visuoperceptual and visuomotor processes, and evaluate and monitor the output with executive functions. In addition, much of the clock-related information to be recalled is highly abstract and conceptually complex (e.g., meaning of the spatial layout of a clock face, meaning of the hands and their relative lengths). The multi-factorial nature of the processes underlying clock drawing is what makes it highly sensitive for detecting cognitive impairment.

Given the breadth of cognitive domains employed in the act of clock drawing, it is anticipated that many different types of clock-drawing errors may occur. It is primarily for this reason that many different systems or methods for administration and scoring clock drawings have emerged in the literature. The two most common administration procedures are (1) a clock drawn free-hand (free-drawn) or (2) a clock drawn using a pre-drawn circle (pre-drawn). Although these procedures result in the activation of similar cognitive processes, they also may differ. For example, it has been argued that pre-drawn clocks primarily tap perceptual functions whereas free-drawn clocks place greater relative demands on language, memory, and executive functions (Freedman, Leach, Kaplan, Winocur, Shulman, & Delis, 1994). According to Freedman et al. (1994), patients may be selectively impaired on one or the other, or both. Although this may be the case, we have found little empirical evidence describing the proportion of cases showing dissociations. A poorly drawn circle (e.g., too small or asymmetrical) necessarily affects the accuracy with which the remainder of the clock can be drawn (e.g., spatial arrangements of numbers) and limits the amount of information available for interpretation. Using a pre-drawn circle as a matter of course may overcome this problem. Pre-drawn circles, approximately 4 in or 10 cm in diameter, are typically provided on a piece of 8 ½ × 11 in. white paper.

The instructions provided for clock drawing also differ such that certain elements are emphasized more or less. Some procedures request the placement of hands (e.g., all of those reviewed below) and others do not (e.g., Friedman, 1991; Ishiai, Sugishita, Ichikawa, & Gono, 1993; Pan et al., 1989; Watson, Arfken, & Birge, 1993; Wolf-Klein, Silverstone, Levy, & Brod, 1989). Some intentionally avoid referring to 'hands' in the instructions (i.e., set the time to 10 past 11; Shulman, 2000). Even when hand placement is required, the time to which hands are set may vary. Typically, times that require hand placement in both sides of hemi-space are used (e.g., "20 after 8" with the placement in inferior visual quadrant or parietal fields, "10 past/after 11" with the placement in superior quadrants or temporal fields; Freedman et al., 1994). It is argued that "10 past 11" places greater demands on executive functions mediated by the frontal lobes: because of the proximity of the "10" and the "11," a stimulus-bound error (i.e., one hand drawn pointing to the 10) may result, potentially indicating executive dysfunction (Freedman et al., 1994). Times on the hour and half-hour have been shown to be easier tasks (i.e., performed correctly more often) than other times (Tuokko, Hadjistavropoulos, Miller, & Beattie, 1992; Tuokko, Hadjistavropoulos, Miller, Horton, & Beattie, 1995).

Depending on the purposes for which clock drawing is being used, scoring systems may be selected to provide a simple scale of severity of impairment (i.e., ranking from best to worst such as the 5-point scale of Shulman et al. or 10-point scale of Sunderland et al.) or to capture error types reflective of deficits in different cognitive domains. Both Shulman (2000) and Lin et al. (2003) argue that clinicians, who are under time constraints and the pressure of a caseload, need to employ the simplest approach to clock drawing that provides reasonably accurate screening information. However, clock drawing provides potentially very rich information about cognitive processing, brain function, and possibly disease status that may not be demonstrated using simplified approaches. For example, it appears that hand placements and even slight errors in the spatial positioning of numbers are important, at least in the context of screening for dementia (e.g., Schramm, Berger, Mueller, Kratzsch, Peters, & Froelich, 2002). These specific error types then may be classified as normal vs. abnormal or summed within and across error types.

Many scoring systems were developed based on clinical observation and judgement as to which errors are important to consider. It is implied in some systems that the spatial location of errors on the clock face is important (i.e., errors in some quadrants weighted more heavily) but there is no empirical evidence to support this contention. Similarly, the sequencing of number placement plays an important role in some scoring systems (e.g., Royall, Mulroy, Chiodo, & Polk, 1999) but it is not clear that placing the numbers 12, 3, 6, and 9 prior to placing the other numbers is actually indicative of a superior performance. Scoring Roman numerals as errors is also a questionable practice unless the instructions to the patient have been specific as to the requirement for Arabic numbers. In fact, the evidence for reliability and screening validity of a variety of Clock-Drawing Tests (CDT) has been compared as have pre- vs. free-drawn clock procedures, and, to date, there is no consistent, cumulative evidence suggesting superiority of any one measure or procedure (e.g., Bourke, Castleden, Stephen, & Dennis, 1995; Brodaty & Moore, 1997; Heinik, Solomesh, Shein, & Becker, 2002b; Juby, 1999; Juby, Tench, & Baker, 2002; Lee & Lawlor, 1995; Lee, Swanwick, Coen, & Lawlor, 1996; Powlishta et al., 2002; Ravaglia et al., 2003; Richardson & Glass, 2002; Royall et al., 1999; Schramm et al., 2002; Souder, O'Sullivan, & Pechenik, 1999; Storey, Rowland, Basic, & Conforti, 2001; Suhr, Grace, Allen, Nadler, & McKenna, 1998; Tuokko, Hadjistavropoulos, Rae, & O'Rourke, 2000).

Only two systems (i.e., Freedman et al., 1994; Tuokko et al., 1995) have taken a normative approach to determining which errors and/or how many errors are indicative of impairment. This approach may be particularly important for the identification of cognitive impairment in later life because the normal aging process is associated with certain types of decline in cognitive processing; scoring systems need to be able to clearly delineate the effects of age from age-related pathology. By examining error types, we are provided with the opportunity to learn more about how clock drawing reflects underlying cognitive impairment and how this, in turn, is related to global and specific areas of brain damage. All clock-drawing approaches require the same amount of time for administration (i.e., to have a clock drawn), and differences that occur in the amount of time required for reliable scoring are minimal. O'Rourke et al. (1997) note that the time taken for scoring was no more than 3–5 min for each of five different scoring systems.

The clock-drawing measures selected for review here are those that have taken a quantified process approach to the development of a scoring system and provide reliability data. Others, such as those resulting in scales of severity (e.g., Lam et al., 1998; Libon, Swenson, Barnoski, & Sands, 1993; Shulman, Shedletsky, & Silver, 1986; Spreen & Strauss, 1998; Sunderland, Hill, Mellow, & Lawlor, 1989; Wolf-Klein et al., 1989), are not included. Finally, we did not include Watson et al.'s (1993) system, as it is solely based on the placement of numbers within the four quadrants, Ishiai et al.'s (1993) clock system, because of the limited reliability evidence, or Solomon et al.'s (1998) clock system because, to date, the limited research concerns its use in combined screening batteries (Robert et al., 2003; Solomon et al., 1998).

Initially, clock procedures that use a free-drawn clock are reviewed, followed by those for which a pre-drawn clock is provided. Table 11.1 provides a summary of these clock-drawing tasks and defines abbreviations for participant samples used throughout this chapter. In some instances, multiple clocks are drawn (e.g., Freedman et al., 1994; Royall, Cordes, & Polk, 1998); in other instances, clock drawing is administered in the context of a more fulsome assessment of time-related concepts (e.g., Tuokko et al., 1995). Where appropriate, we include descriptions of these broader clock activities.

Overall, it appears that clock drawing lends itself well to the quantified process approach for scoring. A number of clinicians and researchers have developed or adopted this approach in recent years but the full extent of its utility has yet to be determined. In most instances, the adoption of this approach has led to the development of procedures that are objective and this is evident in the reported high levels of inter-rater reliability. An advantage of these methods over the typical process approach where one must witness the drawing is that, with minimal training, many members of the health care team can administer and score clock drawing reliably and this information can be shared.

In the future, it will be important to consider cultural, language, and educational variables as they relate to clock drawing (e.g., Lin et al., 2003). It will also be important to determine the conditions under which clock drawing contributes unique information to the screening process. Some researchers have begun to combine clock-drawing systems with other tests (e.g., the Mini-Mental State Examination [MMSE]) to create screening batteries, and have investigated the accuracy of these combined batteries for detecting dementia (Borson, Scanlan, Brush, Vitaliano, & Dokmak, 2000; Robert et al., 2003; Scanlan & Borson, 2001; Solomon et al., 1998) or predicting motor outcomes following stroke rehabilitation (Adunsky, Fleissig, Levenkrohn, Arad, & Noy, 2002). Schramm et al. (2002) found that adding various clock tasks to the MMSE resulted in increased sensitivity compared to the MMSE alone, but did not report the change in specificity, if any. It will also be important to determine in what other contexts clock drawing can play a role. For example, Seigerschmidt et al. (2002), in differentiating very mild dementia from normal aging, note that relatively simple scoring systems may not be adequate to detect subtle differences in performance and a more detailed scoring system may prove most beneficial in this regard.

Table 11.1 Summary of clock-drawing tasks reviewed in this chapter

Clock task	*Administration*		*Total score*	*Participant samples in addition to 'cognitively normal' older adults*
	Circle	*Time*		
CDIS (Mendez, Ala, & Underwood, 1992)	Free-drawn	11:10	20	Dementia (mixed), Alzheimer's disease (AD), stroke, mood/anxiety disorders, and schizophrenia
CLOX (Royall et al., 1998)	Free-drawn	1:45	15	AD
Rouleau (Rouleau, Salmon, Butters, & Kennedy, 1992)	Free-drawn	11:10	Quantitative 10	Dementia (mixed), AD, Vascular dementia (VaD), Diffuse Lewy body disease (DLBD), Huntington's disease (HD), Parkinson's disease (PD), stroke, and schizophrenia
			Qualitative—errors	AD, HD, VaD, and stroke
Freedman (Freedman et al., 1994)	Free-drawn	6:45	15	AD, PD, VaD, mood/anxiety disorders, stroke, schizophrenia, and young/middle-aged adults
	Pre-drawn	6:05	13	AD, PD, schizophrenia, and young/middle-aged adults
Lin (Lin et al., 2003)	Pre-drawn	10:10	16	AD
Manos (Manos & Wu, 1994)	Pre-drawn	11:10	8	Dementia (mixed), AD, VaD, Fronto-temporal dementia (FTD), rehabilitation outpatients, and surgical inpatients
Tuokko (Tuokko et al., 1992)	Pre-drawn	11:10	Error tally	Dementia (mixed) and AD

Free-drawn clocks

Clock-Drawing Interpretation Scale

Source

No specific materials are provided.

Description

The Clock-Drawing Interpretation Scale (CDIS) was originally developed by Mendez et al. (1992) as a measure of constructional ability in patients with AD.

Administration

To administer CDIS, present a blank piece of paper (8 ½ × 11 in.) along with written and oral instructions to draw a clock (the specific instructions were not provided). After completion, instruct the person (both orally and in writing) to set the time to 10 after 11 (again, the specific instructions were not provided; Mendez et al., 1992).

Scoring

The total score for CDIS is 20 points, where one point is awarded for each element completed correctly (see Table 11.2).

Comment

Reliability: Overall, there is sufficient evidence for CDIS reliability. Inter-rater reliabilities range between r of 0.91 and 0.97 (Bourke et al., 1995; Esteban-Santillan, Praditsuwan, Ueda, & Geldmacher, 1998; Heinik, Vainer-Benaiah, Lahav, & Drummer, 1997; Mendez et al., 1992; Powlishta et al., 2002; Suhr et al., 1998) with a Kendall rank-order coefficient of 0.93 (Storey, Rowland, Basic, & Conforti, 2002). Test–retest reliability was high over 6 months (gamma statistic = 0.94; Storey et al., 2001), but moderate over 12 (rs 0.70–0.78) and 24 weeks for AD patients (r = 0.76; Mendez et al., 1992). Finally, the internal consistency was high (r = 0.95; Mendez et al., 1992).

Construct validity: CDIS correlations were moderate to large with MMSE scores (i.e., rs range from 0.34 to 0.76; Ben-Yehuda, Bentur, & Friedman, 1995; Bourke et al., 1995; Mendez et al., 1992; Royall et al., 1999; Souder, O'Sullivan, & Pechenik, 1999); the CAMCOG, which is the cognitive part of the Cambridge Examination for Mental Disorders for the Elderly (r = 0.67; Bourke et al., 1995); the Clinical Dementia Rating (CDR, rs = − 0.71; Powlishta et al., 2002) scale; and the Executive Interview (EXIT25), a structured interview that elicits self-reports about behaviours that might indicate executive dysfunction (r = −0.73; Royall et al., 1999). CDIS scores were

Table 11.2 CDIS scoring criteria[a]

(1) There is an attempt to indicate time	(11) Seven or more of the same symbol type are ordered sequentially
(2) All marks or items can be classified as part of the circle, a hand, or a symbol for clock numbers	(12) There are no repeated or duplicated number symbols
(3) The clock circle is totally enclosed with no gaps if numbers or symbols representing numbers are present, score items 4–15	(13) The numbers do not go beyond the number 12
(4) All symbols are within the circle	(14) A "2" is present and is pointed out in some way
(5) All symbols lie about equally adjacent to the clock circle edge	(15) An "11" is present and is pointed out in some way if the clock contains one or more hands, score items 16–20
(6) Only Arabic or Roman numerals are present (no substitutions)	(16) All hands radiate from the direction of a circle's centre
(7) All numbers 1–12 are present	(17) All hands are totally within the clock circle
(8) Three or more of the four quadrants contain the appropriate numbers (12–3, 3–6, 6–9, or 9–12 in each quadrant)	(18) There are exactly two distinct and separable hands
(9) Most numbers (symbols) are distributed throughout the circle without major gaps	(19) One hand is visibly longer than another hand
(10) Most numbers (symbols) are ordered in a clockwise direction	(20) There is an attempt to indicate a time with one or more hands

[a]Adapted from Mendez et al. (1992).

moderately correlated with the Global Deterioration Scale (GDS; $r = 0.40$; Mendez et al., 1992), and only accounted for a small proportion of variance in Neurobehavioral Cognitive Status Exam (NCSE) construction subtest scores ($r = 0.28$; Souder et al., 1999). Finally, CDIS had small-to-large correlations with neuropsychological tests (see Table 11.3 for correlations and definitions of abbreviated test names).

Criterion validity: CDIS scores adequately differentiate between cognitively normal older adults and those with dementia. The overall accuracy of CDIS scores for identifying cognitively normal and demented older adults was 0.78 (95% CI 0.70–0.85) for older adults whose first language was English (Storey et al., 2001) and 0.70 (95% CI 0.60–0.80) for those whose first language was not English (Storey et al., 2002). When a CDIS score of 18 or below was used as indicative of dementia (i.e., cut-off 18/19), the sensitivity and specificity ranged from 75 to 98% and 16 to 77%, depending on the sample (Lee et al., 1996; Storey et al., 2001, 2002). When patients with dementia were grouped by severity (based on CDR scores), the sensitivity (at a cut-off of 18/19) was lower (between 44 and 60%) for patients with very mild dementia (CDR of 0.5) than for those with mild-to-moderate dementia (CDR 1.0 or more; sensitivity = 82–97%; Lee

Table 11.3 Correlations of CDIS with neuropsychological tests

Neuropsychological test[a]	*r*	*Source*
Wechsler Memory Scale (WMS) mental control (MC)	0.23	Suhr et al. (1998)
WMS logical memory (LM)	0.11	Suhr et al. (1998)
WMS visual reproduction (VR)	0.12	Suhr et al. (1998)
WMS orientation	0.41	Suhr et al. (1998)
Wechsler Adult Intelligence Scale—Revised (WAIS-R) Block Design (BD)	0.46	Souder et al. (1999)
Boston Naming Test (BNT)	0.29	Suhr et al. (1998)
Controlled Oral Word Association Test (COWAT)	0.33–0.36	Mendez et al. (1992), Suhr et al. (1998)
Hooper Visual Orientation Test (HVOT)	0.42	Suhr et al. (1998)
Greek cross drawing	−0.42	Suhr et al. (1998)
Letter cancellation total time	−0.44	Mendez et al. (1992)
Letter cancellation errors	−0.53	Mendez et al. (1992)
Grooved Pegboard left	−0.44	Mendez et al. (1992)
Grooved Pegboard right	−0.49	Mendez et al. (1992)
Benton Facial Recognition Test	0.47	Mendez et al. (1992)
Symbol Digit Modalities Test (SDMT)	0.65	Mendez et al. (1992)
Rey–Osterrieth Complex Figure Test (RCFT) copy	0.66	Mendez et al. (1992)
RCFT delayed recall long-term storage	0.49	Mendez et al. (1992)
Buschke Selective Reminding Test (SRT)	0.21	Mendez et al. (1992)
SRT long-term retrieval	0.27	Mendez et al. (1992)
SRT recognition	0.31	Mendez et al. (1992)

[a]See Spreen and Strauss (1998) for a description of each.

et al., 1996; Powlishta et al., 2002). When a cut-off of 17/18 was used, the sensitivity of the CDIS was 46% and the specificity was 79% for AD patients with a CDR < 1.0 (Esteban-Santillan et al., 1998).

CDIS scores were similar for individuals with left- vs. right-sided strokes, suggesting that CDIS scores were not able to lateralize stroke-related deficits (Suhr et al., 1998). Many depressed older adults scored below the 18/19 cut-off (Lee & Lawlor, 1995), as did many older patients with schizophrenia (Heinik, Lahav, Drummer, Vainer-Benaiah, & Lin, 2000; Heinik et al., 1997). Further, mean CDIS scores were similar for older patients with schizophrenia and older patients with AD (Heinik, Reider-Groswasser, Solomesh, Segev, & Yoram Bleich, 2000), suggesting that using CDIS as a dementia screen in older schizophrenic patients may be problematic (Heinik et al., 1997).

Normative data

No normative data are provided. When screening, however, it may be possible to use a cut-off score of 19 or above to indicate normality, but note the low specificities obtained when identifying cognitively normal vs. demented older adults (Lee et al., 1996; Powlishta et al., 2002; Storey et al., 2001, 2002). Since age, but not education (Heinik et al., 1997; Royall et al., 1999; Storey et al., 2002), is related to CDIS scores (Royall et al., 1999), ideal comparisons would be made with cognitively normal adults of similar age. However, in the absence of these data, the overall CDIS scores for cognitively normal older adults can be used: $M = 18.2$, $SD = 0.8$, $N = 26$ (Mendez et al., 1992); or $M = 18.2$, $SD = 2.3$, $N = 15$ (Powlishta et al., 2002); or $M = 16.2$, $SD = 3.7$, $N = 52$ (Royall et al., 1999); or $M = 18.33$, $SD = 1.9$, $N = 71$ (Suhr et al., 1998).

CLOX

Source

The CLOX form is required for administration (also includes scoring) and can be copied from the source Royall et al. (1998) (see Royall et al., 2003 for a Spanish version).

Description

CLOX was developed by Royall et al. (1998) as a measure of executive function, and it includes both free-drawn (CLOX1) and copy (CLOX2) conditions.

Administration

The CLOX form has a pre-drawn circle in the bottom left-hand corner and is required for administration. To administer CLOX1, present the blank (back) side of the CLOX form and state: "Draw me a clock that says 1:45. Set the hands and numbers on the face so that a child could read them." After completion, draw a clock in the pre-drawn circle that is on the CLOX (front) form while the person watches. According to Royall et al. (1998), first set the hands to 1:45; then write the numbers 12, 6, 3, and 9; and finally make the hands into arrows. Then ask the person to copy this clock (the specific instructions for CLOX2 were not provided).

Scoring

The scoring procedure is the same for CLOX1 and CLOX2. Points are awarded for the features as shown in Table 11.4, for a maximum score of 15 points.

Table 11.4 CLOX scoring criteria

Scoring description	*Points*
(1) Figure resembles a clock	/1
(2) Outer circle is present	/1
(3) Circle diameter > 1 in.	/1
(4) All numbers (1–12) are present in the circle	/1
(5) Numbers 12, 6, 3, and 9 are placed first	/1
(6) Only Arabic numerals	/1
(7) Only numbers 1–12 are present	/1
(8) Sequence of 1–12 intact without omissions or intrusions	/1
(9) Only two hands are present	/1
(10) All hands represented as arrows	/1
(11) Hour hand between 1 and 2 o'clock	/1
(12) Minute hand longer than hour hand	/1
(13) Number spacing is intact (or if spacing errors exist and there are signs of correction or erasure)	/2 OR (/1)
(14) If all of the following are NOT present: hand pointing to 4 or 5, "1:45," intrusions from "hand" or "face" (e.g., eyes), letters or words or pictures, or intrusions from the circle on the front side of CLOX form	/1
	Total /15

Comment

Reliability: Inter-rater reliability was high for both CLOX1 (r = 0.94) and CLOX2 (r = 0.93; Royall et al., 1998). Cronbach's α for CLOX was 0.82 for both the English (Royall et al., 1998) and Spanish CLOX versions (Royall et al., 2003).

Construct validity: CLOX scores correlate highly with both MMSE (r = 0.76−0.82 for CLOX1 and r = 0.80−0.85 for CLOX2), and EXIT25 scores (r = − 0.78 to − 0.83 for CLOX1 and r = − 0.74 to − 0.79 for CLOX2; Royall et al., 1998, 1999).

Criterion validity: Combined CLOX scores correctly identified 83.1% of older adults, who were either cognitively normal or had AD. When the AD patients were further grouped based on their MMSE pentagons' drawings (i.e., those with and without errors), the combined CLOX scores correctly categorized 91.9% of the two AD subgroups. When used to predict functional ability in cognitively normal older adults, CLOX1 significantly predicted living situation (i.e., independent living apartments vs. congregate high rises where laundry, housecleaning, meals, and medication supervision were provided), and CLOX2 significantly predicted instrumental activities of daily living (IADLs; Royall, Chiodo, & Polk, 2000).

Table 11.5 Means and standard deviations for cognitively normal elderly persons on CLOX

Source	*CLOX1*	*CLOX2*
Royall et al. (2000); $N = 561$	$M = 10.3$, $SD = 3.3$	$M = 13.3$, $SD = 2.1$
Royall et al. (1999); $N = 52$	$M = 11.6$, $SD = 2.8$	$M = 14.0$, $SD = 1.2$
Royall et al. (1998); $N = 45$	$M = 12.1$, $SD = 2.6$	$M = 14.2$, $SD = 1.0$

Normative

No normative data are provided. There is a small, but significant effect of age on CLOX scores (Royall et al., 2003). Level of education is related to CLOX scores (Royall et al., 1998, 1999, 2003). Despite the relation between demographic variables and CLOX scores, only overall mean scores are provided. For cognitively normal older adults the means and standard deviations for CLOX1 and CLOX2 are shown in Table 11.5 (see Royall et al., 2003, for the mean of a Hispanic sample, 72.5% of whom were administered CLOX in Spanish).

Rouleau

Source

No materials are provided.

Description

Rouleau et al. (1992) developed quantitative and qualitative clock scoring for both free-drawn and copy administrations in order to investigate the visuospatial and visuoconstructional impairments associated with AD and HD. Cahn and colleagues (Cahn & Kaplan, 1997; Cahn, Salmon, Monsch, & Butters, 1996; Cahn-Weiner, Williams, Grace, Tremont, Westervelt, & Stern, 2003) modified Rouleau's qualitative scoring system to assess eight error types, but this will not be reviewed here.

Administration

To administer the Rouleau clock-drawing task, present a blank piece of paper (8 ½ × 11 in.) and state "I would like you to draw a clock and put in the numbers, and set the hands for 10 after 11." After completion, present an 8 ½ × 11 in. paper that has a fully drawn clock on the top portion (this "model" clock is 3 in. in diameter and has its hands set to 10 after 11) and ask the person to copy this model clock as accurately as possible onto the bottom portion of the paper (Rouleau et al., 1992; the specific instructions were not provided).

Scoring

Rouleau et al. (1992) propose two scoring systems: a quantitative and a qualitative scoring system. The quantitative system awards up to 10 points, and involves quality rankings for each of the following qualitative features of clock drawing: integrity of the clock face, the numbers, and the hands (see Table 11.6). The qualitative scoring system is summarized in Table 11.7 (see Rouleau et al., 1992 for more details and illustrative examples).

Comment

QUANTITATIVE SCORING SYSTEM

Reliability: Ample evidence for inter-rater reliability of the quantitative scoring system exists: correlations ranged between $r = 0.92$ and 0.97 (Cahn & Kaplan, 1997; Esteban-Santillan et al., 1998; Powlishta et al., 2002; Rouleau et al., 1992; South, Greve, Bianchini, & Adams, 2001). The inter-rater intra-class correlations (ρ_Is) were high for each of the three qualitative features: integrity of clock face, 0.70; numbers, 0.93; and hands, 0.92, as were intra-rater ρ_Is (i.e., each

Table 11.6 Quantitative scoring criteria for Rouleau

Qualitative feature	*Rating*
Integrity of clock face	2 points—if it is present without major distortion
	1 point—if it is incomplete or with some distortion
	0 points—if it is absent or totally inappropriate
Numbers	4 points—all present, in right order, with minimal error in spatial arrangement
	3 points—all present, but errors in spatial arrangement
	2 points—missing or added numbers, but no gross distortion of remaining numbers, or—numbers placed in counterclockwise direction, or—numbers all present, but gross distortions in spatial layout (e.g., hemi-neglect, numbers outside the clock)
	1 point—missing or added numbers and gross spatial distortion
	0 points—absence or poor representation of numbers
Hands	4 points—hands are in correct position and the appropriate size difference is represented.
	3 points—slight errors in the placement of the hands, or no representation of size difference
	2 points—major errors in the placement of the hands
	1 point—only one hand or poor representation of both hands
	0 points—no hands or perseveration on hands

Table 11.7 Rouleau's qualitative scoring system

Qualitative error	*How defined*
Size	Size of clock was small if < 1.5 in. or large if more than 5 in.
Graphic difficulty	Mild—some distortions present in the lines of the clock face and/or hands and/or numbers, but overall performance is adequate
	Moderate—distortions are evident, but overall performance is interpretable
	Severe—distortions are evident and in some cases make it very difficult to interpret the overall performance
Stimulus bound	A—hands are set to 10 to 11 instead of 10 after 11 (in free-drawn condition)
	B—time is written in letters or numbers, hands are either absent, or present but pointed between the numbers 10 and 11
Conceptual deficit	A—misrepresentation of the clock itself
	B—misrepresentation of the time set on the clock or time is written on the clock
Spatial/planning	A—neglect on left side of clock
	B—deficit in planning—with gap before 12, 3, 6, or 9
	C—deficit in spatial layout of numbers without any pattern
	D—numbers written outside clock circle
	E—numbers written counterclockwise
Perseveration	A—perseveration of hands (more than 2 hands)
	B—perseveration of numbers or writing numbers beyond 1–12

rater's consistency of scoring): integrity of clock face, 0.71; numbers, 0.93; and hands, 0.91 (South et al., 2001).

Construct validity: The quantitative scoring system had small to large correlations with the MMSE (i.e., between $r = 0.27$ and 0.69; Kitabayashi, Ueda, Narumoto, Nakamura, Kita, & Fukui, 2001; Royall et al., 1999; Souder et al., 1999; Ueda et al., 2002), a large correlation with the EXIT25 ($r = -0.69$; Royall et al., 1999), a large correlation with the CDR ($r = -0.74$; Powlishta et al., 2002), and a small correlation with the NCSE construction subtest ($r = 0.18$; Souder et al., 1999).

The correlation of the quantitative scoring system with the Dementia Rating Scale (DRS) is less clear: DRS and quantitative scores were not correlated at time 1 in a longitudinal study of AD patients, but were highly correlated at years 2 and 3 ($r = -0.61$ and $r = -0.72$; Rouleau et al., 1996).

The quantitative scores accounted for a moderate proportion of the variance in the following neuropsychological test scores: WAIS-R BD (0.45; Souder et al., 1999), WMS orientation (0.38), COWAT (0.33), HVOT (0.49), and Greek cross (−0.42; Suhr et al., 1998). In WMS MC (0.23), WMS LM

(0.11), WMS VR (0.12), and BNT (0.29) there was only a small amount of shared variance with quantitative clock scores (Suhr et al., 1998). Finally, after stepwise multiple regression analysis of SPECT regional cerebral blood flow in patients diagnosed with AD, quantitative clock scores were predicted only by MMSE scores and measures from the left posterior temporal region (Ueda et al., 2002).

Criterion validity: Various studies have found differences between the quantitative clock performance of cognitively normal older adults and other groups. Normal older controls performed better than patients with either AD (Kitabayashi et al., 2001; Rouleau et al., 1992), HD (Rouleau et al., 1992), or VaD (Kitabayashi et al., 2001). Although quantitative scores appear to differ between cognitively normal older controls and patient groups, the total scores did not appear to differentiate between types of patient groups: mean scores for patients with AD, PD, and DLBD were very similar (Cahn-Weiner et al., 2003). Finally, when the quantitative scoring system was used with middle-aged schizophrenics, it appeared that a small proportion was categorized as cognitively impaired (Tracy, de Leon, Doonan, & Musciente, 1996).

In addition to comparing mean group performance on the quantitative clock test, other researchers have investigated its use when screening for AD. Cahn et al. (1996) found that optimal sensitivity and specificity was obtained when using a cut-off of ≤ 7 (i.e., 88 and 63%, respectively). Esteban-Santillan et al. (1998) report a sensitivity of 93% and specificity of 42% at a cut-off of < 10 when detecting mild AD (i.e., CDR = 1). Powlishta et al. (2002) concluded that the quantitative scoring system was insensitive to very mild dementia because at a cut-off of < 5, the sensitivity of the quantitative clock-drawing scores varied with CDR scores: 20% for CDR = 0.5 and 86% for CDR = 1. On the other hand, Powlishta et al. found that the specificity appeared to be high (98%; but $N = 15$ cognitively normal).

QUALITATIVE SCORING SYSTEM

Reliability: The evidence for inter-rater reliability of the qualitative scoring system was low for the stimulus bound feature ($r = 0.73$), but excellent for the other five features scored: size $r = 1.00$, graphic difficulty $r = 0.89$, conceptual difficulty $r = 0.82$, spatial/planning $r = 0.82$, and perseveration $r = 1.00$ (Suhr et al., 1998).

Construct validity: Suhr et al. reported correlations with subscales of the WMS (orientation, MC, LM, and VR), the BNT, the COWA, the HVOT, and the Greek cross drawing for all error types except Perseverations. The qualitative feature of Size had a trivial correlation ($r < 0.1$) with WMS MC, BNT, COWA, and WMS LM scores and small correlations (rs ranged between 0.1 and 0.3) with WMS orientation, WMS VR, HVOT, and Greek cross scores. Graphic Difficulties had a trivial correlation with WMS MC, HVOT, and Greek cross scores, and it had a small correlation with WMS orientation, WMS LM, WMS VR, BNT, and COWA scores. Stimulus Bound errors had a trivial correlation with all scores, except with WMS MC, COWA, HVOT, and Greek cross, where it accounted for a small proportion of variance in each. Conceptual Deficit errors accounted for a small proportion of variance in WMS MC, WMS LM, WMS VR, BNT, and Greek cross, but accounted for a moderate proportion of variance (r ranged between 0.3 and 0.5) in WMS orientation, COWA, and HVOT scores. Finally, Spatial/Planning errors accounted for a moderate proportion of variance in WMS orientation and Greek cross scores, a small amount of variance in BNT, COWA, HVOT, and WMS VR, but a trivial amount of variance in WMS MC and WMS LM.

Criterion validity: Rouleau et al. (1992) suggested that the qualitative scoring system is able to differentiate between patients diagnosed with AD and those diagnosed with HD, and that the clock drawing can differentiate between AD and HD groups who were matched for dementia severity with the DRS. They found that AD patients were more likely to draw large clocks (seven with AD and two with HD), more had difficulties with Spatial/Planning (i.e., four AD patients and only one HD patient wrote numbers outside the clock face), and were more likely to have Conceptual Deficits (13 DAT vs. 3 HD patients with Conceptual Deficits). HD patients, in contrast, were more likely to draw small clocks (seven HD and vs. three AD patients), make Graphic Difficulty errors (20 HD vs. 6 AD patients), and have difficulties with Spatial/Planning (i.e., eight HD and one AD patient had a deficit in planning).

Another study by Kitabayashi et al. (2001) compared the ability of the Rouleau qualitative scoring system to differentiate between AD and VaD. AD patients were most likely to make Conceptual errors (more than 60% of the 67 AD patients made this error) and Spatial/Planning errors (40–60%), and the types of errors made by patients with AD did not differ according to severity of dementia as measured by MMSE scores. Patients with MMSE scores above 24 and who had VaD had similar error types to patients with AD. However, the error types of VaD patients with lower MMSE score were different from VaD patients with higher MMSE scores and from those with AD. Patients with MMSE scores between 18 and 24 and VaD (i.e., more ‘mild’ dementia) were more likely to make Spatial/Planning errors (68% of the 19 mild VaD group), and those with lower MMSE scores (i.e., more ‘moderate’ dementia) were more likely to make Conceptual Deficit errors (90% of the 10 with moderate VaD) and have Graphic Difficulties (60%).

Rouleau et al. (1996) investigated error types over 3 years for a group of AD patients and found that Conceptual errors increased in frequency over time, and it appeared that Spatial/Planning deficits also increased over time (even though this could not be scored for many with more severe AD because they were not able to correctly write numbers). Finally, they found that patients with AD who made Conceptual errors during the first assessment (year 1) had more rapidly declining DRS scores over the 3-year period than patients who did not make Conceptual clock errors at year 1.

Suhr et al. (1998) analyzed errors in the qualitative scoring system by comparing mean number of errors for each group, as opposed to the analyses

Table 11.8 Normative data for Rouleau's quantitative scoring system

Source	*M*	*SD*	*N*
Cahn et al. (1996)	8.7	1.2	237
Kitabayashi et al. (2001)	9.8	0.7	8
Powlishta et al. (2002)	8.0	1.9	15
Rouleau et al. (1992)	8.94	1.12	25
Royall et al. (1999)	7.2	2.5	52
Suhr et al. (1998)	8.59	1.5	71

above that were tallies of the number of people in each group making specific error types. Suhr et al. found that the types of qualitative errors differed significantly for groups of stroke patients. Specifically, patients with right-sided strokes performed more poorly than those with left-sided strokes on Graphic Difficulty and Spatial/Planning. Patients with subcortical strokes had more errors of Graphic Difficulty than patients with cortical strokes, but patients with cortical strokes had more errors of Perseveration. Although these differences were significant and the effect sizes of the mean group differences were large (i.e., d between 0.50 and 0.63), there is likely too much overlap between the groups to recommend using the qualitative scoring system to differentiate stroke types.

Normative

Although age has a trivial relationship with quantitative total score ($r = -0.08$; Cahn & Kaplan, 1997; Cahn et al., 1996), Cahn et al. (1996) provide normative data for 65- to 75-year-olds ($M = 8.8$, $SD = 1.1$, $N = 91$), 76- to 84-year-olds ($M = 8.7$, $SD = 1.3$, $N = 97$), and those aged 85 and over ($M = 8.5$, $SD = 1.2$, $N = 49$). Other normative data, along with the source are provided in Table 11.8.

Free-drawn and pre-drawn

Freedman

Source

No specific test materials are provided.

Description

Freedman and colleagues (1994) devised a normative-based clock-drawing system that includes free-drawn, pre-drawn administrations, and an 'examiner' condition, which involves setting fully drawn clocks at three different times. Paganini-Hill, Clark, Henderson, and Birge (2001) provide a modified version of Freedman's clock-drawing task with a total score of seven points that will not be reviewed here.

Administration

To administer the Freedman et al. (1994) free-drawn clock, present a blank piece of paper (8 ½ × 11 in.) and say, "I would like you to draw a clock and put in the numbers." After completion say "Now I would like you to set the time at a quarter to seven." To administer the pre-drawn clock, present a paper with a pre-drawn circle (i.e., 11.7 cm or 4 5/8 in. diameter circle) and state: "Put the numbers on the clock and set the time to 5 after 6." The 'examiner' clock is not reviewed here.

Scoring

Scoring the pre- and free-drawn clocks involves determining the presence or absence of critical items, which are summarized in Table 11.9. To score pre-drawn clocks, items 1–13 are scored for a total of 13 possible points, and for free-drawn clocks, the clock circle is also scored (i.e., items 14 and 15), for a total of 15 points.

Comment

Reliability: Inter-rater reliability for total free-drawn (r = 0.865; Freedman et al., 1994; r = 0.98; Suhr et al., 1998) and pre-drawn scores were high (r = 0.841; Freedman et al., 1994). The inter-rater reliability (ρ_I) of subtest scores were also high for both free-drawn (numbers = 0.75, hands = 0.91, centre of clock = 0.91, and clock circle = 0.51) and pre-drawn clocks (numbers = 0.88, hands = 0.95, and centre of clock = 0.60). Further, the intra-rater reliability (ρ_I) of the subtests were high: numbers = 0.80, hands = 0.92, centre of clock = 0.91, and clock circle = 0.54 for free-drawn; and for pre-drawn clocks numbers = 0.91, hands = 0.96, and centre of the clock = 0.58 (South et al., 2001). Although the time interval between testing sessions was unspecified, Freedman et al. (1994) reported that the total scores test–retest reliability (rs) of the free- and pre-drawn clocks were low, stating that this was potentially due to a restricted range of scores, but did not provide further data.

Convergent validity: Most research, to date, has been conducted on Freedman et al.'s free-drawn clocks. Free-drawn total scores were highly correlated with MMSE scores (i.e., between r = 0.526 and 0.73; Heinik et al., 2000, 2002b; Heinik, Solomesh, Bleich, & Berkman, 2003; Souder, O'Sullivan, & Pechenik, 1999) and CAMCOG scores (between r = 0.612 and 0.80; Heinik et al., 2000, 2002, 2003). Free-drawn scores were moderately correlated with CDR scores (r = 0.477; Heinik et al., 2000) and only had a small

Table 11.9 Freedman scoring criteria[a]

Subtest	*Critical items*	*Points*
Numbers	(1) Numbers 1–12 only without additions or omissions	/1
	(2) Arabic characters	/1
	(3) Written in correct order	/1
	(4) No rotations of paper while drawing numbers	/1
	(5) Correct position of numbers	/1
	(6) All numbers included inside circle	/1
		Subtotal /6
Hands	(7) Clock has 2 hands or marks	/1
	(8) Hour target indicated	/1
	(9) Minute target indicated	/1
	(10) Hands in correct proportion	/1
	(11) No superfluous marking	/1
	(12) Hands joined or within ½' of joining	/1
		Subtotal /6
Centre of clock	(13) Clock has a centre—either drawn or inferred	/1
		Subtotal /1
		Pre-drawn total /13
Clock circle	(14) Acceptable circle drawn	/1
	(15) Circle is not too small or big, nor reproduced repeatedly	/1
		Subtotal /2
		Free-drawn total /15

[a]Adapted from Freedman et al. (1994)

correlation with the construction subtest of the NCSE ($r = 0.24$; Souder et al., 1999). Free-drawn total scores have also been correlated with a wide variety of neuropsychological test scores (see Table 11.10).

Despite correlations with cognitive tests, free-drawn total score did not correlate with measures of instrumental activities of daily living or basic activities of daily living in patients with mild and moderate AD (Heinik et al., 2002b). Free-drawn scores were, however, correlated with linear CT images, and they appeared to be most highly correlated with linear CT images of caudal atrophy in AD patients ($r = -0.427$; Heinik et al., 2000).

Criterion validity: Mean pre- and free-drawn scores were lower for patients with either AD or PD with dementia (PDD) than for patients with PD or normal controls (Freedman et al., 1994). VaD patients were shown to have lower average free-drawn scores than patients with AD (Heinik et al., 2000;

Table 11.10 Correlations of Freedman's free-drawn scores with neuropsychological scores

Neuropsychological test score (see Table 11.3 for abbreviations)	*r*	*Source*
WMS orientation	0.36	Suhr et al. (1998)
WMS mental control	0.27	Suhr et al. (1998)
WMS logical memory	0.09	Suhr et al. (1998)
WMS visual reproduction	0.18	Suhr et al. (1998)
BNT	0.27	Suhr et al. (1998)
COWAT	0.20–0.40	Freedman et al. (1994), Suhr et al. (1998)
HVOT	0.52	Suhr et al. (1998)
Greek cross drawing	–0.43	Suhr et al. (1998)
WAIS-R BD	0.31–0.41	Freedman (1994), Souder et al. (1999)
WAIS-R INFO	0.26	Freedman et al. (1994)
WAIS-R ARITH	0.18	Freedman et al. (1994)
WAIS-R PC	0.21	Freedman et al. (1994)
RCFT copy	0.27	Freedman et al. (1994)
RCFT immediate recall	0.37	Freedman et al. (1994)
RCFT delayed recall	0.30	Freedman et al. (1994)
Wisconsin Card Sorting Test (WCST) errors	–0.16	Freedman et al. (1994)
WCST perseverative responses	–0.18	Freedman et al. (1994)
WCST perseverative errors	–0.17	Freedman et al. (1994)
WCST number of cards sorted	–0.12	Freedman et al. (1994)
WCST number of categories	0.10	Freedman et al. (1994)
WCST correct	0.14	Freedman et al. (1994)

Heinik, Solomesh, Raikher, & Lin, 2002a), and VaD patients appeared to have difficulty with the Hands subscore but not the other subscores relative to patients with AD (Heinik et al., 2002a). Nevertheless, Heinik and colleagues found that the total score was the only significant predictor of AD/VaD diagnosis using stepwise discriminant function analysis, and with the total score they were able to correctly identify 79.6% of the AD patients and 50% of the VaD patients. Finally, Suhr et al. (1998) did not find that the free-drawn total score differentiated between left, right, or bilateral strokes.

AD patients had lower average free-drawn scores than older depressed and cognitively normal older adults (Herrmann et al., 1998), and free-drawn scores accurately differentiated between patients with dementia or a psychiatric disorder (i.e., mood or anxiety disorder). At a cut-off of 12 the sensitivity was 85% and specificity was 89%, and over all possible cut-off points, the

Table 11.11 Freedman et al.'s (1994) normative information for different age groups

Age group	*Free-drawn (out of 15)*	*Pre-drawn (out of 13)*
20–29 (n = 40)	M = 14.70 (SD = 0.61)	M = 12.72 (SD = 0.50)
30–39 (n = 40)	M = 14.75 (SD = 0.49)	M = 12.70 (SD = 0.56)
40–49 (n = 40)	M = 14.77 (SD = 0.43)	M = 12.56 (SD = 0.94)
50–59 (n = 52)	M = 14.50 (SD = 0.83)	M = 12.54 (SD = 0.73)
60–69 (n = 76)	M = 14.28 (SD = 0.88)	M = 12.38 (SD = 0.80)
70–79 (n = 59)	M = 13.68 (SD = 0.88)	M = 11.46 (SD = 1.55)
80–90 (n = 41)	M = 13.34 (SD = 2.09)	M = 11.22 (SD = 1.93)

accuracy was 93% (Heinik et al., 2003). Finally, Freedman free- and pre-drawn clocks have been researched for patients with schizophrenia. Young to middle-aged adults with schizophrenia obtained lower mean clock-drawing scores than age-matched normal controls (Herrmann et al., 1999). Further, middle-aged to older adults with schizophrenia obtained similar mean clock scores to older adults with dementia, but both groups obtained lower scores than cognitively normal middle-aged to older controls. Of interest, the clock scores for patients with schizophrenia were similar to the normal controls after controlling for MMSE scores (Bozikas et al., 2003).

Normative data

Freedman et al. (1994) provide normative data for 348 cognitively normal participants between the ages of 20 and 90 years old. Total scores for pre- and free-drawn clocks appear to be influenced by age; consequently, Freedman et al. provide separate normative information for different age groups (see Table 11.11). However, on inspection, this only has practical relevance for those over age 70.

Pre-drawn

Clock-Drawing Test

Source

No specific materials are provided.

Description

This measure, the CDT, was developed as a simplified screening test for persons with AD (Lin et al., 2003). The CDT has two parts: clock drawing (CDT-D) and clock copy (CDT-C).

Administration

To administer the CDT-D, present a piece of paper on which a circle 10 cm in diameter is printed and say, "Draw a clock. Put in all the numerals and show the time 10:10." Instructions can be repeated but no additional prompting is given and the person is allowed to revise the drawings without any time limit. For the clock copy component, have the person copy a printed clock and draw in the hands to show the time of 10:10 (the specific instructions were not provided; Lin et al., 2003).

Scoring

A scoring system was devised based on those developed by Watson et al. (1993), Wolf-Klein et al. (1989), Tuokko et al. (1992), and Förstl, Bruns, Levy, and Cairns (1993). The clock face is divided into quadrants by drawing one line through the centre and the 12, and a second line perpendicular to the first one through the centre. If a number is placed on the reference line, it is included in the quadrant clockwise to the line. Placing three numerals in a quadrant is considered correct. For both CDT-D and CDT-C, a score of 1 is given for an affirmative answer to each of the questions in Table 11.12 (maximum = 16; Lin et al., 2003).

Table 11.12 The CDT scoring system

Scoring description	*Points*
(a) Does the drawing resemble a clock?	/1
(b) Are all numerals inside the circle?	/1
(c) Are numerals 12, 3, 6, and 9 placed first?	/1
(d) Is 12 placed correctly?	/1
(e) Are all numerals spaced equally and symmetrically?	/1
(f) Are 3 numbers included in the first quadrant?	/1
(g) Are 3 numbers included in the second quadrant?	/1
(h) Are 3 numbers included in the third quadrant?	/1
(i) Are 3 numbers included in the fourth quadrant?	/1
(j) Is the sequence 1–12 correct and complete?	/1
(k) Are both hands presented?	/1
(l) Are both hands presented as arrows?	/1
(m) Is the minute hand longer than the hour hand?	/1
(n) Is the hour hand pointing to 10 o'clock?	/1
(o) Is the minute hand pointing to the numeral 2?	/1
(p) 10:10, words or counterclockwise direction not used?	/1
	Total /16

Comment

Reliability: The inter-rater reliabilities for both CDT-D and CDT-C ranged from 0.98 to 0.99 (mean $r = 0.99$). A second CDT-D and CDT-C measure was obtained from these patients 1–3 months later with test–retest reliabilities ranging from 0.86 to 0.91 (mean = 0.90) for CDT-D and 0.86 to 0.91 (mean 0.88) for CDT-C (Lin et al., 2003).

Construct validity: CDT-D and CDT-C scores were correlated strongly with the MMSE ($r = 0.73$ and 0.67, respectively) but only moderately with the CDR ($rs = -0.47$ and –0.37, respectively). CDT-D and CDT-C scores showed strong correlations with performance on the Cognitive Abilities Screening Instrument (CASI; $r = 0.75$ and 0.67, respectively). Only the CASI remained significantly associated with the CDT-D and CDT-C scores when age and education level, both of which correlated weakly with the CDT scores, were included in a stepwise regression analysis (Lin et al., 2003).

Criterion validity: The CDT-D and CDT-C scores differed between persons with and without AD but only CDT-D scores differed between groups showing no dementia (CDR = 0), questionable dementia (CDR = 0.5), or mild dementia (CDR = 1). When the individual CDT-D scoring items (i.e., 0 or 1 for each of the 13 scoring questions) were used to discriminate between the CDR groups, only three items contributed to the discrimination: "Is the hour hand pointing to 10 o'clock?," "Is the minute hand longer than the hour hand?," and "Is 12 placed correctly?" Using scores derived from just these three items (simplified scoring or CDT-S, range 0–3), 74.9% of the cases were correctly classified. Cut-off scores of 10/11 and 2/3 for the CDT-D and CDT-S, respectively, resulted in levels of sensitivity (66.7 and 72.9%, respectively) and specificity (74.5 and 65.6%) that did not differ significantly (Lin et al., 2003).

Normative data

No normative data are provided. All participants were recruited from individuals with memory complaints who visited a memory clinic (Lin et al., 2003). Thus, using the means derived from this study for the nondemented control sample may be lower than would otherwise be expected because this sample included those persons with a CDR score of 0.5. It may be most appropriate to refer to the CDT-D and CDT-C scores for the sample with a CDR score of 0 as a reference for potentially normal performance (CDT-D; $M = 12.42$, $SD = 3.68$; CDT-C; $M = 13.55$, $SD = 2.67$; $N = 142$).

Ten-Point Clock Test (TPCT)

Source

No specific materials are provided.

Description

TPCT was developed to screen for and grade cognitive deficits in adult medical and surgical patients in a tertiary referral centre (Manos & Wu, 1994).

Administration

To administer the TPCT, present a plain white sheet of paper on which a circle of 4 ½ in. in diameter is drawn and say, "Put the numbers in the face of a clock." When the task is complete, say, "Make the clock say ten minutes after eleven" (Manos & Wu, 1994).

Scoring

To score the clock, the number 12 is rotated to the top of the page. The clock face is divided into quadrants by drawing one line through the centre of the circle and the 12, and a second line perpendicular to the first one through the centre. Two more lines are drawn through the centre of the circle, dividing it into eighths. If the 12 is missing, it is assumed to be located counter-clockwise from the number 1, at a distance equivalent to the distance between numbers 1 and 2. See Table 11.13 for a description of the scoring. A plastic template with the circle divided into eighths may be placed over the clock drawing to facilitate scoring (Manos & Wu, 1994).

Comment

Reliability: Both inter-rater and test–retest reliabilities have been shown to be good for the TPCT. Inter-rater reliabilities have ranged from $r = 0.88$ to 0.97 and $r = 0.88$ to 0.95 (Manos & Wu, 1994; Schramm et al., 2002; Seigerschmidt, Moesch, Siemen, Foerstl, & Bickel, 2002). The consistency with which the clock drawings were rated as normal or abnormal was determined using kappa coefficients (i.e., $r_k = 0.88$; Seigerschmidt et al., 2002). When the TPCT scoring was applied to free-drawn clocks, the inter-rater reliability remained good ($r = 0.93$) with a strong weighted kappa coefficient ($r_k = 0.81$; Powlishta et al., 2002). Test–retest reliability, determined using administrations on two successive days, was good ($rs = 0.87$ and 0.94, respectively; Manos & Wu, 1994).

Construct validity: Correlations between TPCT and other cognitive screening measures vary widely depending on the sample investigated. For example, correlations have been shown with the MMSE ranging from 0.32 to 0.68, with the Short Performance Test (SKT; Erzigkeit, 1989) ranging from 0.13 to 0.57 (Moretti, Torre, Antonello, Cazzato, & Bava, 2002; Seigerschmidt et al., 2002) and with the CDR ($r = 0.71$; Powlishta et al., 2002). The TPCT scoring applied to free-drawn clocks correlated strongly with the MMSE ($r = 0.62$) and EXIT25 ($r = -0.57$; Royall et al., 1999).

Table 11.13 Scoring for the TPCT

Scoring description	*Points*	*Comments*
One point is given for each of the following numbers for which at least half of the spatial volume of the number falls in its proper eighth of the circle relative to the number 12:		Numbers placed outside the circle are scored by extending the dividing line and are scored as correct if falling within the lines of the appropriate eighth
1	/1	
2	/1	
4	/1	
5	/1	
7	/1	
8	/1	
10	/1	
11	/1	
	Subtotal /8	
One point is given for each of the following: a short hand pointing to the number 11 and a long hand pointing to the number 2	/1 /1	No points are given for: • Hands of equal length • Hands of any length pointing to numbers other than 11 and 2
	Subtotal /2	• For a short hand pointing to 2 and a long hand pointing to 11
	Total /10	

The TPCT's correlations with neuropsychological measures (i.e., Trails A and B; WAIS-R Digit Span, Block Design, and Similarities—raw and age-adjusted scaled scores) have been shown to range from high (Block Design raw score; $r = 0.56$) to low (WAIS-R Digits forward scaled percentile; $r = 0.22$; Manos & Wu, 1994). Nurses' estimates of cognitive impairment obtained prior to administering the clock-drawing task were strongly related to clock-drawing scores (rs $= -0.68$). Moretti et al. (2002) reported TPCT correlations with semantic fluency, phonological fluency, proverbs and visuospatial skills varied depending on the specific patient group with semantic fluency showing the highest ($r = 0.62$) and lowest ($r = 0.33$) correlations for the Fronto-temporal Dementia (FTD) and AD groups, respectively. These findings suggest that the TPCT is related to different cognitive processes depending on the underlying pathology and speaks to its sensitivity to various forms of cognitive impairment.

Criterion validity: The TPCT has been used to differentiate between people with and without dementia as well as with various forms of dementia. It has also been used with mixed results to identify very mild or questionable dementia. Using a cut-off score of 7/8, 76.3% of dementia cases and 78.3% of elderly controls were correctly classified (Manos & Wu, 1994). This cut-off point identified most patients with delirium or dementia (92 and 90%, respectively) but few with adjustment disorders (5%). Schramm et al. (2002) found this cut-off score yielded a sensitivity of 67% and a specificity of 86%. By changing this cut-off to 8 (i.e., scores of 9 or 10 considered normal), the sensitivity rose to 81% but the specificity dropped to 75%.

Of the AD patients with very mild dementia (i.e., MMSE scores > 23), 71% scored < 8 points on the TPCT (Manos, 1999). Of those with MMSE scores < 24, 80% were identified with this cut-off for a combined sensitivity of 77%. A total of 18% of the control sample scored < 8 on the clock task (i.e., misclassified as impaired). Powlishta et al. (2002) concluded that it was not possible to distinguish between individuals who had very mild dementia (CDR = 0.5) and those who were cognitively normal (CDR = 0) using the TPCT but both of these groups differed from those with mild (CDR = 1), and moderate or severe dementia (CDR = 2 or 3). When a cut-off score of 7/8 was used, the TPCT yielded a specificity of 80% and a sensitivity to dementia of at least mild severity of 97%. However, the sensitivity of this scoring method to very mild dementia was poor (i.e., 44%) with the sensitivity to all dementias dropping to 75%. Seigerschmidt et al. (2002) examined the TPCT in patients with questionable dementia (CDR = 0.5) or no cognitive impairment (CDR = 0) and reported group mean differences ($p < 0.05$), a sensitivity of 66.7%, a specificity of 65.5%, a positive predictive value of 57.9%, and a negative predictive value of 73.4%. Seigerschmidt et al. (2002) also examined the association between the TPCT and co-morbidity using a dichotomous classification (low vs. high co-morbidity) and found no association between them.

Schramm et al. (2002) used the TPCT in conjunction with the MMSE and the SKT and found the sensitivity for detecting dementia increased to 89% (as opposed to the sensitivity of MMSE alone = 80%) and 88% (as opposed to sensitivity of SKT alone = 75%), respectively. For mildly impaired participants (i.e., GDS score of 3), adding the TPCT to the MMSE and SKT resulted in increases of sensitivity from 54 to 68%, and 68 to 88%, respectively. For more severely impaired participants (i.e., GDS > 3), combining the TPCT with that MMSE and SKT resulted in increases in sensitivity from 96 to 100% and 82 to 87%, respectively. No information was provided by the authors as to the effect these combinations had on specificity.

Normative data

No normative data are provided. When screening, it may be possible to use a cut-off score of 8, below which further testing is recommended (Manos, 1999; Manos & Wu, 1994; Powlishta et al., 2002). This cut-off has been shown to be sensitive to cognitive impairment due to various underlying conditions (see above for details). There are some data to suggest that scores may vary in relation to age, gender, and education (e.g., Seigerschmidt et al., 2002). The overall score on the TPCT for cognitively normal older adults are provided by Manos and Wu (1994; $M = 8.5$, $SD = 1.6$, $N = 23$), Powlishta et al. (2002; $M = 8.4$, $SD = 2.4$, $N = 15$), and Seigerschmidt et al. (2002; $M = 8.4$, $SD = 2.5$, $N = 139$).

The Clock Test (CT)

Source

Tuokko et al. (1995). *The Clock Test: Administration and scoring manual.* Toronto, Ontario, Canada: Multi-Health Systems, Inc. This manual was prepared in keeping with the standards for educational and psychological testing jointly developed by the American Psychological Association and the National Council on Measurement in Education (APA, 1985). Record forms with QuikScore templates and a clock reading administrative "tent" are available from Multi-Health Systems (www.mhs.com).

Description

This measure was developed as a standardized tool to assess for the presence of cognitive impairment in elderly persons for use in screening or as part of a more extensive psychological battery. The Clock Test has three components: Clock Drawing (CD), Clocks Setting (CS), and Clock Reading (CR). CS and CR were added to CD to allow for an evaluation of an individual's comprehension and facility with time concepts (e.g., can a person read a clock?), and allows for examination of patterns of performance within and across components. The CT is intended for use as a clinical and research tool (Tuokko et al., 1995).

Administration

QuikScore forms are used to facilitate administration and scoring of each component. On the back of the QuikScore Form, there is a pre-drawn circle 7 cm in diameter. Present the form and say, "Imagine this is the face of a clock. Put the numbers on the clock face." When this is complete, say, "Now put the hands on the clock to indicate 10 past 11." It is permissible to repeat "10 past 11" if asked, but the phrase 10 past 11 must be used. CS is administered using the removable sections from the front of the QuikScore Form. Have the person place the hands on pre-drawn circles to indicate 1 o'clock, 10 past 11, 3 o'clock, 9:15, and 7:30. CR uses an administrative "tent" containing five flip-cards each showing a pre-drawn circle with marks indicating the location of the numbers (no numbers included) and the hands drawn to indicate a specific time (same times as CS but a different order of administration). CS and CR examine facility with time concepts at varying levels of complexity. Administer the components in the above order (Tuokko et al., 1995).

Scoring

A dual scoring system was developed that offers both an overall quantifiable score to assess general level of efficiency of performance and, for CD, a qualitative analysis of specific error types. Seven error categories were determined with subtypes of errors within each category explicitly defined (see Table 11.14). Using this system, all error types can be classified. Given that maximum scores are not pre-determined for all error types, the possible range of scores is very wide. In practice, the upper limit is about 31 errors. For CS and CR, three points are assigned for each clock: one point if the hour hand is correctly placed (CS) or read (CR); one point if the minute hand is correctly placed (CS) or read (CR); and one point for indicating the correct relative lengths of the hands (CS). For CR, the final one point is assigned if both hands are read correctly (Tuokko et al., 1995). The maximum score for CS is 15 points as is the maximum score for CR. We will focus primarily on the CD component of the CT and only make minor reference to the CS and CR components.

Comment

Reliability: Inter-rater, intra-rater, and test–retest reliability estimates have been determined for the various components of the CT. Inter-rater reliabilities have been shown to be good for all three components of the CT (CD ranging from 0.90 to 0.99; CS ranging from 0.95 to 0.98; CR consistently 0.99; Tuokko et al., 1992). Inter-rater reliabilities for the error type categories were: 1.00 for omissions; 0.86 for perseverations; 0.98 for rotations; 0.93 for misplacements; 1.00 for distortions; 0.82 for substitutions; and 0.73 for additions (Kurzman, 1992). Intra-rater reliability for CD was determined by having a rater score all clocks and then re-score a random selection of 50 of the clocks ($r = 0.97$; Tuokko et al., 2000). When CD was administered on two occasions within 4 days to people suspected of dementia (Tuokko et al., 1992), a test–retest reliability coefficient of 0.70 was obtained.

Construct validity: It has been shown that CD scores correlated moderately and significantly with other measures of cognitive functioning (i.e., convergent validity), while they were uncorrelated with measures designed to assess unrelated constructs (i.e., divergent validity; see Table 11.15). This was true for CS and CR as well (Kurzman, 1993; Tuokko et al., 1995). Convergent validity correlations were generally higher when calculated for persons with dementia than when calculated for persons with no cognitive impairment (NCI; Kurzman, 1992). This appeared to be due to the restricted range of scores achieved by those with NCI (Kurzman, 1992).

Criterion validity: All three components of the CT have been shown to differ significantly between AD patients and those with NCI (Tuokko et al., 1992). The AD group made significantly more errors of omission and misplacement. Using a CD error score > 2 resulted in a sensitivity of 86% and a specificity of 92%. When deficits on two or more components of the CT (i.e., CD, CS, and CR) were used, sensitivity and specificity increased to 94

Table 11.14 Summary of error types by category for the CD component of the CT

Omissions	
N = neglect	
Nu = number	
H = hands	
Perseverations	
RNP = repetition of numbers	
HP = hand perseveration	
SNP = sequence of number perseveration	
Rotations	
CR = clock face rotations	
NR = number rotations	
RR = reversal rotations	
HR = hand rotations	
Misplacement	
MN = misplaced hands	
SQ = sequence	
MH = misplaced hand	
Distortions	
Unique	
HV = horizontal/vertical number placement	
C = circularity	
Substitutions	
LW = letter/word	
S = scribble	
W = words	
AN = additional number	
RL = relative lengths	
Additions	
IW = irrelevant words	
IS = irrelevant scribble	
IF = irrelevant figures	

and 93%, respectively. When a CD cut-off of 3 errors was applied in the context of a large epidemiological sample, the sensitivity remained good (91%) but the specificity was relatively low (50%; Tuokko et al., 2000).

CT scores have also been found useful for predicting the development of dementia over time (i.e., 12–24 months) in people attending a dementia clinic

Table 11.15 Correlations of CT with neuropsychological measures

Dimension and test[a]	*r*	*Source*
Convergent validity tests		
Wechsler Adult Intelligence Scale—Revised (WAIS-R) Block Design (BD)	– 0.56 to – 0.57	Kurzman (1992), Tuokko et al. (1995)
WAIS-R Object Assembly (OA)	– 0.56	Kurzman (1992)
WAIS-R Digit Symbol	– 0.56	Kurzman (1992)
WAIS-R Information	– 0.44 to – 0.48	Kurzman (1992), Tuokko et al. (1995)
WAIS-R Similarities	– 0.39 to – 0.41	Kurzman (1992), Tuokko et al. (1995)
Controlled Oral Word Association Test (COWAT)	– 0.47 to – 0.48	Kurzman (1992), Tuokko et al. (1995)
WAIS-R Vocabulary	– 0.45	Kurzman (1992)
Multi-Focus Assessment Scale (MAS)[b] Auditory Receptive Language	– 0.27 to – 0.33	Kurzman (1992), Tuokko et al. (1995)
MAS Visual Receptive Language	– 0.42 to – 0.46	Kurzman (1992), Tuokko et al. (1995)
MAS Mental Status	– 0.50 to – 0.52	Kurzman (1992), Tuokko et al. (1995)
MAS Orientation	– 0.55	Kurzman (1992), Tuokko et al. (1995)
MAS Expressive Language	– 0.32 to – 0.33	Kurzman (1992), Tuokko et al. (1995)
MAS Accessibility	– 0.40	Kurzman (1992)
WAIS-R Digits Forward	– 0.32	Kurzman (1992)
WAIS-R Digit Backward	– 0.46	Kurzman (1992)
WAIS-R Digit Span	– 0.43	Tuokko et al. (1995)
Buschke Cued Recall (BCR) Free Recall (FR) 1	– 0.44	Kurzman (1992), Tuokko et al. (1995)
BCR Retrieval	– 0.47	Tuokko et al. (1995)
BCR Acquisition	– 0.43	Tuokko et al. (1995)
BCR Retention (Total Recall Trial 7)	– 0.27 to – 0.35	Kurzman (1992), Tuokko et al. (1995)
Modified-Mini Mental State (3MS) Examination	– 0.34	O'Connell (2001)
Divergent validity tests		
MAS Memorial University of Newfoundland Scale of Happiness	– 0.04 to – 0.07	Kurzman (1992), Tuokko et al. (1995)
MAS Social Behaviour	– 0.16 to – 0.19	Kurzman (1992), Tuokko et al. (1995)
Tapping Right	– 0.23	Kurzman (1992)
Tapping Left	– 0.17	Kurzman (1992)
Dynamometer Right	– 0.10	Kurzman (1992)
Dynamometer Left	– 0.13	Kurzman (1992)

[a]see Spreen and Strauss (1998) for a description of each.
[b]Coval, Crockett, Holliday, and Koch (1985).

(O'Rourke, Tuokko, Hayden, & Beattie, 1997). Although none met dementia criteria on the first assessment, at second assessment, approximately 1/3 were diagnosed with dementia. Groups differed with respect to CD, CR, and CS scores obtained at their first assessment. Those who developed dementia showed more substitution errors at initial assessment than those who remained dementia free. When impaired performance was identified as falling below the cut-off on two or more subtests of the CT, sensitivity and specificity were found to be 91 and 95% relative to time two diagnoses. When age differences between the groups were controlled using MANCOVA, CS and substitution errors on CD continued to differentiate the groups.

Normative data

Norms for the CT have been developed based on a large normative sample of people who scored > 77 on the 3MS examination and were assumed to be cognitively intact ($N = 1753$). *T*-scores that allow for the direct comparison of one component to another are provided in the manual and on the QuikScore form. The percentage of people falling below each score (i.e., percentiles) is also provided in the manual and on the QuikScore form. In addition, age-based cut-off scores to maximize sensitivity and specificity are provided. For CD, a cut-off score of > 2 errors maximizes sensitivity and specificity for persons aged 65–79, as does a cut-off score > 5 errors for people 80 years of age and older. For CR, a cut-off score < 13 maximizes sensitivity and specificity for persons aged 65–79, as does a cut-off score < 12 for those aged 80 and over. For CS, a cut-off score < 11 maximizes sensitivity and specificity for those aged 65–74, as does a cut-off score < 10 for those aged 75–79, and a cut-off score < 8 for those aged 80 and over (Tuokko et al., 1995).

References

Adunsky, A., Fleissig, Y., Levenkrohn, S., Arad, M., & Noy, S. (2002). A comparative study of Mini-Mental Test, Clock-Drawing task and Cognitive-FIM in evaluating functional outcome of elderly hip fracture patients. *Clinical Rehabilitation*, *16*, 414–419.

American Psychological Association (1985). *Standards for Educational and Psychological Testing*. Washington, DC: American Psychological Association.

Ben-Yehuda, A., Bentur, N., & Friedman, G. (1995). The Clock Drawing Test as a cognitive screening tool for elderly patients in an acute-care hospital. *Aging*, *7*, 188–190.

Borson, S., Scanlan, J., Brush, M., Vitaliano, P., & Dokmak, A. (2000). The Mini-Cog: A cognitive 'vital signs' measure for dementia screening in multi-lingual elderly. *International Journal of Geriatric Psychiatry*, *15*, 1021–1027.

Bourke, J., Castleden, C. M., Stephen, R., & Dennis, M. (1995). A comparison of clock and pentagon drawing in Alzheimer's disease. *International Journal of Geriatric Psychiatry*, *10*, 703–705.

Bozikas, V. P., Kosmidis, M. H., Kourtis, A., Gamvrula, K., Melissidis, P., Tsolaki, M., & Karavatos, A. (2003). Clock Drawing Test in institutionalized patients with schizophrenia compared with Alzheimer's disease patients. *Schizophrenia Research*, *59*, 173–179.

Brodaty, H., & Moore, C. M. (1997). The Clock Drawing Test for dementia of the Alzheimer's type: A comparison of three scoring methods in a memory disorders clinic. *International Journal of Geriatric Psychiatry*, *12*, 619–627.

Cahn, D. A., & Kaplan, E. (1997). Clock drawing in the oldest old. *Clinical Neuropsychologist*, *11*, 96–100.

Cahn, D. A., Salmon, D. P., Monsch, A. U., & Butters, N. (1996). Screening for dementia of the Alzheimer type in the community: The utility of the Clock Drawing Test. *Archives of Clinical Neuropsychology*, *11*, 529–539.

Cahn-Weiner, D. A., Williams, K., Grace, J., Tremont, G., Westervelt, H., & Stern, R. A. (2003). Discrimination of dementia with Lewy bodies from Alzheimer disease and Parkinson disease using the Clock Drawing Test. *Cognitive and Behavioral Neurology*, *16*, 85–92.

Coval, M., Crockett, D., Holliday, S., & Koch, W. (1985). A Multifocus Assessment Scale for use with elderly populations. *Canadian Journal on Aging*, *4*, 101–109.

Critchley, M. (1953). *The parietal lobes*. New York: Hafner.

Erzigkeit, H. (1989). *SKT: Ein Kurztest zur Erfassung von Gedächtnis- und Aufmerksamkeitsstörungen. Manual.* Beltz: Weinheim 4. Auflage.

Esteban-Santillan, C., Praditsuwan, R., Ueda, H., & Geldmacher, D. S. (1998). Clock Drawing Test in very mild Alzheimer's disease. *Journal of the American Geriatrics Society*, *46*, 1266–1269.

Förstl, H., Bruns, A., Levy, R., & Cairns, N. (1993). Neuropathological basis for drawing disability (constructional apraxia) in Alzheimer's disease. *Psychological Medicine*, *23*, 399–403.

Freedman, M., Leach, L., Kaplan, E., Winocur, G., Shulman, K. I., & Delis, D. C. (1994). *Clock drawing: A neuropsychological analysis*. London: Oxford University Press.

Friedman, P. J. (1991). Clock drawing in acute stroke. *Age & Ageing*, *20*, 140–145.

Goodglass, H., & Kaplan, E. (1972). *The assessment of aphasia and related disorders*. Philadelphia: Lea & Febiger.

Heinik, J., Lahav, D., Drummer, D., Vainer-Benaiah, Z., & Lin, R. (2000). Comparison of a Clock Drawing Test in elderly schizophrenia and Alzheimer's disease patients: A preliminary study. *International Journal of Geriatric Psychiatry*, *15*, 638–643.

Heinik, J., Reider-Groswasser, I., Solomesh, I., Segev, I., & Yoram Bleich, A. (2000). Clock Drawing Test: Correlation with linear measurements of CT studies in demented patients. *International Journal of Geriatric Psychiatry*, *15*, 1130–1137.

Heinik, J., Solomesh, I., Bleich, A., & Berkman, P. (2003). Are the Clock-Drawing Test and the MMSE combined interchangeable with CAMCOG as a dementia evaluation instrument in a specialized outpatient setting? *Journal of Geriatric Psychiatry & Neurology*, *16*, 74–79.

Heinik, J., Solomesh, I., Raikher, B., & Lin, R. (2002a). Can Clock Drawing Test help to differentiate between dementia of the Alzheimer's type and vascular dementia?: A preliminary study. *International Journal of Geriatric Psychiatry*, *17*, 699–703.

Heinik, J., Solomesh, I., Shein, V., & Becker, D. (2002b). Clock Drawing Test in mild and moderate dementia of the Alzheimer's type: A comparative and correlation study. *International Journal of Geriatric Psychiatry*, *17*, 480–485.

Heinik, J., Vainer-Benaiah, Z., Lahav, D., & Drummer, D. (1997). Clock Drawing Test in elderly schizophrenia patients. *International Journal of Geriatric Psychiatry*, *12*, 653–655.

Herrmann, N., Kidron, D., Shulman, K. I., Kaplan, E., Binns, M., Leach, L., & Freedman, M. (1998). Clock tests in depression, Alzheimer's disease, and elderly controls. *International Journal of Psychiatry in Medicine*, *28*, 437–447.

Herrmann, N., Kidron, D., Shulman, K. I., Kaplan, E., Binns, M., Soni, J., Leach, L., & Freedman, M. (1999). The use of clock tests in schizophrenia. *General Hospital Psychiatry*, *21*, 70–73.

Horton, A. M., & Roberts, C. (2003). Demographic effects on the Trail Making Test in a drug abuse treatment sample. *Archives of Clinical Neuropsychology*, *18*, 49–56.

Ishiai, S., Sugishita, M., Ichikawa, T., & Gono, S. (1993). Clock-Drawing Test and unilateral spatial neglect. *Neurology*, *43*, 106–110.

Juby, A. (1999). Correlation between the Folstein Mini-Mental State Examination and three methods of clock drawing scoring. *Journal of Geriatric Psychiatry & Neurology*, *12*, 87–91.

Juby, A., Tench, S., & Baker, V. (2002). The value of clock drawing in identifying executive cognitive dysfunction in people with a normal Mini-Mental State Examination score. *Canadian Medical Journal*, *167*, 859–864.

Kitabayashi, Y., Ueda, H., Narumoto, J., Nakamura, K., Kita, H., & Fukui, K. (2001). Qualitative analyses of clock drawings in Alzheimer's disease and vascular dementia. *Psychiatry & Clinical Neurosciences*, *55*, 485–491.

Kurzman, D. (1992). *The construct validity of the Clock Test in normal and demented adults*. Unpublished Master's thesis, University of Victoria, Victoria, BC, Canada.

Lam, L. C. W., Chiu, H. F. K., Ng, K. O., Chan, C., Chan, W. F., Li, S. W., & Wong, M. (1998). Clock-face drawing, reading and setting tests in the screening of dementia in Chinese elderly adults. *Journals of Gerontology*, *53B*, P353–P357.

Lee, H., & Lawlor, B. A. (1995). State-dependent nature of the Clock-Drawing task in geriatric depression. *Journal of the American Geriatrics Society*, *43*, 796–798.

Lee, H., Swanwick, G. R. J., Coen, R. F., & Lawlor, B. A. (1996). Use of the clock-drawing task in the diagnosis of mild and very mild Alzheimer's disease. *International Psychogeriatrics*, *8*, 469–476.

Libon, D. J., Swenson, R. A., Barnoski, E. J., & Sands, L. P. (1993). Clock drawing as an assessment tool for dementia. *Archives of Clinical Neuropsychology*, *8*, 405–415.

Lin, K. N., Wang, P. N., Chen, C., Chiu, Y. H., Kuo, C. C., Chuang, Y. Y., & Liu, H. C. (2003). The three-item Clock-Drawing Test: A simplified screening test for Alzheimer's disease. *European Neurology*, *49*, 53–58.

Manos, P. J. (1999). Ten-Point Clock Test sensitivity for Alzheimer's disease in patients with MMSE scores greater than 23. *International Journal of Geriatric Psychiatry*, *14*, 454–458.

Manos, P. J., & Wu, R. (1994). The Ten Point Clock Test: A quick screen and grading method for cognitive impairment in medical and surgical patients. *International Journal of Psychiatry in Medicine*, *24*, 229–244.

Mendez, M. F., Ala, T., & Underwood, K. L. (1992). Development of scoring criteria for the clock-drawing task in Alzheimer's disease. *Journal of the American Geriatrics Society*, *40*, 1095–1099.

Mesulam, M. M. (1985). *Principles of behavioral neurology*. Philadelphia: FA Davis Company.

Moore, V., & Wyke, M. A. (1984). Drawing disability in patients with senile dementia. *Psychological Medicine*, *14*, 97–105.

Moretti, R., Torre, P., Antonello, R. M., Cazzato, G., & Bava, A. (2002). Ten-Point Clock Test: A correlation analysis with other neuropsychological tests in dementia. *International Journal of Geriatric Psychiatry*, *17*, 347–353.

O'Connell, M. E. (2001). Two-step screening for cognitive impairment: The Clock Test and the 3MS. Unpublished Master's thesis, University of Victoria, Victoria, BC, Canada.

O'Rourke, N., Tuokko, H., Hayden, S., & Beattie, B. L. (1997). Early identification of dementia: Predictive validity of the Clock Test. *Archives of Clinical Neuropsychology*, *12*(3), 257–267.

Paganini-Hill, A., Clark, L. J., Henderson, V. W., & Birge, S. J. (2001). Clock drawing: Analysis in a retirement community. *Journal of the American Geriatrics Society*, *49*, 941–947.

Pan, G. D., Stern, Y., Sano, M., & Mayeux, R. (1989). Clock-drawing in neurological disorders. *Behavioural Neurology*, *2*, 39–48.

Powlishta, K. K., Von Dras, D. D., Stanford, A., Carr, D. B., Tsering, C., Miller, J. P., & Morris, J. C. (2002). The Clock Drawing Test is a poor screen for very mild dementia. *Neurology*, *59*, 898–903.

Ravaglia, G., Forti, P., Maioli, F., Arnone, G., Pantieri, G., Cocci, C., Nativio, V., Muscari, A., Pedone, V., & Mariani, E. (2003). The Clock-Drawing Test in elderly Italian community dwellers: Associations with sociodemographic status and risk factors for vascular cognitive impairment. *Dementia & Geriatric Cognitive Disorders*, *16*, 287–295.

Richardson, H. E., & Glass, J. N. (2002). A comparison of scoring protocols on the Clock Drawing Test in relation to ease of use, diagnostic group, and correlations with Mini-Mental State Examination. *Journal of the American Geriatrics Society*, *50*, 169–173.

Robert, P. H., Schuck, S., Dubois, B., Olie, J. P., Lepine, J. P., Gallarda, T., Goni, S., & Troy, S. (2003). Screening for Alzheimer's disease with the short cognitive evaluation battery. *Dementia & Geriatric Cognitive Disorders*, *15*, 92–98.

Rouleau, I., Salmon, D. P., & Butters, N. (1996). Longitudinal analysis of clock drawing in Alzheimer's disease patients. *Brain & Cognition*, *31*, 17–34.

Rouleau, I., Salmon, D. P., Butters, N., & Kennedy, C. (1992). Quantitative and qualitative analyses of clock drawings in Alzheimer's and Huntington's disease. *Brain & Cognition*, *18*, 70–87.

Royall, D. R., Chiodo, L. K., & Polk, M. J. (2000). Correlates of disability among elderly retirees with "subclinical" cognitive impairment. *Journals of Gerontology*, *55A*, M541–M546.

Royall, D. R., Cordes, J. A., & Polk, M. (1998). CLOX: An executive clock-drawing task. *Journal of Neurology, Neurosurgery & Psychiatry*, *64*, 588–594.

Royall, D. R., Espino, D. V., Polk, M. J., Verdeja, R., Vale, S., Gonzales, H., Palmer, R. R., & Markides, K. P. (2003). Validation of a Spanish translation of the CLOX for use in Hispanic samples: The Hispanic EPESE study. *International Journal of Geriatric Psychiatry*, *18*, 135–140.

Royall, D. R., Mulroy, A. R., Chiodo, L. K., & Polk, M. J. (1999). Clock drawing is sensitive to executive control: A comparison of six methods. *Journals of Gerontology*, *54*, P328–P333.

Scanlan, J., & Borson, S. (2001). The Mini-Cog: Receiver operating characteristics with expert and naive raters. *International Journal of Geriatric Psychiatry*, *16*, 216–222.

Schramm, U., Berger, G., Mueller, R., Kratzsch, T., Peters, J., & Froelich, L. (2002). Psychometric properties of Clock Drawing Test and MMSE or Short Performance Test (SKT) in dementia screening in a memory clinic population. *International Journal of Geriatric Psychiatry*, *17*, 254–260.

Seigerschmidt, E., Moesch, E., Siemen, M., Foerstl, H., & Bickel, H. (2002). The Clock Drawing Test and questionable dementia: Reliability and validity. *International Journal of Geriatric Psychiatry*, *17*, 1048–1054.

Shulman, K. I. (2000). Clock-drawing: Is it the ideal cognitive screening test? *International Journal of Geriatric Psychiatry*, *15*, 548–561.

Shulman, K. I., Shedletsky, R., & Silver, I. L. (1986). The challenge of time: Clock-drawing and cognitive function in the elderly. *International Journal of Geriatric Psychiatry*, *1*, 135–140.

Solomon, P. R., Hirschoff, A., Kelly, B., Relin, M., Brush, M., DeVeaux, R. D., & Pendlebury, W. W. (1998). A 7 minute neurocognitive screening battery highly sensitive to Alzheimer's disease. *Archives of Neurology*, *55*, 349–355.

Souder, E., O'Sullivan, P., & Pechenik, G. (1999). Comparison of scoring criteria for Clock Drawing Test. *Journal of Clinical Geropsychology*, *5*, 139–145.

South, M. B., Greve, K. W., Bianchini, K. J., & Adams, D. (2001). Interrater reliability of Three Clock Drawing Test scoring systems. *Applied Neuropsychology*, *8*, 174–179.

Spreen, O., & Strauss, E. (1998). *A compendium of neuropsychological tests: Administration, norms and commentary*. New York: Oxford University Press.

Storey, J. E., Rowland, J. T. J., Basic, D., & Conforti, D. A. (2001). A comparison of five clock scoring methods using ROC (receiver operating characteristics) curve analysis. *International Journal of Geriatric Psychiatry*, *16*, 394–399.

Storey, J. E., Rowland, J. T. J., Basic, D., & Conforti, D. A. (2002). Accuracy of the Clock Drawing Test for detecting dementia in a multicultural sample of elderly Australian patients. *International Psychogeriatrics*, *14*, 259–271.

Suhr, J., Grace, J., Allen, J., Nadler, J., & McKenna, M. (1998). Quantitative and qualitative performance of stroke versus normal elderly on six clock drawing systems. *Archives of Clinical Neuropsychology*, *13*, 495–502.

Sunderland, T., Hill, J. L., Mellow, A. M., & Lawlor, B. A. (1989). Clock drawing in Alzheimer's disease: A novel measure of dementia severity. *Journal of the American Geriatrics Society*, *37*, 725–729.

Tracy, J. I., de Leon, J., Doonan, R., & Musciente, J. (1996). Clock drawing in schizophrenia. *Psychological Reports*, *79*, 923–928.

Tuokko, H., Hadjistavropoulos, T., Miller, J. A., & Beattie, B. L. (1992). The Clock Test: A sensitive measure to differentiate normal elderly from those with Alzheimer Disease. *Journal of the American Geriatrics Society*, *40*, 579–584.

Tuokko, H., Hadjistavropoulos, T., Miller, J. A., Horton, A., & Beattie, B. L. (1995). *The Clock Test: Administration and scoring manual*. Toronto: Mental Health Systems.

Tuokko, H., Hadjistavropoulos, T., Rae, S., & O'Rourke, N. (2000). A comparison of alternative approaches to the scoring of clock drawing. *Archives of Clinical Neuropsychology*, *15*(2), 137–148.

Ueda, H., Kitabayashi, Y., Narumoto, J., Nakamura, K., Kita, H., Kishikawa, Y., & Fukui, K. (2002). Relationship between Clock Drawing Test performance and regional cerebral blood flow in Alzheimer's disease: A single photon emission computed tomography study. *Psychiatry & Clinical Neurosciences*, *56*, 25–29.

Watson, Y. I., Arfken, C. L., & Birge, S. J. (1993). Clock completion: An objective screening test for dementia. *Journal of the American Geriatrics Society*, *41*, 1235–1240.

Wolf-Klein, G. P., Silverstone, F. A., Levy, A. P., & Brod, M. S. (1989). Screening for Alzheimer's disease by clock drawing. *Journal of the American Geriatrics Society*, *37*, 730–734.

12 Quantitative approaches to the analysis of block design performance

Paula K. Shear and Amy J. Jak

Introduction

Block design is a timed test of visuospatial construction and nonverbal problem-solving that was first developed by Kohs (1923) as a measure of intelligence. Modifications of Kohs' blocks have been incorporated into the Wechsler scales of intelligence for both adults and children and are therefore widely used in clinical practice (Kaufman, 1990). Performance on this task is strongly correlated with Performance and Full Scale IQ measures (Sattler, 2001). In addition to its high *g* loading and importance as a component in intellectual assessment, block design is also known to be sensitive to visuospatial deficits and to cerebral dysfunction (Lezak, 1995), a finding that has led to a prominent place for this task in neuropsychological assessment. Throughout this chapter, "block design" will be used to refer to the standardized Wechsler versions of the task, unless otherwise specified.

On the block design task, the examinee is required to reproduce two-dimensional square arrays by properly and rapidly arranging either four (for 2×2 designs) or nine (for 3×3 designs) three-dimensional blocks. All blocks comprise sides that are colored solid white, solid red, or a combination of red and white areas that are divided along the diagonal. The traditional scoring of block design involves assigning a set number of points for each correct design, including bonus points for speed, and zero points for incorrect designs. The resulting total score is informative for the purposes of understanding the overall level of performance on the task. It does not, however, provide information about the integrity of the component cognitive processes that are required for successful completion of the designs and that may be selectively impaired in specific forms of brain dysfunction.

This distinction between the "process" of completing a task and final "achievement" as summarized by overall performance scores was articulated by Hans Werner (1937), who described qualitative aspects of apraxic patients' efforts to make skilled movements as an "unfolding" over time. Edith Kaplan and her colleagues have subsequently applied this process-oriented approach to the study of a wide range of cognitive and motors skills, which has included extensive qualitative descriptions of block design performances in patients with cognitive dysfunction (Kaplan, 1983, 1988; Kaplan, Palmer, Weinstein, Baker, & Weintraub, 1981). Those aspects of block design performance that received most attention in these initial descriptive papers include a relative preference to attend to the square configuration of the design or, rather, to the internal details (a preference thought to be indicative of lateralization of cerebral dysfunction); the side of the design on which the examinee begins his or her construction (also related to lateralization); and the speed and efficiency of the steps taken toward task completion (nonspecific indicators). Each of these aspects of performance will be discussed in greater detail later in this chapter.

Despite the widespread impact that this process model of assessment has had on clinical practice, there were, until relatively recently, few empirical studies in patient samples that were designed to examine the generalizability of these qualitative observations by Kaplan and colleagues, most of which were derived from individual case studies. Equally problematic, until recently there has been a near absence of normative studies on which to base clinical judgments about the degree to which the presence of these qualitative features of performance are typical or atypical in the general population. The goal of this chapter is to provide quantitative information about component processes of block design performance, in order to inform clinical practice, research and test development. We will begin with an overview of studies that explore the cognitive mechanisms that are invoked during block design performance and their relationship to stimulus parameters of the Wechsler versions of the task, and then we will move to a discussion of the available normative data.

Component processes contributing to block design performance

It is intuitively clear that, like most visuospatial measures, block design performance is dependent in part on foundational skills such as the ability to understand and retain the test instructions, attend to the task, and see the stimuli adequately. In addition, there are components of successful performance that are tied to the demand characteristics of this particular test.

Hierarchical visuospatial processing

Of these components, by far the most thoroughly studied is the requirement that the final correct design be in a square configuration (2×2 or 3×3 matrix). Configural errors on block design may appear in the form of designs that are placed flat on the desktop but that break the square matrix (broken configurations), square matrices that are rotated out of alignment with the model (whole design rotations), and blocks that are stacked upon each other vertically (stacking).

Broken configuration errors on block design are best understood within the context of "global–local" visuospatial processing theory. Visuospatial abilities have long been considered to be mediated by the right cerebral hemisphere, although there is abundant evidence that each hemisphere actually plays a unique role in visuospatial processing. Specifically, it appears that the right hemisphere processes global, configural information preferentially, while the left hemisphere selectively processes information from the smaller local elements of a visual array. Stated differently, patients with damage to the left hemisphere (who are putatively relying disproportionately on the right hemisphere for processing) tend to make errors in which they miss the local elements in an array but show relative preservation of the global configuration. In contrast, patients with right-hemisphere damage (putatively relying more on the left hemisphere for processing) tend to make errors in which they violate the global configuration but show relative preservation of the local elements (Delis, Kiefner, & Fridlund, 1988; Delis, Robertson, & Efron, 1986; Lamb, Robertson, & Knight, 1990; Robertson & Delis, 1986; Robertson, Lamb, & Knight, 1988). This pattern is evident not only in focal lesion patients but also in those with diffuse disease, among whom those with more impaired verbal than visual skills (i.e., evidence of greater left-hemisphere dysfunction) show preferential configural processing, whereas those with more impaired verbal than visual skills (i.e., greater right-hemisphere dysfunction) show preferential local processing (Bihrle, Bellugi, Delis, & Marks, 1989; Delis et al., 1992). This dissociation has typically been studied using hierarchical stimuli that are designed to have unambiguous configural and local components, such as the one illustrated in Figure 12.1.

These replicable findings from experimental paradigms with hierarchical global–local stimuli are consistent with the case study reports on block design performance, which suggest that individuals with left-hemisphere damage tend to adhere adequately to the square configuration of the designs but make errors in the internal placement of the blocks (local errors), whereas those with right-hemisphere damage show the opposite pattern (Kaplan, 1983, 1988; Milberg, Hebben, & Kaplan, 1986). Focusing for a moment only on the broken configuration aspect of block design errors, the observation of increased numbers of broken configurations in patients with right-hemisphere involvement has now been confirmed in empirical studies of adults (Akshoomoff, Delis, & Kiefner, 1989; Ben-Yishay, Diller, Madleberg, Gordon, & Gerstman, 1971; Fischer & Leavell, 1995) and children (Schatz, Ballantyne, & Trauner, 2000) with focal lesions due to stroke and in populations with focal damage superimposed on more widespread cognitive dysfunction, such as individuals

```
      X
     X X
    X   X
   X X X X
  X       X
 X         X
```

Figure 12.1 In this hierarchical stimulus, the global or configural level is the letter A, and the local elements are the letter X.

with epilepsy (Zipf-Williams, Shear, Strongin, Winegarden, & Morrell, 2000) and traumatic brain injury (Wilde, Boake, & Sherer, 2000). The presence of broken configuration errors is related to poorer visuospatial processing skill, as measured by lower block design scaled scores in healthy children (Kramer, Kaplan, Share, & Huckeba, 1999) and lower Visual Form Discrimination Test scores in adults with traumatic brain injuries (Wilde et al., 2000).

The most compelling link, however, between the experimental literature on global–local processing and broken configurations on block design comes from a study by Kramer and colleagues (Kramer, Kaplan, Blusewicz, & Preston, 1991). This study examined a mixed group of healthy volunteers and patients in an alcohol treatment program and found that those individuals with a relatively weaker tendency to process global as compared to local information on the experimental hierarchical stimuli were also more likely to break configuration on block design. Kramer et al. (1999) later replicated these findings in a group of healthy children. In contrast to these results for broken configuration errors, whole design rotations on the block design are not significantly related to performance on the hierarchical stimuli (Kramer et al., 1991). Thus, it may be inaccurate to merge counts of broken configuration and whole block rotation errors into one index, as several investigators have done in the past, because they may reflect different underlying cognitive mechanisms.

Taken together, the literature suggests that the robust demonstration of a configural processing weakness in patients with right-hemisphere damage on hierarchical global–local tasks translates well to the presence of broken configurations on the Block Design Test. There are, however, fewer empirical studies that have tested the complementary premise by Kaplan and colleagues that, similar to the global–local results, patients with left-hemisphere damage show a selective tendency to make single-block errors on block design that nevertheless preserve the square configuration of the design (Kaplan, 1983, 1988; Milberg et al., 1986). The vast majority of the published block design studies report qualitative observations regarding broken configurations but not single-block errors. It is possible that this trend in the literature reflects either the presence of negative findings for these variables or, more likely, the fact that in order to examine errors in a comprehensive fashion, it is necessary to record not only the examinee's final solution to a block design problem but also every move that was made on the way to that solution (Kaplan, Fein, Morris, & Delis, 1991). While it is a relatively simple task to count the number of broken configuration errors made *en route* to a solution, because the number of errors is relatively small, it is a much more labor-intensive effort to record every block placement in a way that allows for subsequent analysis of single-block errors.

A second area of complexity in measuring local errors on the block design tasks is that, in contrast to the hierarchical stimuli such as that illustrated in Figure 12.1, it is not always clear on block design which aspects of the figure are "global" and which are "local." Aside from the unambiguous configural nature of the square matrix, the remaining aspects of the design could be perceived by the examinee as being entirely local or, rather, as relating to the configural portions of the inner details. For example, in the design that features a chevron pattern, the blocks that form the chevron could be conceptualized as either local elements relative to the entire matrix or global features within the chevron portion of the array. Therefore, while we can define single-block rotations or substitutions as a unique error category in terms of scoring, it is not clear if all of these errors reflect the same underlying mechanism that mediates the local processing deficits identified in studies of hierarchical stimuli.

Finally, even if single-block errors are indeed an accurate index of local processing failures, the test itself is constructed in such a way that scoring of broken configurations and single-block errors are confounded. That is, it is only possible to identify single-block errors in productions that preserve the square configuration of the design. In the absence of this structure, individual blocks cannot be mapped onto the target figure. In an extreme case in which an individual breaks configuration on each design that is attempted, no single-block errors would be identifiable. This situation stands in contrast to the experimentally constructed hierarchical figures in which the global and local components are orthogonal.

We have identified only three empirical studies of patients with relatively lateralizing disorders that report data for single-block errors. Of these, all demonstrate significant results for this measure. Specifically, both adults with strokes (Fischer & Leavell, 1995) and children with pre- or perinatal strokes (Schatz et al., 2000) have been shown to display the full double-dissociation wherein those with left-hemisphere damage show preserved global configuration in the presence of an inflated number of single-block errors, and those with right-hemisphere damage show the opposite pattern. In a related study, Vasterling and colleagues (Vasterling, Rogers, & Kaplan, 2000) have demonstrated a significant but modest elevation in the number of single-block errors made by patients with post-traumatic stress disorder (PTSD), again in the absence of abnormalities in the number of broken configurations. Individuals with PTSD are believed to have left-hemispheric hypoactivity, which is consistent with the observation of single-block errors . This finding is consistent with a report that young, healthy men with relatively greater levels of depressive symptoms and trait anxiety demonstrated a local bias on a hierarchical global–local task. In contrast, those with relatively greater positive mood and optimism showed a global processing bias (Basso, Schefft, Ris, & Dember, 1996).

Thus far, the studies that have been reviewed indicate that the Block Design Test is sensitive, at least at the group level, to the patterns of global–local visuospatial processing deficits that are known from the experimental literature to exist in lateralized cerebral dysfunction. Now we turn to a discussion of experiments with novel block design tasks that provide information about the specific stimulus parameters that have been found to affect the frequency with which individuals display global or local processing biases and the efficiency with which they solve block design tasks.

Strategy and stimulus complexity

Wechsler and other theorists have suggested that examinees approach Block Design Tests with one of two strategies: analytic or synthetic (Wechsler, 1958). An analytic strategy requires the examinee to segment the matrix into components that correspond to the individual blocks and then to systematically place each block into the correct location. To give one of a number of possible examples, an examinee who solves a 3×3 block design item by placing the blocks one at a time, working from left to right, top to bottom, is using an analytic strategy. A synthetic approach, in contrast, refers to attempts to move the blocks until they match the gestalt of the target figure, without first trying to segment the design into its component elements. Several studies have examined analytic vs. synthetic approaches to novel block design tasks.

In a representative study, Schorr and colleagues (Schorr, Bower, & Kiernan, 1982) replicated and extended earlier work by Royer (Royer & Weitzel, 1977) by presenting undergraduates with partially completed items from the WAIS Block Design Test using a tachistoscope, and requiring them to select the block from an array (solid red, solid white, mixed block in each of the four possible orientations) that would complete the design correctly. They demonstrated an effect of task uncertainty, whereby subjects selected correct solid blocks (having to decide only between red or white) more rapidly than correct mixed blocks (having to decide among four possible orientations). Independent of task uncertainty, there was also an effect of perceptual cohesiveness: performance was more rapid for designs with higher numbers of interior edge cues. Edge cues refer to aspects of the patterns that provide implicit information about the demarcation between blocks (see Figure 12.2). The finding that the number of internal edge cues affects processing speed and accuracy has now been replicated several times, using novel versions of the block design task (Akshoomoff, 1996; Royer, Gilmore, & Gruhn, 1984; Rozencwajg & Corroyer, 2001).

Together, these findings have been interpreted as demonstrating that healthy young adults tend to adopt an analytic approach to the block design task, an approach that is made more challenging as fewer internal edge are available. The assumption is that, if examinees were working from a gestalt-driven approach, they would not be hindered by an increase in perceptual

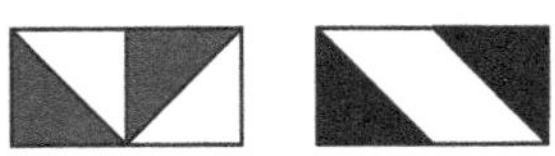

Figure 12.2 The 2×1 design on the left has internal edge cues that speed construction (low perceptual cohesiveness), whereas the design on the right has no internal edge cues (high perceptual cohesiveness).

cohesiveness (reduction of edge cues). A related finding is that, on a novel block design task, participants make an increasing number of broken configuration errors when they are faced with designs that have higher perceptual cohesiveness (Akshoomoff, 1996). The number of broken configurations on these same designs is reduced when examinees are provided with a superimposed grid that provides the missing edge information (Akshoomoff, 1996). Even when edge cue information is held constant, however, certain types of visual gestalts are more difficult to reproduce than others. Specifically, stripe patterns are harder to construct than are triangles or diamonds that are similar in terms of the number of edge cues, and subjects must spend a greater amount of time referring to the target stimulus while constructing these more difficult figures (Rozencwajg & Corroyer, 2001).

It must be emphasized that the Wechsler block design stimuli were not designed with attention to these perceptual contributors to task difficulty (with the exception of the optional stimuli on the WISC-III PI, described below). Thus, on the Wechsler scales, broken configuration errors would not be expected to be distributed equally across items; rather, they should occur more frequently on items that include fewer internal edge cues or that have diagonal lines. There is evidence that such an item-specific pattern is evident in healthy children (Kramer et al., 1999) and healthy elderly people (Joy, Fein, Kaplan, & Freedman, 2001; Troyer, Cullum, Smernoff, & Kozora, 1994), although there is not yet information about how performance in clinical populations may vary across individual blocks in the task. The varying perceptual complexity and gestalts of the different stimuli become a substantial confound also in developmental work, because older children and more visuospatially skilled elders are more likely to advance to items with stimulus features that pull more strongly for broken configuration errors, whereas those who meet earlier discontinuation rules are not tested on these items. Thus, expressing broken configuration errors as a percentage of the number of items completed corrects only for the length of the test and not for its stimulus characteristics.

Developmental and demographic effects on qualitative block design performance

Children as young as 4.5 years of age make planful attempts to solve block design problems (Akshoomoff, 1996), and their Wechsler block design raw scores increase systematically between the ages of 6 years, 0 months and 13 years, 11 months (Kramer et al., 1999). Using novel versions of the block design stimuli that vary systematically in terms of the degree of perceptual cohesiveness, Akshoomoff and colleagues (Akshoomoff, 1996) have demonstrated that children's errors are related both to their age and to the stimulus characteristics of the target figures. Within a sample of children who were 4.5–8.9 years of age, younger children were more likely to make errors than their older peers, and their errors were more likely to include broken configurations. However, in all age groups studied, children were most likely to make single-block errors on designs with extensive edge cues and most likely to make broken configuration errors on designs with few edge cues. Furthermore, the provision of a superimposed grid led children throughout the studied age range to make fewer errors overall and fewer broken configurations.

Thus, while young children are more error-prone, the effect of stimulus features on error types is similar across the early childhood years. Rozencwajg and colleagues (Rozencwajg & Corroyer, 2001) expanded this line of inquiry by testing healthy 12- and 17-year-old children as well as adults, using a computer program that recorded moves. Younger children were more likely than the older participants to use a global strategy, that is, to place the blocks in an order that reflected the gestalt of the pattern rather than an analytic attempt to segment the patterns into individual blocks. Furthermore, certain types of gestalts, such as diagonal patterns, were more challenging for all participants, but particularly for the younger age group. This study also demonstrates that stimulus features of the design affect performance in children.

Turning now to adult development, block design performance declines significantly with advancing age (Kaufman, 1990). Aging is associated with motor slowing on the block design task, as assessed by the speed with which participants are able to construct solid (all red or all white) square figures, and with disproportionately reduced speed when task uncertainty is greater (i.e., when there are a higher number of mixed blocks), even after controlling for motor speed (Royer et al., 1984). Thus, it appears that both motor speed and processing speed task components are affected by aging. In contrast, perceptual cohesiveness did not affect age cohorts differentially across the range from 49 to over 75 years of age (Royer et al., 1984).

On the Wechsler scales, within a sample ranging in age from 50 to 90, age affects not only the speed with which blocks are placed, but also the proportion of block placements that are accurate. Participants over age 60 are somewhat more likely than younger individuals to break configuration or commit whole design rotation errors than those 50–59 years of age (Joy et al., 2001). Visual inspection of the data does not suggest, however, that configural errors increase systematically with age beyond the sixth decade of life. When time constraints are removed, the presence (Troyer et al., 1994) or absence (Joy et al., 2001) of age effects may depend in part on the scoring system that is selected. That is, reduced age effects are present when performance is expressed as the percentage of blocks placed that are correct, rather than as the sum of points for correct solutions. More specifically, some investigators have scored designs that are correct overtime by crediting the participant with the minimum number of points possible for an item (i.e., without time bonus points). Using this system, an individual who completes an item correctly overtime cannot possibly earn the same overtime score as one who completes the design on time and earns bonus points. Time is therefore still confounded with the overtime score using this method.

To summarize, while both young children and the elderly show performance decrements on block design, all age groups show a similar response to perceptual cohesiveness. In the healthy elderly, performance is hampered by motor and processing speed decrements, although there is no evidence that those over 60 years of age show a progressive tendency to make configural errors.

Gender and education

Qualitative block design performance is similar between boys and girls (Akshoomoff, 1996; Kramer et al., 1999). There is a report of modestly higher block design scores for men than women when the time limit is extended, although the men in this sample also had slightly more education than the women (Troyer et al., 1994). Other authors report no gender differences in healthy elderly (Paolo & Ryan, 1994). Little data are available that have examined education effects. In children, broken configurations are more common in individuals whose mothers have lower levels of education and in African-American as compared to White or Hispanic participants (Kramer et al., 1999).

Standardized versions of qualitative block design assessment

Although the Wechsler versions of the Block Design Test were not designed to assess all possible parameters optimally (e.g., the edge cues are not systematically controlled, and the assessment of single-block errors is confounded with the presence of broken configurations), the existing literature does in general support the sensitivity of block design to impairments in several of the component processes of visuospatial perception and construction that have been identified in the experimental literature. In order to evaluate the clinical significance of the observed group differences in patients, however, it is necessary to have a normative database for qualitative aspects of the block design task. There are several well-designed normative studies of qualitative aspects of block design performance, which will be reviewed below. It is noteworthy, however, that none of these studies provide data for the most recent versions of the Wechsler scales for children and adults. Therefore, while the results likely generalize well to the newer versions of the test, they do not perfectly predict the expected findings on the most recently appended designs. In addition, because there is not yet a standardized protocol for collecting quantitative block design data that reflects a process approach, the measures differed somewhat across studies.

With regard to the issue of systematic data collection, there are now two published measures designed to supplement the standardized administration of the block design. The WAIS-R as a Neuropsychological Instrument (WAIS-R NI; Kaplan et al., 1991) was developed to provide additional qualitative information about each Wechsler subscale, including block design. Unfortunately, the WAIS-R NI block design protocol calls for the examiner to give the participant 12 blocks for each of the designs. This procedure is intended to provide additional information about performance by forcing the examinee to select the correct number of blocks from those presented; however, it also means that standard WAIS-R scaled scores cannot be derived from the test administration. Additional features of the NI administration include a sequential record of each block placement that the examinee makes, an examination of the ability to complete designs correctly beyond the standard time limit, an assessment of the examinee's subjective judgment about whether solutions are correct, and a version of the stimuli with an explicit grid overlay to use on items that are failed. The authors suggest describing the integrity of the final design as the percentage of blocks in the design that are correctly placed. They also suggest tallying the number of errors that occur in left vs. right hemispace, the side on which the examinee began his or her construction, the number of broken configurations, single-block rotation errors, single-block errors in selecting the wrong surface (wrong solid color or solid vs. mixed), whole design rotations, and the amount of scatter among item scores on the subtest.

While the recording method and the variables of interest potentially provide a standardized assessment method for future work, the WAIS-R NI itself is largely an aspirational measure in that normative data are not provided for these indices. The authors write in the test manual, "… it is important for future research to provide normative data for the varieties of error types described in this Manual. The other major area of needed research … concerns the reliability with which constituent observations and scores can be generated and the validity of the proposed interpretations" (Kaplan et al., 1991). In the decade since this instrument was published, however, extremely few studies have been conducted with the WAIS-R NI protocol. The WAIS-R NI was given in its entirety (all subtests) in a study of patients with Parkinson's disease, and the authors reported that the test administration required 4 h for the patients and 2 h for healthy volunteers (Peavy et al., 2001). Hence, in terms of feasibility, it will be important for instruments developed in the future to quantify component processes of performance to be more time efficient.

More recently, the WISC-III PI (Kaplan, Fein, Kramer, Delis, & Morris, 1999) was developed and designed to provide supplemental qualitative information based on the intellectual assessment. In contrast to the WAIS-R NI, the WISC-III PI manual does provide normative data based on a standardization sample of 550 children between the ages of 6 and 16 years. The manual calls for the standardized administration of the WISC-III Block Design Subtest, and normative data are provided for the total number of blocks correctly placed, broken configuration errors *en route* to the final solution, and broken configurations in the final solution. An optional Block Design PI task provides six additional stimuli, designed to have greater perceptual cohesiveness than the original stimuli and to be administered by providing the examinee with 12 blocks from which to select the correct number for the final solution. Those Block Design PI items that are failed are then repeated with explicit grid information. These additional items are theoretically interesting in that they are designed specifically to control the empirical literature on visuospatial processing. We are not aware of published studies that have utilized these additional stimuli.

Reliability data

The most complete block design data come from protocols in which the examiner records each move that the examinee makes throughout the task, rather than simply the final production. In our experience, this type of recording requires extensive practice and can be difficult to accomplish when the examinee works rapidly or makes many corrections. There are no published data on the reliability with which individual examiners record this type of flow diagram of patient data, with the possible exception of one study for which it is not completely clear whether the reliability data that are provided refer to the recording of responses or to the classification of already recorded responses (Ben-Yishay et al., 1971).

The only definite reliability data on the accuracy with which examinees diagram patient responses comes from a study with novel block design stimuli that used videotaping to record children's responses. Thus, in contrast to clinical work with patients, the raters could presumably rewind the tape if they needed more time to do their recordings. These authors report reliability of over 90% between two independent raters on measures of total time, single-block errors in the final production, whole design rotations in the final production, and incomplete designs in the final production (Akshoomoff, 1996).

Once responses are recorded, independent raters are highly reliable in the accuracy with which they are able to code *en route* and final errors of whole design rotations, broken configurations, and single-block errors in adult patient groups (Kramer et al., 1991; Vasterling et al., 2000; Zipf-Williams et al., 2000), with most reliability coefficients at the level of 0.90 and higher. (The exceptions are from one study in which intraclass correlations of 0.80 are reported for whole design rotations *en route* and in the final configuration; Vasterling et al., 2000.)

The WISC-III PI manual (Kaplan et al., 1999) provides test–retest reliability data for certain of the block design indices in healthy children assessed with an average inter-test interval of 23 days. The number of correctly placed blocks (WISC-III Block Design partial score) has reliability coefficients that range from 0.79 to 0.92 across the 8–16-year-old age groups, with somewhat lower values for 6- and 7-year-olds (0.73 and 0.68, respectively). Reliability coefficients are slightly higher overall for the same index drawn from the Block Design PI (the six new optional stimuli), with coefficients ranging from 0.60 to 0.93. No test–retest reliability data are provided for the error categories.

To summarize, the existing data suggest that adequate inter-rater reliability exists when raters make error judgments from pre-recorded protocols, although the ideal study that compares multiple raters' recordings of the designs as they are being constructed as well as coding of the data into error types has not yet been conducted. There is also a clear need for more information about the stability of quantitative error scores over time.

Normative data

WISC-III

In a sample of children aged 6–13 years that represent a subset of the WISC-III PI normative sample (Kramer et al., 1999), over half of the participants at all ages broke the square configuration of at least one design. It was not uncommon to see two broken configurations *en route* to a final solution even in the older children (13.6% of 12- and 13-year-olds broke configuration twice *en route*), although three or more such errors were unusual even in young children. Thus, the presence of as many as two broken configurations *en route* are unlikely to be clinically meaningful. Broken configurations in the final constructions were uncommon across all age groups, however, with only 2.8% of the sample offering a broken configuration as the final solution twice or more. Thus, the presence of a multiple of such errors in the final construction is of possible clinical significance.

In the full WISC-III PI normative sample, the number of broken configuration errors reportedly declines beyond the age of 13 (Kaplan et al., 1999), with 16-year-olds showing a mean of only 0.66 broken configurations *en route* to the final solution and 0.16 on the final production (as compared to 1.24 and 0.28, respectively, in the 13-year-olds). The frequencies of these errors are so low, however, that it is difficult to accurately examine age-related changes. Again, it is important to emphasize that older and more visuospatially skilled children would have been administered a larger number of designs with perceptual features that pull for broken configurations; designs 10 and 11 elicited a particularly high number of broken configurations (Kramer et al., 1999).

WAIS-R

No normative block design data are available for qualitative performance in younger adults. There are, however, three published normative studies of aging, all drawn from WAIS-R administrations (Joy et al., 2001; Paolo & Ryan, 1994; Troyer et al., 1994). Troyer and colleagues (Troyer et al., 1994) report data from 145 highly educated, healthy individuals 50–95 years of age (70% female). For 71 of the participants, qualitative measures were available in addition to standard scores. These investigators identified the expected performance decline with age. Older subjects continued to earn lower scores even when the time limit was extended, but these data used a methodology that confounds speed credit with overtime scores. Broken configurations *en route* to the final design occurred on average in only 7.5% of the trials that were administered, and broken configurations in the final design in only 3.1%.

Single- and multi-block rotation errors (the latter referring to situations in which two or more blocks were aligned correctly with each other but placed incorrectly within the design) were more common, occurring in 43.3 and 20.3% of the trials, respectively, when errors made *en route* to or at the final solution were combined. The majority of trials were begun on the right (48.1%), with another 38.5% begun on the left. The authors note, however, that certain designs elicited similar start positions across examinees (particularly designs 7–9). It is remarkable that a full 89% of the participants began design 9 in the middle, which is consistent with experimental data suggesting that the specific design gestalts influence the order of block placement (Rozencwajg & Corroyer, 2002). Only 11% of participants consistently started on one side, excluding the design with the high incidence of center starts. Finally, only one person in the entire sample demonstrated "closing in" by stacking blocks on top of the model.

Paolo and Ryan (1994) studied 225 healthy people between 75 and 96 years of age (67% female) with average Full Scale IQs (mean = 03.57, standard deviation = 14.27). Broken configuration errors were infrequent in their sample, with only 8.4% of participants making one or more broken configurations *en route* to the final design and 4.9% making one or more broken configurations in the final production. Whole design rotations were also uncommon, with only 4.8% of the sample making one or more of these errors in a final construction. It was extremely rare for the participants to make errors in which they stacked blocks on top of each other or on top of the model, with less than 1% of participants demonstrating each of these error types.

Finally, Joy and colleagues (Joy et al., 2001) present data drawn from 177 individuals between the ages of 50 and 90 (71% female). Age was again associated with declines in overall score, although this effect was greater for the regular block design raw score than it was for a novel index of the percentage of blocks correctly placed. Older participants were found to make more single-block errors but not more configural errors than less elderly participants. They report that broken configurations *en route* to a final solution occurred in 5.84% of the designs attempted, which corresponds to an average of less than one error per protocol. They found that 7.3% of the participants made two broken configurations and only 2.3% made more than two. Whole design rotations occurred in 10.2% of the sample. Broken configuration errors that involved placing blocks at odd angles were rare. In terms of single-block errors, 47.5% of the sample made between one and four placement errors, and 55.4% made between one and four rotation errors *en route* to or in their final solution. Single-block errors were elicited more strongly on certain items than others. For example, the diagonal stripes in design 7 seemed to pull more strongly for single-block errors than did other items. In terms of clinical interpretation, the authors suggest that two or more broken configuration errors should raise a concern about clinical impairment, and any errors that include blocks placed at odd angles reflect an abnormal approach to the task.

In terms of time limits, 9.0% of the sample completed all items within time. An additional 56.1% were able to complete more designs with additional time compared to the standardized administration, with the majority completing one additional design overtime. Examinees were most likely to begin their constructions on the left, although it was unusual for people to begin all of the designs in the same location. Consistent with the Troyer et al. (1994) report, Joy and colleagues found that start points varied across designs.

Concluding comments

The existing literature provides empirical support for the relationship between several different types of qualitative block design variables and cerebral functioning. The most robust findings are that broken configuration errors, which are relatively infrequent in healthy adults, are significantly more prevalent in patients with right- rather than left-hemisphere involvement. Individuals making a large number of broken configuration errors, particularly in their final productions, should be evaluated for corroborative evidence of right-hemisphere compromise, although the lack of such an error pattern has no lateralizing significance. Fewer empirical studies have evaluated the supposition that left-hemisphere damage is associated with disproportionate numbers of single-block errors, although those that are available are consistent and support the presence of these patterns in individuals with lateralized cerebral dysfunction.

There are a number of studies that, taken together, support the fact that groups of patients with comparable overall scores on the block design task may, nevertheless, show significant differences in qualitative aspects of performance such as the incidence of broken configuration and single-block errors (Akshoomoff et al., 1989; Fischer & Leavell, 1995; Schatz et al., 2000; Vasterling et al., 2000; Zipf-Williams et al., 2000). These quantitative process measures, then, provide information about block design performance that is distinct from what is available on the basis of traditional scores alone, and that enhances an understanding of the mechanisms that underlie performance decrements.

Thus, although original descriptions of expected performance on process-oriented measures (Kaplan, 1983, 1988; Milberg et al., 1986) have justifiably been criticized for a lack of empirical support, more recent research has supported many of the major premises described in these earlier papers. One type of block design performance, however, deserves mention in this regard. Kaplan and her colleagues have often written that among patients with right-hemisphere damage who break the square configuration of the design, those with anterior lesions are more likely to generate errors that preserve the primary gestalt of the design, whereas those with more posterior lesions generate errors that are less closely tied to the main gestalt elements. This observation may well be demonstrated to be accurate in future work, but the current literature does not include empirical studies that either support or refute this contention.

There is a clear need for further reliability work to establish the consistency with which examiners can record individual block movements as well as examine whether the identified error patterns are stable over time in healthy individuals and in patients across the lifespan. In addition, the existing normative data are incomplete, with a particular gap in information about early and middle adulthood. Given that error rates are relatively low in both children and in elderly populations, it is probably reasonable to infer that they are also low in the intervening age groups. However, data in this age range will be important for the most accurate study of changes with normal aging. The current normative database is made complex by the wide variety of variables that individual research teams have chosen to record, as well as by the different recording methods (e.g., running record of all block placements; consideration only of the final design; sampling block placements every 15 s throughout the construction). The effect of these differences is that results can be compared only approximately across studies.

In terms of the design of future work in this area, there is evidence that it is useful to distinguish between the presence of certain errors *en route* to the final design and those in the final production, meaning that information is lost when only the final product is analyzed. In addition, it is helpful for normative studies to provide descriptions of the frequency with which individuals made different numbers of errors, as opposed to simply providing mean error counts (which tend to be too low to be analyzed in a meaningful way). The existing data also suggest that it is important to examine item-specific differences in error patterns, because the Wechsler items vary in terms of perceptual cohesiveness, task uncertainty and the gestalts that must be reproduced, stimulus parameters that are known to be related to task difficulty, error rates, error types, and start positions. A final aspiration would be to work in future modifications of the Wechsler scales toward the inclusion of block design items constructed with attention to stimulus parameters known from cognitive science to affect task performance and to error types that have now been shown to be present in patients with many forms of cerebral dysfunction.

References

Akshoomoff, N. A., Delis, D. C., & Kiefner, M. G. (1989). Block constructions of chronic alcoholic and unilateral brain-damaged patients: A test of the right hemisphere vulnerability hypothesis of alcoholism. *Archives of Clinical Neuropsychology*, *4*, 275–281.

Akshoomoff, N. A., & Stiles, J. (1996). The influence of pattern type on children's block design performance. *Journal of the International Neuropsychological Society*, *2*, 392–402.

Basso, M. R., Schefft, B. K., Ris, M. D., & Dember, W. N. (1996). Mood and global–local visual processing. *Journal of the International Neuropsychological Society*, *2*, 249–255.

Ben-Yishay, Y., Diller, L., Madleberg, I., Gordon, W., & Gerstman, L. J. (1971). Similarities and differences in block design performance between older normal and brain-injured persons: A task analysis. *Journal of Abnormal Psychology*, *78*, 17–25.

Bihrle, A., Bellugi, U., Delis, D. C., & Marks, S. (1989). Seeing either the forest or the trees: Dissociation in visuospatial processing. *Brain and Cognition*, *11*, 37–49.

Delis, D. C., Kiefner, M., & Fridlund, A. J. (1988). Visuospatial dysfunction following unilateral brain damage: Dissociation in hierarchical and hemispatial analysis. *Journal of Clinical and Experimental Neuropsychology*, *10*, 421–431.

Delis, D. C., Massman, P. J., Butters, N., Salmon, D. P., Shear, P. K., Demadura, T., & Filoteo, J. V. (1992). Spatial cognition in Alzheimer's disease: Subtypes of global–local impairment. *Journal of Clinical and Experimental Neuropsychology*, *14*, 463–477.

Delis, D. C., Robertson, L. C., & Efron, R. (1986). Hemispheric specialization of memory for visual hierarchical stimuli. *Neuropsychologia*, *24*, 205–214.

Fischer, R. S., & Leavell, C. A. (1995). Analysis of configural and detail errors on block design (abstract). *Journal of the International Neuropsychological Society*, *1*, 178.

Joy, S., Fein, D., Kaplan, E., & Freedman, M. (2001). Quantifying qualitative features of block design performance among healthy older adults. *Archives of Clinical Neuropsychology*, *16*, 157–170.

Kaplan, E. (1983). Process and achievement revisited. In S. Wapner & B. Kaplan (Eds.), *Toward a holistic developmental psychology* (pp. 143–156). Hillsdale, NJ: Lawrence Erlbaum Associates, Inc.

Kaplan, E. (1988). A process approach to neuropsychological assessment. In T. Boll & B. K. Bryant (Eds.), *Clinical neuropsychology and brain function* (pp. 129–167). Washington, DC: American Psychological Association.

Kaplan, E., Fein, D., Kramer, J., Delis, D., & Morris, R. (1999). *WISC-III PI*. San Antonio, TX: The Psychological Corporation.

Kaplan, E., Fein, D., Morris, R., & Delis, D. C. (1991). *WAIS-R as a Neuropsychological Instrument*. San Antonio, TX: The Psychological Corporation.

Kaplan, E., Palmer, E. P., Weinstein, C., Baker, E., & Weintraub, S. (1981). *Block design: A brain-behavior based analysis*. Paper presented at the International Neuropsychological Society, Bergen, Norway.

Kaufman, A. S. (1990). *Assessing adolescent and adult intelligence*. Boston, MA: Allyn and Bacon.

Kohs, S. C. (1923). *Intelligence measurement: A psychological and statistical study based upon the Block-Design Tests*. New York: Macmillan.

Kramer, J. H., Kaplan, E., Blusewicz, M. J., & Preston, K. A. (1991). Visual hierarchical analysis of block design configural errors. *Journal of Clinical and Experimental Neuropsychology*, *13*, 455–465.

Kramer, J. H., Kaplan, E., Share, L., & Huckeba, W. (1999). Configural errors on WISC-III block design. *Journal of the International Neuropsychological Society*, *5*, 518–524.

Lamb, M., Robertson, L., & Knight, R. (1990). Component mechanisms underlying the processing of hierarchically organized patterns: Inferences from patients with unilateral cortical lesions. *Journal of Experimental Psychology: Learning, Memory and Cognition*, *16*, 471–483.

Lezak, M. D. (1995). *Neuropsychological assessment* (3rd ed.). New York: Oxford University Press.

Milberg, W. P., Hebben, N., & Kaplan, E. (1986). The Boston process approach to neuropsychological assessment. In I. Grant & K. M. Adams (Eds.), *Neuropsychological assessment of neuropsychiatric disorders* (pp. 65–86). New York: Oxford University Press.

Paolo, A. M., & Ryan, J. J. (1994). Base rates of WAIS-R qualitative information for persons 75 years and older. *Assessment, 1*, 83–88.

Peavy, G. M., Salmon, D. P., Bear, I., Paulsen, J. S., Cahn, D. A., Hofstetter, C. R., Kaplan, E. F., Delis, D. C., & Shults, C. W. (2001). Detection of mild cognitive deficits in Parkinson's disease patients with the WAIS-R NI. *Journal of the International Neuropsychological Society, 7*, 535–543.

Robertson, L., & Delis, D. (1986). "Part-whole" processing in unilateral damaged patients: Dysfunction of hierarchical organization. *Neuropsychologia, 24*, 363–370.

Robertson, L., Lamb, M., & Knight, R. (1988). Effects of lesions of temporal-parietal junction on perceptual and attentional processing in humans. *Journal of Neurosciences, 8*, 3757–3769.

Royer, F. L., Gilmore, G. C., & Gruhn, J. J. (1984). Stimulus parameters that produce age differences in block design performance. *Journal of Clinical Psychology, 40*, 1474–1485.

Royer, F. L., & Weitzel, K. (1977). Effect of perceptual cohesiveness on pattern recoding in the block design task. *Perception and Psychophysics, 21*, 39–46.

Rozencwajg, P., & Corroyer, D. (2002). Strategy development in a block design task. *Intelligence, 30*, 1–25.

Sattler, J. M. (2001). *Assessment of children, cognitive applications* (4th ed.). San Diego, CA: Jerome M. Sattler, Publisher, Inc.

Schatz, A. M., Ballantyne, A. O., & Trauner, D. A. (2000). A hierarchical analysis of block design errors in children with early focal brain damage. *Developmental Neuropsychology, 17*, 75–83.

Schorr, D., Bower, G. H., & Kiernan, R. (1982). Stimulus variables in the Block Design Test. *Journal of Consulting and Clinical Psychology, 50*, 479–487.

Troyer, A. K., Cullum, C. M., Smernoff, E. N., & Kozora, E. (1994). Age effects on block design: Qualitative performance features and extended-time effects. *Neuropsychology, 8*, 95–99.

Vasterling, J. J., Rogers, C., & Kaplan, E. (2000). Qualitative block design analysis in posttraumatic stress disorder. *Assessment, 7*, 217–226.

Wechsler, D. (1958). *The measurement and appraisal of adult intelligence* (Vol. 53). Baltimore: Williams & Wilkins.

Werner, H. (1937). Process and achievement: A basic problem of education and developmental psychology. *Harvard Educational Review, 7*, 353–368.

Wilde, M. C., Boake, C., & Sherer, M. (2000). Wechsler Adult Intelligence Scale-Revised block design broken configuration errors in nonpenetrating traumatic brain injury. *Applied Neuropsychology, 7*, 208–214.

Zipf-Williams, E. M., Shear, P. K., Strongin, D., Winegarden, B. J., & Morrell, M. J. (2000). Qualitative block design performance in epilepsy patients. *Archives of Clinical Neuropsychology, 15*, 149–157.

13 New indices of planning abilities using the Tower of London task

W. Keith Berg, Dana L. Byrd, Joseph P. H. McNamara, and Christine A. MacDonald

The structure of executive functions or frontal-lobe functions remains an active debate (see Miyake et al., 2000). Whether executive functions are considered separate abilities or a unified ability, planning ability is consistently included among the ranks of executive functions. A common variety of tasks used to assess planning are tower-transform problem-solving tasks. The classic tower-transform task is the Tower of Hanoi (TOH), but a tower-transform task that is gaining prominence both in clinical and research settings is the Tower of London (TOL; Berg & Byrd, 2002). The objective of the TOL is to rearrange a set of three differently colored balls or beads placed on three pegs of the game board to exactly match the balls in color and position on a separate goal board (see Figure 13.1). The balls may only be moved one at a time from one peg to another, and the length of the three pegs is designed to hold only 3, 2, or 1 ball, respectively. With different arrangements of game and goal balls, problems may vary in difficulty, with optimal solutions requiring from 1 to 8 moves.

The TOL task, developed over 20 years ago by Shallice (1982), is now widely used to assess planning ability and has largely replaced the TOH task in the neuropsychological literature as an assessment of spatial planning. Much of the popularity of this task stems from the fact that, unlike the TOH, there is no single "trick" or subgoal (repeatable sequence of moves) with which one can solve problems. This task is prominent in clinical use because of Shallice's initial finding that performance on this task deteriorates markedly in lesion patients with predominately left-frontal damage, compared to those with right-frontal or more posterior damage. Furthermore, the deterioration in performance was most evident with the more difficult problems. These data were important because they demonstrated that execution of an efficient plan on a task with clear spatial demands was more influenced by left-frontal than by right-frontal or parietal lesions (Shallice, 1982).

Since Shallice's development of the task, a large group of studies has made use of it, testing both clinical (e.g., Cockburn, 1995; Levin et al., 1997; Murji & DeLuca, 1998) and nonclinical groups (e.g., Dagher, Owen, Boecker, & Brooks, 1999; Kafer & Hunter, 1997; Morris, Ahmed, Syed, & Toone, 1993),

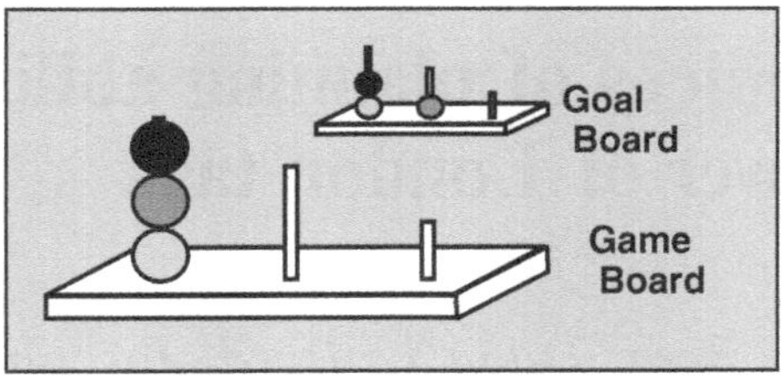

Figure 13.1 Illustration of the TOL task. In the standard version balls are red, blue, and green. Participants must move balls on the game board, one at a time, to match the color and position of the balls on the goal board. A ball underneath another ball cannot be moved until the one above it is placed in a different position. The tall peg holds three balls, the middle peg holds two balls, and the small peg holds one ball.

and testing both young children (e.g., Byrd, van der Veen, McNamara, & Berg, 2004; Luciana & Nelson, 1998) and older adults (e.g., Dagher, Owen, Boecker, & Brooks, 1999). Furthermore, the task has been incorporated into a number of published and standardized executive functioning test batteries (e.g., Cambridge Neuropsychological Test Automated Battery, Colorado Neuropsychology Tests and NEPSY).

Although the TOL task has the potential to provide a very rich source of information about the cognitive processes involved in planning, our review of clinically oriented as well as research-oriented studies of planning (Berg & Byrd, 2002) found two issues to be of concern. The first is a lack of consistency across studies with regard to the measure of performance that is employed, and the second is a failure to take advantage of the wealth of information available from an evaluation of the problem-solving approach or strategy use. The second issue is a general lack of attention to what Poreh (2000) identifies as the "composition" aspect of the quantified process approach. According to Poreh, this aspect is, "an approach by which data on a given test that have been largely overlooked are compiled and subsequently analyzed, resulting in new indices that are believed to reflect underlying constructs accounting for test performance" (Poreh, 2000, p. 214). This type of information could be particularly beneficial to the neuropsychologist. Generally speaking, the body of research associated with the TOL task suggests a somewhat haphazard approach to the measurement of performance.

This chapter reviews the categories of performance measures that have been employed with the TOL, focusing on the unique information each measure provides. We will include information on some new measures we have been developing that may be especially useful in evaluating the cognitive processes that are unique to planning. Thus, our approach is focused on the composition paradigm of the quantified process approach (Poreh, 2000). Finally, we will present the work from two new studies, one that illustrates an evaluation of strategy use and the second that examines the value and comparability of employing computerized testing of the TOL task. As will be indicated, moving toward computerized testing is critical to being able to expand the type and complexity of measures in a feasible manner. We conclude the chapter with a summary of recommendations for the neuropsychologist interested in maximizing the value of the TOL to assess their research participants and clinical clients. This chapter intends to offer valuable information to the clinician as well as to the research investigator.

TOL measures of performance

Measures of performance in common use for the TOL task can be categorized into three broadly defined groups: (1) success or accuracy of solution; (2) efficiency of the solution; and (3) speed of performance and planning during the solution (Berg & Byrd, 2002). We will discuss each of these and will add to this list one additional class of measurements that is rarely examined but is important to be considered, strategy measures. Strategy measures can include general indicators of planning efficiency but can also provide more specific information on the tactics that an individual develops to solve a complex problem and how these strategies evolve with repeated experiences. Such strategy measures may provide valuable new information about the cognitive and neurological capabilities of the individual for both clinicians and researchers.

Success or accuracy of solution

Success measures, sometimes referred to as accuracy measures, are most commonly reflected in the proportion or percent of the problems solved. Measures of success would seem to be fairly straightforward but can actually vary considerably depending in part on the particular test procedure employed. Two distinctly different test procedure approaches have been utilized. One typically involves limiting participants to a fixed number of attempts to reach a "perfect" solution of a particular problem. A perfect solution is one that is achieved in the minimum number of "moves" possible. We will refer to this approach as the performance-limit procedure. In this procedure, success rate is usually determined by the percent of all problems presented that is solved either in the first attempt (e.g., Anderson & Lajoie, 1996; Luciana & Nelson, 1998) or in a fixed number of additional attempts (e.g., Levin et al., 1996).

The second procedure, which we will refer to as the time-limit procedure, limits the time participants are allowed for a single attempt at a solution, but does not require perfect solutions. That is, it allows participants to complete problems with solutions taking more than the minimum moves necessary. With the time-limit procedure, success is commonly defined as the percent of problems solved within the time limit regardless of the number of moves beyond the minimum needed to achieve that solution (e.g., Byrd & Berg, 2002; Culbertson & Zillmer, 1998a, 1998b, 1998c). Note that across studies, there are variations in the numbers of solution attempts allowed in the performance-limit procedure and variations in time limits in the time-limit procedure, and each of these variations can have significant effects on success rate.

A major advantage of the performance-limit procedure is that it underscores the need for careful planning, as participants are required to solve the problems in the minimum moves possible. A major advantage of the time-limit procedure is in portraying the quality of planning in more detail. The imperfect solutions that may occur under the time-limit procedure can offer a wider range of patterns of solutions, errors, and recovery from errors. These latter measures are important to evaluating both efficiency and strategy, as will be explained later in the chapter. Furthermore, the time-limit approach may be maximally flexible because one can still calculate success measures from the proportion of both the perfect solutions that spontaneously occur as well as the proportion correct among all solutions, perfect or not.

Clearly, the distinction between these procedures is not trivial. Baker, Segalowitz, and Ferlisi (2001) evaluated the relationship among scoring versions of both these procedures and found that though they were quite high, $r = 0.76$, among 7-year-olds, they dropped precipitously for older groups, to an $r = 0.46$ for adults.[1] But regardless of the correlation, a more significant question, especially for the quantified process approach, is the extent of valuable information that can be obtained from each test procedure.

Efficiency of the solutions

The measurement of the efficiency of problem solving also differs with the test procedure employed. When the time-limited procedure is used, TOL solution efficiency can be measured from the number of moves required to solve a problem relative to the minimum number possible. When using the performance-limited procedure, solution efficiency might be reflected by the number of attempts required to achieve a perfect solution to a particular problem, provided that multiple attempts to achieve a perfect solution are allowed (e.g., Levin et al., 1996). More efficient solutions would produce fewer moves on any given problem, or fewer attempts to achieve a perfectly solved problem.

Measuring efficiency by assessing the number of attempts required to achieve a perfect solution in the performance-limited procedure may be problematic because it requires repeated exposure to the same problem. In this case learning would be expected to occur and as a result it might confound our measure of efficiency. This is further complicated since learning rates may well differ with age or clinical group. The time-limit approach avoids this drawback because each problem is presented only once. One then evaluates

[1] Some caution in interpreting these results is warranted since quite different scoring schemes were necessarily used to assess the two methods of testing. See Baker et al. (2001) for details.

efficiency by measuring the number of moves required to solve a problem above the minimum number required. Further, using this definition for efficiency, one can directly compare problems varying in difficulty. Berg and Byrd (2002) provide further suggestions for improving this measure of efficiency to correct for increased chances of errors as the number of moves required for solution is increased. Regardless of the test procedure, efficiency might also be conceptualized as the time taken to achieve a solution. However, we have found that such temporal measures can be better conceptualized separately, as a measure of speed of processing, as is done in the treatment presented below.

Speed of performance and planning during the solution

Cognitive psychologists widely report that across a variety of tasks speed of processing is inversely related to accuracy of performance (e.g., Dennis & Evans, 1996; Osman, Lou, Muller-Gethmann, Rinkenauer, Mattes, & Ulrich, 2000). Planning tasks also show this speed-accuracy tradeoff function, both in normal and in frontally-lesioned adults (Davies, 2000; Luria, 1966). Thus, measures of speed are a likely candidate for providing important information about planning capability and have therefore been employed by a number of investigators using the TOL (e.g., Culbertson & Zillmer, 1998a, 1998b; Luciana & Nelson, 1998; Morris et al., 1993). Separating out the various components of the speed measure of the planning process may further enhance the information available from measures of temporal performance.

Although measuring the total time taken to reach a solution is a common method of evaluating the general problem of solution speed, the solution time can be separated into more meaningful measures of specific cognitive abilities. Total solution time is the time spent on planning prior to initiating a solution, which we refer to as the solution initiation time, and the subsequent time spent achieving that solution, which we refer to as the solution completion time. Furthermore, the latter period can be subdivided into the time taken to pause and think about the moves during solution, referred to as pause time, and the time taken to execute the actual moves during solution, the movement time. A series of alternating pause times and movement times would comprise the solution completion time, and the series of pause time and movement times could be pooled into a total pause and total move times for any given solution completion time. Thus, the entire period from the point when the problem is initiated until it is completed can be conceived of as comprising: solution initiation time, total pause time, and total movement time.

When interpreting the two basic temporal measures, solution initiation time and solution completion time, it is important to consider that these measures are not necessarily independent of one another, and are possibly reciprocally related. For example, Davies (2003) suggests that participants might employ one of two different strategies when planning. One approach would be to take more time to plan prior to problem solving and less pause time to plan "online," which would increase solution initiation time and decrease the pause portion of solution completion time. At the other extreme one could do the reverse, planning little before the initial move but frequently pausing during the solution completion time. Either approach might be successful, as might an intermediate approach that balances each. Yet they do represent different strategies or styles for achieving a solution. Unfortunately, few data are available to address this possibility, since most often these different approaches are not assessed. Solution initiation time, solution completion time, and the pause and movement time components of solution completion time are now considered separately.

Solution initiation time

The time from the presentation of the problem to the time of the first move has been called solution initiation latency, first move time, planning time, first move latency, or initiation time. This time period may or may not include the completion of the first move. When solution initiation time includes the time to actually complete the first move it can be influenced by motor abilities. With normal adults, however, the time to reposition the ball is usually far shorter than the initial planning time. As a result, for normal adults solution initiation time is not contaminated seriously by the motor component when the placement of the first ball is included.

Nonetheless, employing the solution initiation time measurement procedure that defines the end of this period when the ball movement is initiated rather than completed could eliminate any motor component, and would therefore appear to be the preferred procedure. However, at times participants extend the ball motion time by briefly holding the selected ball above the pegs or by moving the ball quite slowly toward its destination. The delay in ball placement may occur because of continued planning or error checking during ball repositioning. Because the time involved in completing the ball motion may include continued cognitive processes, we recommend that the measurement of solution initiation time continue until the completion of the actual ball repositioning unless comparing across wide age ranges or patient groups where movement time differences might be substantial.

When evaluating groups such as clinical patients, young children, the elderly, or others with limited motor ability, the portion of solution initiation time related to actual ball positioning could be considerably greater than with adult control groups. In these cases, independently determining the time needed to reposition a ball and subtracting this time from the solution initiation time would be important. A yoked motor task could be given to obtain an estimate of the time required to actually reposition the ball (e.g., Owen, Downes, Sahakian, Polkey, & Robbins, 1990). This underscores the value of using a procedure that includes ball repositioning time when contrasting populations with varied motor ability.

Once factors such as motor ability are controlled, examination of solution initiation time allows us to address either the extent to which the participants take time to carefully consider a plan before initiating a solution or whether the participants can quickly develop an effective plan. Based on a factor analysis, Levin et al. (1996) reported that solution initiation time loads heavily on a different factor than do the measures of the percent solved and the number of rule violations, suggesting the importance of separately considering the latter measure.[2]

Even if the ball repositioning time is managed, there remains a serious interpretative problem in considering just what cognitive aspect of planning is represented by the solution initiation time. For example, one possible interpretation of solution initiation time is that it becomes longer if participants plan more future moves or if they plan each move more carefully. In this case, longer solution initiation time would indicate more deliberative and thorough planning. This is consistent with the interpretation of factor analyses by Levin et al. (1996) from their study of head-injured children. Similarly, Kafer and Hunter (1997) reported longer planning (solution initiation) times with more difficult problems, suggesting that solution initiation time could be longer because the difficulty forces the participant to form a longer and more thorough plan. However, Kafer and Hunter also suggest that solution initiation time may be longer when a participant is struggling to formulate a plan. It is also true in these cases that a longer solution initiation time may not necessarily indicate any particular deliberateness or thoroughness, but possibly ineffective planning. This becomes clear when solution initiation time of the participants becomes shorter as they gain experience, and presumably become more effective with the TOL task, even with problem difficulty held constant (Berg & Byrd, in press).

A correction for the number of moves in the problem as well as a comparison of solution initiation time with other measures, such as success or efficiency, can help clarify whether group or individual differences in solution initiation time are due to variation in deliberateness, ineffective planning, or replanning. Ward and Allport (1997) provide an example of the value of comparing solution initiation time with other performance measures. These researchers found an inverse relationship between solution initiation time and solution errors. These results underscore the necessity of separately scored, multiple measures of TOL performance to expose the sources of performance differences.

Solution completion time

Solution completion time is the time taken to complete the solution after the end of the solution initiation time. This has been termed subsequent move

[2] The factor analysis of Levin et al. (1996) results in two aspects of planning. There is both a "planning and execution" factor, labeled "planning" in their Table 3, and a "planning and deliberation" factor, labeled "inhibition" in that table. Solution initiation time loads heavily onto the "inhibition" factor.

time, solution time, or move time. The solution completion measure has utility but is limited because, as noted above, it combines the actual moves and the pauses for online planning. It is, however, preferable to the other common timing measure, the total time taken to solve the problem, which is the solution initiation time plus solution completion time.

Components of solution time: pause time and move time

Another way to measure planfulness during problem solving is to examine the amount of planning time taken between consecutive moves. Researchers have used a number of methods to measure what may be considered "online planning pauses" but most of these measures do not distinguish any pause to plan from the time to complete a repositioning of the ball. However, previous research (Spitz, Minsky, & Bessellieu, 1985) using the TOH has demonstrated that the simple measure of median move time may serve well when comparing groups who are unlikely to differ in motor abilities. Similarly, other studies have recorded mean move time, calculated as the solution completion time divided by the number of moves. In these cases the terms "median move time" or "mean move time" here actually refer to the combination of any pause for online planning and the actual time taken to reposition the ball. When the actual time to position the ball can be assumed to be relatively constant, variation in such measures could be argued to reflect variations in pause time. Adding to the confusion, in some studies mean move time may also include the time taken to make the first move, i.e., the solution initiation time. In such cases variation in mean move time could be sensitive to manipulations of problem-solving instructions, such as the opportunity or encouragement to plan prior to starting problem solving (Davies, 2003). As a result, we recommend mean or median move time to be based only on solution completion time and exclude solution initiation time.

When comparing two groups of comparable motor ability, such as two equivalent groups of college students, mean move time can offer a window on the planfulness of moves (Davies, 2003). However, comparing groups that differ on motor speed, such as children and adults or clinical and nonclinical populations, making inferences on planning from mean move time may be more difficult. In studies comparing groups likely to differ in motor ability, as described above, a yoked motor control procedure may be useful to correct for differences in motor speed or motor initiation. For example, Owen and colleagues (1990) employed their computerized "One Touch Tower of London" and subtracted move times during a yoked motor control task from the move times during a problem solution. This resulted in a more pure measure of planning time. With this measure, Owen and colleagues discriminated between planning times in Parkinson's diagnosed and control adults.

Our laboratory has taken a different approach to the comparison of groups that differ on motor speed, an approach that does not require additional testing time needed for yoked motor controls. In comparing children and adults' TOL performance, we examined the time between each of the participant's moves to look for instances of unusually long pauses, on the reasoning that these delays usually occur because of online planning rather than any need for more time to reposition a ball. Thus far, we have found that both the number of planning pauses and the proportion of planning pauses differentiate the performance of children and adults (Byrd & Berg, in preparation). However, thus far, we have used this procedure only as a measure of the frequency of planning pauses, not of the length of planning pauses. This measure can be more difficult to interpret with preschool children or individuals with ADHD because long pauses may be indicative of planning or could indicate that the participant was off-task.

Strategy measures

When a time-limited procedure is used and participants are allowed to make moves beyond the minimum required, general information about the quality of problem-solving abilities can be determined from efficiency measures such as the number of extra moves taken over the minimum required. However, provided with the detailed functional structure of the TOL task, such as the problem space (see Berg & Byrd, 2002), and data for individual moves, more specific information can be gathered about the planfulness of the participants and the strategies that they may have employed. These strategies then in turn may provide more specific information about participants' executive functioning abilities. Our laboratory has explored a number of approaches to measure the strategy during problem solving on the TOL; three of these approaches to be discussed here are: measures that divide the solution into two distinct and qualitatively meaningful phases, measures that examine the ability to identify and remove obstacles to an efficient solution, and measures of attempted rule violation. Attempts to violate task rules can be viewed as a type of strategy, though not an ineffective one.

Two phases of a solution: exploratory and goal-focused

Using a time-limit procedure, Kotovsky, Hayes, and Simon (1985) found that in normal adults[1] solutions on the TOH task commonly contain two phases indicative of two different cognitive processes. The first phase they refer to as "exploratory behavior" where the participants make seemingly random moves, some that move one closer to the goal and others that move one further away. Kotovsky and colleagues (1985) and Zhang (1997) suggest that during this first phase individuals explore the aspects of the problem and the possible moves within it, forming a representation of the problem. Kotovsky and colleagues also refer to the second phase of adults' solutions as "final path behavior." During this second or goal-focused phase participants "see" a solution, "close in on the goal," and unerringly execute the final sequence using a series of moves that consistently brings them closer to the goal.

These two phases of problem solving have been differentiated by how they respond to changes in the visual presentation of task elements known as isomorphic transformations (Kotovsky et al., 1985). The exploratory phases of the solutions are lengthened or shortened considerably by isomorphic changes to the presentation of the task.[3] In contrast, the final path is quite consistent across isomorphic changes, though it can be lengthened or shortened by versions of the task that change the working memory load of the task (e.g., Klahr & Robinson, 1981). Kotovsky and colleagues suggest that working memory capacity affects how far ahead the participants can "see" in the solution to the problem and is therefore an important limiting factor in the final path length.

The conceptualization of the two phases of TOH solutions by Kotovsky et al. (1985) can be adapted for application to the TOL, provided that the time-limit rather than the performance-limit procedure is used. To calculate these measures, we examined each move of the solution and determined if it moved the game-board ball arrangement closer, further, or the same number of moves away from the goal. All of these three stages are possible within the TOL problem space (Berg & Byrd, 2002). The distance from the goal at any position is determined by the minimum number of moves necessary to reach the goal from that position. From this information, we calculated the two phases of the TOL solutions.

The first phase of problem solution, what Kotovsky and colleagues (1985) refer to as the exploratory phase, we refer to with the more neutral term, pre-goal phase. The pre-goal phase is defined as the number of moves made prior to initiating the goal phase (see below). It begins with the first move of the solution and ends with the first move of the goal phase. During this period participants inconsistently move the ball closer to, further away from, or stay the same number of moves from the goal. The minimum pre-goal phase length is zero, which can occur when there is a perfect solution, because, by definition each move of this solution takes the participant unerringly to the goal position. In this circumstance the entire solution is comprised of the goal phase. The maximum pre-goal phase length is limited only by the number of moves possible in the time allotted for solving a problem. A shorter pre-goal phase length may indicate that fewer moves are required to develop an accurate solution plan and therefore an earlier focus on reaching the goal. This is consistent with the view of Kotovsky and colleagues (1985) regarding this phase. Hence, the more complete and accurate the plan developed prior to the initial move—i.e., during the solution initiation time—the shorter the exploratory phase can be expected to be. Similarly, well-developed strategies should yield short exploratory phases.

---

[3] An isomorphic change to a task is one that alters the appearance of the task but not the problem space (Zhang, 1997). That is, a given problem is solved with an identical set of moves as for the isomorph of the problem. An example of this is the Monsters and Globe task and the TOH.

We refer to our adaptation of Kotovsky and colleagues' (1985) final path phase as the goal phase. The goal phase is the sequence of moves that lead to the solution wherein every move brings the participant closer to the goal. The goal phase length has the possible range of 1 to 8 moves. The maximum is 8 since in the Shallice's TOL Problem Space,[4] one can never be more than 8 optimal moves away from any other position. For perfectly solved problems, the goal phase is always equal to the minimum number of moves for the problem being solved, and the pre-goal phase is equal to 0. However, with nonoptimal solutions the goal phase length may exceed the minimum number of moves of the problem since the participant may have moved further from the goal during the pre-goal phase prior to seeing the direct path to the goal. Of course, it may also be shorter than the minimum number of moves to the problem, as is more commonly the case, since during the exploratory phase one can move somewhat closer to the goal but not in an unerring manner. In general, a longer goal phase may be indicative of a plan that involves a deeper solution search; that is, a plan that considers the consequences of a greater number of moves in advance of the current position. Details of calculating the goal and pre-goal path phase lengths may be found in Appendix 1.

These two phases of solution, the pre-goal phase and the goal-path phase, are responsive to developmental differences and may also be sensitive to clinical differences. Preschoolers' planning deficits and development are evident in a number of aspects of their planning task performances. Preschool children present solutions on the TOH indicative of a large number of nongoal-focused or exploratory moves (Bidell & Fischer, 1994; Welsh, 1991), possibly due to a lack of focus on the goal of the task or repetitions of the same error in their solutions (Welsh, 1991). Preschoolers' solutions also demonstrate a very shallow depth of search for the goal, a measure of thinking ahead multiple steps to the solution. Preschoolers improve between the ages of 3 and 5 years in their ability to provide solutions that require planning of a number of steps (Welsh, Pennington, & Groisser, 1991). Klahr and Robinson (1981) examined the children's solutions to an isomorph[4] of the TOH task in detail and found increases in depth of search across preschool years. These data on the development of preschoolers' planning task performance, the demonstration of an increased focus on the goal and an increased depth of search for the goal, map well onto Kotovsky and colleagues' (1985) research regarding two separable phases of TOH solutions.

Kotovsky et al. (1985) and Zhang (1997) argue that the two phases of problem solving reflect very different cognitive processes. As such, we might expect that clinical differences in planning and problem-solving abilities

[4] Berg and Byrd (2002) distinguish Shallice's TOL version from several other tasks identified as TOL, such as the five disk TOL (e.g., Gillhooly, Phillips, Wynn, Logie, & Della Sala, 1999; Ward & Allport, 1997) because these versions of the TOL do not have the same problem space, and are essentially different tasks despite the similarity in name.

could also be reflected in the relative lengths of these two separate phases of problem solution in the TOL. Thus far, these measures for the TOL have not been used with disordered populations. However, evidence from other planning tasks and from other TOL measures (e.g., Colvin, Dunbar, & Grafman, 2001; Shallice, 1982) allow us to predict that populations with damage to the left dorso-lateral prefrontal cortex or other areas related to planning would generate solutions with longer pre-goal paths as well as shorter goal paths.

The use of pre-goal and goal phase assessments provide relatively general assessments of strategy; basically, planful vs. nonplanful approaches to planning. However, more specific measures of strategy use can also be explored so as to focus on cognitive processes of interest. One of these is to recognize the need to temporarily move a ball that is an obstacle in TOL problem solving. Here we present preliminary evidence from a study that examined the ability to employ this strategy.

A study of specific strategy use

The examination of specific problem-solving strategy has been fruitful in finding important developmental differences on tasks other than the TOL (e.g., Rittle-Johnson & Siegler, 1999). The study of strategy use and development is important because the effective use of particular strategies may reduce the overall cognitive load that is experienced by an individual when faced with a problem. The attenuation of cognitive load is particularly efficacious for individuals who may have reduced cognitive resources to allocate to problem solving because of immaturity, normal aging, or brain damage such as of the frontal lobes.

Although strategy use with the TOL remains largely unexplored, hypotheses generated by developmental changes in strategy use on other tasks suggest that strategy development underlies developmental improvement on the TOL. Rittle-Johnson and Siegler (1999) found that compared to first graders, second graders were more likely to use an efficient spelling strategy, retrieval, and tended to stray from using an inefficient, back-up strategy throughout the spelling session, resulting in faster solving time and more accurate answers. The evidence of efficient strategy use in older children on spelling problems by these investigators parallels the developmentally associated performance changes reported by Luciana and Nelson (1998) on the TOL. Finding that older preschool children are more likely to display a high accuracy, minimum move performance combination on the TOL, Luciana and Nelson suggested the use of efficient strategies. In comparison, the younger-preschool-aged problem solver who typically displays low accuracy and frequent extra moves does not appear to display the use of, or recognize the advantage of, an efficient strategy throughout the problem-solving session.

Identifying the strategy that is optimal for rapid and efficient problem solving allows us to decompose more completely the use of elements of planful problem solving. One particular strategy requirement of many tower problems is obstacle-removal subgoal, the ability to move one ball or disk temporarily out of the way so that other balls may be moved to their goal positions (see, e.g., MacDonald, Garner, & Spurgeon, 2002). All problems requiring a minimum of 4 or more moves require this strategy at least once, as do some of the problems that require a minimum of 3 moves. We refer to problems that have this characteristic as "obstacle problems." To solve an obstacle problem in the TOL task the participant must first remove the obstacle ball from a peg and place it in a position other than its final goal position after which the ball underneath becomes unobstructed and can be placed in its final goal position (see Figure 13.2). Therefore, to solve an obstacle problem successfully it is essential that the problem solver recognizes and deals

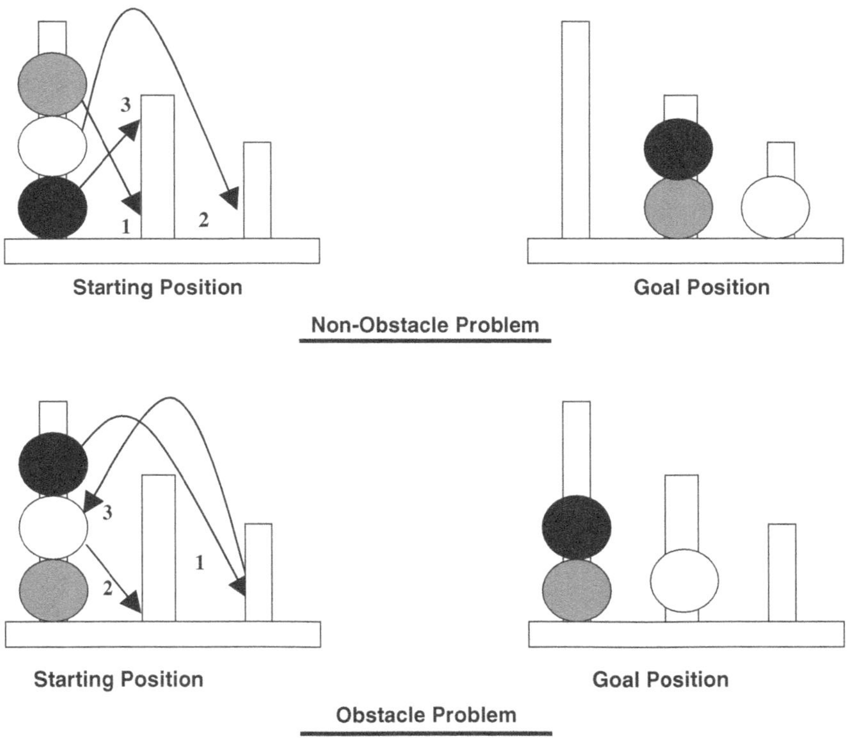

Figure 13.2 Example of nonobstacle and obstacle 3-move problems. Each move in order is shown here by numbered arrows. The optimal solution for each is achieved by moving the balls from their starting position on the game board on the left in the order shown by the numbered arrows. Note that for the nonobstacle problem each move puts a ball into its final goal position, whereas in the obstacle problem, at least one ball must be moved temporarily out of the way (Step 1 in this example) to a position that is not its final goal position. This allows for the placement of other ball(s) directly into their goal positions. In Step 3 of this example the obstacle ball can be moved from its temporary position to its final goal position.

with the obstacle appropriately by making a move that appears to take them away from the goal, but actually moves them closer to the goal. It requires not focusing on the result of a single move but on the overall result of a series of moves it facilitates. Because the obstacle component serves to conceal an obvious path to the goal state, it requires a more complex, less obvious strategy to solve the problem efficiently, and thus requires thinking ahead multiple steps and the willingness to make a move that appears to take the solver away from the solution.

In order to examine developmental differences in the ability to manage problems requiring identification and removal of an obstacle, we tested two groups of preschoolers ($N = 23$), young (3-year-olds) and old (4-year-olds), on their problem-solving efforts. We presented 3-move obstacle and nonobstacle problems and used move-by-move analysis to determine the use of either an efficient or an inefficient strategy over the session. The efficient strategy for an obstacle problem was defined by moving an obstacle ball to a temporary location, called a "holding peg," that is not its final goal location (see Figure 13.3).

Problems requiring removal of an obstacle were more challenging for all of the preschoolers. Accuracy, solution initiation time, solution completion time, total moves, and rule violations all displayed significantly poorer performance for obstacle vs. nonobstacle, 3-move problems (see Table 13.1). The differences were especially striking for the timing measures. For example, solution initiation times, mostly comprised of the time to plan a solution approach, were almost twice as long for obstacle problems as for the nonobstacle problems, despite the same minimum number of moves required for each.

The development of the ability to manage obstacle problems was exemplified by the older children performing better on obstacle problems than

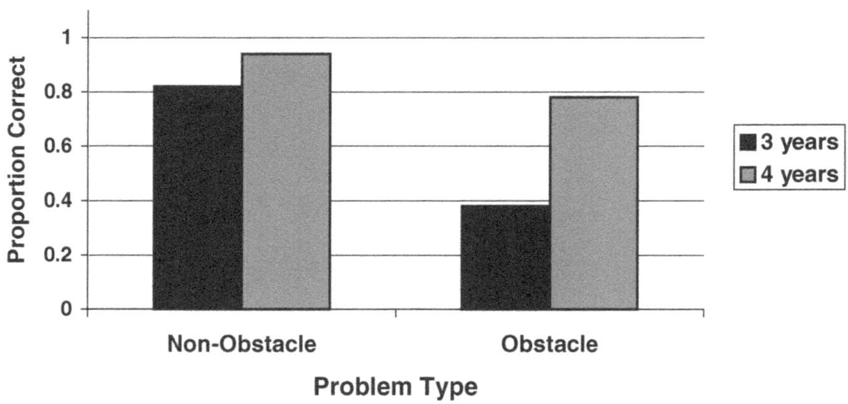

Figure 13.3 Comparison of 3- and 4-year-old preschool children's accuracy at solving TOL problems. Data are shown for problems that have an obstacle ball that must be removed and for all nonobstacle problems. The nonobstacle problems include 1-, 2- as well as 3-move problems, but results restricted to 3-move problems were similar.

Table 13.1 Performance by problem type (3-move nonobstacle, 3-move obstacle)

Performance measure	*Problem type*			
	Nonobstacle		*Obstacle*	
	M	*SD*	*M*	*SD*
Proportion solved**	0.89	0.17	0.63	0.41
Total moves**	3.07	0.76	3.48	1.15
Solution initiation time**	8.81	3.49	17.56	6.95
Solution completion time*	19.07	10.15	28.15	3.05
Rule violations**	0.06	0.09	0.46	0.25

Note: All time information is presented in seconds.

* Difference between nonobstacle and obstacle is significant at $p < 0.05$.
** Difference between nonobstacle and obstacle is significant at $p < 0.01$.

younger children, but the two age groups performed similarly on nonobstacle problems, resulting in a significant interaction of age with the type of problem, $F(1, 21) = 5.14$, $p < 0.04$. Analyses of individual moves during the solution was identified to be due to the older children's greater use of the efficient holding peg strategy on the obstacle problems (58%) compared to the younger children's use of this strategy (25%), $t(21) = 2.45$, $p < .03$. Kaller, Unterrainer, Rahm, and Halsband (2004) have also undertaken an evaluation of 3-move obstacle problems and found that manipulations of various problem characteristics of such problems differentially influence adults' ability to solve them.

An obstacle problem, which notably challenges the participants' planning and problem-solving ability, may emphasize the problem-solving differences between younger and older preschoolers. Obstacle problems frequently require one to inhibit the tendency to move the obstacle ball immediately to its goal state, an impossible event in obstacle problems without a nonoptimal solution. This suggests one might expect to see effects of obstacle vs. nonobstacle problems for some clinical groups who have problems with inhibitory control.

It should also be recognized that not only correct or efficient strategies can be identified but also incorrect or inefficient strategies. Among the most inefficient strategies is the rule violation. Rule violations provide an interesting insight on problem solving because although not legal, they can nonetheless be viewed as a strategy.

Rule violations

During problem solving on the TOL task, participants may attempt to break any one of the three rules that state: (1) do not place more than the allowed number of balls on any peg; (2) do not place the balls anywhere other than on a peg; and (3) reposition only one ball at a time. In scientific literature, rule violation behavior has been handled in a variety of ways. Many studies do not measure instances of this behavior or simply do not allow the participant to make illegal moves. For example, all of the computerized tests currently available take this approach by making such illegal moves impossible. We are currently developing a computerized TOL task designed to assess attempts to violate rules (Schlorholtz & Berg, 2003). A few studies with clinically-diagnosed patients, such as children with closed head injury and adults with dementia, have measured a combined score for all types of rule violations and found more frequent violations in clinical groups (Carlin, Bonerba, Phipps, Alexander, Shapiro, & Grafman, 2000; Levin et al., 1997). Furthermore, we have informally observed numerous rule violations with preschool children and Culbertson and Zillmer (1998b) include a measure of rule violations in their standardized TOL task designed for use with children as well as adults. To our knowledge, different types of rule violations have either been scored separately, or not been scored separately but subsequently combined as a sum score in the reported analyses (e.g., Culbertson & Zillmer, 1998b).

An important issue in the interpretation of rule violation scores is that they could occur for two reasons: either the participant is unable to remember the rules or, alternatively, the participant knows the rules but chooses to disregard them as an expedient to solving the problem. In the case where participants could not remember the rule, a violation would not be considered a strategy. In the literature on neurologically disabled adults (Carlin et al., 2000; Levin et al., 1997), it is suggested that rule violations occur because participants forget the rules or have problems acting within the rules. A similar explanation may be valid for young children. However, when testing non-clinical older children or adults, it is less likely that they have forgotten the rules. To help interpret measures of rule violations with any population, we recommend the use of procedures that help insure that participants understand the rules and assess the extent of this understanding. These procedures include the use of sufficient practice problems to insure a clear knowledge of the rules, and/or the use of a series of questions that require the participant to either explain the rules back to the examiner or to identify illegal moves. The latter are especially informative at the end of the test session since they can assess the memory of the participants.

By noting when and how often rule violations occur, researchers can add important new information to the participant's or client's profile of problem-solving ability. In an analysis of rule violations in our study of obstacle problems described above, preschoolers produced a significantly higher proportion of rule violations on obstacle than on nonobstacle problems (see Table 13.1). These data suggest that younger children may select illegal strategies rather than make a move that on the surface appears to move them away from the goal. Similar effects might occur with some clinical groups. It would be of interest to determine if this or other deficits in strategy use could be overcome with training. This could be advantageous for both children and certain clinical populations such as those diagnosed with ADHD or those who have experienced frontal-lobe lesions, which have been recognized to be deficient in problem-solving abilities (for a review, see Anderson et al., 1996).

Effects of computerized testing on response measures

Both the speed measures and the strategy measures described above would be difficult to obtain accurately without making use of the assistance of computerized testing. However, the most common method of presenting the TOL task is with a physical apparatus, an actual set of balls and pegs as opposed to a virtual set presented on a computer screen. The physical test method limits one to assessing speed with a stopwatch, a procedure that seriously limits precision. This is especially relevant for the brief solution initiation time and the pause times during the solution. Thus, computerized testing (e.g., Owen et al., 1990; Schlorholtz & Berg, 2003) allows one to more readily obtain complete and accurate timing information. An additional advantage of computerized testing is the assurance of standardized instruction, participant practice, and other test methods; provided these are incorporated into a well-designed computer program.

Clearly there are practical advantages of using computerized administration and recording of data. But exactly what is the impact of moving from the now commonly used procedure of using a physical apparatus to test neuropsychological clients to using a computer-based testing procedure? Do both testing methods produce comparable results or should the literature derived from each be considered independently? We provide preliminary results of a methodological study to examine this issue.

We compared the solutions of 42 undergraduate students on the 4- to 7-move problems under two administration conditions: the widely used physical version using actual balls, boards, and pegs, and a computer version simulating this physical version and utilizing a computer mouse to "move" the balls. The same 12 problems were presented in each method, but with colors permuted in order to give the illusion of new problems. The time-limit procedure was employed wherein each problem ended when it was either solved or a 3-min time limit had expired.

In the physical testing condition, two boards were presented, a game board and a goal board (see Figure 13.1). This procedure is the one commonly used to test with the TOL task (e.g., Hughes, 1998), and was the basic procedure originally employed by Shallice (1982). In the computerized testing condition, we used a program developed in our laboratory that was designed to closely match the physical testing in both appearance and movement of the balls (see Appendix 2 for details).

As expected, use of the computer vs. physical test method affected response speed measures because balls could generally be moved more quickly with a mouse than when physically moving a ball. However, a more critical test was whether important variables such as the difficulty of the problem produced similar effects on each of the measures for computer and physical methodologies. With problem difficulty defined by the minimum number of moves required, we found linear effects of difficulty for each of six different measures for both test conditions; no interactions were found between difficulty and mode of testing (see Figure 13.4 for two examples).

Another way to look at the comparability of procedures is by determining the correlation of the performance measures between testing modes. If changing

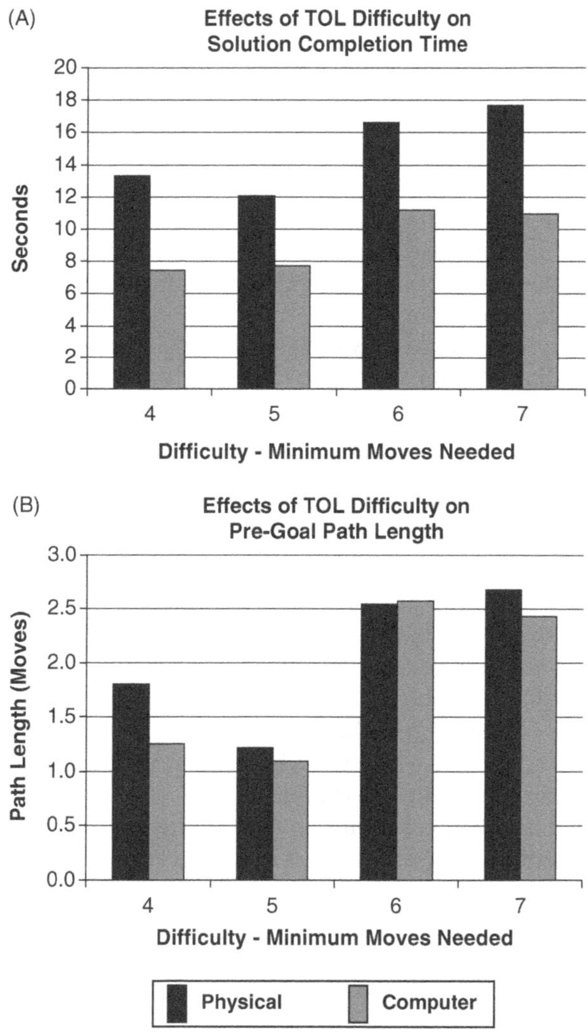

Figure 13.4 Effects of test mode (physical apparatus vs. computer and mouse) and problem difficulty on solution completion and pre-goal phase. Note the parallel effects of difficulty for the physical and computer test modes.

the testing mode fundamentally alters the task, one might expect the correlations among the timing to be reduced. When examining five different dependent variables, we found all correlations between these testing modes were positive and for four of the five were significant. The correlation for the two highest, solution initiation time and pre-goal path, were both at $r = 0.53$.

What we conclude from this is that at least for young adults computer testing is not only very much feasible, but that the data obtained from this test method are consistent with that for physical methods of testing (see Appendix 2 for further information). This suggests that the cognitive demands of the task remain reasonably constant across computer and physical testing procedures. Further work of this sort with clinical groups and groups of children and older adults are also warranted and needed as they may have more difficulty in physically interacting with the physical apparatus or computer interface. However, this study suggests that it is promising to utilize computerized testing of this sort so as to allow for easier and more consistent administration and calculation of detailed measures from the TOL.

Summary and conclusions

We have outlined four classes of performance measures: (1) success or accuracy measures; (2) efficiency measures; (3) timing measures; and (4) strategy measures. Assessment of the first of these, success or accuracy measures, is included in almost every report using the TOL task, whereas the others are inconsistently reported. For example, rule violations are often not reported and when reported are sometimes combined with other measures that make them difficult to evaluate. Other strategy measures are the most recent addition and are now beginning to appear in TOL reports. We believe these strategy measures could become the most critically important for a clinician hoping to specify the nature of a client's disabilities and for the investigator trying to understand the normative nature of planning and executive functioning.

We would argue that the inconsistency in use of all of these measures in the past clinical and research literature is fostering an ignorance of the full potential of the TOL as a cognitive assessment. A survey of the research in the area quickly makes it evident that there is a bewildering array of measures, subsets of measures, combinations of measures, most of which appear to lack a clear rationale (Baker et al., 2001; Berg & Byrd, 2002). An effort should be made to report the information from at least the first three (success, efficiency, and timing) of the categories we have outlined to provide a comprehensive view of performance. The past literature is also lacking normative data using a very complete set of these measures. Until we have such a set, the clinician and clinical researcher are left helpless to make any rational choices of which measures to select for a given client or study or to determine if clients' performance is sub-normal. Composite measures, especially those that combine different classes of measures, also create problems in comparing across studies. We believe that reporting of multiple measures will prove more fruitful and suggest that researchers and clinicians alike conceive of TOL evaluation in terms of a profile of measures, including measures of strategy, rather than a single composite measure of limited meaning.

Efforts to improve the use of multiple measures in a profile would be greatly enhanced by a movement toward computerized testing, which would have the potential for providing more detailed information needed for strategy and timing. For those who prefer the benefits of testing with a physical apparatus, Appendix 2 outlines procedures to utilize computerized methods offline to obtain this information indirectly from video.

The benefits of any combination of measures depend greatly on the choice of TOL problems included in the test. We suggest a two-pronged approach to this selection: (1) select problems not simply by the number of moves, but by the extent and type of strategies they require; and (2) evaluate the details of the participant's solutions including their employment of optimal strategies, their avoidance of nonstrategic moves, and their attempts to avoid the need for task-specific strategies by attempting rule violations. We believe this approach could greatly enhance the value of the task for clinicians and research investigators alike.

The approach we have suggested here is consistent with Poreh's (2000) Composition Paradigm, and with the development of new measures for existing paradigms. In addition to reviewing some newer variants of existing measures of the TOL, we have identified and exemplified a new class of measures for the TOL task: the strategy measures. Our view that investigators and clinicians consider employing multiple measures, as in a profile, rather than single measures or composites of multiple measures, also fits with the Composition Paradigm approach. What remains is further testing with the strategy measures to explore the extent of their clinical and normative value.

Author note

Portions of the research reported here were supported by an Esther Katz Rosen grant from the American Psychological Foundation and a grant from the the Evelyn F. and William T. McKnight Brain Institute to W. Keith Berg at the University of Florida and by an NIMH Training Postdoctoral Fellowship number T32 MH18264 awarded to Dana L. Byrd at Columbia University.

References

Anderson, P., Anderson, V., & Lajoie, G. (1996). The Tower of London test: Validation and standardization of pediatric populations. *The Clinical Neuropsychologist*, *10*, 54–65.

Baker, K., Segalowitz, S. J., & Ferlisi, M. (2001). The effect of differing scoring methods for the Tower of London task on developmental patterns of performance. *The Clinical Neuropsychologist*, *15*, 309–313.

Baker, S. C., Rodgers, R. D., Owen, A. M., Frith, C. D., Dolan, R. J., Frackowiak, R. S. J., & Robbins, T. W. (1996). Neural systems engaged by planning: A PET study of the Tower of London task. *Neuropsychologia*, *34*, 515–526.

Berg, W. K., & Byrd, D. L. (2002). The Tower of London spatial problem solving task: Enhancing clinical and research implementation. *Journal of Experimental and Clinical Neuropsychology*, *25*, 586–604.

Berg, W. K., & Byrd, D. L. (in press). Examining cognitive development using psychophysiological correlates: Evidence of a hierarchy of future-oriented processes across measures. Invited chapter contribution to L.A. Schmidt and S.J. Segalowitz (Eds.), *Developmental psychophysiology: Theory, systems, and applications*. Cambridge: Cambridge University Press.

Bidell, T. R., & Fischer, K. W. (1994). Developmental transitions in children's early on-line planning. In M. M. Haith & J. B. Benson (Eds.), *The development of future-oriented processes*. The John D. and Catherine T. MacArthur Foundation series on mental health and development (pp. 141–176). Chicago, IL: University of Chicago Press.

Byrd, D. L., & Berg, W. K. (2002). The relationship between age and the preparatory heart rate response: Childhood through adulthood. *Biological Psychology*, *61*, 271–276.

Byrd, D. L., van der Veen, T., McNamara, J. P. H., & Berg, W. K. (2004). Preschoolers don't practice what they preach: Preschoolers' planning performances with manual and spoken response requirements. *Journal of Cognition and Development*, *5*, 427–449.

Carlin, D., Bonberba, J., Phipps, M., Alexander, G., Shapiro, M., & Gagman, J. (2000). Planning impairments in frontal lobe dementia and frontal lobe lesion patients. *Neuropsychologica*, *38*, 655–665.

Cockburn, J. (1995). Performance on the Tower of London test after severe head injury. *Journal of the International Neuropsychological Society*, *1*, 537–544.

Colvin, M. K., Dunbar, K., & Grafman, J. (2001). The effects of frontal lobe lesions on goal achievement in the water jug task. *Journal of Cognitive Neuroscience*, *13*, 1129–1147.

Culbertson, W. C., & Zillmer, E. A. (1998a). The construct validity of the Tower of LondonDX as a measure of the executive functioning of ADHD children. *Assessment*, *5*, 215–226.

Culbertson, W. C., & Zillmer, E. A. (1998b) The Tower of LondonDX: A standardized approach to assessing the executive functioning in children. *Archives of Clinical Neuropsychology*, *13*, 285–301.

Culbertson, W. C., & Zillmer, E. A. (1998c). *The Tower of LondonDX Manual*. Multi–Health Systems, Inc. (Available at www.mhs.com)

Dagher, A., Owen, A. M., Boecker, H., & Brooks, D. J. (1999). Mapping the network for planning: A correlational PET activation study with the Tower of London task. *Brain*, *122*, 1973–1987.

Davies, S. P. (2000). Memory and planning processes in solutions to well-structured problems. *Quarterly Journal of Experimental Psychology: Human Experimental Psychology*, *53A*, 896–927.

Davies, S. P. (2003). Initial and concurrent planning in solutions to well-structured problems. *The Quarterly Journal of Experimental Psychology*, *56A*, 1147–1164.

Dennis, I., & Evans, J. St.B. T. (1996). The speed-error trade-off problem in psychometric testing. *British Journal of Psychology*, *87*, 105–129.

Gillhooly, K. J., Phillips, L. H., Wynn, V., Logie, R. H., & Della Sala, S. (1999). Planning processes and age in the five-disc Tower of London task. *Thinking and Reasoning*, *5*, 339–361.

Hughes, C. (1998). Finding your marbles: Does preschoolers' strategic behavior predict later understanding of mind? *Developmental Psychology*, *34*, 1326–1339.

Kafer, K. L., & Hunter, M. (1997). On testing the face validity of planning/problem-solving tasks in a normal population. *Journal of the International Neuropsychological Society*, *3*, 108–119.

Kaller, C. P., Unterrainer, J. M., Rahm, B., & Halsband, U. (2004). The impact of problem structure on planning: Insights from the Tower of London task. *Cognitive Brain Research*, *20*, 463–472.

Klahr, D., & Robinson, M. (1981). Formal assessment of problem-solving and planning processes in preschool children. *Cognitive Psychology*, *13*, 113–148.

Kotovsky, K., Hayes, J. R., & Simon, H. A. (1985). Why are some problems hard? Evidence from the Tower of Hanoi. *Cognitive Psychology*, *17*, 248–294.

Levin, H. S., Fletcher, J. M., Kufera, J. A., Harward, H. J., Lilly, M. A., Mendelsohn, D., Bruce, D., & Eisenberg, H. (1996). Dimensions of cognition measured by the Tower of London and other cognitive tasks in head-injured children and adolescents. *Developmental Neuropsychology*, *12*, 17–34.

Levin, H. S., Song, J., Scheibel, R. S., Fletcher, J. M., Harward, H., Lilly, M., & Goldstein, F. (1997). Concept formation and problem-solving following closed head injury in children. *Journal of the International Neuropsychological Society*, *3*, 598–607.

Luciana, M., & Nelson, C. A. (1998). The functional emergence of prefrontally-guided working memory systems in four- to eight-year-old children. *Neuropsychologica*, *36*, 273–293.

Luria, A. R. (1966). *Higher cortical functions in man*. New York: Basic Books, Inc.

MacDonald, C., Garner, E., & Spurgeon, J. (2002). Prefrontally-guided planning abilities of preschool children using the Tower of London task. *Psi Chi Undergraduate Journal*, *7*, 107–121.

Miyake, A., Friedman, N. P., Emerson, M. J., Witzki, A. H., & Howerter, A. (2000). The unity and diversity of executive functions and their contributions to complex 'frontal lobe' tasks: A latent variable analysis. *Cognitive Psychology*, *41*(1), 49–100.

Morris, R. G., Ahmed, S., Syed, G. M., & Toone, B. K. (1993). Neural correlates of planning ability: Frontal lobe activation during the Tower of London test. *Neuropsychologia*, *31*, 1367–1398.

Morris, R. G., Downes, J. J., Sahakian, B., Evenden, J. L., Heald, A., & Robbins, T. W. (1988). Planning and spatial working memory in Parkinson's disease. *Journal of Neurology, Neurosurgery, & Psychiatry*, *51*, 757–766.

Murji, S., & DeLuca, J. W. (1998). Preliminary validity of the cognitive function checklist: Prediction of Tower of London performance. *The Clinical Neuropsychologist*, *12*, 358–364.

Osman, A., Lou, L., Muller-Gethmann, H., Rinkenauer, G., Mattes, S., & Ulrich, R. (2000). Mechanisms of speed-accuracy tradeoff: Evidence from covert motor processes. *Biological Psychology*, *51*, 173–199.

Owen, A. M., Downes, J. J., Sahakian, B., Polkey, C. E., & Robbins, T. W. (1990). Planning and spatial working memory following frontal lobe lesions in man. *Neuropsychologia*, *28*, 1021–1034.

Poreh, A. M. (2000). A quantified process approach: An emerging methodology to neuropsychological assessment. *The Clinical Neuropsychologist*, *14*, 212–220.

Rittle-Johnson, B., & Siegler, R. S. (1999). Learning to spell: Variability, choice, and change in children's strategy use. *Child Development*, *70*, 332–348.

Schlorholtz, E., & Berg, W. K. (2003). *Tower of London Software* [*Computer Software*]. Gainesville, FL: Mini Enterprises.

Shallice, T. (1982). Specific impairments of planning. *Philosophical Transactions of the Royal Society of London, Biology*, *298*, 199–209.

Spitz, H. H., Minsky, S. K., & Bessellieu, C. L. (1985). Influence of planning time and first-move strategy on Tower of Hanoi problem-solving performance of mentally retarded young adults and nonretarded children. *American Journal of Mental Deficiency*, *1*, 46–56.

Ward, G., & Allport, A. (1997). Planning and problem-solving using the five-disc Tower of London task. *The Quarterly Journal of Experimental Psychology*, *50A*, 49–78.

Welsh, M. C. (1991). Rule-guided behavior and self-monitoring on the Tower of Hanoi disk-transfer task. *Cognitive Development*, *6*, 59–76.

Welsh, M., Pennington, B. F., & Groisser, D. B. (1991). A normative-developmental study of executive function: A window on prefrontal function in children. *Developmental Neuropsychology*, *7*, 131–149.

Zhang, J. (1997). The nature of external representations in problem solving. *Cognitive Science*, *21*, 179–217.

Appendix

Appendix 1: Calculation of pre-goal and goal phases

In order to clarify how the pre-goal and goal phase lengths are determined, we present two example solutions. The first example is a 4-move problem that is solved perfectly. Here, the participant begins 4 moves away from the goal and proceeds directly to the goal (from 4 moves away from the goal to 3, 2, 1, and then 0 moves away from the goal). For this perfect solution path, the goal phase length would be 4 and the pre-goal phase length is 0. As a second example, consider the same 4-move problem with a less than perfect solution. The participant might make 7 moves to solve this problem. This solution may involve moving from the initial 4 moves from the goal to 5, 4, 3, 3, 2, 1, and then 0 moves away from the goal. The goal phase is calculated as the sequence of moves where the participant moves the balls directly to the goal, which in this case is 3-moves long (from 3 to 2 moves, from 2 to 1 move, and from 1 to 0 moves away from the goal). The pre-goal phase is the number of moves before the goal phase, and is, in this case, 4 moves long (from 4 to 5 moves, 5 to 4 moves, 4 to 3 moves, and 3 to 3 moves away from the goal).

One can determine from these example solutions that the pre-goal and goal phase lengths are not necessarily reciprocal to each other because the total number of moves made is not fixed. Also, the goal phase and pre-goal phase measures can only be calculated on problems where the solution is eventually reached (the game board is successfully transformed to be like the goal board). One may also notice from these examples that, unlike the TOH, the TOL allows for a participant to move a ball to another position while the number of moves from the goal still remains the same, resulting in sequences such as seen in the second example (4–3 moves and then 3–3 moves to the goal).

Appendix 2: Obtaining comparable data from computerized and physical apparatus testing methods

The computerized testing that we utilized was designed to closely match the physical testing both in appearance and in movement of the balls. In the computerized testing, participants moved a ball by selecting it with a mouse button press and then dragging it to a different peg. If desired, a pause between problems can be interposed to mimic the time it takes the experimenter to rearrange the balls on the boards for each new problem in the physical testing condition. Performance data for the computerized testing are measured and recorded directly by the computer program.

When circumstances require use of physical test methods, it is still possible to get most if not all of the advantages of computerized testing. This can be done by video recording the test session with the camera directed toward the participant's goal board. Once video recorded, this recording may be played back, optimally at carefully calibrated slower speeds while test personnel use a computerized version of the TOL to mimic the movements of the participant during replay. Replay at a slow speed using conventional consumer videotape recorders may produce variable speeds of playback or be slowed down by unknown amounts. More expensive units are available that allow calibrated slow motion playback. Use of digital video may also allow this with the proper computer software during replay. We have used a precision video editing machine to replay videotapes at exactly one-quarter speed to improve timing accuracy. In our experience, this procedure produced inter-rater reliability for position of moves of 100% and for timing of moves within 0.25-s accuracy of 91%. We successfully used this procedure with studies of both children and adults.

Though this procedure does allow one to use physical testing methods and still get considerable accuracy and detail for some of the new measures proposed, it comes at a cost of some considerable time and effort in scoring of videotapes, especially when significantly slowed down. Thus, careful consideration must be given to the cost/benefit ratio of this approach.

Our computer testing procedure differs from that used in the widely used Cambridge Neuropsychological Test Automated Battery (e.g., Owen et al., 1990) in two ways: (1) in our program the appearance of the balls and pegs closely approximated with that seen in the physical model, whereas the Cambridge version used balls in hanging "pockets" in place of upright pegs; and (2) in our program participants moved a ball by selecting it with a mouse button press and then dragging it to a different peg, visually simulating the physical ball movement, whereas in the Cambridge version balls were relocated by a series of two mouse clicks, one to the pocket (peg) that holds the ball intended to be moved and a second mouse click on the pocket to receive that ball. The computer then executes the indicated ball movement. Thus, the results we report by comparing computerized testing and physical testing methods may not generalize to the Cambridge computerized version.

Part IV

The Decomposition Paradigm

The Decomposition Paradigm involves the development of new subscores that depict underlying facets and patterns of performance. In Chapter 14, Amir M. Poreh describes the decomposition of the Rey–Osterrieth Complex Figure using a novel multiple dimensional scaling procedure. In Chapter 15, Daniel N. Allen, Joshua E. Caron, and Gerald Goldstein describe the application of more traditional factor analytical techniques toward the development of new process index scores for the Halstead Category Test.

14 Quantification and validation of the Rey–Osterrieth global-local indices

Amir M. Poreh

Introduction

The sum bit-scoring of the Rey–Osterrieth Complex Figure (ROCF; Osterrieth, 1944) has repeatedly been shown to be sensitive to brain injury (Binder, 1982; Hamby, Wilkins, & Barry, 1993; Osterrieth, 1944; Shorr, Delis, & Massman, 1992). Clinical observations suggest, however, that in some cases, it is useful to decompose the ROCF sum score and use the resulting indexes for the evaluation of specific neurocognitive deficits. Such indexes are thought to tap into underlying constructs such as visual spatial memory, graphomotor coordination and planning deficits (Lezak, 1983).

The most well known of these indexes involves the distinction between global and local portions of the figure. These two indexes were qualitatively described by Edith Kaplan and her associates (Goodglass & Kaplan, 1981; Kaplan, 1988). They reported that patients with documented right hemisphere brain injury (RHI) exhibit deficits in analyzing and remembering the global features of the figure. Patients with documented left hemisphere injury (LHI), on the other hand, are able to copy and recall the general features of the figure, yet exhibit higher than expected errors in copying its fine details (Binder, 1982; Delis, Kramer, & Kiefner, 1988; Goodglass & Kaplan, 1981).

In spite of the appeal of the qualitative distinction between global and local errors on the ROCF, a number of researchers have noted that it is difficult to explicitly demarcate between such features (i.e., De Renzi, 1982; Kimchi, 1992; Moscovitch, 1979). Several case studies show that the errors evidenced on the ROCF may interact with the regional location of the elements in the patient's visual field (Kaplan, 1988). Furthermore, in recent years a number of studies have criticized the distinction between global and local processing showing that complex visual-perceptual stimuli require the activation of both right- and left-brain regions (Hübner, 1998), and that other brain regions may be involved in the performance of the ROCF.

The value of regional indices in the assessment of head-injured patients is exemplified in patients suffering from injures to the frontal lobes and related subcortical areas, such as the basal ganglia. Case studies show that such damage may result in hemi-neglect and rightward oriented bias, although these two phenomena may be dissociated (Weintraub & Mesulam, 1988).

To address this issue, Rapport et al. (1995) developed empirical criteria for left-middle and right-sided demarcation of the Osterrieth items. Using qualitative analysis they identified a number of data sets and presented several case studies to support the utility of right/middle/left indices for detecting unilateral neglect. In a more recent study, Rapport and Webster (2003) recommended that two or more omissions on the Osterrieth copy production may serve as an optimal cut-off for the classification of a neglect syndrome.

Although the validation of the demarcation and classifiability of the indices might be examined using a well-defined clinical population and specified cut-offs, most cognitive deficits may be depicted along a continuum. Furthermore, it is important to provide norms as well as to evaluate all of the possible indexes and compare their classifiability for different patient populations.

Toward the assessment of classifiability

When describing or analyzing a variable, the statistical test chosen should be based on that variable's sampling distribution. The normality of the variable distribution will depend on the sample size, problems of measurement (such as ceiling or floor effect), and the type of data (ordinal or interval). Some researchers take for granted that the data obtained by neuropsychologists are normally distributed. However, this is rarely the case. Hence, parametric methodologies for decomposing neuropsychological tests are inauspicious, and could lead to spurious findings. Furthermore, these methodologies are exploratory and due to their instability, might not produce replicable findings.

One promising nonmetric method that is used for assessing the classificability of indexes is Faceted Smallest Space Analysis (F-SSA).

This nonmetric statistical technique allows for the formulation of regional hypotheses regarding the interrelationships between the various items of a scale (Shye, 1988, 1994; Shye & Elizur, 1994). For example, it is hypothesized that one may be able to partition the space of the ROCF scale into distinct homogeneous regions, each containing one class of items (global/local or right/middle/left). These partition patterns are expected to substantially conform to one of the three partition models specified by the F-SSA (Axial, Radial or Medial; Borg & Shye, 1995; Shye, 1991). Poreh and Shye (1998) confirmed this hypothesis and showed that during the copying and recall stages of this test, the subjects made differential errors on the predetermined facets. Additional analysis using conventional statistics showed that these errors differentially correlated with the loci of the brain injury, and that only the right-side portion of the figure provides an index for distinguishing between patients, providing support for Rapport et al. (1995) and Rapport and Websters' (2003) observations.

Normative data and classifiability of the ROCF indices in the elderly population

To examine the utility of the ROCF indices in the general population, a random sample of 197 older adults was obtained from the Israeli Department of Interior (65–90 years of age). The majority of the older adults were right-handed (81.8%) as determined by the Annett Handedness Inventory. The average score on the Mini-Mental Status Exam, a gross measure of general cognitive functioning, was 28.15 ($SD = 3.17$), with no differences among the ethnic groups. Seventy three of the subjects completed the ROCF tests of copy.

Table 14.1 depicts the demarcation of the ROCF along the two said dimensions (global/local and right/middle/left). Table 14.2 provides normative data for the elderly as well as some reliability data for the different

Table 14.1 The ROCF composites scoring criteria

ID	*Description*		*Global*	*Local*	*Right*	*Middle*	*Left*
1	Cross in upper left corner, outside of rectangle		■		■		
2	Large rectangle		■			■	
3	Diagonal cross		■			■	
4	Horizontal midline of 2			■		■	
5	Vertical midline			■		■	
6	Small rectangle, within 2 to the left			■	■		
7	Small segment above 6			■	■		
8	Four parallel lines within 2, upper left			■	■		
9	Triangle above 2 upper right			■			■
10	Small vertical line within 2, below 9			■			■
11	Circle with three dots within 2			■			■
12	Five parallel lines within 2, crossing 3, lower right			■			■
13	Sides of triangle attached to 2 on right			■			■
14	Diamond attached to 13			■			■
15	Vertical line within triangle 13 parallel to right vertical of 2			■			■
16	Horizontal line within 13, continuing 4 to right			■		■	
17	Cross attached to 5 below 2			■		■	
18	Square attached to 2, lower left		■		■		
	ROCF Total	■					
	Global/Local		■	■			
	Right/Middle/Left				■	■	■

Table 14.2 Normative data of the ROCF subscales in the elderly

Division		*Number of items*	*Mean*	*SD*	*Reliability (alpha)*
Copy	Local	13	21.7	4.8	0.94
	Global	4	7.3	1.6	0.89
	Right	5	8.9	2.2	0.86
	Middle	5	9.2	4.1	0.90
	Left	8	14.7	3.2	0.94
Recall	Local	13	13.3	5.9	0.80
	Global	4	6.5	2.3	0.84
	Right	5	5.0	2.8	0.72
	Middle	5	7.2	2.6	0.78
	Left	8	8.1	3.6	0.64

indexes for this population. One sees that using Cronbach's alpha, the resulting internal consistencies of the sum total copy condition scores of these subscales was high (0.94 and 0.80, respectively). The internal consistencies of the recall condition scale were much lower (0.72–0.84). Clearly, the lower reliability on the recall condition suggests the need for caution when using these indices in various populations.

Following Poreh and Shye (1998), the ROCF was decomposed using a confirmatory multidimensional nonmetric statistical technique (F-SSA). Since these subjects did not have any known neurological conditions, we did not expect the decomposition to yield as high separation values as had been found in patients with lateralized brain injury. Table 14.3 shows the resulting data. Figures 14.1–14.3 and Tables 14.1 and 14.2 correspond to Table 14.3's results.

Table 14.3 Comparison of separation indexes

Condition	*Model*	*Separation index (Poreh and Shye's data/present data)*	
		Global vs. local	*Right/middle/left*
Copy	Axial	0.835/0.570	0.761/0.631
	Angular	0.935/0.614	0.822/0.617
	Radial	0.720/0.764	0.611/0.617
Recall	Axial	0.790/0.382	0.560/0.681
	Angular	0.906/0.468	0.562/0.511
	Radial	0.807/0.665	0.676/0.551

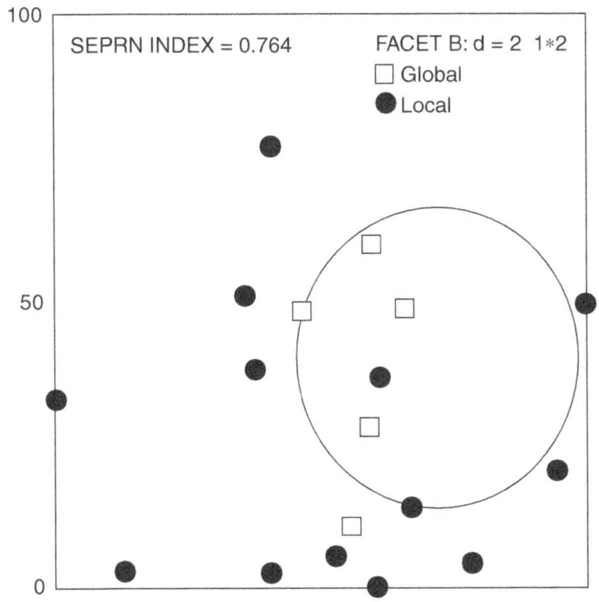

Figure 14.1 FSSA map for all subjects during the copy stage for global and local elements.

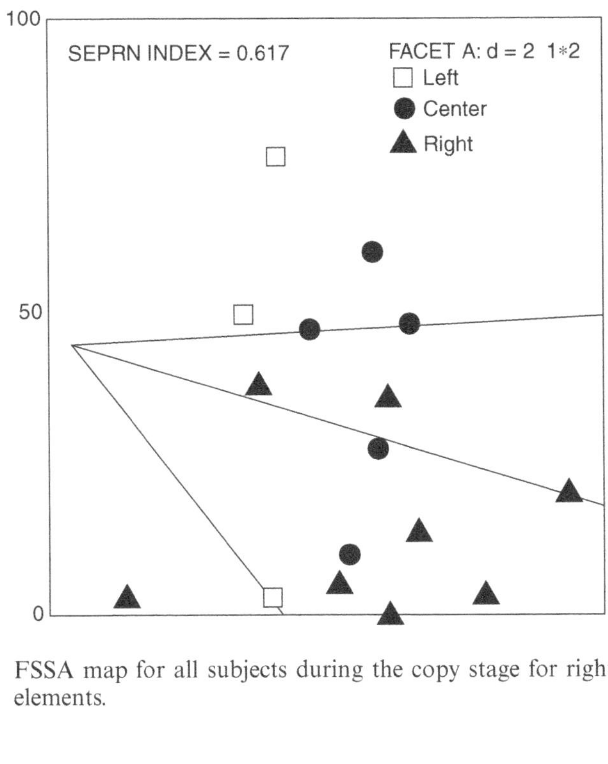

Figure 14.2 FSSA map for all subjects during the copy stage for right/middle/left elements.

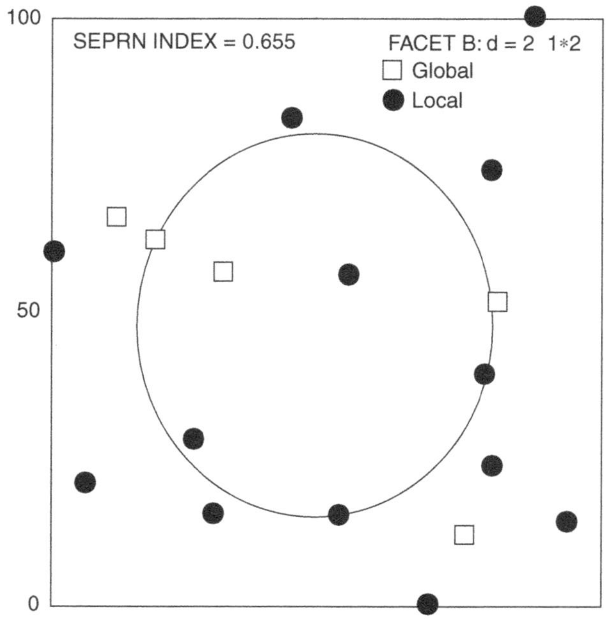

Figure 14.3 FSSA map for all subjects during the recall stage for global and local elements.

Figure 14.1 shows that the global ROCF items intercorrelate, whereas the local elements appear to be uncorrelated. The use of the right/left/middle distinction not only does not improve our analysis, but also makes the interpretation of the data more complex (see Figure 14.2). The radial solution appears to be the most appropriate for the copy condition in the global/local demarcation whereas the angular solution was most appropriate for the right/middle/left demarcation. In the recall condition, the radial solution was appropriate in both studies. A similar pattern was noted in the recall stage of the ROCF. One sees that the global/local distinction using the radial facet separation provided the most comprehensive distinction between the ROCF elements. The use of the right/middle/left distinction did not add much to the interpretations and required an angular solution, which is much more complex to interpret.

Discussion

The present chapter illustrates the use of modern multidimensional techniques for decomposing existing neuropsychological tests. One sees that by employing such methods, it is not only possible to evaluate the contributions of these dimensions to the final product but it may also be possible to assess their reliability and provide normative data.

However, patients who have suffered an injury to a specific module are very different from the patients in the present study. Thus, our findings of a lower separation between the elements in the general elderly population were not surprising. Moreover, it confirms that the use of these indices should be used with great caution, particularly since they are moderately reliable. Furthermore, it confirms Delis et al.'s conclusion that the use of factor analysis for the assessment of constructs, as in the case of the CVLT, requires the use of homogenous patient groups.

Finally, this chapter emphasizes the importance of using nonparametric statistics for the analysis of neuropsychological data. It demonstrates the robustness of such methods for assessing indices. Namely, such procedures are not dependent on single items. Rather, they assess the general spatial "pattern" of the elements as a whole. Therefore, slightly different divisions of the elements are likely to result in similar results. Hence, such statistical techniques may help quantify and examine many of the clinical observations that have been put forth by clinicians who adhere to the "process" approach and open new windows for examining notions that may have been previously regarded as "clinical lure".

References

Binder, L. (1982). Constructional strategies on complex figure drawings after unilateral brain damage. *Journal of Clinical Neuropsychology*, *4*, 51–58.

Borg, I., & Shye, S. (1995). *Facet theory: Form and content*. Thousand Oaks, CA: Sage.

De Renzi, E. (1982). *Disorders of space exploration and cognition*. New York: Wiley.

Delis, D. C., Kramer, J. H., & Kiefner, M. G. (1988). Visuospatial functioning before and after commissurotomy: Disconnection in hierarchical processing. *Archives of Neurology*, *45*, 462–465.

Goodglass, H., & Kaplan, E. (1981). Assessment of cognitive deficits in the brain-injured patient. In M. S. Gazzaniga (Ed.), *Handbook of behavioral neurology* (Vol. 2). *Neuropsychology*. New York: Plenum.

Hamby, S. L. Wilkins, J. W., & Barry, N. S. (1993). Organizational quality on the Rey–Osterrieth and Taylor Complex Figure Tests: A new scoring system. *Psychological Assessment*, *5*, 27–33.

Hübner, R. (1998). Hemispheric difference in global/local processing revealed by same–different judgements. *Visual Cognition*, 15, 457–478.

Kaplan, E. (1988). A process approach to neuropsychological assessment. In T. Boll & B. K. Bryant, *Clinical neuropsychology and brain functioning: Research, measurement, and practice* (pp. 129–166). Washington, DC: American Psychological Association Press.

Kimchi, R. (1992). Primacy of holistic processing and global/local paradigm: A critical review. *Psychological Bulletin*, *112*, 24–38.

Lezak, M. D. (1983). *Neuropsychological assessment* (2nd ed.). New York: Oxford University Press.

Moscovitch, M. (1979). Information processing and cerebral hemispheres. In M. S. Gazzaniga (Ed.), *The handbook of behavioral neurobiology* (pp. 187–208). New York: Springer.

Osterrieth, R. (1944). Le st de copie d'une figure complex: Contribution a l'etude de la perception et de la memoire. *Archives de Psychologie*, *30*, 286–356.

Poreh, A., & Shye, S. (1998). Examination of the global and local features of the Rey–Osterrieth complex figure using faceted smallest space analysis. *The Clinical Neuropsychologist*, *12*(4), 453–467.

Rapport, L. J., Dura, R. L., & Webster, J. S. (2003). Assessment of unilateral neglect using the ROCF. In J. A. Kinght (Ed.), *The handbook of Rey–Osterrieth Complex Figure usage: Clinical and research applications.* Lutz, Florida: Psychological Assessment Resources, Inc.

Rapport, L. J., Dura, R. L., Webster, J. S., Charter, R., & Morrill, B. (1995). Indices of hemispatial deficits on the Rey–Osterrieth Complex Figure. *The Clinical Neuropsychologist*, *9*, 169–179.

Shorr, J. S., Delis, D. C., & Massman, P. J. (1992). Memory for the Rey–Osterrieth complex figure: Perceptual clustering, encoding, and storage. *Neuropsychology*, *6*, 43–50.

Shye, S. (1988). Inductive and deductive reasoning: A structural reanalysis of ability tests. *Journal of Applied Psychology*, *73*, 308–311.

Shye, S. (1991). *Faceted smallest space analysis: A computer program for the PC.* Jerusalem: The Israel Institute of Applied Social Research.

Shye, S. (1998). Modern facet theory: Content design and measurement in behavioral research. *European Journal of Psychological Assessment*, *14*, 160–171.

Shye, S., & Elizur, D. (1994). *Introduction to facet theory: Content design and intrinsic data analysis in behavioral research.* Thousand Oaks, CA: Sage.

Weintraub, S., & Mesulam, M. M. (1988). Visual hemispatial inattention: Stimulus parameters and exploratory strategies. *Journal of Neurology Neurosurgery and Psychiatry*, *51*, 1481–1488.

15 Process index scores for the Halstead Category Test

Daniel N. Allen, Joshua E. Caron, and Gerald Goldstein

Introduction

The Halstead Category Test (HCT; Halstead & Settlage, 1943) is a core test in the Halstead–Reitan Neuropsychological Test Battery and is generally considered to be a measure of abstraction ability, concept formation, and problem solving. It continues to be widely used for the assessment of these abilities (Lees-Haley, Smith, Williams, & Dunn, 1996). The common approach to interpretation focuses on the total number of errors that are made across 208 test items grouped into seven separate subtests (Reitan & Wolfson, 1993). While the practice of interpreting a total error score has proven highly effective in identifying individuals with brain damage, a number of studies suggest that the HCT assesses more than one neurocognitive construct and performance may best be represented by two or more scores that reflect these constructs rather than one total error score. Early indications of the test's multifactorial nature were provided by Simmel and Counts (1957), who used item analysis to demonstrate that the HCT items assessed a number of diverse cognitive abilities including counting, perceptual organization, set maintenance, and learning. In essence, their early work emulated the quantified process approach, by providing a basis for the development of indexes that could assist in the interpretation of the HCT. Their work also clearly demonstrated that the HCT was not solely a measure of abstraction ability, raising the possibility that adequate performance on the HCT could occur despite impaired abstraction ability.

Since then, investigators have reported that the HCT total error score is associated with a number of other diverse cognitive constructs including intelligence, memory, and problem solving (Goldstein & Shelly, 1971, 1972; Halstead, 1947; Lansdell & Donelly, 1977; Leonberger, Nicks, Goldfader, & Munz, 1991). More recent findings from factor analysis have indicated that the seven HCT subtests load on three factors that have been designated as Symbol Recognition and Counting, Spatial Positional Reasoning, and Proportional Reasoning (Allen, Goldstein, & Mariano, 1999; Johnstone, Holland, & Hewett, 1997). Additional evidence for the complex nature of the HCT has been provided by studies examining performance on individual HCT subtests (Caron, Allen, & Goldstein, 2002; Goldstein & Shemansky,

1995; Reitan, 1959) and by the development of scales using items selected across the seven subtests (Minassian, Perry, Carlson, Pelham, & DeFilippis, 2003). Thus, while a total error score has been traditionally used as an indicator of brain function, it is apparent that the HCT provides useful and clinically relevant information that is not fully reflected by this score.

In this chapter, we review the literature that has examined the construct validity of the HCT, including studies of total score correlations with other neuropsychological tests, those examining factor scores and individual subtest scores, as well as scoring procedures that span individual subtests to arrive at specific indexes of neurocognitive functioning. The literature review is organized according to the three major paradigms discussed by Poreh (2000) for the quantified process approach, including the satellite testing paradigm, composition paradigm, and the decomposition paradigm. The satellite paradigm pertains to tasks that have been developed to clarify performance on the HCT. Few if any satellite procedures have been developed for the HCT. The composition paradigm develops new indexes by examining existing data in order to provide unique information regarding the abilities assessed by the test. In most cases, studies of the HCT involving the composition paradigm have focused on interpretation of individual subtest scores or combinations of subtests scores, although some studies have examined reaction times as a unique source of information. Finally, the decomposition paradigm, which emphasizes the development of new indices that are based on analyses of individual items, has also been used to develop a number of unique indexes for the HCT. Prior to reviewing these approaches, however, a brief historical background and description of the HCT are provided.

Historical background and description of the Halstead Category Test

The HCT was one of a large number of tests that were originally selected by Ward Halstead at the University of Chicago who was attempting to identify tests that could differentiate between individuals with and without brain damage. The HCT proved to be one of the more effective tests in differentiating these groups (Reitan & Davison, 1974), and so, was retained as one of the core tests of the Halstead–Reitan Neuropsychological Test Battery (HRNB; Reitan & Wolfson, 1993). Choca, Laatsch, Wetzel, and Agresti (1997) recently provided an extensive review of the HCT, including its historical development. Briefly, they note that Halstead originally experimented with sorting tasks (Halstead, 1940) but abandoned these techniques in favor of an approach that eventually resulted in the development of the HCT. By 1947, with the publication of *Brain and intelligence* (Halstead, 1947), the HCT testing apparatus and 360 test items were developed, and by 1958 the 208 items that make up the current version of the test were selected (Shure & Halstead, 1958).

Halstead's approach was to present a number of novel learning trials in an effort to assess concept formation ability. Test items consist of Roman numerals, letters, solid and dashed lines, simple human stick figures, and geometric figures varying in size, shape and color. A box-like apparatus resembling a large computer monitor is used to present individual items, which are projected onto a 10×10 in opaque screen using a slide projector. Four keys, which are sequentially numbered 1–4, are positioned below the opaque screen. Test subjects are instructed to indicate the number that the item reminds them of by pressing the key with the corresponding number. Before the test begins, participants are also told that there will be seven subtests and that a single principle runs through each subtest. During each subtest, the examiner does not provide any clues or instructions as to what the correct principle is; rather, a pleasant chime follows correct responses while a rasping buzzer follows incorrect responses. The subject must use this feedback to determine the correct principle for each subtest. At the end of each subtest, the examiner informs the test subject that the subtest is over and a new subtest will begin that might use the same or a different principle.

The principles required to complete the first two subtests are simplistic. Subtest I requires participants to match Roman numerals with the numbered keys on the front of the projection apparatus, while Subtest II requires participants to match the number of items on the screen with the correct key. Even persons with moderate-to-severe brain damage generally perform these subtests without difficulty. For example, Forrest, Allen, and Goldstein (2004) reported a mean error rate of 1.22 (SD = 1.94) for a sample of 177 individuals with heterogeneous forms of brain damage when Subtests I and II were combined. Subtest III is based on the concept of uniqueness. Four geometric shapes are presented simultaneously with one figure being different from the other three figures in some way and the test subject must depress the key corresponding to the unique shape. The principle guiding Subtest IV is the quadrant–key relationship. Figures are presented that have four quadrants with each quadrant associated with either key one, two, three, or four. A correct response occurs when the subject pushes the key corresponding to the missing quadrant. Subtests V and VI are guided by the principle of proportion. A figure is presented that has a proportion of solid and dotted lines. When the figure is completely solid, the test subject should depress key four, while a half-solid figure corresponds with key two, and so on. Subtest VII does not present any new principles or items, but instead reviews the principles previously presented in Subtests I–VI.

As can be clearly seen from this brief description of the HCT, it is composed of markedly different items and requires a number of cognitive abilities to successfully complete. While it was originally thought to be uniquely sensitive to frontal-lobe damage, it has become apparent that it is also sensitive to lesions in other brain regions (Reitan & Wolfson, 1994), which is consistent with the multifaceted nature of the test. These observations have led some to criticize the use of a total error score, because it averages across a variety of underlying neurocognitive functions and limits the amount of information that can be derived from the test (Choca et al., 1997). This criticism has prompted several investigations examining constructs assessed by individual HCT subtests, as well as the application of factor analysis to determine the unique neurocognitive functions it assesses (Allen et al., 1999; Caron et al., 2002; Goldstein & Shemansky, 1997; Johnstone et al., 1997; Minassian et al., 2003; Reitan, 1959).

Since the development of the original version of the Category Test, a number of revisions have occurred, including the development of downward extensions of the test to make it appropriate for use with young children (Boll, 1993) and older children and adolescents (Kilpatrick & Spreen, 1973; Reed, Reitan, & Klove, 1965). Short forms have also been developed because of concern regarding the amount of time it takes to administer all 208 items (Boyle, Ward, & Steindl, 1994; Gelowitz & Paniak, 1992; Kilpatrick, 1970; Russell & Levy, 1987; Wetzel & Boll, 1987), although these shortened versions may have some limitations (Taylor, Goldman, Leavitt, & Kleinmen, 1984). Finally, because the original apparatus to administer the test is expensive and bulky, a number of alternative administration methods have been developed, including booklet (DeFilippis & McCampbell, 1979), card (Kimura, 1981), pen and paper (Adams & Trenton, 1981), and computerized versions (Choca, 1987; DeFilippis, 1993). While some concern has arisen about the comparability of the various versions, most studies suggest that scores derived from the standard, computerized, and booklet forms of the test are comparable. While lacking the portability of the booklet version, computerized versions have a number of distinct advantages over the original and booklet forms of the HCT. For example, because the test is administered by a computer, examiner errors during the administration and scoring are essentially eliminated, while standardization of administration is potentially increased. Additionally, because scores are recorded by the computer, additional information (e.g., reaction times) can be collected and detailed scores can be calculated with ease. These considerations have led many practitioners to opt for computerized or booklet versions of the Category Test over the original version.

Satellite testing paradigm

To our knowledge, there has been little research conducted on the HCT that would fall within the strictest definition of the satellite testing paradigm, and there are no published studies reporting the development or evaluation of satellite tests. However, when administered as part of the HRNB, interpretation of the HCT total error score is accomplished within the context of performance on other tests in the battery (Reitan & Wolfson, 1993). Clarification of the deficient ability contributing to poor performance on the HCT is thus attained by noting poor or adequate performance on other tests in the battery. The actuarial approach to test interpretation has been applied to the HRNB (Russell, Nurringer, & Goldstein, 1974). While this approach has been characterized as diametrically opposed to the process approach, implicit in actuarial approaches is the idea that patterns of performance across tests are suggestive of impairment of discrete neurocognitive abilities, which are in turn reflective of lesions of discrete brain regions or neural circuits. In the broadest sense then, the core tests of the HRNB could be considered satellite testing procedures in that they help to clarify the abilities assessed by the HCT. Of course, an important distinction is that the tests of the HRNB were not designed as complimentary procedures to the HCT but rather were selected because of their ability to differentiate between brain-damaged and nonbrain-damaged individuals. It is clear then that interpretation of the HCT is greatly facilitated by examination of performance on other tests. Therefore, satellite procedures, which are currently absent from the literature, could be very useful in understanding performance deficits on the HCT.

The composition paradigm

There have been many studies that have used composition-based approaches to develop more sensitive and specific indexes of impairment for the HCT. Studies have primarily focused on combining various subtest error scores through factor analysis or on interpreting error scores for individual subtests in order to reflect the specific cognitive domains assessed by the HCT. However, reaction times have also been investigated.

Factor analyses

A number of factor analytic studies have been carried out, with some examining the factor structure of the HRNB including the HCT, and others examining the factor structure of the HCT itself. In Halstead's (1947) original factor analysis of the HRNB, the Category Test loaded on a factor with a test of nonverbal intelligence and the Memory and Location measures from the Tactual Performance Test. Halstead called this an "Abstraction" factor. The HCT also had a secondary loading on a learning and memory factor, termed the "Central Integrative Field". Since that time, Goldstein and Shelly (1971) also found that the HCT total error score loaded on an abstraction and problem-solving factor. Other studies report loadings on factors assessing general intellectual functioning and memory abilities, with stronger associations with perceptual organization and visual memory, than verbal comprehension or auditory/verbal memory (Boyle, 1988; Goldstein & Shelly, 1972; Klonoff, 1971; Lansdell & Donnelly, 1977; Leonberger et al., 1991). These studies strengthen the impression that the HCT does not measure a unitary ability. They also provide a rationale for factor analysing separate subtests of the HCT.

Studies using a variety of factor and principal component analytic techniques have consistently found that the HCT subtests load on three distinct factors including a Symbol Recognition and Counting factor (Subtests I and II), a Spatial Positional Reasoning factor (Subtests III and IV), and a

Proportional Reasoning factor (Subtests V and VI) (Donders, 2001; Fischer & Dean, 1990; Johnstone et al., 1997; Kelly, Kundert, & Dean, 1992; Livingston, Gray, & Haak, 1996). Johnstone et al. (1997) demonstrated that these factors differ from other cognitive abilities, as they tended to load on separate factors when the HCT subtests were simultaneously analysed with tests of cognitive flexibility, verbal and visual memory, and verbal and nonverbal intelligence. Because factor structure may vary based on the unique characteristics of the sample under investigation (Russell, 1974), Allen et al. (1999) used confirmatory factor analyses to compare the factor structure of the HCT across three samples, including a brain-damaged, psychiatric, and nonbrain-damaged comparison group. Analyses were initially performed with all seven subtests to establish comparability with prior studies. However, because very few errors were made on Subtests I and II, their score distributions violated assumptions of multivariate normality, and so the confirmatory analyses were conducted again excluding Subtests I and II. In the analysis with all HCT Subtests, a three-factor model was optimal for all groups, providing a significantly better fit of the data than the null, one- and two-factor models. Subtests I and II formed one factor (Counting), Subtests III and IV loaded on the second factor (Spatial Positional Reasoning), and Subtests V and VI loaded on the third factor (Proportional Reasoning). In contrast to exploratory factor analyses that have found Subtest VII to load with Subtests III and IV, our confirmatory work indicated that Subtest VII loaded on both Factors 2 and 3, which is reasonable given that it is a review of the concepts presented in the first six subtests. When Subtests I and II were excluded, a two-factor solution was optimal, consisting of the Spatial Positional (Subtests III and IV) and Proportional Reasoning (Subtests V and VI) factors, with Subtest VII again loading on both factors. HCT factor structures were identical for the brain-damaged, psychiatric, and nonbrain-damaged groups.

While it was clear that three factors could be extracted from the HCT subtests, the underlying abilities that they assessed remained unclear, so correlations were calculated between the HCT factors and the WAIS and other tests of the HRNB. All correlations were significant ($p < 0.01$) and were of the same order of magnitude in all three groups. There were no marked variations among the three factors with regard to pattern of correlations with the WAIS or HRNB tests. Based on these findings, it appeared that while the Category Test was a multidimensional procedure, some question could be raised concerning the construct validity of the factors. It was suggested that the factors may not be differentially associated with the neurocognitive abilities assessed by traditional neuropsychological tests, but may be associated with other measures or outcomes. Consistent with this suggestion, Donders (2001) found that the Proportional Reasoning factor was sensitive to severity of brain injury, while the Spatial Positioning factor was not. Additional research is necessary to establish the construct and criterion validity of the HCT factors, which will facilitate their use in brain-damaged samples.

Subtest indexes

Effort

Because Subtests I and II were originally developed to familiarize participants to the testing procedure, items are easy and very few individuals make errors on these subtests. In our study of 601 patients, 97% of the total sample made one error or less on Subtest I, whereas on Subtest II, 83.5% of the sample made one error or less (Forrest et al., 2004). The simplicity of the subtests was further demonstrated by Laatsch and Choca (1991) who used item analysis to evaluate item difficulty on the HCT in a sample of rehabilitation patients, some of whom were impaired and others who were not. In all, 40 items were identified as being too easy to provide any meaningful discrimination. All of the items on Subtests I and II were identified as too simple as almost all participants, whether impaired or unimpaired, passed these items. As a result, error scores on Subtests I and II have little sensitivity to brain damage, except in very severe cases, where failure on these subtests indicates that the subject is incapable of comprehending or following test instructions. Given their insensitivity to brain damage, it might seem reasonable to drop Subtests I and II from administration or reduce them in length (Laatsch & Choca, 1991, 1994). However, a number of recent studies suggest that these subtests may be particularly useful as measures of effort and as such, can identify individuals who are malingering neurocognitive deficits (DiCarlo, Gfeller, & Oliveri, 2000; Forrest et al., 2004; Mittenberg, Rotholc, Russell, & Heilbronner, 1996; Tenhula & Sweet, 1996). A discussion of these studies is included here because poor scores reflect the underlying process (i.e., dissimulation) that is used to complete the subtests.

Mittenberg et al. (1996) reported that simulated malingering groups made significantly more errors on the HCT than did head-trauma patients. Tenhula and Sweet (1996) also found that, compared to brain-injured patients and normal controls, simulated malingerers made more errors on all of the HCT subtests, with errors on Subtests I and II being the most sensitive to malingered performance. DiCarlo et al. (2000) reported that number of errors on Subtests I and II combined, number of errors on Subtest VII, total HCT errors, and number of errors on 19 "easy" items were all useful in detecting malingered performance. However, a total of two or more errors on Subtests I and II provided the best discrimination between groups as this criterion correctly classified all of the normal controls and brain-damaged patients, as well as 76% of all simulated malingerers. Recently, Forrest et al. (2003, 2004) compared individuals with brain damage to coached malingerers and normal controls on a variety of indexes thought to be sensitive to malingered HCT performance. Stepwise discriminant function analysis indicated that errors of Subtests I and II were the most effective in discriminating between groups, with controls and brain-damaged groups making approximately one error, compared to the simulated malingerers who made an average of five errors. Thus, while Subtests I and II are not sensitive to brain injury of mild-to-moderate severity, they do provide an index of effort that is highly sensitive to malingered test performance and more generally, inadequate effort. Given that they also serve to familiarize participants with the testing procedure and take a relatively short time to administer, we are of the opinion that these subtests should be given to all individuals who are being evaluated for brain injury, and are essential when litigation is an issue.

Learning and executive functions

Learning has been examined in a number of ways with some investigations examining improvement in performance as the test progresses (Bertram, Abeles, & Snyder, 1990), and others comparing subtest scores with the expectation that improvement should occur when a principle is repeated from one subtest to the other (Goldstein & Shemansky, 1997; Reitan, 1959). These two methods have produced contradictory findings, with the former suggesting that learning does not have a substantial impact on HCT performance, and the latter suggesting that it does.

In a number of studies using the latter approach (Forrest et al., 2003; Goldstein & Shemansky, 1997; Reitan, 1959) researchers hypothesized that since the same concept is used to solve Subtests V and VI, and these subtests have the same number of items, relatively fewer errors should be made on Subtest VI. In fact, when compared to Subtest V, significant improvement in performance was noted on Subtest VI in all of these studies, not only for individuals without brain damage, but also for those with schizophrenia and those with heterogeneous forms of brain damage. Improvement in performance for the brain-damaged, schizophrenia, and nonbrain-damaged comparison groups from Forrest et al. (2003) are presented in Figure 15.1. As expected, the nonbrain-damaged comparison group made fewer overall errors than the schizophrenia group, who in turn made fewer errors than the brain-damaged group. However, all groups exhibited significant improvement ($p < 0.001$) in performance on Subtest VI, suggesting that learning does occur from Subtests V to VI in most individuals.

Forrest and coworkers (2003, 2004) also examined learning effects on Subtest VII, which is a review of the items and principles used for Subtests I–VI. However, because direct comparisons of error scores are not practical given the substantially different number of items among subtests, two average error scores were developed, the first by dividing the total number of combined errors for Subtests I through VI by the total number of items on Subtests I–VI (avI–VI), and the second by dividing the total number of errors on Subtest VII by the total number of items on Subtest VII (avVII). Again, as can be seen in Figure 15.2, a significant decrease ($p < 0.001$) in average number of errors was noted from avI–VI to avVII for the nonbrain-damaged, schizophrenia, and brain-damaged groups, with expected differences in overall performance between the three groups. Results are largely consistent across these studies with regard to improvement from Subtests V–VI (Forrest

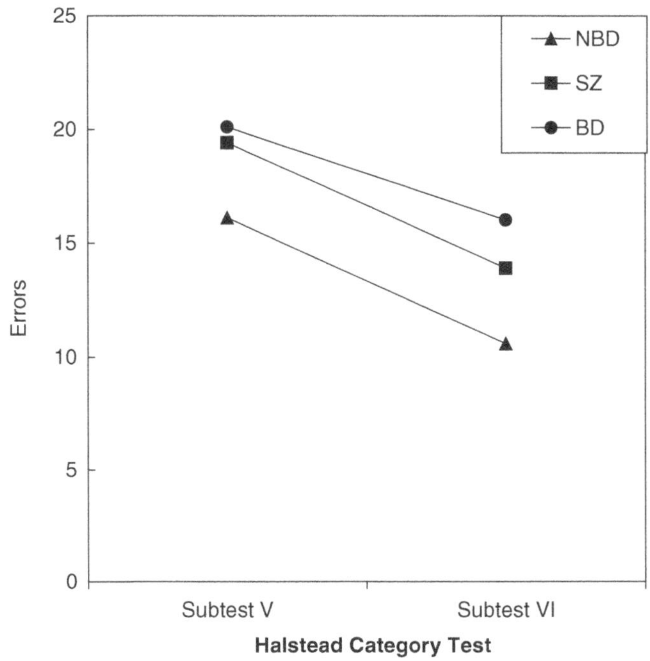

Figure 15.1 Error scores for the nonbrain-damaged, schizophrenia, and brain-damaged groups on the Halstead Category Test (Subtests V and VI). NBD, non-brain-damaged comparison group; SZ, schizophrenia group; BD, brain-damaged group.

et al., 2003, 2004; Goldstein & Shemansky, 1997; Reitan, 1959), although the method of comparing average error scores for Subtests I–VI to Subtest VII is a new methodology for examining learning effects on Subtest VII.

While these results are promising, validation studies are needed in order to determine the sensitivity of these learning effects to brain damage. While it is apparent that learning does occur, it is counter-intuitive that individuals with schizophrenia, who are known to have mesial temporal-lobe dysfunction and declarative memory deficits, would learn as much in relative terms as non-brain-damaged comparison samples. A similar observation is relevant to the brain-damaged group. Thus, these studies provide little clarification of the memory systems that are responsible for improved performance. Procedural memory could account for these findings, as dissociations between declarative and procedural memory have been reported for amnestic patients. Also, the HCT may have a motor learning component, which may differentially favor the procedural memory system as the test progresses. Alternatively, sample heterogeneity may have obscured the sensitivity of these indexes to declarative memory deficits in both schizophrenia and brain-damaged samples, by combining individuals who have declarative memory impairment with those who

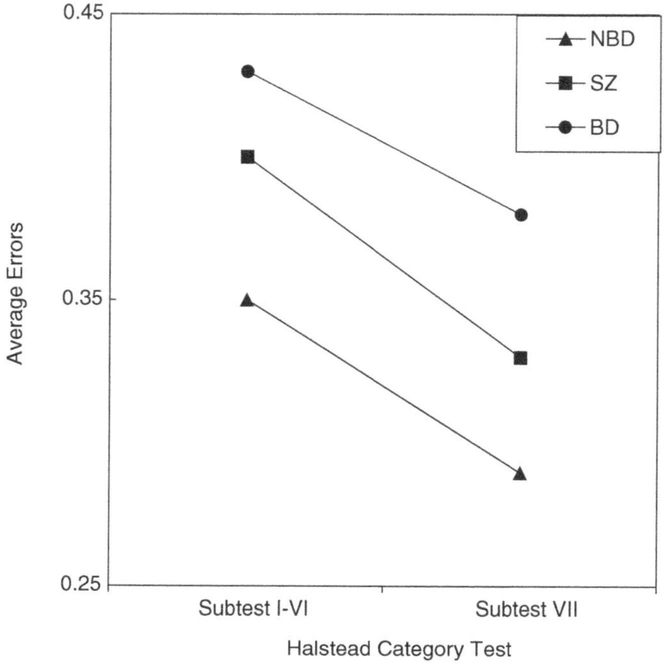

Figure 15.2 Averaged error scores for the nonbrain-damaged comparison, schizophrenia, and brain-damaged groups on Halstead Category Test (Subtests I–VI and VII). NBD, nonbrain-damaged comparison group; SZ, schizophrenia group; BD, brain-damaged group.

do not have impairment. In support of this explanation, Allen, Goldstein, and Weiner (2001) recently reported that some patients with schizophrenia exhibit a profile of neuropsychological deficits consistent with frontal-lobe damage, while others exhibit temporal-lobe profiles, and still others have mixed fronto-temporal profiles. This heterogeneity may have allowed for overall improvement in performance to be observed for the schizophrenia group, even though some individuals with declarative memory deficits did not improve.

In a preliminary investigation of this issue, Caron et al. (2002) compared Subtests V and VII performance of individuals with temporal-lobe lesions to those with frontal-lobe lesions, as well as to a group with schizophrenia and to a nonbrain-damaged comparison sample. Subtest VII was included as an index of learning, while Subtest V was included as an index of perseveration. It was reasoned that because the test stimuli for Subtest V bear a strong resemblance to those on Subtest IV, individuals may attempt to use the strategy from Subtest IV to complete Subtest V. However, Subtests IV and V require different strategies, so individuals who are prone to perseveration due to frontal-lobe damage are expected to make more errors on Subtest V. It was hypothesized that a double dissociation would be present wherein the frontal-lobe group would make more errors on Subtest V (perseveration) and fewer errors on Subtest VII (memory) compared to the temporal-lobe group who would exhibit the opposite pattern. Patients with schizophrenia should perform poorly on both subtests given that frontal- and temporal-lobe abnormalities have been identified as cardinal features of the disorder. Significant interaction effects were found ($p < 0.01$) and consistent with the hypothesis, a double dissociation was present in which the frontal-lobe group made more errors on Subtest V while the temporal-lobe group made more errors on Subtest VII (see Figure 15.3). The results provide additional evidence supporting the usefulness of Subtest VII as an index of learning and memory, and further suggest that Subtest VII is sensitive to declarative memory deficits, which arise from temporal-lobe lesions. Results also provide preliminary support for the usefulness of Subtest V as a measure of perseveration. Limitations include small numbers of participants in the frontal- and temporal-lobe groups. Additionally, the specific types of errors that each group made on Subtests V and VII were not examined. Research that has used decomposition approaches to investigate error types is discussed in the next section, which extends the current findings to some extent. However, additional research is

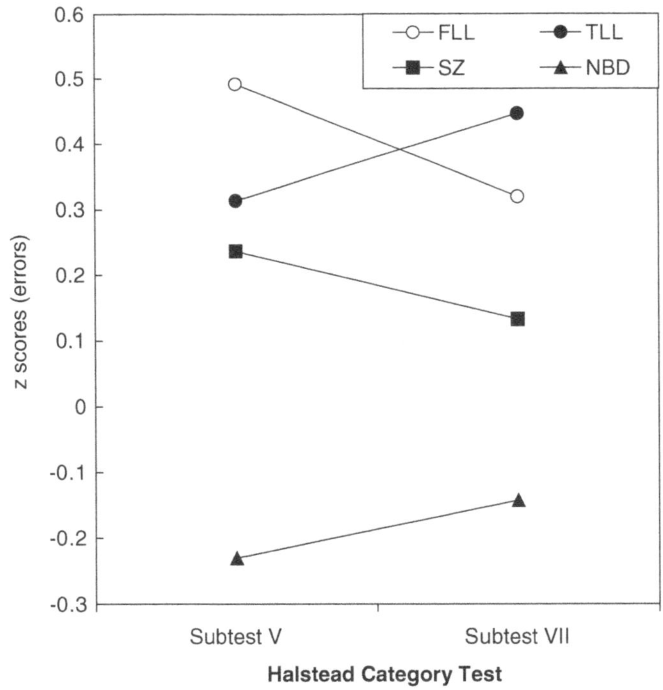

Figure 15.3 Standard error scores for the frontal-lobe lesion, temporal-lobe lesion, schizophrenia, and nonbrain-damaged patient comparison groups on the Halstead Category Test (Subtests V and VI). FLL, frontal-lobe lesion group; TLL, temporal-lobe lesion group; NBD, nonbrain-damaged comparison group; SZ, schizophrenia group.

necessary to determine the construct validity of Subtests V and VII when used as measures of perseveration and memory, respectively.

Response times

Response times to HCT items vary significantly from subject to subject, with individuals who have brain damage taking longer to complete the test than those without damage (Finlayson et al., 1986). Given the sensitivity of total response times to brain damage, response times to individual items have also been examined. Studies utilizing the original version of the HCT have recorded response times to individual items using a stop watch, and have calculated scores for total response times, as well as for times averaged across correct responses and incorrect responses (e.g., Rattan, Dean, & Fisher, 1986). When included in a factor analysis with other tests from the HRNB, response times formed their own factor, which accounted for 21.2% of the total variability (Rattan et al., 1986). Response times were also significantly correlated with Full Scale IQ. Taken together, these findings suggest that response times may be associated in a general way with the integrity of information processing capacities, or alternatively may reflect psychomotor speed even in the absence of complex processing requirements. The primary limitations of using the original HCT to gather reaction time information is the need for an additional person to record response times using a stop watch, as well as inevitable imprecision in recording these times. So in order for reaction times to be practical, computerized administration of the HCT is necessary. However, reaction times recorded by computerized versions have not received much attention, although some suggest decreased reaction times accompanied by poor performance may reflect impulsivity (Choca, Laatsch, Garside, & Arnemann, 1994). Preliminary reports have indicated that response times for Subtest III are associated with reading scores in individuals with learning disabilities, which may be a unique relationship derived largely from associations between reading ability and the spatial position concept assessed by Subtest III (Rattan & Coslett, 1999) or by the more general associations between reaction times and verbal IQ. HCT reaction times for correct responses have also been reported to discriminate between children with and without learning disabilities in reading (Rattan, Coslett, & Wood, 2000). Thus, response times appear to provide unique information that is helpful in augmenting the interpretation of the HCT, particularly when computerized versions of the test are used. Additional research is needed in order to clearly identify the neurocognitive abilities being assessed and to demonstrate their usefulness in clinical practice.

The decomposition paradigm

The decomposition paradigm involves examining relationships between individual test items in order to develop new indexes of ability. Factor analysis of individual items is often used in the decomposition approach to create new indexes, but to date there have been no studies that have factor analysed the individual items of the HCT. However, item analysis approaches have been used (Laatsch & Choca, 1991, 1994; Simmel & Counts, 1957). Simmel and Counts (1957) demonstrate that the HCT requires skills such as counting, perceptual organization, set maintenance, and learning. Laatsch and Choca (1991, 1994) used item analysis and cluster-branching methodology to examine item difficulty and develop adaptive versions of the test. These studies have some relevance to the current discussion because they have provided new scales based on rearranging items. For example, based on the observation by Russell and Levy (1987) that some items from Subtests V and VI could be correctly answered by using the principle of counting instead of the principle of proportion, Laatsch and Choca (1994) selected out the counting items to form a separate subtest representing an intermediate difficulty level between Subtest II and the original Subtest III. They also collapsed the remaining items from Subtests V and VI to form one subtest assessing Proportional Reasoning. The sensitivity of scores derived from these new subtests have not been extensively evaluated, and their construct validities are yet to be established. Also, it is unclear whether changing the order in which items are administered alters their difficulty levels or the constructs they assess. However, item analysis approaches hold great promise with regard to developing empirically based decomposition indexes for the HCT.

Effort indexes

The HCT items are consistent with symptom validity testing procedures that use below chance performance on forced-choice items as an index of suboptimal effort (Tenhula & Sweet, 1996). In an application of this methodology to the HCT, Bolter, Picano, and Zych (1985) examined the adequacy of a set of 18 "easy" items, identified as infrequently missed by their sample, in differentiating between normal controls, simulated malingerers, and individuals with traumatic brain injury. The normal control and brain-damaged groups made fewer errors on easy items than did the simulated malingerers, providing some support for this approach. Tenhula and Sweet (1996) also found that Bolter's easy items could discriminate between normal control, brain-damaged, and simulated malingering groups, although error scores on Subtests I and II were more effective at identifying malingerers. Also, Subtests I and II were more effective in identifying malingerers than 19 easy items that Tenhula and Sweet identified from their sample, which differed from the 18 items identified by Bolter et al. (1985).

DiCarlo et al. (2000) replicated the findings from Tenhula and Sweet (1996). However, they extended prior findings by including a coached simulator group, i.e., a group that was specifically instructed in how to avoid being detected as malingering. As previously mentioned, they found that making more than one total error on Subtests I and II was the most consistent and accurate indicator of both coached and uncoached malingering. While the 19 easy items identified by Tenhula and Sweet performed less well, they were still able to accurately classify 80% of uncoached simulators, 53.6% of coached simulators, 100% of controls, and 90% of the brain-damaged group. In summary, despite some criticisms (Ashendorf, O'Bryant, Constantinou, Weber, Palav, & McCaffrey, 2001), these findings generally support the use of easy items as indexes of effort, and are consistent with the widely held belief that individuals who perform more poorly on simple tasks compared to harder tasks are likely to be feigning neurocognitive impairment.

Executive function indexes

There have been a number of attempts to develop indexes reflecting various types of executive function deficits such as perseveration although most of this research has appeared in abstract form (e.g., Miller & Bornstein, 1991; Schutz & Gorman, 1985; Strite, Hannay, & Meyers, 1996) and so, detailed information regarding rationale and scoring procedures is not available. Strite et al. (1996) reported the development of a perseveration index that was sensitive to right-hemisphere lesions. Miller and Bornstein (1991) also found that their perseveration index, in which perseverative errors were defined as a response followed by the same numbered response, was sensitive to right-frontal-lobe lesions. Schutz and Gorman (1996) reported the development of two perseveration scores, one focusing on figure-ground reversals and the second focusing on repeated errors. These scales exhibited correlations with a number of other neuropsychological measures and clinical variables although a specific pattern of association with measures of executive functions was not present. Schutz and Schutz (2000) later reported the development of a scale that had significant associations with important clinical variables, such as duration of coma and post-traumatic amnesia.

In one of the only published studies, Minassian and coworkers (2003) used the decomposition approach to develop scales assessing executive functions, including the abilities to shift and maintain problem-solving sets. The Perseverative Response Index (PRI) reflects the tendency of some individuals with brain damage to continue to use the same problem-solving strategy despite feedback indicating that the strategy is no longer effective. Select items from Subtests III–VII are included in the scoring of this index. An example of a perseverative response would be use of the number principle from Subtest II to solve items on Subtest III, which is governed by the principle of uniqueness. The Loss of Set Index (LSI) evaluates inattentiveness or failure to hold a problem-solving strategy in working memory. The LSI is calculated based on select items from Subtests III–VI. Errors are scored each time a participant makes three correct responses, followed by an incorrect response. To validate these measures, Minassian et al. (2003) administered the Category Test and a number of other neuropsychological tests to individuals with heterogeneous forms of brain damage, as well as to individuals with schizophrenia. In both groups the PRI was significantly correlated with number of perseverative responses on the Wisconsin Card Sorting Test (WCST; Heaton, Chelune, Tallen, Kay, & Curtiss, 1993). The PRI also exhibited significant correlations with measures of learning and memory, indicating that a greater number of perseverative responses was associated with poorer performance on memory measures. These correlations may simply reflect the associations between executive planning abilities, and efficient encoding of information into and retrieval of information out of long-term storage. The LSI was not significantly correlated with the WCST Failure to Maintain Set (FMS) score in the brain damage and schizophrenia groups. The LSI did have a greater range than the WCST FMS, which has limited utility because it occurs with such low frequency even in brain-damaged populations. These findings provide initial support for the construct validity of the PRI. Additional research is necessary to determine if these indexes can discriminate between individuals with and without brain damage, as well as whether or not they are sensitive to localized lesions.

Memory indexes

Minassian and coworkers (2003) also reported the development of a Memory Index (MI) for the HCT. The MI is based solely on responses to Subtest VII, and reflects the retention of strategies learned over Subtests III–VI. The MI is a refinement of the procedure reported by Caron et al. (2002), who simply used the error score from Subtest VII as their Memory Index. This approach assumes that all of the principles presented in Subtests I–VI were mastered. Rather than making this assumption, Minassian et al. (2003) award points only for the MI if it is clear that the individual has mastered the corresponding concepts from Subtests III–VI (items from Subtests I and II are excluded from the MI). Hence, in order for an item on Subtest VII to be scored as a memory retrieval on the MI, five correct answers in a row had to be attained on the subtest in which the concept was originally presented. For patients with schizophrenia or brain damage, significant correlations were present between the MI and measures of memory derived from the Wechsler Memory Scale Revised (Wechsler, 1987) and the California Verbal Learning Test (Delis, Kramer, Kaplan, & Ober, 1987). These correlations provide support for the construct validity of the MI, although further research is needed with clinical and normal populations to determine the sensitivity and specificity of this index to memory dysfunction.

Conclusions

The various satellite, composition, and decomposition approaches to interpreting the HCT are presented in Table 15.1. As can be seen from the table, satellite tests to assist in the interpretation of the HCT have not been developed and at present, HCT performance can only be clarified using neuropsychological tests from the HRNB or other sources. Certainly, satellite testing approaches have proved useful in clarifying interpretation of a number of

Table 15.1 Quantified process approach indexes for the Halstead Category Test

Quantified process approach paradigm	*Ability*	*Reference*
Satellite test paradigm		
—	—	—
Composition paradigm		
Subtest I	Effort	Tenhula and Sweet (1996); DiCarlo et al. (2000)
Subtest II	Effort	Tenhula and Sweet (1996); DiCarlo et al. (2000)
Subtest V	Executive function (perseveration)	Caron et al. (2002)
Subtest VI	Learning	Reitan (1959); Goldstein and Shemansky (1997)
Subtest VII	Learning	Forrest et al. (2003, 2004)
Reaction time	Impulsivity, psychomotor speed, information processing speed, verbal IQ	Rattan et al. (1986); Choca et al. (1994)
Subtests I+II	Symbol Recognition and Counting	Johnstone et al. (1997); Allen et al. (1999)
Subtests III+IV+VII (0.5)	Spatial Positional Reasoning	Allen et al. (1999)
Subtests V+VI+VII (0.5)	Proportional Reasoning	Allen et al. (1999)
Decomposition paradigm		
Easy items 18	Effort	Bolter et al. (1985)
Easy items 19	Effort	Tenhula and Sweet (1996)
Perseverative response index	Executive function	Minassian et al. (2003)
Loss of set index	Attention, set maintenance	Minassian et al. (2003)
Memory index	Long-term memory (visual and verbal)	Minassian et al. (2003)
Subtest III revised	Counting	Laatsch and Choca (1994)
Subtest V+VI revised	Proportional Reasoning	Laatsch and Choca (1994)

other commonly used neuropsychological measures (Poreh, 2000) and should also prove useful when applied to the HCT.

Unlike the satellite approach, the composition paradigm has been successfully used to develop indexes that can greatly assist in the interpretation of the HCT. Indexes have been developed that reflect effort, simple counting and symbol recognition, memory, executive function, and various aspects of reasoning ability, with some evidence supporting reaction times as measures of impulsivity, reading comprehension, psychomotor speed, and information processing speed. For a number of these indexes, additional research is necessary to refine them and fully understand their psychometric properties, including construct-and-criterion related validities. However, these studies have provided substantive evidence suggesting that the composition paradigm can be very useful in developing indexes to clarify performance on the HCT. In a similar manner, decomposition approaches have provided a number of useful indexes that should aid in interpreting the HCT. As can be seen from the table, substantial overlap exists between indexes developed using composition and decomposition techniques. Direct comparisons have not been made between these indexes although these types of comparisons would be helpful in determining the amount of variance shared by the various indexes, as well as their associations with other commonly administered neuropsychological tests and relative sensitivities to brain damage. Composition approaches, such as examination of individual subtest scores, have the advantage of simplicity in that they are easy to calculate. However, this simplicity can make them less sensitive or less pure measures of underlying cognitive abilities because items composing some HCT subtests are not homogeneous. Decomposition approaches can address this shortcoming by selecting homogeneous sets of items based on their unique characteristics, with the selection process driven by specific theoretical assumptions regarding the ability under investigation. One approach that has not been used but that would be helpful in developing decomposition indexes would be the application of factor analysis to the individual HCT items, rather than the subtest scores. Such an analysis would require an extensive amount of data, but would provide a strong statistical–empirical basis for specifying items as measures of distinct constructs, thus providing support for the construct validity of currently available decomposition indexes.

Finally, a relatively new development that is receiving an increased amount of attention is the use of quantified process approaches to develop indexes of effort for the HCT, as well as for a large number of other commonly used tests. For the HCT, most studies indicate that indexes developed using the composition approach are more effective than currently available decomposition indexes. Specifically, poor performance on Subtests I and II appear more sensitive to inadequate effort than performance on "easy" items. However, the latter approach may be augmented by using the easy items identified by Laatsch and Choca (1994) through item analysis. Not only were the items empirically selected based on item difficulty levels, but there are more items (45) that are more broadly distributed throughout the HCT, so they should provide a more adequate sampling of behavior and be more sensitive to fluctuations in motivation as the test progresses.

References

Adams, R. L., & Trenton, S. L. (1981). Development of a paper-and-pen form of the Halstead Category Test. *Journal of Consulting and Clinical Psychology*, *49*, 298–299.

Allen, D. N., Goldstein, G., & Mariano, E. (1999). Is the Category Test a multidimensional instrument? *Journal of Clinical and Experimental Neuropsychology*, *21*, 237–244.

Allen, D. N., Goldstein, G., & Weiner, C. L. (2001). Differential neuropsychological patterns of frontal- and temporal-lobe dysfunction in patients with schizophrenia. *Schizophrenia Research*, *48*, 7–15.

Ashendorf, L., O'Bryant, S. E., Constantinou, M., Weber, M., Palav, A., & McCaffrey, R. J. (2001). An empirical examination of Bolter's Validity Index for the Halstead Category Test (abstract). *Archives of Clinical Neuropsychology*, *16*, 847.

Bertram, K. W., Abeles, N., & Snyder, P. J. (1990). The role of learning in performance on Halstead's Category Test. *The Clinical Neuropsychologist*, *4*, 244–252.

Boll, T. (1993). *Children's Category Test*. San Antonio, TX: The Psychological Corporation.

Bolter, J. F., Picano, J. J., & Zych, K. (1985). *Item error frequency on the Halstead Category Test: An index of performance validity*. Paper presented at the annual meeting of the National Academy of Neuropsychology, Philadelphia, PA.

Boyle, G. J. (1988). What does the neuropsychological Category Test measure? *Archives of Clinical Neuropsychology*, *3*, 69–76.

Boyle, G. J., Ward, J., & Steindl, S. R. (1994). Psychometric properties of Russell's short for of the Booklet Category Test. *Perceptual and Motor Skills*, *79*, 128–130.

Caron, J., Allen, D. N., & Goldstein, G. (2002). Perseveration and memory scores for the Halstead Category Test (abstract). *Archives of Clinical Neuropsychology*, *17*, 775.

Choca, J. P. (1987). *Category Test computer program*. Ontario, Canada: Multi-Health Systems.

Choca, J., Laatsch, L., Garside, D., & Arnemann, C. (1994). *Computer Category Test*. Ontario, Canada: Multi-Health Systems.

Choca, J. P., Laatsch, L., Wetzel, L., & Agresti, A. (1997). The Halstead Category Test: A Fifty Year Perspective. *Neuropsychology Review*, *7*, 61–75.

DeFilippis, N. A. (1993). *Category Test: Computer version research edition*. Odessa, FL: Psychological Assessment Resources.

DeFilippis, N. A., & McCampbell, E. (1979). *The Booklet Category Test*. Odessa, FL: Psychological Assessment Resources.

Delis, D. C., Kramer, J. H., Kaplan, E., & Ober, B. A. (1987). *California Verbal Learning Test*. New York: The Psychological Corporation.

DiCarlo, M. A., Gfeller, J. D., & Oliveri, M. V. (2000). Effects of coaching on detecting feigned cognitive impairment with the Category Test. *Archives of Clinical Neuropsychology*, *15*, 399–413.

Donders, J. (2001). Clinical utility of the Category Test as a multidimensional instrument. *Psychological Assessment*, *13*, 592–594.

Finlayson, M. A., Sullivan, J. F., & Alfano, D. P. (1986). Halstead's Category Test: Withstanding the test of time. *Journal of Clinical & Experimental Neuropsychology*, *8*, 706–709.

Fischer, W. E., & Dean, R. S. (1990). Factor structure of the Halstead Category Test by age and gender. *International Journal of Clinical Neuropsychology*, *12*, 180–183.

Forrest, T. J., Allen, D. N., & Goldstein, G. (2003). Evaluation of new malingering indexes for the Halstead Category Test (abstract). *Archives of Clinical Neuropsychology*, *18*, 783.

Forrest, T. J., Allen, D. N., & Goldstein, G. (2004). Detection of malingered brain damage on the Halstead Category Test. *The Clinical Neuropsychologist*, *18*, 334–347.

Gelowitz, D. L., & Paniak, C. E. (1992). Cross-validation of the Short Category Test-booklet format. *Neuropsychology*, *6*, 287–292.

Goldstein, G., & Shelly, C. H. (1971). Field dependence and cognitive, perceptual, and motor skills in alcoholics: A factor-analytic study. *Quarterly Journal of Studies on Alcohol*, *32*, 29–40.

Goldstein, G., & Shelly, C. H. (1972). Statistical and normative studies of the Halstead Neuropsychological Test Battery relevant to a neuropsychiatric hospital setting. *Perceptual and Motor Skills*, *34*, 603–620.

Goldstein, G., & Shemansky, W. J. (1997). Patterns of performance by neuropsychiatric patients on the Halstead Category Test: Evidence for conceptual learning in schizophrenia. *Archives of Clinical Neuropsychology*, *12*, 251–255.

Halstead, W. C. (1940). Preliminary analysis of grouping behavior in patients with cerebral injury by the method of equivalent and non-equivalent stimuli. *American Journal of Psychiatry*, *96*, 1263–1294.

Halstead, W. C. (1947). *Brain and intelligence: A quantitative study of the frontal lobes.* Chicago: University of Chicago Press.

Halstead, W. C., & Settlage, P. (1943). Grouping behavior of normal persons and persons with lesions of the brain. *Archives of Neurology and Psychiatry*, *49*, 489–506.

Heaton, R. K., Chelune, G. J., Tallen, J. L., Kay, G. G., & Curtiss, G. (1993). *Wisconsin Card Sorting Test manual revised and expanded.* Odessa, FL: Psychological Assessment Resources.

Johnstone, B., Holland, D., & Hewett, J. E. (1997). The construct validity of the Category Test: Is it a measure of reasoning or intelligence? *Psychological Assessment*, *9*, 28–33.

Kelly, M. D., Kundert, D. K., & Dean, R. S. (1992). Factor analysis and matrix invariance of the HRNB-C Category Test. *Archives of Clinical Neuropsychology*, *7*, 415–418.

Kilpatrick, D. L. (1970). The Halstead Category Test of brain dysfunction: Feasibility of a short form. *Perceptual and Motor Skills*, *30*, 577–578.

Kilpatrick, D. L., & Spreen, O. (1973). A revision of the Halstead Category Test for children aged 9 to 15. *Psychology in the Schools*, *10*, 101–106.

Kimura, S. D. (1981). A card form of the Reitan-Modified Halstead Category Test. *Journal of Consulting and Clinical Psychology*, *49*, 145–146.

Klonoff, H. (1971). Factor analysis of a neuropsychological battery for children aged 9 to 15. *Perceptual and Motor Skills*, *32*, 603–616.

Laatsch, L., & Choca, J. (1991). Understanding the Halstead Category Test by using item analysis. *Psychological Assessment: A Journal of Consulting and Clinical Psychology*, *3*, 701–704.

Laatsch, L., & Choca, J. (1994). Cluster-branching methodology for adaptive testing and the development of the adaptive Category Test. *Psychological Assessment*, *6*, 345–351.

Lansdell, H., & Donnelly, E. F. (1977). Factor analysis of the Wechsler Adult Intelligence Scale subtests and the Halstead–Reitan Category and Tapping Tests. *Journal of Consulting and Clinical Psychology*, *45*, 412–416.

Lees-Haley, P. R., Smith, H. H., Williams, C. W., & Dunn, J. T. (1996). Forensic neuropsychological test usage: An empirical survey. *Archives of Clinical Neuropsychology*, *11*, 45–51.

Lefevre, C., Rattan, G., Sujansky, R., & Griffith, R. (1991). *Response time on the older children's Category Test: A more sensitive index of learning*. Paper presented at the annual convention of the National Academy of Neuropsychology, Dallas, TX.

Leonberger, F. T., Nicks, S. D., Goldfader, P. R., & Munz, D. C. (1991). Factor analysis of the Wechsler Memory Scale—Revised and the Halstead–Reitan Neuropsychological Battery. *The Clinical Neuropsychologist*, *5*, 83–88.

Livingston, R. B., Gray, R. M., & Haak, R. A. (1996). Factor analysis of the intermediate Category Test. *Perceptual and Motor Skills*, *83*, 851–855.

Miller, H. B., & Bornstein, R. A. (1991). *Development of component measure of perseveration for the Halstead Category Test*. Paper presented at the annual convention of the American Psychological Association, San Francisco, CA.

Minassian, A., Perry, W., Carlson, M., Pelham, M., & DeFilippis, N. (2003). The Category Test Perseveration, Loss of Set, and Memory Scales: Three new scales and their relationship to executive functioning measures. *Assessment*, *10*, 213–221.

Mittenberg, W., Rotholc, A., Russell, E., & Heilbronner, R. (1996). Identification of malingered head injury on the Halstead–Reitan Battery. *Archives of Clinical Neuropsychology*, *11*, 271–281.

Poreh, A. M. (2000). The quantified process approach: An emerging methodology to neuropsychological assessment. *The Clinical Neuropsychologist*, *14*, 212–222.

Rattan, G., & Coslett, J. A. (1999). Response time measures on the Category Test in differentiating LD and regular readers (abstract). *Archives of Clinical Neuropsychology*, *14*, 685–686.

Rattan, G., Coslett, J. A., & Wood, T. (2000). The relative efficacy of response time measures on the Category Test in identifying LD readers (abstract). *Archives of Clinical Neuropsychology*, *15*, 800.

Rattan, G., Dean, R. S., & Fisher, W. E. (1986). Response time as a dependent measure on the Category Test of the Halstead–Reitan Neuropsychological Test Battery. *Archives of Clinical Neuropsychology*, *1*, 175–182.

Reed, H. B. C., Reitan, R. M., & Klove, H. (1965). The influence of cerebral lesions on psychological test performances of older children. *Journal of Consulting Psychology*, *29*, 247–251.

Reitan, R. M. (1959). Impairment of abstraction ability in brain damage: Quantitative versus qualitative changes. *Journal of Psychology*, *48*, 97–102.

Reitan, R. M., & Davison, L. A. (1974). *Clinical neuropsychology: Current status and applications.* Washington: V.H. Winston and Sons.

Reitan, R. M., & Wolfson, D. (1993). *The Halstead–Reitan Neuropsychological Test Battery: Theory and clinical interpretation.* Tucson, AZ: Neuropsychology Press.

Reitan, R. M., & Wolfson, D. (1994). A selective and critical review of neuropsychological deficits and the frontal lobes. *Neuropsychology Review*, *4*, 161–198.

Russell, E. W. (1974). The effect of acute lateralized brain damage on Halstead's biological intelligence factors. *Journal of General Psychology*, *90*, 101–107.

Russell, E. W., & Levy, M. (1987). Revision of the Halstead Category Test. *Journal of Consulting and Clinical Psychology*, *55*, 898–901.

Russell, E. W., Neuringer, C., & Goldstein, G. (1974). *Assessment of brain damage: A neuropsychological key approach.* New York: John Wiley & Sons.

Schutz, L. E., & Gorman, P. (1996). Process subscales for the Halstead Category Test (abstract). *Archives of Clinical Neuropsychology, 11*, 445–446.

Schutz, L. E., & Schutz, J. A. (2000). New findings for Category Test subscales (abstract). *Archives of Clinical Neuropsychology, 15*, 821.

Shure, G., & Halstead, W. (1958). Cerebral localization of intellectual processes. *Psychological Monographs, 72* (no. 465).

Simmel, M. L., & Counts, S. (1957). Some stable response determinants of perception, thinking, and learning: A study based on the analysis of a single test. *Genetic Psychology Monographs, 56*, 3–157.

Strite, D., Hannay, J., & Meyers, C. A. (1996). *The Category Test revisited: An analysis of memory, perseveration, and localization*. Paper presented at the 24th annual meeting of the International Neuropsychological Society, Chicago.

Taylor, J. M., Goldman, H., Leavitt, J., & Kleinmen, K. M. (1984). Limitations of the brief form of the Halstead Category Test. *Journal of Clinical Neuropsychology, 6*, 341–344.

Tenhula, W. N., & Sweet, J. J. (1996). Double cross-validation of the Booklet Category Test in detecting malingered traumatic brain injury. *The Clinical Neuropsychologist, 10*, 104–116.

Wechsler, D. (1987). *Wechsler Memory Scale-Revised manual.* New York, NY: The Psychological Corporation.

Wetzel, L., & Boll, T. (1987). *Short Category Test, booklet format.* Los Angeles: Western Psychological Services.

Part V

Combining paradigms

The division of the Quantified Process Approach into three paradigms aids the conceptualization of this new paradigm. In reality, however, the understanding of a particular task typically requires the combination of several paradigms. Anita M. Hubley describes in Chapter 16 the use of all three approaches toward capturing process in complex figure scoring. In Chapter 17, Daniel J. Slick and Esther Strauss describe the application of the Quantified Process Approach to the development of new measures for the assessment of suboptimal performance on traditional neuropsychological tests.

16 Capturing process in complex figure scoring

Anita M. Hubley

Introduction

Complex figures are commonly used to assess visuospatial abilities and executive functioning in children and adults and there has been a steady increase in studies using such figures since 1976 (Knight, 2003a). While the most commonly used complex figure is the Rey–Osterrieth Complex Figure (ROCF; Osterrieth, 1944; Rey, 1941), other figures include the Taylor Complex Figure (TCF) (Taylor, 1969), Modified TCF (Hubley, 1996; Hubley & Tremblay, 2002), Medical College of Georgia Complex Figures (Loring & Meador, 2003), Mack Visual Design (Frazier, Adams, Strauss, & Redline, 2001), Modified ROCF (Saxton, Becker, & Wisniewski, 2003), and the complex figures from the Memory Test for Older Adults (Hubley & Tombaugh, 2002; Hubley, Tombaugh, & Hemingway, 2003).

Advantages associated with complex figure tests are that: (1) they are complex enough to access both process (i.e., sequencing, organization, and strategy) and outcome (i.e., accuracy, placement, and error); (2) they can be used with children or adults; (3) they have been found to be useful with both nonclinical and a wide variety of clinical populations; and (4) they can be used to assess visuospatial construction, learning, recall, and recognition as well as executive functioning.

General administration procedures

Traditional administration of complex figure tests uses an incidental procedure in which the examinee is first instructed to draw a copy of the figure while viewing it. The person is then asked to reproduce the figure from memory, either immediately afterwards or after a delay interval. Immediate recall may occur from 0 to 3 min after the copy trial. Delayed recall may occur from 5 to 60 min after the most recent trial (copy or immediate recall), but is typically about 20–40 min. In the incidental procedure, the person is not informed in advance that there will be a memory component to the task. Thus, it is assumed that any information recalled is learned incidentally during the copy trial (Hubley & Tombaugh, 2003; Knight, 2003b). Alternatively, one of two intentional procedures can be used. In the first procedure, the same administration order is used as seen in the incidental procedure except that the examinee is told in advance that memory will be assessed (e.g., Sadeh, Ariel, & Inbar, 1996). In the second procedure, the examiner informs the person that memory will be assessed and starts with a number of learning trials. The examinee first studies the figure for a set period of time (e.g., 60 s); then it is removed and the person is immediately asked to reproduce the figure from memory. Typically, there are three to four such learning trials. These are followed by a delayed recall trial and then the copy trial. There are a number of benefits of using an intentional procedure, but at the very least it permits the assessment of learning in addition to memory and controls for exposure time to the figure (see Hubley & Tombaugh (2003) and Tombaugh, Schmidt, & Faulkner (1992) for a more detailed discussion).

Regardless of whether an incidental or intentional procedure is used when administering complex figures, many clinicians and researchers also attempt to record the process used by examinees to draw the figure at least on copy if not on all trials. There are two main approaches used to record process: (1) coloured pen switching and (2) process flowcharts using numbers. Knight, Kaplan, and Ireland (2003) reported that 60% of their survey respondents reported using a coloured pen-switching approach wherein examinees complete the drawing using different coloured pens that are switched at set time intervals or when particular components of the figure are completed. Process flowcharts in which the examiner numbers the components of the figure according to the order in which the examinee draws them were used by 27% of their survey respondents.

Scoring of complex figures

Complex figures tend to be scored using one or both of the two general types of scoring systems: quantitative and qualitative (Knight, 2003b). Quantitative, or point-based, scoring systems focus on the accuracy of the appearance and placement of figure components. Qualitative scoring systems focus on the process used to copy, and sometimes recall, the figure. The term 'qualitative' in this case is misleading as the majority of these scoring system have, in fact, *quantified* the variables (e.g., alignments, sequencing, clustering, and errors) being measured. Better terms for the general categories of quantitative and qualitative scoring systems might be 'accuracy' and 'process', respectively. Of course, some scoring systems (e.g., Boston Qualitative Scoring System [BQSS]) incorporate both accuracy and process measures.

Knight et al. (2003) reported that the majority of their survey respondents used an accuracy system to score the ROCF. Specifically, 76% of respondents reported using the standard 36-point accuracy system reported in Spreen and Strauss (1998) and Lezak (1995).[1] This scoring system was first published by

---

[1] For information on scoring by using Lezak's text, readers are referred to its most recent edition (i.e., Lezak, Howieson, & Loring, 2004).

Osterrieth (1944) and was modified by Taylor (1959). Another 12% of respondents reported using Denman's (1984) 72-point accuracy system. A total of 11% did not use a scoring system, choosing instead to interpret performance via visual inspection. The survey did not specify many qualitative scoring systems but did ask participants to record the system they used. Six percent used Bernstein and Waber's (1996) Developmental Scoring System for the ROCF and only 14% reported using other systems.

While the number of respondents from the Knight et al. (2003) survey using a qualitative scoring seems low, there is no shortage of interest in the more qualitative or process aspects of complex figure performance judging from the number of different scoring systems that have emerged to quantify these aspects of performance. Unlike accuracy scoring, for which the 36-point system is clearly the most commonly used system, there is no single process scoring system that is commonly accepted and used.

One of the reasons for the interest in qualitative or process aspects of complex figure drawing is that two figures drawn using different processes and perhaps containing different types and numbers of errors can produce the same accuracy score. While accuracy scores can provide important information about the output of visuospatial construction, learning, and memory, many researchers and clinicians believe that information about the process (i.e., strategies, sequencing, and errors) used when constructing or recalling a complex figure provides additional unique information. The reason no single process scoring system has emerged as dominant is probably owing to the disagreement over exactly what to measure and how to measure it.

This chapter provides an overview of scoring systems, tasks, or procedures designed to capture or provide insight into the process used by examinees when copying a complex figure (i.e., construction) or reproducing it from memory (i.e., recall). Nearly all the process scoring systems have been designed for use specifically with the ROCF in mind. This review is organized according to the three paradigms or methodologies presented by Poreh (2000) as comprising the Quantified Process Approach. These three paradigms are the Satellite Testing Paradigm, the Composition Paradigm, and the Decomposition Paradigm.

Satellite Testing Paradigm

The concept of satellite tests emerged out of the Boston Process Approach (Milberg, Hebben, & Kaplan, 1996). Poreh (2000) described the Satellite Testing Paradigm as consisting of new tasks designed to complement existing tests and provide additional information about examinees' skills. There appear to be five types of satellite tasks that have been developed for the ROCF: recognition tasks, match-to-sample task, spatial assembly task, spatial discrimination task, and procedures to model organizational structure or strategy. These tasks appear to have arisen from limitations associated with traditional ROCF tasks. One limitation of the ROCF is the reliance on constructional ability. That is, a person who experiences motor difficulties may, at best, have difficulty with aspects of copying the figure accurately (e.g., producing particular shapes like a diamond or drawing lines) or, at worst, be unable to draw the figure at all (e.g., due to severe rheumatoid arthritis or to paralysis). Moreover, poor constructional abilities make it difficult, if not impossible, to determine if poor recall performance is due to memory difficulties, constructional difficulties, or both. Supplementary measures such as recognition, match-to-sample, spatial assembly, and spatial discrimination tasks may require relatively little or no motor involvement. Another limitation of traditional ROCF tasks is that they do not allow the examiner to discriminate between deficits in encoding vs. retrieval. Tasks such as recognition, spatial assembly, and spatial discrimination allow the examiner to compare performance on these tasks to the traditional (free) recall trials.

The work of four groups of researchers who have produced one or more satellite tasks is highlighted here. John Meyers and colleagues (Meyers & Lange, 1994; Meyers & Meyers, 1995) created a recognition recall task as part of a commercial version of the ROCF. Philip Fastenau and colleagues (Fastenau, 2002; Fastenau, Denburg, & Hufford, 1999) developed the Extended Complex Figure Test (ECFT), which includes a recognition task, match-to-sample trial, and an ECFT-Motor Independent (ECFT-MI) version that removes the fine motor requirements of the ECFT. Finally, both Deborah Waber and colleagues (Waber, Isquith, Kahn, Romero, Sallan, & Tarbell, 1994) and Bruce Diamond and colleagues (Diamond, DeLuca, & Kelley, 1997) produced different structured procedures for modelling and shaping an organized approach to ROCF reproduction.

Rey Complex Figure Test and Recognition Trial

John Meyers and colleagues (Meyers & Lange, 1994; Meyers & Meyers, 1995) created a recognition task as part of the commercially produced Rey Complex Figure Test and Recognition Trial to better discriminate between encoding and retrieval difficulties in visuospatial memory and to assist with differential diagnosis and the development of treatment strategies. Copy, 3-min and 30-min delayed recall trials are administered first and followed by the recognition recall task. In this task, the examinee is presented with 24 complex figure components presented on a page. These components consist of unique shapes taken from the ROCF (i.e., target items) and the TCF (i.e., distractor items). The examinee is asked to identify the 12 shapes from the ROCF. Scores on the recognition task consist of True and False Positives, True and False Negatives, and Recognition Total Correct. The entire test can be purchased from Psychological Assessment Resources (PAR).

An advantage of this version of the ROCF is that norms, based on a sample of 601 men and women aged 18–89 years and 505 boys and girls aged 6–17 years, are available. The sample represents both urban and rural areas as well as all geographic regions of the United States. Knight (2003b) suggests that the recognition task, given its use of both ROCF and TCF components, could potentially be used with the TCF as well. In a review of this test, Cohen (2001) noted that, while the recognition task is easy to administer, recording and calculating the relevant scores are somewhat cumbersome.

In terms of validity evidence, Meyers and Meyers (1995) reported that recognition scores were significantly related to age, but not to gender or education. When the copy accuracy, copy time, 3- and 30-min delayed recall accuracy scores, and recognition measures were used to discriminate among brain-injured patients, psychiatric patients, and healthy normal subjects, it was found that a total of 78% of the subjects were correctly classified, with recognition performance providing an incremental validity of 16.7%.

Extended Complex Figure Test

Philip Fastenau and colleagues (Fastenau, 2002; Fastenau et al., 1999) developed the ECFT, which includes a Recognition task, Matching task, and an ECFT-Motor Independent version (ECFT-MI). The focus here will be on these tasks because they assess aspects of ROCF performance (e.g., attention, retrieval, and visuoperception) that may contribute to our understanding about process. Norms for adults aged 30–85 years were presented by Fastenau et al. The ECFT is commercially available and can be purchased from Western Psychological Services.

The Recognition task contains 30 items. For each item, examinees must select the ROCF constructional element from among five options. Options are always presented with the base rectangle or the outer perimeter of the ROCF as a referent. Items used in the task were based on Waber and Holmes' (1985, 1986) classification of ROCF components into the base rectangle, main substructure, outer configuration, and internal detail (Fastenau, 2003). The distractor items represent common errors such as rotation, incorrect alignment, poor integration, incorrect proportion or placement, and hemi-inattention. There are 7 items in the Global Scale (base rectangle and main substructure components) and 23 items in the Detail Scale (outer configuration and internal detail components). Of the Detail Scale items, 9 are specific to the left side of the figure and 11 are specific to the right side.

The Matching task was created using 10 of the 30 Recognition items; these items consist of one base rectangle item, one main substructure item, four left-detail items, and four right-detail items. A vertical array of five options is presented next to a target item. Examinees must select the option that matches the target item.

Some research has been conducted that provides evidence suggesting that ECFT scores can discriminate between clinical and control groups or among clinical groups. Most of this research is being conducted by Fastenau and his colleagues. Such clinical groups include individuals with temporal-lobe epilepsy (TLE), depression, Alzheimer's disease, and acute lateralized stroke (Fastenau, 2003).

The main feature of the ECFT-MI is that it uses an administration procedure that removes the fine motor requirements of the ECFT so it can be used with individuals who have limited motor skills. Rather than copying the ROCF, examinees are instructed to imagine drawing the figure by tracing it in their minds. A fixed time interval of 3 min is used for this procedure. Once the ROCF model is removed, the Recognition and Matching tasks are administered. Fastenau (2003) reported that recognition performance does not differ based on whether the standard or motor-independent administration procedure is used. Furthermore, he reported that the ECFT-MI can discriminate between neurological patients and healthy controls.

Further research needs to be conducted with the ECFT and ECFT-MI to evaluate their usefulness with nonclinical and clinical populations and, specifically, to what degree measures such as recognition and matching can contribute to our understanding of the process in ROCF recall.

Turbo Rey

Waber et al. (1994) developed a structured procedure for modelling and shaping an organized approach to ROCF reproduction for children. In this procedure, the child is shown a transparency containing a portion of the ROCF. The child is asked to copy these components. Next, a second transparency is placed over the previous one and more components of the ROCF are added. The child is asked to add these components to his/her drawing. Finally, a third transparency is placed over the other two and the rest of the ROCF components are displayed. The child then adds these components to his/her drawing.

Two different presentation types can be modelled: (1) configuration presentation and (2) linear presentation (Waber et al., 1994). In the configuration presentation, the first transparency contains the large rectangle, intersecting diagonals, and horizontal and vertical midlines. The second transparency includes the outer components of the ROCF: small triangle at top, large triangle at the right with horizontal and vertical lines and diamond, stem and bottom cross, square with diagonal line, and stem and cross at the left. Finally, the third transparency adds the inner components: short vertical line in the upper right quadrant, circle with dots, five short diagonal lines, rectangle with diagonal lines, short horizontal line in the upper left quadrant, and four short horizontal lines. In the linear presentation, the first transparency contains the left half of the figure including the stem and half of the lower cross. The second transparency contains the right half of the figure except the large triangle and diamond, and the third transparency contains the large triangle with the horizontal and vertical lines and the diamond.

Little other information about the Turbo Rey and its use is available. Further research examining how each of the configuration and linear presentations assist in the understanding process with the ROCF or other complex figures is needed.

Rey organizational and extended memory procedure

Diamond et al. (1997) developed the Rey organizational and extended memory (R-OEM) procedure in an attempt to identify whether impairments on the ROCF are due to encoding, consolidation, or retrieval problems. This procedure is administered in four stages. In Stage 1, examinees are administered the ROCF in the standard manner using a copy and immediate recall trial. If immediate recall accuracy using the standard Taylor 36-point scoring system is 21 or less, then the organizational component of the R-OEM is administered in Stage 2. The goal of this procedure is to improve immediate recall accuracy performance by providing examinees with an organizational structure to aid in learning the figure. The materials for the R-OEM procedure consist of five transparent acetate sheets, one sheet for each of the five 'subunits' into which the ROCF has been divided. No rationale is provided for the particular selection of subunits. However, the first subunit consists of the main configural components: the large rectangle with the intersecting diagonals and the horizontal and vertical midlines. The second subunit consists of all components to the right and outside the figure: the large triangle on the right with the horizontal and vertical lines contained within it and the diamond attached at the apex. The third subunit includes components within the right half of the figure: the short vertical line in the upper right quadrant, the circle with dots, and the five short diagonal lines. The fourth subunit consists of components above and below the large rectangle: the small triangle above the rectangle, the square with diagonal line, and the stem and cross at the bottom of the figure. Finally, the fifth subunit consists of components in the left half of the figure: stem and cross, four short horizontal lines, the small rectangle with diagonal lines contained within it, and the small horizontal line above the small rectangle. In the R-OEM procedure, the first subunit transparency is presented and the examinee is asked to trace the subunit with his/her finger. The transparency containing the next subunit is presented in its correct position over top of the previous transparency and the examinee is again asked to trace the subunit. This process continues until all five subunits have been presented. Immediately afterwards, the examinee is asked to draw the ROCF from memory. The R-OEM procedure and reproduction of the ROCF continue until an accuracy score of at least 22 is achieved or until the R-OEM procedure has been administered five times.

A 30-min delayed recall trial is administered in Stage 3. Stage 4 consists of the extended memory component of the R-OEM. There are four tasks in this component. The first extended memory measure consists of a five-trial two-alternative forced choice recognition task in which the examinee is presented with one of the subunits seen earlier along with a foil consisting of a somewhat similar, but previously unseen figure. The examinee must identify the subunit viewed earlier. The second measure consists of a spatial assembly task in which the examinee is provided with each of the five subunits and must reassemble them into their proper spatial position. The third measure consists of a five-trial spatial discrimination task in which examinees must identify the component in a ROCF copy that is incorrectly positioned. Finally, the fourth measure consists of a whole figure recognition task in which the examinee must identify the correct complete ROCF from among five alternatives.[2] The maximum score for the entire extended memory component is 20. While much information related to the R-OEM procedure is provided in Diamond et al. (1997), not all of the materials and details about scoring are presented.

The purpose of the Diamond et al. (1997) study was to examine the roles of encoding, consolidation, and retrieval in impaired memory performance by individuals with an anterior communicating artery (ACoA) aneurysm using the organizational procedure and extended memory tasks. Both the organizational procedure and the extended memory tasks appeared to be useful for this purpose. However, little other information (e.g., administration time, scoring time, reliability evidence, and correlations among measures) was provided. Further exploration of the validity (i.e., meaningfulness, usefulness, and appropriateness) of inferences made from the organizational procedure and the extended memory tasks presented by Diamond et al. would be beneficial.

Composition Paradigm

According to Poreh (2000), the Composition Paradigm involves the development of new indices from existing data with the goal of capturing the abilities or skills underlying performance. Usually, obtaining these indices does not impact the testing time and does not modify the standardized administration procedures. In the case of the complex figure, developments in the Composition Paradigm consist of new scoring systems that quantify the process in copying or reproducing the ROCF from memory. At least 17 scoring systems (not including modifications) have been developed to score complex figures for process-related variables.

Generally, these scoring systems will be presented in chronological order. There are two exceptions to this general organization. The first exception is that scoring systems designed to be used with adult populations are presented first, followed by systems designed for use with children. It is important to keep in mind, however, that some of the adult-focused scoring systems have been used with figures drawn by children and some of the child- or developmental-focused scoring systems have been used to score figures drawn by adults. The second exception is that modifications to systems are presented immediately following the original scoring system.

---

[2] A whole figure recognition task is also described in Seidman, Lanca, Kremen, Faraone, and Tsuang (2003) wherein the examinee must identify the correct ROCF from among five alternatives. The four distractor figures differ from the correct figure in details, organizational features, or both.

Osterrieth's classification system

According to Corwin and Bylsma (1993), both Rey and Osterrieth were just as interested in the qualitative aspects of the process examinees used to copy the ROCF as they were in the accuracy of the drawings. To track the process used, Rey (1941, 1993) proposed the use of seven or eight coloured pens. Osterrieth (1944, 1993) provided what he referred to as a preliminary scheme of seven qualitative categories or descriptions for classifying the approach to drawing the ROCF. These descriptions provide a nice summary of the various types of approaches to drawing the ROCF by nonclinical and clinical examinees. In Type I, the large rectangle is copied first and provides the basic structure to guide the addition of all other elements. In Type II, a detail (e.g., cross at the left) attached to the rectangle is drawn first followed by the large rectangle or the rectangle is drawn but encloses another detail (e.g., square at the bottom). Subsequently, the rest of the elements are added using the rectangle as an organizing structure. Type III drawings begin by reproducing the outside contour of the figure without differentiating the large rectangle. In Type IV drawings, details are drawn side by side (like a puzzle) without an overarching plan. Type V drawings consist of some recognizable details but with little or no structure. Type VI drawings have been reduced to a familiar shape or object (e.g., house and boat) with only a general resemblance to the ROCF. Finally, Type VII drawings consist only of unrecognizable scribble. Importantly, Osterrieth cautioned that these seven categories did not imply a ranking.

Ska and Nespoulous (1988) reported that their sample of 150 adults aged 20–84 years tended to use one of three approaches to their copy and recall drawings: (1) a piecemeal approach in which details are juxtaposed one next to the other without an overarching plan (Type IV; 26–60% of subjects); (2) a configural approach in which a large rectangle is drawn first (Type I; 20–52% of subjects); and (3) a modified configural approach in which examinees may start with a detail such as the upper left cross but then proceed as in Type I (Type II; 0–23% of subjects). While Ska and Nespoulous treated the Osterrieth (1944) classifications as categorical data, Silverstein, Osborn, and Palumbo (1998) chose to treat them as ordinal data. They found that their chronic schizophrenia group ($n = 14$) produced poorer copying strategies than did the psychotic nonschizophrenic ($n = 12$) and outpatient schizophrenic ($n = 10$) groups. Correlations between copy strategy scores and residualized recall score (controlling for copy performance) were moderate in magnitude ($r = -0.49$ to -0.50) for the psychotic non-schizophrenic and outpatient schizophrenic groups, but very small ($r = -0.10$ to -0.12) for chronic and acute schizophrenia groups, suggesting that strategy plays a much smaller role in recall for these latter two groups.

Seidman et al. (2003) modified Osterrieth's (1944) classification system and created six groups. The first three groups matched Osterrieth's Types I–III. Group 4 represented the use of a gestalt approach (as seen in the first three groups) that produced an essentially incorrect design. Groups 5 and 6 represented detail-oriented approaches that resulted in correct and incorrect designs, respectively. Seidman et al. also treated these groups as ordinal data. Their study sample consisted of 84 healthy controls, 79 schizophrenic patients, and 14 individuals with bipolar disorder with psychotic features. The entire sample consisted of men and women aged 19–75 years. Patients with schizophrenia were significantly more impaired than controls on copy organization, and used a more detail-oriented and less configural approach. Notably, differences between schizophrenia patients and controls in copy and recall accuracy remained significant even after controlling for copy organization.

Visser's sequence scoring

Visser (1973) published a manual for the Complex Figure Test that focused on the sequence of copying the ROCF rather than on the accuracy of the copy. His interest stemmed from observations that some brain-damaged individuals copied the figure in a bizarre manner, which led him to believe that sequence of copying the figure, and specifically the degree of fragmentation or a piecemeal approach, could be used as an index of brain damage. In this version of the ROCF, the figure is rotated 90° so the diamond is at the top. A preprinted image of the ROCF is used to document the sequence in which the figure is drawn. Visser identified 35 lines (or components, e.g., diamond) in the ROCF; thus, when recording the order in which each of these lines is drawn, there are 35 sequence numbers. If an error is made in recording the sequence, the examiner is instructed to interrupt testing to correct the record. Extra lines are not noted in the sequence and identifiable lines that are placed incorrectly are treated as though they have been placed correctly.

Four types of scores are provided: Interruptions, Omissions, Poor Sequencing, and Total. While it is possible for a line to be interrupted multiple times, only one interruption per line is scored. With respect to omissions, a whole line or parts of a line may be omitted but only one omission per line is scored. Seventeen poor sequence orders were identified that discriminated between male brain-damaged nonepileptic and control groups. One point is given for each poor sequence order present. The Total score is the sum of the Interruption, Omission, and Poor Sequencing scores and ranges from 0 (indicating a good result with low fragmentation and a more global approach) to some theoretical maximum above 30 (indicating a poor result with high fragmentation and a piecemeal approach). The highest score obtained in Visser's sample was 29.

Importantly, the development and standardization group consisted only of males: 140 normal controls, 38 patients with no brain damage, 52 patients with dubious brain damage, and 86 patients with brain damage. Females and epileptic patients originally considered in the research were excluded when individuals with and without brain damage could not be discriminated in these groups during item selection. Further research would be useful to examine the validity of inferences made using this scoring system with different clinical groups and, particularly, with female examinees.

Troyer and Wishart (1997), in their study using 85 community dwelling men and women aged 60–91 years, found scores using Visser's (1973) system to be negatively skewed with a significant positive kurtosis coefficient which reflected an excessive peak in scores at the low (i.e., near ceiling) level of performance. This may suggest that Visser's system will be more sensitive with clinical samples such as the brain-damaged patients in which he was interested, although he also acknowledged that his scores from brain-damaged samples were not normally distributed (Visser & Hermans, 1973). According to Troyer and Wishart, inter-rater reliability for two raters scoring half of the copy drawings was 0.96. The average time to score the last 10 drawings was more than 2 min each. Troyer and Wishart reported that scores using Visser's system showed small, but significant, positive correlations with raw delayed recall accuracy scores[3] ($r = 0.30$). Low, nonsignificant correlations were found with corrected delayed recall accuracy scores, the Visual Verbal Test, the Regard version of the Stroop Task, WAIS-R Vocabulary raw scores, and maximum Digit Span Forward scores.

Binder's Configural, Fragmentation, and Delayed Lateral Attention scores

By using a process flowchart with numbered line sequences on the ROCF copy trial, Binder (1982) developed a scoring system that identified the frequency of Configural, Fragmented, and Missing Units. These units were based on the following five structural or configural ROCF components that were drawn as a single or whole unit by 'normal males' in a pilot study: horizontal and vertical midlines, each of the two diagonals, and the two lines forming the triangle attached to the right side of the large rectangle. Each component that was drawn in a continuous line (or contiguously in the case of the two lines forming the triangle) received a point as a Configural Unit. Those that were drawn separately were scored as Fragmented Units. If a component was not drawn at all, it was scored as a Missing Unit. This scoring system has been referred to as Binder's 5-point scoring system. Although Binder claimed that the purpose of the Configural Units score was to quantify the sequencing strategy in drawing the figure, this scoring system is more accurately viewed as a measure of perceptual clustering or fragmentation of major structural units of the ROCF that stems from previous research describing piecemeal vs. gestalt approaches to figure construction (e.g., Gainotti & Tiacci, 1970; Visser & Hermans, 1973). Binder also used the process flowchart to identify if an examinee attended more to one side of the ROCF when initially copying the figure. That is, if 10 or more consecutive components of the ROCF were drawn on

[3] Accuracy scores were obtained using Taylor's scoring criteria for the 36-point system as reported in Spreen and Strauss (1991). These scores will also be referred to as 'standard accuracy scores'.

one side of the vertical midline before a single line was drawn on the other side, Delayed Lateral Attention (DLA) was indicated, unless the examinee showed total neglect for one side of the figure. The criterion of 10 components was based on pilot testing with 'normals'. DLA was scored dichotomously as present or not. Inter-rater reliability between the two raters was 100% for both the Fragmented Units score and the ratings of DLA.

Binder's (1982) study was comprised of 42 right-handed males aged 46–73 years: 14 left brain-damaged (LBD) stroke patients, 14 right brain-damaged (RBD) stroke patients, and 14 controls. He found that the two brain-damaged groups had similar Configural Units scores, but the LBD group had higher Fragmented Units scores and the RBD group had higher Missing Units scores. While Binder noted that a 'piecemeal' or 'chaining' approach tended to be seen with the LBD group and the 'grossest distortions' tended to be viewed with the RBD group and those with neglect, he also acknowledged that the Fragmented Units score was not able to quantify all unusual strategies used in copying the ROCF. Notably, the control group had no Missing Units and produced few Fragmented Units.

Bosbach, Kornblum, Schröder, and Wagner (2003) showed that 'organization' scores obtained using the Binder system on ROCF copy, 3-min immediate recall, and 30-min delayed recall were able to differentiate between 22 male and female patients with chronic progressive external ophthalmoplegia or Kearns–Sayre syndrome and 20 matched healthy controls. Unfortunately, it is not clear whether Bosbach et al.'s organization scores referred to just Configural Units or all of Binder's measures.

Troyer and Wishart (1997) found Configural Unit scores using Binder's system to be negatively skewed. This suggests that Binder's system may be more sensitive with clinical samples than cognitively intact older adults. Inter-rater reliability was 0.86. The average time to score each of the last 10 drawings was 1 min or less. Scores using Binder's system showed small to moderate, but significant, positive correlations with raw delayed recall accuracy scores ($r = 0.36$) and with the Visual Verbal Test ($r = 0.29$). Low, non-significant correlations were found with corrected delayed recall accuracy scores, the Stroop Task, WAIS-R Vocabulary, and maximum Digit Span Forward scores.

Binder's (1982) scoring system has been criticized for using only five components of the ROCF when there are several other components that could also have been included (Hamby, Wilkins, & Barry, 1993; Shorr, Delis, & Massman, 1992), for using dichotomous (i.e., correct vs. incorrect) scoring (Shorr et al., 1992), and for not being sensitive to a diversity of organizational strategies (Shorr et al., 1992). There are four scoring systems that can be considered modifications of Binder's (1982) system: Binder and Wonser's (1989) 12-point system, Sullivan, Mathalon, Ha, Zipursky, and Pfefferbaum's (1992) 5-point system, the organizational strategy score (OSS) presented by Savage, Baer, Keuthen, Brown, Rauch, and Jenike (1999), and Lange, Waked, Kirshblum, and DeLuca's (2000) system. These will each be described in turn.

Binder and Wonser's 12-point system

Binder and Wonser (1989) revised the 5-point scoring system by modifying the components to be evaluated. Specifically, eight components could be drawn as a single whole unit (i.e., a gestalt): four sides of the main rectangle, the horizontal midline, the vertical midline, and each of the two diagonals. In addition, pilot research also showed that 'normals' tended to draw the midlines and diagonals after the rectangle so one point was assigned for each midline and diagonal line that was drawn after the rectangle. This 12-point system consisted of the sum of the lines drawn as single units plus the number of midlines and diagonal lines drawn after the rectangle. Five scores were reported: Gestalt (similar to Configural Units), After (number of midlines and diagonal lines drawn after the rectangle), Sequencing Total (sum of Gestalt + After), Fragments, and Missing Units.

Binder and Wonser (1989) conducted a study with 58 men and women aged 50–74 years: 20 LBD stroke patients, 26 RBD stroke patients, and 12 controls. They found that the LBD patients had the lowest scores on Sequencing Total, Gestalt, and After and the highest score on Fragments. Both brain-damaged groups had more Missing Units than the control group. Notably, there were no sex differences on Sequencing Total; this was the only sex difference examined.

Janowsky and Thomas-Thrapp (1993) used the 12-point scoring system in their comparison of constructional strategy in healthy older adults (49 men and women aged 60–90 years) and younger adults (20 men and women aged 19–23 years). They found that the two age groups did not differ in their Sequencing Total score; there were also no sex differences in this score. They suggested that organizational strategy may be more important in abnormal, rather than normal, processes in ageing. In a pilot study, using a small group of cognitively impaired older adults originally excluded from their study, they found that this group obtained a considerably lower mean Sequencing Total score than their other two groups.

Sullivan and colleagues' organizational strategy score

Sullivan et al. (1992) were interested in evaluating the role of organizational strategy in nonverbal recall in schizophrenia and chronic alcoholism. Organizational strategy was assessed using coloured pen switching and a 5-point scoring system based on the organization of the five components of the ROCF that form its main framework: the large rectangle, the horizontal midline, the vertical midline, the intersecting diagonals, and the two lines forming the large triangle on the right. This scoring system focuses on the sequencing of figure components, continuity of lines, and quality of form (e.g., distortions or misplacements). Five points are awarded if the main framework is drawn first and all five components are constructed of continuous lines. Four points are awarded if the main framework is drawn first and the rectangle and three other components are constructed of continuous lines. Three points are awarded if the framework is drawn using continuous lines but parts are distorted or misplaced (i.e., poor form). Two points are awarded if either the rectangle or two or more of the other components are drawn without continuous lines. Finally, one point is awarded if either the rectangle or two or more of the other components are drawn without continuous lines and the drawing has poor form. Intra-rater reliability for a single rater was 0.94 for copy drawings and 0.90 for recall drawings. Sullivan et al.'s study of 28 schizophrenic patients, 68 male chronic alcoholism patients, and 69 controls (all males) showed the two patient groups used less holistic approaches than controls, but did not differ from one another, at copy. No group differences were found at recall.

Savage and colleagues' organizational strategy score

Savage et al. (1999) identified five components that could be drawn as a single unit: the main rectangle, the horizontal midline, the vertical midline, the intersecting diagonals, and the two lines forming the triangle attached to the right side of the large rectangle. Two points were assigned if the rectangle was drawn as a single, unfragmented unit and one point was assigned if the other components were drawn as single units; scores could range from 0 to 6 points. An organizational strategy score was obtained for each of copy, immediate recall, and 30-min delayed recall based on the examinee's use of coloured pencils that were changed every 15 s. The order in which the components were drawn was not a consideration in this score, although Savage et al. did note descriptively whether examinees produced one of the five main components within the first three units drawn.

Savage et al. (1999) examined organizational strategy in 20 right-handed patients (mean age of 32.7 years) with obsessive–compulsive disorder (OCD) and 20 healthy right-handed controls (mean age of 31.9 years). They found that individuals with OCD produced significantly more fragmented drawings of the ROCF than controls on copy, immediate recall, and delayed recall. Copy organization strategy scores were significantly related to ROCF copy ($r = 0.54$), immediate recall ($r = 0.67$), delayed recall ($r = 0.75$), and percent recall from copy to immediate recall ($r = 0.63$) accuracy scores based on Denman's (1984) scoring system in their OCD group. They also showed that group differences (OCD vs. controls) on percent recall from copy to immediate recall trials were mediated by organization strategy scores at copy. Notably, adding copy accuracy scores to the model did not significantly improve the explanatory power of the model.

Savage et al.'s (1999) descriptive analysis of order showed that 75% of the OCD group, compared to 50% of controls, began construction with a detail that was not one of the five main components. By the third unit drawn, 65% of the OCD group continued to focus on details whereas only 15% of controls continued to do so. In the OCD group alone, Savage et al. reported that copy organization strategy scores were significantly related to shifting errors on the Visual Verbal Test ($r = -0.45$) and the total score on the Mental Rotations Test ($r = -0.49$). Copy organization strategy scores were not significantly related to initiation errors on the Visual Verbal Test ($r = 0.02$) or errors on the Odd-Man-Out Test ($r = -0.17$). Furthermore, a considerably larger correlation was reported between copy organization strategy scores and scores on a measure of obsessions ($r = -0.41$) than compulsions ($r = -0.08$) from the Yale–Brown Obsessive–Compulsive Scale.

Savage et al. (2000) reported an inter-rater reliability of 0.96 for organizational strategy scores from two raters using a subset of drawings from the copy trial. In this study of 33 OCD patients and 30 controls, OCD patients obtained significantly lower organizational strategy scores than the controls. Group differences between OCD and controls on percent recall from copy to immediate recall trials were mediated by the organizational strategy scores at copy.

Deckersbach et al. (2000a) examined the psychometric properties of the organizational strategy score scale and compared this scoring system to one by Shorr et al. (1992) using a sample of 71 men and women (mean age of 36.1 years) with OCD and 55 healthy controls (mean age of 35.1 years). Most of the sample consisted of the combined samples from Savage et al. (1999) and Deckersbach, Otto, Savage, Baer, and Jenike (2000c). Inter-rater reliability, using Cohen's κ coefficients, was high for the total score ($\kappa = 0.94$) and for all of the main components ($\kappa = 0.84$ to 0.92), except the two lines of the triangle ($\kappa = 0.69$). The Savage et al. and Shorr et al. organizational scoring systems were correlated 0.80. Deckersbach et al. (2000a) reported that Savage et al.'s copy organization strategy scores were significantly related to ROCF copy ($r = 0.40$) and immediate recall ($r = 0.60$) accuracy scores based on the Meyers and Meyers (1995) scoring system in a combined OCD and controls sample. Copy organization strategy scores explained a significant amount of variance in immediate recall accuracy scores. Adding copy accuracy scores did not significantly increase the amount of explained variance in immediate recall accuracy scores.

Deckersbach et al. (2000a) also examined the relative contributions of each of the five main components in the Savage et al. organizational strategy scoring system to immediate recall accuracy scores. All of the components, except the two lines of the triangle, made a significant contribution. Given that the main rectangle did not make a larger contribution than the other components, the authors suggest that their scoring system could be revised so that the main rectangle is not weighted more heavily and thus total scores would range from 0 to 5.

A couple of other studies conducted by this research group with clinical samples such as females with body dysmorphic disorder (Deckersbach et al., 2000b) and individuals with bipolar disorder (Deckersbach, McMurrich, Ogutha, Savage, Sachs, & Rauch, 2004) also provide some evidence supporting the utility of the Savage et al. (1999) scoring system.

Lange and colleagues' organizational scoring system

Lange et al. (2000) claimed to use an organizational scoring procedure similar to Binder (1982). In fact, the main components used are the same as those in Binder and Wonser (1989): four sides of the main rectangle, the horizontal and vertical midlines, and each of the two diagonals. Lange et al., however, describe these eight lines as three components (i.e., rectangle, midlines, and diagonal lines). A score of 50 is assigned for each component that is not complete; otherwise, one sums the number of lines drawn by the examinee to create the three components. The lowest possible score is 8 points; lower scores indicate a more configural approach whereas higher scores indicate a more fragmented approach. Unlike the systems developed by Binder, each of the three components could be completed in any order and there was no requirement that the lines comprising a component be completed contiguously. No rationale was provided for modifying the scoring system or for the particular changes made.

Lange et al. (2000) examined the organizational strategy used by patients with left (LH; $n = 15$) and right (RH; $n = 20$) hemisphere strokes as well as those with cortical ($n = 11$) and subcortical ($n = 19$) stroke lesions. Patients ranged in age from 29 to 75 years. Contrary to the findings of Binder (1982) and Binder and Wonser (1989), they found that those with RH stroke copied the ROCF using a significantly more fragmented approach than those with LH stroke. While it is not clear from the article, this finding may be due to a greater number of incomplete components by patients with RH stroke as this scoring system penalizes heavily for incomplete components and Binder (1982) noted that the number of missing units was higher in his RBD group. An even more striking result was the substantially more fragmented approach used by those with cortical stroke lesions relative to those with subcortical stroke lesions. Organizational strategy scores were highly negatively correlated with copy accuracy scores based on Denman's (1984) scoring ($r = -0.87$ to -0.93) for patients with LH or RH strokes or with cortical or subcortical stroke lesions. Organizational strategy scores were also highly negatively correlated with immediate and delayed recall accuracy scores ($r = -0.76$ to -0.95) for patients with either RH strokes or with cortical stroke lesions but only moderately negatively correlated with immediate and delayed recall accuracy scores ($r = -0.50$ to -0.54) in patients with LH strokes or with subcortical stroke lesions. This indicates that a more fragmented approach to copying the ROCF was related to lower construction accuracy in all groups and lower recall accuracy performance particularly in patients with RH strokes or with cortical stroke lesions.

Summary

Binder's (1982) scoring system has formed the basis for a number of process scoring systems. Most of the interest has focused on whether the approach to drawing the ROCF has been more configural or more fragmented. Binder produced two separate scores for configural and fragmented units whereas others have viewed these as being at two ends of the same continuum. The different scoring variations have also counted, or scored, the Configural Units somewhat differently. There has been relatively less interest in Binder's measures of After, Missing Units, and DLA.

Copy strategy scoring system

Bennet-Levy (1984) developed a measure of copying strategy for the ROCF based on the Gestalt principles of good continuation and symmetry. Good continuation was demonstrated when a line was drawn as a single unit that continued until it was intercepted by another line. Bennet-Levy identified 17 points of good continuation and one point of poor continuation in the ROCF for a maximum score of 18 points. These points of good and poor continuation were selected out of many potential points precisely because they were the only ones on which subjects in their sample showed poor continuation. Symmetry refers to the successive construction of symmetrical components in the figure and rests on the assumption that the order in which the components of the ROCF are drawn accurately reflects the structure and symmetry that the examinee perceives within the figure. Scoring of symmetry is based on the combination of three complex rules. These rules focus on the order in which the following 11 components of the figure are drawn: the main rectangle, the horizontal and the vertical midlines, the intersecting diagonals, the two lines forming the triangle, the horizontal and vertical lines within the triangle, the small square attached to the bottom left quadrant of the figure, the diagonal line within the small square, the small rectangle in left half of figure, and the diagonals within the small rectangle. While there are other symmetrical units (e.g., the diamond and two crosses) in the ROCF, these were excluded from the scoring system because almost all of the subjects constructed these components consecutively. The maximum score for symmetry is 18.

Scoring of good continuation and symmetry was based on a process flowchart with numbered line sequences for the ROCF copy trial. The Strategy Total Score is the sum of the Good Continuation and Symmetry Scores. The maximum possible score is 36 but, interestingly, this cannot actually be achieved because good continuation and symmetry strategies are in direct conflict at three points in the construction of the figure.

Bennet-Levy's (1984) study was comprised of 107 men and women aged 17–49 years, who were car assembly line workers or nonemergency orthopaedic admissions from a hospital. Strategy Total Scores made an independent contribution to the prediction of both copy and 40-min delayed recall accuracy scores based on the Taylor 36-point criteria reported in Spreen and Strauss (1998), even after controlling for age, sex, estimated IQ, and figure completion times. Moreover, both Good Continuation and Symmetry scores made independent contributions to the prediction of copy and 40-min delayed recall accuracy scores when entered into the model instead of Strategy Total Scores. Men obtained significantly better Good Continuation, Symmetry, and Strategy Total Scores than women.

While the importance of Bennet-Levy's (1984) study is well recognized and details of the system are provided in the article, there is little evidence that this particular scoring system is used in the literature. The relatively detailed description of the three rules guiding the scoring of symmetry is difficult to follow and makes the scoring system appear to be highly complex, as has been noted by other researchers (e.g., Hamby et al., 1993; Knight, 2003b; Lezak et al., 2004). Knight questioned whether independent researchers and clinicians could obtain good inter-rater agreement using this scoring system. Troyer and Wishart (1997) reported a very high inter-rater reliability of 0.93 for the Strategy Total Score. However, it is also possible that two raters could obtain high agreement (especially if the raters learned the scoring system together or one rater trained the other), but still not understand or apply all rules of the scoring system as originally intended.[4] Troyer and Wishart reported that the time required to score each of the final 10 copy drawings was only 1–2 min. They also noted that Strategy Total Scores for their older adult sample were relatively normally distributed. These scores showed significant and moderate positive correlations with raw ($r = 0.47$) and corrected ($r = 0.34$) delayed recall accuracy scores, and with the Visual Verbal Test ($r = 0.40$). Low, nonsignificant correlations were found with the Stroop Task, WAIS-R Vocabulary, and maximum Digit Span Forward scores.

A benefit of Bennet-Levy's (1984) scoring system is that it appears to be sensitive to a range of performance in young and middle-aged healthy adults. More research needs to be conducted to determine its usefulness with clinical samples. Specifically, the points of good continuation and the symmetrical units were selected on the basis of performance by healthy and relatively young adults. It is not clear if these particular points and units will be appropriate for use with different clinical groups. On a related note, it will be important to establish whether floor effects are found with clinical groups or older adults. Simplification of the scoring system through the provision of more explicit criteria and examples would be useful.

Scoring system of qualitative errors

Loring, Lee, and Meador (1988) were interested in developing a scoring system for the ROCF that would be sensitive to the types of errors (e.g., distortion and misplacement) frequently observed at recall in patients with right TLE and could be used to classify patients with right TLE. This scoring system is quite different from previous ones that focused on ROCF copy and the

---

[4] This observation is not meant to be specific to this scoring system or to Troyer and Wishart (1997); rather, this potential difficulty with inter-rater reliability could apply to any of the systems described in this chapter.

configural components of the figure (e.g., main rectangle and intersecting diagonals). In developing this scoring system, 30-min delayed recall reproductions of six right TLE patients were examined and qualitative errors suggestive of right TLE dysfunction were identified. Next, the delayed recall reproductions of five left TLE patients were examined and only the 11 errors that appeared to discriminate between the two groups were retained. These errors tend to focus on the following components of the ROCF: the diamond, the four horizontal lines, the five short diagonal lines, the main rectangle, the upper right triangle, and both crosses. The types of errors could be described as misplacements (errors II, V, VIII, and IX), rotations (error III), distortions (errors IV and V), and additions/perseverations (errors I, VI, VII, X, and XI). A table describing each of the 11 errors is available in Loring et al. (1988). Errors such as major mislocation (IX) can be scored multiple times for different components of the figure (D. Loring, personal communication, 12 January 2005). The total score is the number of errors made.

A cross-validation group of nine right and nine left TLEs was used to examine the new scoring system. While no significant difference was found between the right and left TLE groups on standard accuracy scores, the two groups did differ significantly on the basis of qualitative errors; patients with right TLE produced more errors. To examine predictive validity, patients were classified as right TLE if they produced two or more errors. A total of 83% of the patients were correctly classified. A closer look shows that 78% of those with right TLE and 89% of those with left TLE were correctly identified. No clear pattern existed to explain the misclassifications. It was noted that if an error was made by a left TLE patient, it tended to be either a misplacement of one or both crosses (VIII) or a major mislocation (IX). Interestingly, however, such errors were made twice as often by right TLE patients. In fact, observation of the individual subject data shows that the most frequent errors by the right TLE group were: distortion of the rectangle (IV), misplacements of one or both crosses (VIII), and major mislocations (IX). An important restriction in Loring et al. (1988) was that subjects who scored less than 34 on copy accuracy were excluded from the study as the authors felt that visuospatial construction had to be intact to consider these errors as evidence of lateralized temporal dysfunction. It would be interesting to see if this system of errors would be of use with other samples. Barr (2003) questioned whether qualitative scoring systems, such as this one, provide enough unique information to be worth the extra time to score.

Piquet, Saling, O'Shea, Berkovic, and Bladin (1994) conducted a replication study with 44 men and women with TLE before and after anterior temporal lobectomy. They noted that it is not clear, in the scoring of major mislocations (IX), to what extent a component must be misplaced to be treated as a major mislocation. They decided that a component that was incorrectly placed but still in the correct quadrant received an error rating. They reported an interrater reliability of 0.84 for error scores based on 20 5-min delayed recall reproductions from a preliminary study. As with Loring et al. (1988), no significant difference was found between the right ($n = 18$) and left ($n = 26$) TLE groups on standard accuracy scores, but the right TLE group produced significantly more qualitative errors (which they referred to as 'distortion scores'). A logistic regression was used to predict right vs. left TLE using the error scores; 66% of the patients were correctly classified. Only 50% of those with right TLE and 77% of those with left TLE were correctly identified. The authors claimed that this result was equivalent to that obtained when patients with two or more errors are classified as right TLE. Unlike Loring et al., subjects were not excluded if their copy accuracy score was less than 34; thus, five of their patients obtained copy accuracy scores ranging from 19 to 33. None of these individuals were misclassified. The most frequently occurring error was major mislocation (IX). As with Loring et al., this error was made by both right and left TLE patients with almost equal frequency. Four types of errors (i.e., adding a stem to the diamond [I], misplacement of the diamond [II], rotation of the four horizontal lines [III], and additional horizontal lines [VII]) were most characteristics of right TLE subjects. The authors concluded that the Loring et al. scoring system was useful for capturing left/right TLE differences not included in accuracy scoring, but was not sensitive enough to classify left/right TLE. More research is needed to examine the validity of inferences from this scoring system for TLE and other clinical samples.

Complex figure qualitative rating system

The primary source for Bachtler, Roth, Smith, and Weber's (1990) qualitative rating system (QRS) is Knight and Kaplan's (2003) classic text given that Bachtler and colleagues only appear to have presented this scoring system at a conference. In this system, eight variables measuring the presence of configural and detail elements, execution or planning of configural and detail elements, placement of detail elements, perseveration, confabulation, and extent of left/right asymmetry are each rated on a 5-point scale. A ninth variable, presence of left/right asymmetry, is rated on a 3-point scale. A copy of this rating system is available in Knight (2003b).

Bachtler et al.'s (1990) study was comprised of 39 patients receiving surgical treatment for complex partial seizures. They found that, not only did patients with right foci/resection obtain poorer ROCF accuracy scores, but they also did poorly on ratings of configuration, detail placement, and detail execution at 6 months post-surgery. This finding suggests the QRS may have potential for describing visuospatial deficits in some clinical samples.

No information is provided about the development of this rating system, inter-rater reliability, or the time it takes to use. An examination of the straightforward-looking 5-point rating scales suggests the potential for disagreement among raters in interpreting phrases (i.e., vague quantifiers) such as 'a few' vs. 'some' and 'mildly poor', 'moderately poor', and 'significantly poor'. Finally, more validity evidence is needed to support the use of this scale with clinical and nonclinical samples.

Perceptual cluster index

Shorr et al. (1992) were interested in developing a finer, more sensitive measure of the process by which examinees copy the ROCF than seen in Binder (1982). This process was named 'perceptual clustering' by Delis (1989) as a visuospatial analogue to the semantic clustering process observed in verbal measures such as the California Verbal Learning Test. In this case, the interest is in whether examinees recognize subwholes within the ROCF and draw each of these subwholes in a continuous or contiguous manner.

Using a process flowchart with numbered line sequences on the ROCF copy trial, Shorr et al.'s (1992) scoring system centred around the following 10 components or 'subwholes' of the figure: the main rectangle, the horizontal and the vertical midline, the intersecting diagonals, the two lines forming the triangle, the horizontal and vertical lines within the triangle, the small square attached to the bottom left quadrant of the figure, the small rectangle in the left half of the figure, and the diagonals within the small rectangle. On the basis of these 'subwholes', 20 junctures and lines of interest where breaks in the continuous drawing of the subwholes can occur were identified. A figure showing each of the junctures is available in Shorr et al. A point was given if the lines on each side of the juncture were drawn continuously or contiguously with a maximum perceptual cluster score (PCS) of 20. In addition, a perceptual cluster ratio (PCR) consisting of the PCS divided by the number of junctures in the examinee's drawing while controlling for missing junctures was computed.

The sample in Shorr et al. (1992) consisted of 50 male neuropsychiatric veterans aged 23–83 years. Inter-rater reliability exceeded 0.98 based on two raters' scoring of 15 randomly selected copies of the ROCF. PCR was found to correlate significantly with copy accuracy scores obtained using the Taylor 36-point system ($r = 0.53$) and an encoding score that consisted of immediate recall accuracy divided by copy accuracy ($r = 0.55$). In addition, the PCR made a significant, unique contribution to the variance explained in the encoding score even when it was entered after copy accuracy in a regression analysis. The correlation between PCR and a savings score that consisted of 20-min delayed recall accuracy divided by immediate recall accuracy was near-zero and nonsignificant.

In the other research, Deckersbach et al. (2000a) reported that inter-rater reliability, using Cohen's κ coefficient, was 0.94 in a sample of 126 OCD and control subjects. Scores obtained using the Savage et al. (1999) and Shorr et al. (1992) organizational scoring systems correlated 0.80. Troyer and Wishart (1997) reported that inter-rater reliability was 0.95. The average time to score each of the last 10 drawings was 1 min or less.

Troyer and Wishart (1997) reported that scores using Shorr et al.'s (1992) system were negatively skewed in a sample of older adults. This suggests that Shorr et al.'s system may be more sensitive with clinical samples than cognitively intact older adults. Scores showed small to moderate, but significant, positive correlations with the raw ($r = 0.42$) and corrected ($r = 0.33$) delayed recall accuracy scores. Low, nonsignificant correlations were found with the Visual Verbal Test, the Stroop Task, WAIS-R Vocabulary, and maximum Digit Span Forward scores. Deckersbach et al. (2000a) also reported significant correlations between scores obtained using Shorr et al.'s system and Meyer and Meyer's (1995) accuracy scores at copy ($r = 0.42$) and immediate recall ($r = 0.53$).

Deckersbach et al. (2000a) also examined whether three components (small rectangle in the left half of the figure, diagonals within the small rectangle, and small square attached to the bottom left quadrant of the figure) present in Shorr et al.'s (1992) system, but not Savage et al.'s (1999) OSS, would improve the explanatory power of the OSS in immediate recall accuracy scores. While the inter-rater reliability for each of these three components was very high ($\kappa > 0.90$), the amount of variance explained in immediate recall accuracy scores actually decreased by a nonsignificant amount.

Research is needed that examines the utility of Shorr et al.'s (1992) PCR with a variety of clinical samples. Furthermore, it would be useful to obtain evidence examining whether the PCR provides a more sensitive index than Binder's (1982) system.

Organizational scoring system

Chervinsky, Mitrushina, and Satz (1992) wanted to develop an organizational scoring system for the ROCF copy trial that did not confound organization with accuracy of reproduction. They defined organization as "the way in which the subject subdivides the complex figure into component parts in order to achieve the final copy" (p. 269). To record organization, they had the examinee switch pens whenever the examiner perceived that there was a natural break in the reproduction and a chunk of the figure was completed. With this approach, six to twelve different coloured pens were typically used. The organizational scoring system is broken into a total of seven sections that include different components of the figure. In the first six sections, points are assigned based on whether components were completed in only one colour or not. Section 1 includes the large rectangle, the diagonals, and the horizontal and vertical midlines. Section 2 involves the large triangle to the right of the figure and the horizontal and vertical lines within it. Section 3 focuses on the lower cross (note: the stem is not mentioned), the square and the diagonal within it. Section 4 involves the small rectangle and the diagonal lines within it. Section 5 includes the upper cross and stem attaching it to the large rectangle and Section 6 focuses on the triangle on top of the rectangle. In the last section, entitled the Scoring Penalty Section, points are subtracted if two or more colours are used to complete each of the following: circle with three dots, the five short diagonal lines, the four horizontal lines, and the diamond. The total score is obtained by subtracting the points in the Scoring Penalty Section from the sum of the points obtained in Sections 1–6. A detailed copy of this straightforward scoring system is available in Chervinsky et al. The authors report that it takes less than 1.5 min to score each copy reproduction.

Chervinsky et al. (1992) examined the sensitivity of the organizational scoring system to age and sex differences in a sample of 156 healthy older adults (62 men and 94 women) aged 57–85 years. There were no significant sex differences in organizational scores; nor were there significant age differences when the sample was divided into four different age groups. Correlations between organizational scores and both age and education were low and nonsignificant. Low, but significant, correlations were reported between organizational scores and both WAIS-R Performance IQ ($r = 0.32$) and Full Scale IQ ($r = 0.25$). Research is needed that provides the validity evidence with a variety of clinical samples. In addition, evidence regarding inter-rater reliability is needed.

Complex figure organizational quality scoring system

By using a pen-switching approach with three different coloured pens, Hamby et al. (1993) developed a scoring system that focuses on the use of both configural elements to structure the drawing and a parsimonious and systematic approach whereby lines are not broken into more segments than necessary. This system uses the presence and number of configural, secondary, and detail errors to rate the organizational quality of ROCF or TCF copy performance. Organizational quality is scored on a 5-point ordinal scale with higher scores indicating better organization. Configural errors involve the four lines of the main rectangle, the horizontal and the vertical midlines. If there are three or more configural errors, an organizational quality score of 1 (very poor organization) is given. Secondary errors involve the intersecting diagonals for the ROCF and the horizontal line in the top half of the square for the TCF. If there are two or less configural errors, the examiner checks for a secondary error and sums the configural and secondary errors. A sum of 3 is assigned an organizational quality score of 1, a sum of 2 receives a score of 2 (poor organization), and a sum of 1 receives a score of 3 (fair organization). The rest of the components of the figure are considered to be details. If there are no configural and secondary errors, one checks for detail errors. If there are one or more detail errors, an organizational quality score of 4 (good organization) is given whereas if there are no detail errors, then an organizational quality score of 5 (excellent organization) is assigned. According to the authors, most protocols take less than 1 min to score. A detailed copy of the scoring system is available in Hamby et al. (1993).

The sample in Hamby et al. (1993) consisted of 63 predominantly male HIV-infected individuals with an average age of 33.7 years. A total of 36 subjects were asymptomatic and 27 were symptomatic. Subjects were randomly assigned to receive either the ROCF or TCF. Inter-rater reliability, using κ, was 87.6% for two of the authors. A κ of 79.3% was obtained between a graduate student rater, who had experience scoring complex figures for accuracy and received 1 h of training on the new scoring system, and the consensus scores from the previous two raters. A κ of 75% was obtained between an undergraduate student rater, who had no exposure to neuropsychological assessment but received 1 h of training on the new scoring system, and the consensus scores between the original two raters for 20 protocols. Organizational quality scores were significantly correlated with the accuracy scores for copy, 30-min delayed recall, and percent retained recall. The TCF produced significantly higher organizational scores than did the ROCF. Finally, organizational quality scores for the ROCF, but not the TCF, significantly discriminated asymptomatic from symptomatic HIV subjects. Copy and delay accuracy scores were unable to discriminate asymptomatic and symptomatic HIV subjects.

Cornell, Roberts, and Oram (1997) examined organizational quality in ROCF copies in 110 male prison inmates aged 20–53 years. Inter-rater reliability for two raters on the Hamby et al. system, using an intraclass correlation, was 0.96. Organizational quality was significantly related to both copy ($r = 0.42$) and recall ($r = 0.52$) accuracy scores. Organizational quality was not significantly related to age, but was related to minority status (which was not clearly defined; $r = 0.23$). Finally organizational quality was significantly and positively related to impulsiveness ($r = 0.26$), WAIS-R Block Design ($r = 0.44$), Trails A ($r = 0.22$), Trails B ($r = 0.27$), and Category Test performance ($r = 0.25$); it was not related to psychopathy, anger, WAIS-R Vocabulary, or social desirability. Controlling for age, education, and/or minority status had little to no effect on the magnitude of these correlations. Because 62% of examinees received the lowest possible score of 1, Cornell et al. modified the scoring criteria in an attempt to better discriminate among the lowest scoring individuals. This modification did not change the correlational findings.

Troyer and Wishart (1997) found that scores using Hamby et al.'s system were positively skewed, indicating that average scores for this sample of healthy older adults were at floor levels. Inter-rater reliability was 0.80. The average time to score each of the last 10 drawings was 1–2 min. Scores using Hamby et al.'s system showed a small, but significant, negative correlation with the Stroop Task ($r = -0.28$), which indicates that response inhibition and ability to overcome interference was related to better organizational quality on the ROCF. Low, nonsignificant correlations were found with raw and corrected delayed recall accuracy scores based on the Taylor 36-point criteria, WAIS-R Vocabulary raw scores, and maximum Digit Span Forward scores.

The three studies conducted using the Hamby et al. (1993) process scoring system have produced variable results for inter-rater reliability and correlations with accuracy scores. More importantly, two studies reported possible floor effects with two nonclinical samples, which suggest a potential problem in applying this scoring system with clinical samples.

Boston Qualitative Scoring System

Stern and colleagues' (Stern et al., 1994; Stern et al., 1999) BQSS is well recognized as the most comprehensive system for quantifying the qualitative aspects of examinees' ROCF productions (Boone, 2000; Cohen, 2003; Hartman & Potter, 1998; Leark, 2003). The selection of the qualitative features to be included in the BQSS emerged out of the Boston Process Approach (Kaplan, 1988; Milberg et al., 1996) as well as from discussions with experienced clinicians. The authors divided the ROCF components hierarchically into configural elements, clusters, and details. Configural elements include the main rectangle, the intersecting diagonals, the horizontal and the vertical midlines, and the large triangle on the right. Configural elements are scored for presence, accuracy, and fragmentation. Clusters consist of the following nine secondary elements that are comprised of multiple lines or shapes that appear to form a unit: small rectangle with diagonal lines, small square with diagonal line, small triangle at top, diamond, circle with dots, cross at left, cross at bottom, four horizontal lines, and five short diagonal lines. Clusters are scored for the presence, accuracy, placement, and fragmentation. Details consist of the following six line segments: short vertical line in upper right quadrant, vertical line within large triangle, horizontal line within large triangle, stem connecting cross at left, stem connecting cross at bottom, and short horizontal line above small rectangle. Details are scored for presence and placement. The sequence of drawing the ROCF can be recorded using either a process flowchart using numbers or a coloured pen-switching process, with Stern et al. (1999) offering detailed advice on each approach.

In total, there are 17 'qualitative' scores provided. There are three presence scores (for configural elements, clusters, and details), two accuracy scores (for configural elements and clusters), two placement scores (for clusters and details) as well as scores for fragmentation, planning, neatness, vertical expansion, horizontal expansion, reduction, rotation, perseveration, confabulation, and asymmetry. It is the latter grouping of scores that are of the greatest interest in obtaining information about the process used in drawing the ROCF. The raw scores are all based on a 5-point scale (from 0 to 4), except asymmetry which uses a 3-point scale. In all cases, higher scores represent better performance. In addition to the 17 qualitative scores, there are 6 summary scores, which consist of presence and accuracy (for copy, immediate recall, and delayed recall), organization (based on fragmentation and planning scores at copy), immediate retention, and 30-min delayed retention. The organization summary score is of the greatest interest in this chapter on process scoring.

There are three different scoring approaches described in the manual: Comprehensive Scoring Method (CSM), Quick Scoring Guide (QSG), and Combination Method. In the CSM, the examiner follows the detailed scoring criteria provided in the manual. The authors estimated that it takes 10–15 min to score the three drawings from copy, immediate recall, and delayed recall. The QSG is provided as a quick alternative for experienced examiners who do not seek the precision of the CSM. It is estimated to take 5 min to score the copy, immediate recall, and delayed recall drawings with this method. The Combination Method is recommended for examiners seeking greater precision for accuracy scores but less precision for qualitative scores. It is worth noting that the BQSS has been refined since its initial inception; thus, examiners are encouraged to use the commercially available version of the scoring system and norms. The BQSS can be purchased from PAR and is accompanied by a detailed manual.

Stern et al. (1999) reported that inter-rater reliability for the CSM was obtained for the 17 qualitative scores using two trained research assistants who scored 62 copy trial reproductions selected from normal and patient research populations. Weighted κ coefficients calculated for the 16 5-point scores ranged from 0.53 to 1.00. Ten of the scores obtained κ coefficients of 0.82 and higher. However, κ coefficients of 0.76 and below were obtained for configural accuracy, planning, neatness, rotation, cluster placement, and detail placement, which suggest that the scoring guidelines for these variables could use further refinement. A percent agreement of 100% was obtained for the 3-point asymmetry score. Inter-rater reliabilities for the summary scores were 0.90 and higher except for delayed retention, which was 0.77. Inter-rater reliability for the QSG was obtained using two trained research assistants, who scored 30 copy trial reproductions. Weighted κ coefficients ranged from 0.34 to 1.00. Only four of 16 scores were higher than 0.80 whereas eight scores had κ coefficients of less than 0.70. On the basis of this information, the use of the QSG for diagnostic purposes is highly questionable. In many studies using the BQSS, authors do not report the scoring method (i.e., CSM and QSG) they have used. It is therefore recommended that such information be included to better judge inter-rater reliability. Hartman and Potter (1998) reported inter-rater reliabilities (using intraclass correlations) for two scorers who scored a subsample of 22 protocols selected randomly in a sample of younger and older community-dwelling adults. These estimates ranged from 0.87 to 0.91 for summary scores and from 0.79 to 1.00 for all qualitative scores, except perseveration (0.65), neatness (0.39), and confabulation (0.26). Troyer and Wishart (1997) reported an inter-rater reliability of 0.87 for fragmentation but only 0.62 for planning. The average time to score each of fragmentation and planning for the last 10 drawings was 1 min or less.

Norms for the BQSS are based on 433 healthy men and women ranging in age from 18 to 94 years (Stern et al., 1999). While some reviewers have viewed this large standardization sample as an advantage of this scoring system (e.g., Boone, 2000), others have criticized the sample for not reflecting US Census data with respect to socioeconomic status and ethnicity (e.g., Leark, 2003). Stern et al. reported that neither the age by gender interaction nor the age effect was significant for the organization summary score in the standardization sample. There was, however, a significant gender difference on the organization score, with women performing more poorly. The organization score was not related significantly to education. Hartman and Potter (1998) also note a lack of relationship between age and the organization summary score.

Troyer and Wishart (1997), in their study of 85 older men and women, examined BQSS fragmentation and planning scores. They reported that fragmentation scores showed a significant moderate positive correlation with the raw delayed recall accuracy scores based on the Taylor criteria ($r = 0.41$) and a small, but significant, negative correlation with the Stroop Task ($r = -0.31$). Low, nonsignificant correlations were found with corrected delayed recall accuracy scores, the Visual Verbal Test, WAIS-R Vocabulary, and maximum Digit Span Forward scores. Planning scores, on the other hand, showed significant small to moderate positive correlations with the raw delayed recall accuracy scores ($r = 0.39$) and Visual Verbal Test ($r = 0.34$). Low, nonsignificant correlations were found with corrected delayed recall accuracy scores, the Stroop Task, WAIS-R Vocabulary, and maximum Digit Span Forward scores. Hartman and Potter (1998) reported that organizational quality was correlated with standard accuracy scores for older ($r = 0.57$) but not younger ($r = 0.02$) examinees at copy, but for neither age group at immediate recall.

A number of studies have been conducted that provide evidence suggesting that BQSS scores can discriminate between clinical and control groups or among clinical groups. Many of these studies involve the authors themselves. Such clinical groups include high- and low-IQ groups (Fujii, Lloyd, & Miyamoto, 2000), attention-deficit/hyperactivity disorder (Schreiber, Javorsky, Robinson, & Stern, 1999), depression (Elderkin-Thompson, Boone, Kumar, & Mintz, 2004; Elderkin-Thompson, Kumar, Mintz, Boone, Bhang, & Lavretsky, 2004), traumatic brain injury (Stern et al., 1999), HIV (Stern, Silva, Chaisson, & Evans, 1996; Stern et al., 1992), dementia (Stern et al., 1999), and alcohol abuse (Dawson & Grant, 2000). Some research has also been conducted using the BQSS with children (e.g., Akshoomoff, Feroleto, Doyle, & Stiles, 2002; Akshoomoff & Stiles, 1995a, 1995b; Cahn, Marcotte, Stern, Arruda, Akshoomoff, & Leshko, 1996).

The strengths of the BQSS are also its shortcomings. This is a comprehensive scoring system, but it does take a considerable amount of time to first learn the BQSS and then to apply it to the ROCF. Given the relatively low inter-rater reliabilities for some scores (e.g., cluster placement, detail placement, rotation, neatness, and confabulation), the scoring guide for these variables needs further improvement. In addition, Boone (2000) noted the need for stronger convergent validity evidence, particularly given the modest correlations with measures of executive functioning.

Rey-O organizational scoring system

As with Bachtler et al.'s (1990) QRS, the primary source for the Rey-O organizational scoring system (R-OOSS) is Knight (2003b) as information about this scoring system has otherwise only appeared at conferences. With the R-OOSS, Lott, Petersen, Capitano, and Spiteri (1996) were primarily interested in creating a quick index of executive functioning that could be used in conjunction with traditional accuracy scores. This scoring system yields an organization score that focuses on the order in which configural elements (i.e., large rectangle, intersecting diagonals, and vertical and horizontal midlines) of the ROCF are completed. Scores range from 0 to 10, with higher points reflecting better organization. Inter-rater reliability, using Cronbach's alpha, was reported to be 0.97 for copy and 0.98 for recall across three raters who scored 30 protocols. A couple of unpublished studies have been conducted that provide some preliminary evidence supporting the validity of inferences using the R-OOSS. R-OOSS scores correlated 0.77 for copy and 0.72 for recall with BQSS organizational scores. Preliminary research suggests that R-OOSS scores can discriminate among individuals with different levels of adaptive daily functioning (Petersen, Guarino, & Weller, 1998) and between learning disabled and nonlearning disabled groups (Petersen, Soliman, & Lott, 2001). While this scale appears to be relatively straightforward, there is the potential for disagreement among raters in how to assign scores to "overall integration". Considerably more work needs to be conducted and published before this scoring system can be recommended for use clinically.

Organizational scoring system

Kixmiller, Verfaellie, Mather, and Cermak (2000) developed a 9-point organizational scoring system (OSS) for the copy trial. Coloured pen switching was used to record examinees' process for reproducing the ROCF. Six items focus on drawing components as units: the large rectangle (which can include the large triangle on the right), the intersecting diagonals, the horizontal and vertical midlines, the small rectangle, the diagonals within the small rectangle, and the correct angling of the upper diagonal lines for the two triangles. Three items focus on good temporal sequencing of components; that is, each of the respective triangular structures should be drawn before (1) the circle with dots, (2) the small rectangle, and (3) the four horizontal lines. One point is given for each item that demonstrates good organization as described. Higher scores indicate greater organization. Inter-rater reliability was reported to be 0.90. A short scoring guide for this straightforward scoring system is provided in Kixmiller et al. Very little information is available on this scoring system as the primary purpose of the study was to determine the contribution of visuoperceptive processing problems to visual memory impairments in amnesic Korsakoff, medial temporal, and ACoA aneurysm patients. Korsakoff and ACoA patients obtained significantly lower copy organization scores than medial temporal patients and control groups. More validity evidence is needed to support the use of this scale with clinical and nonclinical samples.

Detailed scoring of Presence, Organization, and Approach

Klicpera (1983) expanded on Osterrieth's (1944) scoring of presence and placement by using a process flowchart to record the sequence and direction of each line drawn and conducting a more detailed analysis of Presence, Organization, and Approach in children's ROCF drawings. Presence consisted of a count of elements comprising each of (1) the external configuration (i.e., 13 segments of lines around the edges of the figure that incorporate the triangle at the top, the large triangle to the right, and the square at the bottom); (2) the main rectangle (i.e., 10 segments of lines); (3) the internal structural components (i.e., 8 segments of lines); and (4) internal and external details (i.e., 13 lines, figures, or clusters). The authors also combined the main rectangle and internal structural components into one category. Organization involves intersections (i.e., the number of correctly copied lines at seven intersections in the figure), alignments (i.e., the number of important lines in the figure that were aligned), and arrangement of details (i.e., the number of perseverations or figure components drawn in an incorrect location). Finally, Approach consisted of order (i.e., percentage of external configuration, main rectangle, and inner structure parts drawn prior to inner details; number of external details drawn prior to parts of the external configuration), continuity (i.e., whether important lines in the figure had been drawn as units), and segmentation (i.e., number of elements drawn isolated from their context).

Klicpera (1983) was interested in comparing coding strategies and planning using the ROCF in 33 boys who were poor readers and 18 boys without learning problems; the sample consisted of boys aged 11 ½–14 ½ years. He found that poor readers generally produced fewer elements, left out significantly more details, drew a smaller percentage of structural elements before details, produced fewer correct intersections, showed less continuity in their drawings, showed poorer placement of details, and showed greater perseveration than the control subjects. Klicpera's scoring categories were less able to discriminate among poor readers with better verbal than nonverbal ability, better nonverbal than verbal ability, and equal verbal and nonverbal ability as determined using the WISC-R; however, it must be noted that, with only 10 subjects per group, statistical power was poor.

A major barrier limiting the use of this scoring system is that not enough detail is provided in Klicpera's (1983) article to enable different researchers to apply the system reliably. For example, it is not clear what the possible range of scores is for alignments or how continuity was actually scored.

Strategy, accuracy, and error scoring system

Kirk and Kelly (1986) presented another of the early scoring systems for children's copy reproductions of the ROCF. This system is divided into two sections: (1) strategies and (2) accuracy and error. The strategies component was designed to evaluate the type of strategy used to copy the figure as well as the level of organization (i.e., structured or nonstructured) associated with the strategy used. According to Kirk and Kelly, strategy is recorded using a process flowchart with numbered line sequences and arrows indicating the directionality of each line, although Kirk (1985) used a coloured pen-switching approach. Under strategies, both the starting strategy and the progression strategy are considered. The starting strategy focuses on where the child initiates the reproduction, whereas the progression strategy focuses on the number of lines used to complete the reproduction. Kirk argued that the starting and progression strategies provide different information about the degree of fragmentation or integration that characterizes the process of reproduction. Both starting and progression strategies are categorized as configurational, part–whole, or piecemeal based on the score achieved. Starting strategies are further categorized as structured or nonstructured in organizational level. Concordance of the strategy between starting and progression can also be noted.

Accuracy is measured using three indicators: number of lines present, alignment of structural elements, and proportional planning. The first indicator is clearly a measure of accuracy as traditionally conceptualized and will not be discussed further here. As noted by Kirk (1985), alignment (maximum score of 51) and proportional planning (maximum score of 9) involve some aspect of spatial planning. Frequencies for a variety of errors are summed to provide a total error score. Under errors, Kirk mentioned only duplication of lines, conflation, and rotation as errors; however, Kirk and Kelly (1986) add omissions and displacement to that list. A detailed copy of this scoring system, with examples and preliminary norms, is available in Kirk and Kelly (1986).

In a study of 282 boys and girls aged 6–16 years, Kirk (1985) reported that inter-rater reliability estimates by two independent scorers ranged from 0.87 to 0.96 across grade levels. An age-related shift from a piecemeal to configurational approach for starting, progression, and concordance of strategy was observed. A shift in the organizational level from nonstructured to structured also appeared to occur at age 12. Research that examines the validity of inferences made using the scoring system with a variety of clinical and nonclinical samples is needed as well as evidence regarding inter-rater reliability with other researchers.

Developmental Scoring System for the Rey–Osterrieth Complex Figure

The Developmental Scoring System for the Rey–Osterrieth Complex Figure (DSS-ROCF) is a comprehensive scoring system that has been normed for children aged 5–14 years (Bernstein and Waber, 1996). The authors noted that the development of this system stemmed from clinical observations that children referred for learning difficulties appeared to perceive the ROCF quite differently than brain-damaged adults even though they produced similar ROCF drawings with considerable distortion and disorganization. In subsequent research, Waber and Holmes (1985, 1986) described the normal developmental progression in copy and recall productions of the ROCF by children. The DSS attempts to capture this developmental progression through four aspects of performance: Organization, Style, Accuracy, and Errors. Given the focus in this chapter on the process approach to scoring complex figures, only the Organization, Style, and Error Scores will be discussed here. A coloured pen-switching procedure is used to record the child's process in drawing the figure.

The Organization Score measures figural organization, which is indicated by whether segments of lines are accurately aligned or whether lines accurately intersect. There are 24 such points of alignment or intersection (i.e., 'criterial features') in the copy trial and 16 such points in the immediate recall and 15–20 min delayed recall trials. Specific sets of criterial features are used to determine the basal organizational level, which ranges from I to V. The basal organizational level indicates the highest level at which all of the criterial features, specified for that level, were correct. Extra points are awarded for any correct criterial features beyond the basal level. Using a table, these points are converted into an Organization Score ranging from 1 (poorly organized) to 13 (highly organized). Different features of the ROCF are weighted differently in the Organization Scores for different ages to reflect developmental changes. Both copy and recall are scored because the similarity (or dissimilarity) of organization on these trials can provide important information about process (e.g., impulsivity, dependence on external structure, and ability to develop or alter strategy).

The Style Score measures not only whether two segments of a line are accurately aligned, but also whether they are drawn in one continuous stroke. Eighteen criterial features are used to rate style in the copy trial. Different weights are assigned to each feature based on the basal organizational level; the sum of these weights for the 18 criterial features provides the Style Score. Based on this score, the copy may be categorized as part-oriented, intermediate, or configurational. Reproductions categorized as intermediate can be subcategorized as either outer configuration/inner part or outer part/inner configuration for the copy trial only. For the recall trials, fewer features tend to be recalled so only six criterial lines are considered. Different criterial lines are used depending on the basal organizational level. First, one rates whether any segment of each required criterial line is present and then whether the lines were drawn in one continuous stroke. Each recall reproduction is categorized as part-oriented, intermediate, or configurational. Generally, the Style Score is meant to characterize the child's preferred cognitive style in drawing the ROCF. That is, this score indicates whether the child tends to favour a more global and integrated orientation or a more detailed and focal orientation.

The Error Score consists of the summed frequency of the following four types of errors observed in the normative sample: rotation, perseveration, misplacement, and conflation (i.e., when one line is used to represent more than one element). Importantly, individual components of the figure can be scored for more than one type of error and both an entire component or segments of a component can be scored for errors. Relatively few errors were made by the normative sample. Waber et al. (1994) suggest that errors may result from poorly developed metacognitive strategies and a failure to appreciate the organizational relationships among the components of the figure.

Waber and Holmes (1985) reported an inter-rater reliability, using two raters, of 0.95 for Organization Scores and 0.88 for Style Scores on 52 randomly selected copy reproductions. Waber and Holmes (1986) reported an inter-rater reliability, using two raters, of greater than 94% for Organization, Style, and Error Scores on 50 randomly selected immediate or delayed recall drawings. Sadeh et al. (1996) reported an inter-rater reliability of 94% for the Organization Score. Bernstein and Waber (1996) claimed that, based on a variety of studies, reliability of raters' ability to identify criterial features in children's drawings ranged from 0.91 to 0.96. Troyer and Wishart (1997) reported an inter-rater reliability for two raters of 0.97.

Quite a few studies have been conducted that provide evidence suggesting that DSS-ROCF scores can discriminate between clinical and control groups of children, although it must be noted that several of these studies involved the authors themselves. Such clinical groups include children with learning disabilities (Chen, Cermak, Murray, & Henderson, 1999; Waber & Bernstein, 1995), attention-deficit/hyperactivity disorder (Grodzinsky & Diamond, 1992; Sadeh et al., 1996; Sami, Carte, Hinshaw, & Zupan, 2003; Seidman et al., 1995), leukaemia (Waber et al., 1990), head injury (Yeates, Patterson, Waber, & Bernstein, 2003), and low birth weights (Waber & McCormick, 1995). A number of studies have also been conducted with clinical and non-clinical samples of adults (e.g., Kalinowski, Weinstein, & Seidman, 2003; Ska, Dehaut, & Nespoulous, 1987; Troyer & Wishart, 1997; Weinstein, Kaplan, Casey, & Hurwitz, 1990). The DSS-ROCF can be purchased from PAR and is accompanied by a detailed manual.

Akshoomoff and Stiles' Planning scores for children

In their examination of developmental trends for copying and recalling the ROCF using the original BQSS (Stern et al., 1994), Akshoomoff and Stiles (1995a, 1995b) noted that the Planning score was not sensitive to developmental trends in children. After reviewing previous literature on children's ROCF copy drawings, they identified three starting strategies (i.e., perimeter, partial perimeter, and nonperimeter) and four progression strategies for children aged 6–12 years. The perimeter starting strategy involves drawing the outer contour of the ROCF and must include drawing the large triangle on the right, the upper triangle, or the lower square prior to drawing any internal elements. In the partial perimeter strategy, parts of the outer contour are drawn followed by some inner or outer details before completing the outer contour. Starting strategies that do not follow one of the two approaches (including the small percentage who start with the rectangle) are classified as a nonperimeter strategy. The four progression strategies are as follows: (1) the main rectangle is complete and the horizontal and vertical midlines were each drawn continuously; (2) the remainder of the figure was broken into two units and was constructed unit by unit; (3) the remainder of the figure was broken into three or more units and constructed unit by unit; and (4) piecemeal and inconsistent placement of remaining units. In Akshoomoff and Stiles's (1995a) study, there was 90% agreement between the two raters across 120 copy trial drawings for starting and progression strategies. Akshoomoff and Stiles (1995a, 1995b) found no significant differences in starting strategies used among the seven age groups of children (aged 6–12 years) at copy or immediate recall; the three strategies were used with nearly equal probability. Progression strategies at copy and immediate recall did differ with age; children aged 8–12 years used more systematic approaches than children aged 6 and 7 years.

Akshoomoff and Stiles' (1995a, 1995b) research makes an important contribution to developmental studies of process in children's visuospatial construction and recall. While some favourable preliminary research has been conducted with children with unilateral brain injury (Akshoomoff et al., 2002), further research is needed to explore the usefulness of this process scoring system with a variety of clinical samples. In addition, research needs to be conducted comparing results from this scoring system with other related systems (e.g., Anderson, Anderson, & Garth, 2001; Kirk, 1985).

Rey Complex Figure Organizational Strategy Score

Anderson et al. (2001) designed the Rey Complex Figure Organizational Strategy Score (RCF-OSS) to improve upon the scoring systems presented by Kirk (1985) and Akshoomoff and Stiles (1995a, 1995b) for paediatric populations. A coloured pen-switching method is used to record the process of copying the ROCF. Drawings are rated on a 7-point scale that is labelled according to the level of organizational strategy (e.g., Level 6—conceptual organization, Level 4—piecemeal/fragmented organization, and Level 2—poor organization). Criteria for each level focus on both the sequence of drawing and alignments. The authors claim it takes less than 30 s to score each protocol. Detailed scoring instructions are available from Anderson et al. (2001). Four registered psychologists were trained to use the RCF-OSS in a single training session and then independently scored 50 random ROCF copies. Inter-rater reliability, using Spearman's r, ranged from 0.85 to 0.92 among the raters. Three psychologists scored the same 50 reproductions one week later; intrarater reliability coefficients ranged from 0.70 to 0.94.

On the basis of data with 376 boys and girls aged 7–13 years, Anderson et al. (2001) reported that the RCF-OSS showed relatively small correlations ($r = -0.12$ to 0.35) with convergent validity measures of executive functioning such as Trails A and B, Controlled Oral Word Association Test, and the Tower of London Test. Similarly, low correlations ($r = 0.18$ to 0.26) were reported with a variety of discriminant validity memory measures such as Block Span, Digit Span, and Story Recall. These results suggest poor convergent validity evidence and moderate discriminant validity evidence for the RCF-OSS. RCF-OSS scores correlated significantly with copy accuracy ($r = 0.51$) and recall accuracy ($r = 0.42$) scores as well as with Waber and Holmes' (1986) organizational score ($r = 0.52$). The seven organizational levels were collapsed into four levels to examine developmental trends. The percentage of children at each organizational level by age group generally was consistent with previous research on developmental trends in organizational strategies. More research is needed that provides validity evidence with a variety of clinical samples.

Decomposition Paradigm

Poreh (2000) described the Decomposition Paradigm as one in which new indices or subscores are developed to reflect the relationship between item or test performance and underlying latent variables or facets. Given that scores from many neuropsychological measures are not normally distributed, he noted that this approach typically involves theory-driven facet or nonparametric classification techniques. Similar to the Composition Paradigm, this paradigm typically does not impact the length of the testing process or modify standardized administration procedures. Very little work appears to have been conducted with complex figures that would fit under the Decomposition Paradigm. Two approaches will be described here: Hartman and Potter's (1998) work decomposing the standard 36-point accuracy system and Poreh and Shye's (1998) development of global and local indices.

Hartman and Potter's 36-point system extension

The goal of Hartman and Potter's (1998) extension to the 36-point accuracy scoring system was to differentiate errors of omission from errors involving distortion of ROCF components. Instead of treating 0-, ½-, and 1-point scores to each component as part of a unidimensional continuum, Hartman and Potter proposed that they be treated as separate categories and summed. Thus, they suggested that the frequency of 0-point scores provides an index of omission errors and measures the degree of complete information loss. The frequency of ½-point scores, which are assigned when there are both accuracy and placement errors, may be indicative of either serious visuospatial difficulties or mild memory problems. Finally, the frequency of 1-point scores, which are assigned for errors in either the accuracy or placement of a component, may provide an index of visuospatial ability.

In a study of 30 male and female younger university students and 30 male and female older community-dwelling adults, Hartman and Potter (1998) reported inter-rater reliabilities, using intraclass correlations, of 0.99 for 0-point scores, 0.79 for ½-point scores, and 0.85 for 1-point scores for a subsample of 22 randomly selected protocols. They reported that the most prominent age difference in this study, which used the original 36-point scoring system, the extended scoring system, and the BQSS, was in the number of omitted elements (0-point scores) at recall wherein older adults tended to omit more elements. Older adults also tended to have more ½-point scores, suggesting that they tend to retain less information about the form or location of ROCF components.

This is an interesting approach to exploring the 36-point accuracy scoring system that attempts to break down the types of errors made. While this approach does not seem difficult to score and would take little work beyond the usual scoring of the figure, more work needs to be conducted examining the validity of interpretations made from these categories of scores.

ROCF global local indexes

Poreh and Shye (1998) used Faceted Smallest Space Analysis, a statistical technique used to examine similarity among variables, to evaluate whether global and local visuoconstructional abilities could be distinguished using the ROCF. Their study included 20 patients with right hemisphere damage (RHD), 20 patients with left hemisphere damage (LHD), and 15 patients with frontal lobe or subcortical damage (FLD). Patients' ages ranged from 17 to 60 years. Both a copy trial and 5-min delayed recall trial were used. Global features consisted of Binder's (1982) five configural ROCF components. All other ROCF components were considered to be local features. The results showed that ROCF components could be meaningfully divided into global or local features and that processing of the ROCF was dependent on both these features and the location of components (i.e., in the left, middle, or right) of the figure. Importantly, not all components traditionally viewed in the literature as having either global or local properties, respectively, showed those properties in Poreh and Shye's analysis. That is, Binder (1982) treated the large triangle to the right of the figure as a global unit and both the small rectangle to the left and the small triangle at the top as local units but the analysis conducted showed that they possessed the opposite qualities. Poreh and Shye suggest these results might reflect differences in the perception of these components due to the receptive fields in which they are located. Another finding in this study was that local features located on the right side of the ROCF discriminated best between RHD and LHD patients, with 72.6% of patients correctly classified.

This unique study contributes to our understanding of how the ROCF is processed. It would be interesting to see this analysis applied to data from other clinical as well as nonclinical populations.

Conclusion

There has been a proliferation of process-scoring systems for the ROCF, especially those systems that have been developed for the use with adults. Only a few systems appear to have been designed for, or applied to, other complex figures (e.g., Hamby et al. [1993] developed the organizational quality scoring system [OQSS] for use with the ROCF or the TCF). Some process scoring systems focus on only one or a few aspects involved in the process of drawing a complex figure (e.g., Chervinsky et al., 1992; Hamby et al., 1993; Shorr et al., 1992) whereas other scoring systems may include a variety of process variables (e.g., Bernstein & Waber, 1996; Klicpera, 1983; Stern et al., 1999; Visser, 1973).

Many process scoring systems claim to measure 'organization' or 'strategy', but how these terms are operationalized and measured may vary considerably. The most common types of qualitative information included in process scoring systems include: line continuity, sequencing, asymmetry, correct alignment and intersections of lines, recognition of configural or component gestalts, omissions, and a variety of errors (e.g., rotations, perseverations, misplacements, confabulation, and size). Even within these types of qualitative information, there can be different ways of operationalizing terms. For example, 'sequencing' may refer to whether configural components are drawn before details, whether some details are drawn before others, or simply whether the drawing starts with the ROCF's main rectangle, cross at upper left, or some other component. It is also unclear as to whether errors should be viewed as process variables or outcome variables (along with accuracy and placement).

In 1997, Troyer and Wishart concluded that no one process scoring system is universally accepted. This conclusion is still true today and suggests dissatisfaction by researchers and clinicians with how process is being assessed. A critical concern with the sheer number of different process scoring systems for the ROCF means few have a significant body of validity evidence to support their use with clinical or nonclinical samples. Moreover, there has been relatively little systematic evaluation of existing process scoring systems. A notable exception is Troyer and Wishart's (1997) study. Further in-depth work is needed to examine the similarities and differences among existing process scoring systems.

For researchers and clinicians interested in examining the process used by examinees or patients to draw the ROCF, it is recommended that the selection of a process scoring system takes place prior to data collection as some scoring systems rely on, or provide norms based on, different administration procedures (e.g., pen-switching vs. process flowcharts; particular delay intervals; and orientation of figure). Issues to consider in reviewing and selecting a process scoring system include: (1) how comprehensive the information needs to be (i.e., is a wide range of information needed or just one type of information?); (2) the type of information required (e.g., different types of errors, sequencing, and organizational style); (3) the ease with which the system can be learned and inter-rater reliability; (4) the length of time needed to score each figure; (5) the availability of norms; (6) the system's use and utility with a particular clinical population; (7) its use and appropriateness with particular age, education, gender, or ethnic groups; and (8) availability of validity evidence supporting the inferences to be made from the scores.

The present chapter primarily consists of an introduction to the wide range of existing process scoring systems for the ROCF. Future research is needed that (1) explores researchers' and clinicians' interest in, and use of, process scoring systems, (2) further integrates relevant theory, empirical evidence, and clinical knowledge to develop a stronger foundation on which to explore process in complex figures and other visuospatial stimuli, (3) provides further validity evidence to support the use of individual process scoring systems with clinical and nonclinical samples, and (4) systematically evaluates existing process scoring systems.

References

Akshoomoff, N. A., Feroleto, C. C., Doyle, R. E., & Stiles, J. (2002). The impact of early unilateral brain injury on perceptual organization and visual memory. *Neuropsychologia, 40*, 539–561.

Akshoomoff, N., & Stiles, J. (1995a). Developmental trends in visuospatial analysis and planning: I. Copying a complex figure. *Neuropsychology, 9*, 364–377.

Akshoomoff, N., & Stiles, J. (1995b). Developmental trends in visuospatial analysis and planning: II. Memory for a complex figure. *Neuropsychology, 9*, 378–389.

Anderson, P., Anderson, V., & Garth, J. (2001). Assessment and development of organizational ability: The Rey Complex Figure Organizational Strategy Score (RCF-OSS). *The Clinical Neuropsychologist, 15*, 81–94.

Bachtler, S. D., Roth, D. L., Smith, G. E., & Weber, A. M. (1990). Qualitative performance on the Rey–Osterrieth Complex Figure in patients with complex partial seizures. *Journal of Clinical and Experimental Neuropsychology, 12*, 75.

Barr, W. B. (2003). Assessment of temporal lobe epilepsy using the ROCF. In J. A. Knight & E. Kaplan (Eds.), *The handbook of Rey–Osterrieth Complex Figure usage: Clinical and research applications*. Lutz, FL: Psychological Assessment Resources.

Bennet-Levy, J. (1984). Determinants of performance on the Rey–Osterrieth Complex Figure Test: An analysis and a new technique for single case assessment. *British Journal of Clinical Psychology, 23*, 109–119.

Bernstein, J. H., & Waber, D. P. (1996). *Developmental scoring system for the Rey–Osterrieth Complex Figure: Professional manual*. Odessa, FL: Psychological Assessment Resources.

Binder, L. M. (1982). Constructional strategies on complex figure drawings after unilateral brain damage. *Journal of Clinical Neuropsychology, 4*, 51–88.

Binder, L. M., & Wonser, D. (1989). *Constructional strategies on Rey–Complex Figure drawings of stroke patients in rehabilitation*. Presented at the International Neuropsychological Society, Orlando, FL, USA.

Boone, K. B. (2000). The Boston Qualitative Scoring System for the Rey–Osterrieth Complex Figure. *Journal of Clinical and Experimental Neuropsychology, 22*, 430–432.

Bosbach, S., Kornblum, C., Schröder, R., & Wagner, M. (2003). Executive and visuospatial deficits in patients with chronic progressive external ophthalmoplegia and Kearns–Sayre syndrome. *Brain, 126*, 1231–1240.

Cahn, D. A., Marcotte, A. C., Stern, R. A., Arruda, J. E., Akshoomoff, N. A., & Leshko, I. C. (1996). The Boston Qualitative Scoring System for the Rey–Osterrieth Complex Figure: A study of children with attention-deficit/hyperactivity disorder. *The Clinical Neuropsychologist, 10*, 397–406.

Chen, C. C., Cermak, S. A., Murray, E. A., & Henderson, A. (1999). The effect of strategy on the recall of the Rey–Osterrieth Complex Figure in children with or without learning disabilities. *The Occupational Therapy Journal of Research, 19*, 258–279.

Chervinsky, A. B., Mitrushina, M., & Satz, P. (1992). Comparison of four methods of scoring the Rey–Osterrieth Complex Figure Drawing Test on four age groups of normal elderly. *Brain Dysfunction, 5*, 267–287.

Cohen, D. A. (2001). Rey Complex Figure Test and Recognition Trial. In B. S. Plake & J. C. Impara (Eds.), *The fourteenth mental measurements yearbook* (pp. 1018–1020). Lincoln, NB: Buros Institute of Mental Measurements, University of Nebraska-Lincoln.

Cohen, D. A. (2003). The Boston Qualitative Scoring System for the Rey–Osterrieth Complex Figure. In B. S. Plake, J. C. Impara, & R. A. Spies (Eds.), *The fifteenth mental measurements yearbook* (pp. 130–133). Lincoln, NB: University of Nebraska-Lincoln.

Cornell, D. G., Roberts, M., & Oram, G. (1997). The Rey–Osterrieth Complex Figure Test as a neuropsychological measure in criminal offenders. *Archives of Clinical Neuropsychology*, *12*, 47–56.

Corwin, J., & Bylsma, F. W. (1993). Commentary and translations of excerpts from Rey's Psychological examination of traumatic encephalopathy and Osterrieth's The Complex Figure Test. *The Clinical Neuropsychologist*, *7*, 3–21.

Dawson, L. K., & Grant, I. (2000). Alcoholics' initial organizational and problem-solving skills predict learning and memory performance on the Rey–Osterrieth Complex Figure. *Journal of the International Neuropsychological Society*, *6*, 12–19.

Deckersbach, T., McMurrich, S., Ogutha, J., Savage, C. R., Sachs, G., & Rauch, S. L. (2004). Characteristics of non-verbal memory impairment in bipolar disorder: The role of encoding strategies. *Psychological Medicine*, *34*, 823–832.

Deckersbach, T., Otto, M. W., Savage, C. R., Baer, L., & Jenike, M. A. (2000c). The relationship between semantic organization and memory in obsessive–compulsive disorder. *Psychotherapy and Psychosomatics*, *69*, 101–107.

Deckersbach, T., Savage, C. R., Henin, A., Mataix-Cols, D., Otto, M. W., Wilhelm, S., Rauch, S. L., Baer, L., & Jenike, M. A. (2000a). Reliability and validity of a scoring system for measuring organizational approach in the Complex Figure Test. *Journal of Clinical and Experimental Neuropsychology*, *22*, 640–648.

Deckersbach, T., Savage, C. R., Phillips, K. A., Wilhelm, S., Buhlmann, U., Rauch, S. L., Baer, L., & Jenike, M. A. (2000b). Characteristics of memory dysfunction in body dysmorphic disorder. *Journal of the International Neuropsychological Society*, *6*, 673–681.

Delis, D. C. (1989). Neuropsychological assessment of learning and memory. In F. Boller & J. Grafman (Eds.), *Handbook of neuropsychology* (Vol. 3, pp. 3–33). Amsterdam: Elsevier.

Denman, S. B. (1984). *Manual for the Denman Neuropsychology Memory Scale*. Charleston, SC: Author.

Diamond, B. J., DeLuca, J., & Kelley, S. M. (1997). Memory and executive functions in amnesic and non-amnesic patients with aneurysms of the anterior communicating artery. *Brain*, *120*, 1015–1025.

Elderkin-Thompson, V., Boone, K. B., Kumar, A., & Mintz, J. (2004). Validity of the Boston Qualitative Scoring System for the Rey–Osterrieth Complex Figure among depressed elderly patients. *Journal of Clinical and Experimental Neuropsychology*, *26*, 598–607.

Elderkin-Thompson, V., Kumar, A., Mintz, J., Boone, K., Bahng, E., & Lavretsky, H. (2004). Executive dysfunction and visuospatial ability among depressed elders in a community setting. *Archives of Clinical Neuropsychology*, *19*, 597–611.

Fastenau, P. S. (2002). *The Extended Complex Figure Test (ECFT)*. Los Angeles, CA: Western Psychological Services.

Fastenau, P. S. (2003). Extended Complex Figure Test (ECFT): Rationale and empirical support for recognition and matching. In J. A. Knight & E. F. Kaplan (Eds.),

The handbook of Rey–Osterrieth Complex Figure usage: Clinical and research applications (pp. 255–282). Lutz, FL: Psychological Assessment Resources.

Fastenau, P. S., Denburg, N. L., & Hufford, B. J. (1999). Adult norms for the Rey–Osterrieth Complex Figure Test and for supplemental recognition and matching trials from the Extended Complex Figure test. *The Clinical Neuropsychologist*, *13*, 30–47.

Frazier, T. W., Adams, N. L., Strauss, M. E., & Redline, S. (2001). Comparability of the Rey and Mack forms of the complex figure test. *The Clinical Neuropsychologist*, *15*, 337–344.

Fujii, D. E., Lloyd, H. A., & Miyamoto, K. (2000). The salience of visuospatial and organizational skills in reproducing the Rey–Osterrieth Complex Figure in subjects with high and low IQs. *The Clinical Neuropsychologist*, *14*, 551–554.

Gainotti, G., & Tiacci, C. (1970). Patterns of drawing disability in right and left hemispheric patients. *Neuropsychologia*, *8*, 379–384.

Grodzinsky, G. M., & Diamond, R. (1992). Frontal lobe functioning in boys with attention-deficit/hyperactivity disorder. *Developmental Neuropsychology*, *8*, 427–455.

Hamby, S. L., Wilkins, J. W., & Barry, N. S. (1993). Organizational quality on the Rey–Osterrieth and Taylor Complex Figure Tests: A new scoring system. *Psychological Assessment*, *5*, 27–33.

Hartman, M., & Potter, G. (1998). Sources of age differences on the Rey–Osterrieth Complex Figure Test. *The Clinical Neuropsychologist*, *12*, 513–524.

Hubley, A. M. (1996). *Modification of the Taylor Complex Figure: A comparable figure to the Rey–Osterrieth Figure?* Edgeworth Series in Quantitative Behavioural Science, Paper No. ESQBS-96-7. University of Northern British Columbia, Prince George, B.C. Canada.

Hubley, A. M., & Tombaugh, T. N. (2002). *Memory Test for Older Adults (MTOA)*. Toronto, ON, Canada: Multi-Health Systems.

Hubley, A. M., & Tombaugh, T. N. (2003). Comparability of the Rey–Osterrieth and Taylor Complex Figures. In J. A. Knight & E. F. Kaplan (Eds.), *The handbook of Rey–Osterrieth Complex Figure usage: Clinical and research applications* (pp. 283–296). Lutz, FL: Psychological Assessment Resources.

Hubley, A. M., Tombaugh, T. N., & Hemingway, D. (2003). A modification of the Taylor Figure and the development of new figures for older adults. In J. A. Knight & E. F. Kaplan (Eds.), *The handbook of Rey–Osterrieth Complex Figure usage: Clinical and research applications* (pp. 297–311). Lutz, FL: Psychological Assessment Resources.

Hubley, A. M., & Tremblay, D. (2002). Comparability of total score performance on the Rey–Osterrieth Complex Figure and a Modified Taylor Complex Figure. *Journal of Clinical and Experimental Neuropsychology*, *24*, 370–382.

Janowsky, J. S., & Thomas-Thrapp, L. J. (1993). Complex figure recall in the elderly: A deficit in memory or constructional strategy? *Journal of Clinical and Experimental Neuropsychology*, *15*, 159–169.

Kalinowski, A. G., Weinstein, C. S., & Seidman, L. J. (2003). Organizational and retrieval deficits on the ROCF in schizophrenia. In J. A. Knight & E. Kaplan (Eds.), *The handbook of Rey–Osterrieth Complex Figure usage: Clinical and research applications* (pp. 463–475). Lutz, FL: Psychological Assessment Resources.

Kaplan, E. (1988). A process approach to neuropsychological assessment. In T. Boll & B. K. Bryant (Eds.), *Clinical neuropsychology and brain function: Research, measurement, and practice* (pp. 127–167). Washington, DC: American Psychological Association.

Kirk, U. (1985). Hemispheric contributions to the development of graphic skill. In C. Best (Ed.), *Hemispheric function and collaboration in the child* (pp. 193–228). Orlando, FL: Academic Press.

Kirk, U., & Kelly, M. S. (1986). *Scoring scale for the Rey–Osterrieth Complex Figure*. Presented at the International Neuropsychological Society, Denver, CO, USA.

Kixmiller, J. S., Verfaellie, M., Mather, M. M., & Cermak, L. S. (2000). Role of perceptual and organizational factors in amnesics' recall of the Rey–Osterrieth Complex Figure: A comparison of three amnesic groups. *Journal of Clinical and Experimental Neuropsychology*, *22*, 198–207.

Klicpera, C. (1983). Poor planning as a characteristic of problem-solving behavior in dyslexic children. *Acta Paedopsychiatrica: International Journal of Child and Adolescent Psychiatry*, *49*, 73–82.

Knight, J. A. (2003a). The Rey–Osterrieth Complex Figure: Overview of the handbook, current uses, and future directions. In J. A. Knight & E. Kaplan (Eds.), *The handbook of Rey–Osterrieth Complex Figure usage: Clinical and research applications* (pp. 5–25). Lutz, FL: Psychological Assessment Resources.

Knight, J. A. (2003b). ROCF administration procedures and scoring system. In J. A. Knight & E. Kaplan (Eds.), *The handbook of Rey–Osterrieth Complex Figure usage: Clinical and research applications* (pp. 57–191). Lutz, FL: Psychological Assessment Resources.

Knight, J. A., & Kaplan, E. (Eds.) (2003). *The handbook of Rey–Osterrieth Complex Figure usage: Clinical and research applications*. Lutz, FL: Psychological Assessment Resources.

Knight, J. A., Kaplan, E., & Ireland, L. D. (2003). Survey findings of Rey–Osterrieth Complex Figure usage. In J. A. Knight & E. Kaplan (Eds.), *The handbook of Rey–Osterrieth Complex Figure usage: Clinical and research applications* (pp. 45–56). Lutz, FL: Psychological Assessment Resources.

Lange, G., Waked, W., Kirshblum, S., & DeLuca, J. (2000). Organizational strategy influence on visual memory performance after stroke: Cortical/subcortical and left/right hemisphere contrasts. *Archives of Physical Medicine and Rehabilitation*, *81*, 89–94.

Leark, R. A. (2003). The Boston Qualitative Scoring System for the Rey–Osterrieth Complex Figure. In B. S. Plake, J. C. Impara, & R. A. Spies (Eds.), *The fifteenth mental measurements yearbook* (pp. 133–136). Lincoln, NB: University of Nebraska-Lincoln.

Lezak, M. D. (1995). *Neuropsychological assessment* (3rd ed.). New York: Oxford University Press.

Lezak, M. D., Howieson, D. B., & Loring, D. W. (2004). *Neuropsychological assessment* (4th ed.). New York: Oxford University Press.

Loring, D. W., Lee, G. P., & Meador, K. J. (1988). Revising the Rey–Osterrieth: Rating right hemisphere recall. *Archives of Clinical Neuropsychology*, *3*, 239–247.

Loring, D. W., & Meador, K. J. (2003). The Medical College of Georgia (MCG) Complex Figures: Four forms for follow-up. In J. A. Knight & E. Kaplan (Eds.), *The handbook of Rey–Osterrieth Complex Figure usage: Clinical and research applications* (pp. 313–321). Lutz, FL: Psychological Assessment Resources.

Lott, K. P., Petersen, R., Capitano, D., & Spiteri, N. (1996). *A clinical psychological approach to the Rey–Osterrieth Complex Figure Test: An interpretive manual.* Pasadena, CA: Author.

Meyers, J. E., & Lange, D. (1994). Recognition subtest for the complex figure. *The Clinical Neuropsychologist, 8*, 153–166.

Meyers, J. E., & Meyers, K. R. (1995). *Rey Complex Figure Test and Recognition Trial.* Odessa, FL: Psychological Assessment Resources.

Milberg, W. P., Hebben, N., & Kaplan, E. (1996). The Boston Process Approach to neuropsychological assessment. In I. Grant & K. M. Adams (Eds.), *Neuropsychological assessment of neuropsychiatric disorders.* New York: Oxford University Press.

Osterrieth, P. (1944). Le test de copie d'une figure complexe. *Archives de Psychologie, 30*, 206–356.

Osterrieth, P. (1993). The Complex Figure Test. (J. Corwin & F. W. Bylsma, Trans.) *The Clinical Neuropsychologist, 7*, 3–21.

Petersen, R., Guarino, A., & Weller, E. L. (Aug., 2001). *Assessing executive functioning in learning disabled adult students.* Presented at the American Psychological Association, San Francisco, CA, USA.

Petersen, R., Soliman, A., & Lott, K. P. (Aug., 1998). *Rey–Osterrieth organizational scoring.* Presented at the American Psychological Association, San Francisco, CA, USA.

Piquet, O., Saling, M., O'Shea, M., Berkovic, S., & Bladin, P. (1994). Rey Figure distortions reflect nonverbal recall differences between right and left foci in unilateral temporal lobe epilepsy. *Archives of Clinical Neuropsychology, 9*, 451–460.

Poreh, A. M. (2000). The quantified process approach: An emerging methodology to neuropsychological assessment. *The Clinical Neuropsychologist, 14*, 212–222.

Poreh, A. M., & Shye, S. (1998). Examination of the global and local features of the Rey–Osterrieth Complex Figure using faceted smallest space analysis. *The Clinical Neuropsychologist, 12*, 453–467.

Rey, A. (1941). L'examen psychologie dan les cas d'encéphalopathie traumatique (Les problèmes). *Archives de Psychologie, 28*, 286–340.

Rey, A. (1993). Psychological examination of traumatic encephalopathy. (J. Corwin & F. W. Bylsma, Trans.) *The Clinical Neuropsychologist, 7*, 3–21.

Sadeh, M., Ariel, R., & Inbar, D. (1996). Rey–Osterrieth and Taylor Complex Figures: Equivalent measures of visual organization and visual memory in ADHD and normal children. *Child Neuropsychology, 2*, 63–71.

Sami, N., Carte, E. T., Hinshaw, S. P., & Zupan, B. A. (2003). Performance of girls with ADHD and comparison girls on the Rey–Osterrieth Complex Figure: Evidence for executive processing deficits. *Child Neuropsychology, 9*, 237–254.

Savage, C. R., Baer, L., Keuthen, N. J., Brown, H. D., Rauch, S. L., & Jenike, M. A. (1999). Organizational strategies mediate nonverbal memory impairment in obsessive–compulsive disorder. *Biological Psychiatry, 45*, 905–916.

Savage, C. R., Deckersbach, T., Wilhelm, S., Rauch, S. L., Baer, L., Reid, T., & Jenike, M. A. (2000). Strategic processing and episodic memory impairment in obsessive compulsive disorder. *Neuropsychology, 14*, 141–151.

Saxton, J. A., Becker, J. T., & Wisniewski, S. (2003). The ROCF and dementia. In J. A. Knight & E. Kaplan (Eds.), *The handbook of Rey–Osterrieth Complex Figure usage: Clinical and research applications* (pp. 569–582). Lutz, FL: Psychological Assessment Resources.

Schreiber, H. E., Javorsky, D. J., Robinson, J. E., & Stern, R. A. (1999). Rey–Osterrieth Complex Figure performance in adults with attention deficit hyperactivity disorder: A validation study of the Boston Qualitative Scoring System. *The Clinical Neuropsychologist*, *13*, 509–520.

Seidman, L. J., Benedict, K. B., Biederman, J., Bernstein, J. H., Sieverd, K., Milberger, S., Norman, D., Mick, E., & Faraone, S. V. (1995). Performance of ADHD children on the Rey–Osterrieth Complex Figure: A pilot neuropsychological study. *Journal of Child Psychology and Psychiatry*, *36*, 1459–1473.

Seidman, L. J., Lanca, M., Kremen, W. S., Faraone, S. V., & Tsuang, M. T. (2003). Organizational and visual memory deficits in schizophrenia and bipolar psychoses using the Rey–Osterrieth Complex Figure: Effects of duration of illness. *Journal of Clinical and Experimental Neuropsychology*, *25*, 949–964.

Shorr, J., Delis, D., & Massman, P. (1992). Memory for the Rey–Osterrieth Figure: Perceptual clustering, encoding, and storage. *Neuropsychology*, *6*, 43–50.

Silverstein, S. M., Osborn, L. M., & Palumbo, D. R. (1998). Rey–Osterrieth Complex Figure Test performance in acute, chronic, and remitted schizophrenia patients. *Journal of Clinical Psychology*, *54*, 985–994.

Ska, B., Dehaut, F., & Nespoulous, J.-L. (1987). Dessin d'une figure complexe par des sujets ages [Drawing of a complex figure by elderly subjects]. *Revue Belge de Psycologie et Pedagogie*, *XXVII*, 25–42.

Ska, B., & Nespoulous, J.-L. (1988). Encoding strategies and recall performance of a complex figure by normal elderly subjects. *Canadian Journal on Aging*, *7*, 408–416.

Spreen, O., & Strauss, E. (1991). *A compendium of neuropsychological tests: Administration, norms, and commentary*. New York: Oxford University Press.

Spreen, O., & Strauss, E. (1998). *A compendium of neuropsychological tests: Administration, norms, and commentary* (2nd ed.). New York: Oxford University Press.

Stern, R. A., Javorsky, D. J., Singer, E. A., Harris, N. G. S., Somerville, J. A., Duke, L. M., Thompson, J. A., & Kaplan, E. (1999). *BQSS: The Boston Qualitative Scoring System for the Rey–Osterrieth Complex Figure: Professional manual*. Lutz, FL: Psychological Assessment Resources.

Stern, R. A., Silva, S. G., Chaisson, N., & Evans, D. L. (1996). Influence of cognitive reserve on neuropsychological functioning in asymptomatic Human Immunodeficiency Virus-1 infection. *Archives of Neurology*, *53*, 148–153.

Stern, R. A., Singer, E. A., Duke, L. M., Singer, N. G., Morey, C. E., Daughtrey, E. W., & Kaplan, E. (1994). The Boston Qualitative Scoring System for the Rey–Osterrieth Complex Figure: Description and interrater reliability. *The Clinical Neuropsychologist*, *8*, 309–322.

Stern, R. A., Singer, N. G., Silva, S. G., Rogers, H. J., Perkins, D. O., Hall, C. D., van der Horst, C. M., & Evans, D. L. (1992). Neurobehavioral functioning in a nonconfounded group of asymptomatic HIV seropositive homosexual men. *American Journal of Psychiatry*, *149*, 1099–1102.

Sullivan, J. V., Mathalon, D. H., Ha, C. N., Zipursky, R. B., & Pfefferbaum, A. (1992). The contribution of constructional accuracy and organizational strategy to nonverbal recall in schizophrenia and chronic alcoholism. *Biological Psychiatry*, *32*, 312–333.

Taylor, E. M. (1959). *Psychological appraisal of children with cerebral deficits*. Cambridge, MA: Harvard University Press.

Taylor, L. B. (1969). Localization of cerebral lesions by psychological testing. *Clinical Neurosurgery*, *16*, 269–287.

Tombaugh, T. N., Schmidt, J. P., & Faulkner, P. (1992). A new procedure for administering the Taylor Complex Figure: Normative data over a 60-year span. *The Clinical Neuropsychologist*, *6*, 63–79.

Troyer, A. K., & Wishart, H. A. (1997). A comparison of qualitative scoring systems for the Rey–Osterrieth Complex Figure Test. *The Clinical Neuropsychologist*, *11*, 381–390.

Visser, R. S. H. (1973). *Manual of the Complex Figure Test (CFT)*. Amsterdam: Swets & Zeitlinger B.V.

Visser, R. S. H., & Hermans, J. W. J. (1973). Piecemeal approach and complexity. *Nederlands Tijdschrift voor de Psychologie en haar Grensgebieden*, *27*, 792–804.

Waber, D. P., & Bernstein, J. H. (1995). Performance of learning disabled and non-learning disabled children on the Rey–Osterrieth Complex Figure (ROCF): Validation of the Developmental Scoring System. *Developmental Neuropsychology*, *11*, 237–252.

Waber, D. P., Giola, G., Paccia, J., Sherman, B., Dinklage, D., Sollee, N., Urion, D. K., & Sallan, S. E. (1990). Sex differences in cognitive processing in children treated with CNS prophylaxis for acute lymphoblastic leukemia (ALL). *Journal of Pediatric Psychology*, *15*, 105–122.

Waber, D. P., & Holmes, J. M. (1985). Assessing children's copy productions of the Rey–Osterrieth Complex Figure. *Journal of Clinical and Experimental Neuropsychology*, *7*, 264–280.

Waber, D. P., & Holmes, J. M. (1986). Assessing children's memory productions of the Rey–Osterrieth Complex Figure. *Journal of Clinical and Experimental Neuropsychology*, *8*, 563–580.

Waber, D. P., Isquith, P. K., Kahn, C. M., Romero, I., Sallan, S. E., & Tarbell, N. J. (1994). Metacognitive factors in the visuospatial skills of long-term survivors of childhood acute lymphoblastic leukemia (ALL): An experimental approach to the Rey–Osterrieth Complex Figure Test. *Developmental Neuropsychology*, *10*, 349–367.

Waber, D. P., & McCormick, M. C. (1995). Late neuropsychological outcomes in preterm infants of normal IQ: Selective vulnerability of the visual system. *Journal of Pediatric Psychology*, *20*, 721–735.

Weinstein, C. S., Kaplan, E., Casey, M. B., & Hurwitz, I. (1990). Delineation of female performance on the Rey–Osterrieth Complex Figure. *Neuropsychology*, *4*, 117–127.

Yeates, K. O., Patterson, C. M., Waber, D. P., & Bernstein, J. H. (2003). Constructional and figural memory skills following pediatric closed head injury: Evaluation using the ROCF. In J. A. Knight & E. Kaplan (Eds.), *The handbook of Rey–Osterrieth Complex Figure usage: Clinical and research applications* (pp. 383–392). Lutz, FL: Psychological Assessment Resources.

17 Measures of suboptimal performance derived from neuropsychological tests

Daniel J. Slick and Esther Strauss

The use of methods for detecting suboptimal performance (SOP)—instances when an examinee does not perform to the best of his or her ability as directed on neuropsychological tests—has increased greatly over the last 25 years. This is particularly the case among the many clinicians who see cases where secondary gain is a significant issue, such as those involving personal injury litigation, long-term disability, worker's compensation, and criminal prosecution. This trend has been driven in part by increased awareness of the frequency with which SOP may be encountered in practice. For example, a recent survey of neuropsychologists in active practice found that as many as 30% of individuals who present for evaluation in the context of litigation are thought to be feigning impairments (Mittenberg, Patton, Canyock, & Condit, 2002). The increased use of measures of SOP has also been driven by a heightened awareness among those who request and scrutinize neuropsychological assessments of both the frequency of SOP and the increasing variety and utility of detection methods. This has led in turn to increasing requests by referring parties for clinicians to explicitly address SOP and also increasingly stringent evidentiary standards being applied to measures for detecting SOP in the medical–legal arenas where they are most commonly used.

With respect to the methods for detecting SOP that have been developed, these are essentially of two types. The first category, which is the focus of this chapter, encompasses those indices of SOP that have been derived from measures that were originally designed for other purposes (i.e., conventional measures of cognitive functions such as the Wechsler scales). These new measures fall under the rubric of the "Quantified Process Approach" (Poreh, 2000) since they attempt to quantify the process by which individuals negotiate particular tasks in order to increase diagnostic efficiency. Typically, the methods involve generating new indices based on existing data/scores (Composition Paradigm) or through quantification of underlying dimensions of the task (Decomposition Paradigm). On rare occasion, researchers have also created complementary tasks to clarify patient performance (Satellite Testing Paradigm; e.g., Barrash, Suhr, & Manzel, 2004). The second category, which will not be reviewed in this chapter, includes those measures that have been developed specifically for detecting SOP, of which Symptom Validity Tests (SVTs) are the most common (see Bianchini, Mathias, & Greve [2001] for a review of many of these measures).

The indices of SOP that have been derived from conventional neuropsychological tests can be divided into four subgroups based on complexity. The simplest indices represent application of the Composition Paradigm; they are essentially cutoff scores applied to existing measures (e.g., delayed recognition scores from memory tests). These have been developed by comparing score distributions of control or clinical samples of interest (e.g., traumatic brain injury [TBI]) to score distributions of suspected malingerers or analog malingering samples. One problem common to simple cutoff measures is that tests designed for clinical purposes often have an insufficiently low floor for separation of bona fide deficits from SOP. That is, score distributions from bona fide clinical cases may range down to nil (e.g., nothing recalled after a delay), eliminating the possibility of conclusively detecting SOP by virtue of performance below that obtained by any patients. In addition, studies have demonstrated that most people who are instructed to feign deficits associated with mild-to-moderate head injury (the type of case most likely to be seen in litigation) do not perform at a level consistent with severe or profound deficits (i.e., floor level). When any meaningful proportion of a bona fide clinical sample obtains nil or very low scores on a measure, then the specificity of that measure for detection of SOP will usually be marginal.

A more sophisticated approach than the simple cutoff method is one in which new indices are derived by simple combination of existing indices (e.g., subtracting recognition from recall scores, failure on two or more indices). This approach also falls within the Composition Paradigm. The development of these measures has typically been informed by assumptions about the naiveté in the lay population regarding patterns of performance seen in neurological conditions (e.g., recognition is usually better than recall). The advantage of combination indices is that they may be less prone to problems of floor or ceiling effects than single index cutoff scores. Simple combination indices also have the advantage of being easily calculated and applied by clinicians.

A yet more sophisticated, but sometimes less clinically practical approach entails the derivation of new indices via complex statistical methods for combining existing indices from one or more tests. This approach falls within the Decomposition Paradigm. For example, methods such as discriminant function analysis, logistic regression or more advanced and powerful techniques such as Bayesian model averaging (Millis & Volinsky, 2001) are employed to narrow down a large number of potential predictors of group membership into a smaller set that is combined in a prediction formula that best discriminates the groups. This process is often atheoretical; many or all available conventional variables from a test or groups of tests may form the initial pool from which the final subset of predictors is selected. In other cases, a smaller pool of initial variables is selected based on prior research or other a priori assumptions. While indices derived in this way may demonstrate better sensitivity and specificity than more simple indices (though sometimes spuriously, as a result of over-fitting in small samples), they are generally not used clinically due to the complexity of the required calculations.

A fourth approach, also falling within the Composition Paradigm, involves the derivation of new indices of SOP based on within-test patterns of performance. For example, analysis may reveal that particular items from a test are infrequently missed by persons with bona fide injuries or impairment, and that multiple errors across a number of these infrequently missed items are extremely rare. Naïve persons are not likely aware of such normative trends and may therefore be identified by a high "infrequent error" count. This type of index is conceptually similar to certain validity scales on personality measures that most clinicians are already familiar with (e.g., the *F* scale from the Minnesota Multiphasic Personality Inventory [MMPI]). A variation on this theme involves creation of a score based on performance across easier and more difficult items within a single test. Yet another example of this approach involves examination of list-order effects on learning tasks for patterns of performance that differ between clinical and SOP groups (e.g., attenuation of primacy effect in person's feigning memory impairment).

When selecting which measures of SOP from conventional tests to use in clinical practice, clinicians should ensure that validity has been adequately established. Ideally, any SOP measure used clinically can be referenced to a reasonably large and representative clinical sample of a type similar to that seen in practice, but without any significant influence of secondary gain (e.g., nonlitigating mild traumatic brain injury). This, at the very least, provides an indication of the rarity of SOP scores in the "invalid" range among examinees with bona fide injuries, thereby providing an estimate of the likelihood that such scores may in fact be false positives. Unfortunately, data from large, directly applicable nonlitigating clinical samples are not yet available for most SOP measures and so specificity remains inadequately characterized. Complimenting specificity data should be information on sensitivity. However, much of the research/normative data available for measures of SOP are derived from analog samples of convenience (i.e., college students instructed to malinger) rather than true clinical cases of malingering. Such analog samples often do not match the demographics and experiences of those seen clinically and they likely are not as highly motivated to feign dysfunction in a believable manner. Thus, sensitivity, like specificity, remains inadequately characterized for many measures. Where sensitivity and specificity are reasonably well characterized, these validity data should be translated into more clinically relevant positive and negative predictive power values—that is, probabilities that an examinee's score does or does not reflect SOP, given an assumed SOP base rate. By focusing on predicative power (particularly with associated confidence intervals) as opposed to a simple binary positive–negative test score interpretation, clinicians adopt a more sophisticated approach to data analysis that will likely serve them far better in increasingly sophisticated and demanding legal settings. (See Lindeboom [1989],

Millis & Volinsky [2001], Mossman [2003] for excellent discussions of this issue and clinically useful methods for deriving predictive power values; see also Slick, Sherman, & Iverson [1999] for a thorough discussion of the role, use, and limitations of psychometric measures in diagnosing malingering.)

We focus here on indices of SOP derived from some commonly used tests of intelligence, memory, and executive function, with the dual goals of illustrating the various subtypes discussed above and of providing information about the nature of these indices and their utility.

Wechsler Intelligence Scales

The various Wechsler Scales of Intelligence (Wechsler, 1955, 1981, 1997) have been among the most widely used cognitive measures in clinical psychology over the last 50 years (e.g., Camara, Nathan, & Puente, 2000). It is not surprising then that some of the earliest studies on detection of SOP have focused on these scales and the derivation of such indices continues to be a significant area of research. The most well studied and supported of the Wechsler-derived measures are described below.

Digit Span and Forward Digit Span

The Digit Span subtest has been included in all versions of the Wechsler Adult Intelligence Scale (WAIS) (and also the Wechsler Memory Scale, WMS) and a number of simple SOP cutoff scores have been derived. Naïve persons erroneously assume that Digit Span assesses memory and that it is significantly compromised in even mild brain injury. Heaton, Smith, Lehman, and Vogt (1978) were the first to demonstrate the potential utility of Digit Span for detecting SOP, reporting that it was the only subtest from the WAIS on which large group differences in scaled scores (roughly 1 *SD*) emerged between analog malingerers and head-injured patients. Similar or larger effect sizes have been found in other studies using the WAIS-R (Iverson & Franzen, 1994; Trueblood, 1994), WMS-R (Mittenberg, Azrin, Millsaps, & Heilbronner, 1993), and WAIS-III/ WMS-III (Langeluddecke & Lucas, 2003).

Given that the forward component of Digit Span (FDS) may be less affected by brain injury and other neurological conditions than the backward component (but see Table 7 from Iverson & Tulsky [2003], for data from the WAIS-III normative and clinical samples demonstrating that this may not be the case), it may have greater predictive power than the total Digit Span score. Therefore, some researchers have focused on FDS. Iverson and Franzen (1994) compared classification accuracy of the WAIS-R Digit Span total raw score vs. longest spans forward (LSF) and backward (LSB) with a sample of TBI patients vs. analog malingerers. They found that both a total score cutoff of 9 or less and an LSF cutoff of 4 or less yielded excellent overall accuracy (96–97%), while an LSB cutoff of 4 or less was less accurate (87%), though still well above chance.

More recently, Iverson and Tulsky (2003) examined Digit Span score distributions in the WAIS-III standardization sample and select clinical groups (e.g., TBI, Korsakoff's). They generated base-rate tables for the Digit Span scaled score, LSF and LSB. Based on rarity of occurrence in the general population *and* in clinical groups (i.e., < 5th percentile), they suggested the following as indicators of SOP: (1) Digit Span scaled score of 5 or less; (2) LSF of 4 or less (for persons under age 55); or (3) LSB of 2 or less. These tables of cutoff scores should routinely be consulted when Digit Span is administered to litigants or in other contexts where SOP may be encountered.

Reliable Digit Span

In 1994, Greiffenstein, Baker, and Gola introduced *Reliable Digit Span* (RDS) in the hope that it might more effectively detect SOP than standard Digit Span scores. This measure is calculated by summing the longest reliable forward and backward digit strings (both trials must be completed without error) from the Digit Span subtest. For example, a patient who passes both trials of 4 digits forward and 3 digits backward attains an RDS score of 7. When applied to a well-defined sample of patients who were given the WAIS-R as part of an evaluation following head injury, a cutoff score of 7 or less yielded sensitivity/ specificity of 0.70/0.73 for discriminating probable malingerers (n = 3) from persons with TBIs (n = 33), while sensitivity/specificity was 0.68/0.89 for discriminating probable malingerers from persons with persistent post-concussive syndrome (n = 30). Similar findings have also emerged with the WAIS-III. In a sample of persons seen following TBI, the RDS cutoff score of 7 yields sensitivity ranging from about 45–90% with specificity of 57–95% (Mathias, Greve, & Bianchini, 2002; Strauss, Hultsch, Hunter, Slick, Party, & Levy-Bencheton, 2000; Strauss, Slick, Levy-Bencheton, Hunter, Macdonald, & Hultsch, 2002).

Surprisingly, no studies to date have directly compared the more sophisticated index of RDS with either of the simpler indices of Digits Forward or Digit Span to determine if RDS offers any incremental validity. Nevertheless, the evidence to date suggests that RDS is a moderately useful measure of SOP, though inadequate on its own. Because it is easy to calculate, RDS should be routinely examined whenever Digit Span is administered.

Vocabulary–Digit Span difference score

Another combination index is the Vocabulary–Digit Span difference score. Mittenberg, Theroux-Fichera, Heilbronner, and Zielinshi (1995) demonstrated that analog malingerers who were administered the WAIS-R tended to suppress Digit Span scores more than Vocabulary scores, while similar levels of performance across both subtests typified a TBI group. An age-corrected (WAIS-R) scaled score Vocabulary–Digit Span discrepancy of 6 or more scaled score points was associated with a probability of malingering of

0.75 or greater. An overall classification rate of 79% for this cutoff was reported by Millis, Ross, and Ricker (1998). Iverson and Tulsky (2003) presented base-rate tables for Vocabulary–Digit Span difference scores from the WAIS-III normative sample as well as from clinical samples. They suggested that a Vocabulary–Digit Span scaled score difference of 5 or greater may signal SOP. It is important to note that these suspicion indices are based on rarity of occurrence in the general population and in clinical groups (generally ≤ 5th percentile), rather than on ability to discriminate malingerers from persons with legitimate impairment or injuries.

In sum, the evidence to date suggests that various measures derived from Digit Span are moderately useful for detecting SOP, though they are not sensitive enough to be the only measures relied on for such purposes.

Wechsler Memory Scales

Recognition tasks

Although probable malingerers tend to suppress their performance on all WMS-III subtests and indices (Langeluddecke & Lucas, 2003), the recognition tasks appear particularly useful to assess SOP. Langeluddecke and Lucas reported that 80% of probable malingerers obtained raw scores below 43/54 on the Auditory Recognition Delayed Total Score, whereas 8.2% of patients who sustained severe TBIs performed below this cutoff. For Word List II recognition, 81% of probable malingerers obtained scores below the cutoff (18/24) compared to 4.4% of severe TBI subjects. Of note, Langeluddecke and Lucas present data showing that recognition measures were clearly superior to total Digit Span scores. Although differences between recall and recognition would seem to be a promising avenue of exploration, this kind of index has yet to be evaluated with the WMS-III.

Studies have also demonstrated that the Faces I subtest from the WMS-III may be useful for detecting SOP as it is relatively insensitive to TBI. Glassmire, Bierley, Wieniewski, Greene, Kennedy, and Date (2003) studied both item-level and simple cut-score approaches to deriving an SOP index from Faces I with samples of nonlitigating TBI patients and controls under standard and instructed malingering conditions. They found that the total raw score provides stronger classification accuracy than an empirically weighted combination of the five easiest items (i.e., floor effect items—10, 17, 39, 43, 45). A raw score cutoff of 31/48 (corresponding to chance-level performance) yielded the maximum classification accuracy with 93.3% sensitivity and 80% specificity. Differences between indices (e.g., immediate memory minus working memory; FSIQ minus general memory) and "easy" tasks such as (e.g., Digit Span, Spatial Span, and Mental Control) were not very sensitive to SOP.

Rarely Missed Index

Killgore and DellaPietra (2000) used an item analysis approach to derive a SOP index based on the Logical Memory Recognition subtest from the

WMS-III. They observed that six items from the delayed recognition component of Logical Memory were correctly responded to at levels exceeding chance, even among people who had not been previously exposed to the stories. Using discriminant function analysis, they developed the *Rarely Missed Index* (RMI). This is calculated by summing the discriminant function weighted scores on the six rarely missed items (nos. 12, 16, 18, 22, 24, and 29). Wrong answers receive no points. The RMI scores can range from –22 to 226. Using a cutoff score of 136 and below, the RMI demonstrated high sensitivity (97%) and specificity (100%) in discriminating between analog malingerers and patients with neurological impairment.

Category Test

Some efforts to derive SOP indices for this popular measure of executive function have focused on derivation of simple cut scores on the easier subtests, on which low scores may be unlikely, even among persons with brain injuries. Thus, Tenhula and Sweet (1996) suggested that an excessive number of errors on Subtests I, II, and VII might raise the suspicion of malingering. Following up on this, DiCarlo, Gfeller, and Oliveri (2000), using a simulation paradigm, confirmed that a decision rule of more than one error on Subtests I and II was a fairly accurate indicator of malingering. This indicator correctly classified 76% of all simulators and all of the controls as well as individuals who had suffered a TBI. It is worth noting in this context that factor analytic findings (see Donders, 2001; Johnstone, Holland, & Hewett, 1997) reveal Subtests I and II to be conceptually different from the other Category Test (CT) subtests, and unrelated to injury severity. In addition, very few normals or brain-injured individuals make errors on items in these subtests, a fact that had been noted many years earlier by Simmel and Counts (1957; see the excellent review by Sweet & King, 2002).

Other efforts to derive SOP indices for the CT have focused on item-level analyses. Bolter, Picano, and Zych (1985) have identified 14 items on the Halstead Category Test (HCT) that most normal and neurologically impaired individuals pass (note: initially there were 18 items but 4 were eliminated on cross-validation). These 18 items that form the Bolter Validity Index (VI) include one item from Subtest I (6), two items from Subtest II (9, 18), two items from Subtest IV (22, 32), three items in Subtest V (27, 30, 33), five in Subtest VI (4, 18, 21, 24, 30) and three in Subtest VII (6, 10, 13). Approximately 97% of normal and neurologically impaired individuals failed two or less of these items. Tenhula and Sweet (1996) reported that a cutoff of more than three of these infrequently missed items was reasonably effective (86% hit rate) in discriminating brain-injured individuals from normals instructed to malinger (see also DiCarlo et al., 2000). Trueblood and Schmidt (1993), however, did not find a significant difference between suspected malingerers and brain-injured controls in the number of "rare errors." It may be that this indicator occurs rarely, and therefore its presence would suggest invalidity, while its absence would not substantiate a test protocol's validity (Trueblood & Schmidt, 1993).

Extreme test–retest inconsistency has also been evaluated as a potential indicator of SOP. Reitan and Wolfson (1996) gave the CT on two occasions to litigants and nonlitigants, who complained of having suffered a TBI. Nonlitigants improved their performance on the second test session, making on average 10 fewer errors. By contrast, litigants made about 14 more errors on the second administration.

It should be noted that the CT validity indicators described above have been developed for use with TBI in individuals typically with average to above educational achievement. Accordingly, the indicators should be used cautiously with individuals with other neurological conditions or of limited education/IQ. In addition, Sweet and King (2002) advise that the indicators may suggest but do not confirm motivational status and should not be used in isolation.

Wisconsin Card Sorting Test

Performance on the Wisconsin Card Sorting Test (WCST), another popular measure of executive function, may also be useful in detecting malingering. Patients suspected of incomplete effort tend to perform more poorly on WCST variables than those classified as having good effort (e.g., Greve, Bianchini, Mathias, Houston, & Crouch, 2002b; King, Sweet, Sherer, Curtiss, & Vanderploeg, 2002; but see Binder, Kelly, Villanueva, & Winslow, 2003). In addition, a number of formulae have been proposed (Bernard, McGrath, & Houston, 1996; King et al., 2002; Suhr & Boyer, 1999), which rely on the notion that individuals who malinger may suppress performance on obvious measures (e.g., number of categories) in comparison to subtle ones (e.g., perseverative errors) or may avoid too many consecutive correct response (e.g., failure to maintain set). Although specificity tends to be good with these formulae, sensitivity is limited (Greve et al., 2002b; King et al., 2002). The Bernard formula shares a substantial amount of variance with the Suhr formula, suggesting that use of these formulae in combination does not enhance diagnostic accuracy (Greve et al., 2002b). Further, each approach may yield somewhat different results depending upon the chronicity and severity of the brain injury (King et al., 2002). The equations provided by Suhr and Boyer (1999) and King et al. (2002) appear to provide reasonably good classification rates in a variety of traumatically brain-injured samples. However, in older adults (ages 55+) these formulae may result in a high rate of false positives and therefore may be inappropriate for use in this population (Ashendorf, O'Bryant, & McCaffrey, 2003).

Rey Auditory Verbal Learning Test

This very popular measure of auditory verbal learning and memory has a lengthy history in the detection of SOP dating from the work of Claparède in the early 1900s and his student, Rey, in the 1950s (Boake, 2000). These efforts as well as subsequent work have led to the development of both simple cutoff rules as well as more complex measures. Thus, a number of investigators have shown that poorly motivated individuals often exhibit a pattern of excessive impairment on some of the Rey Auditory Verbal Learning Test (RAVLT) recall trials (Binder et al., 2003; Sullivan, Deffenti, & Keane, 2002; Sullivan, Keane, & Deffenti, 2001). In addition, there is evidence that severe RAVLT recognition memory impairment (e.g., scores less than 7) likely reflects motivation to exaggerate deficits in patients with closed head injury (Binder, Villanueva, Howieson, & Moore, 1993; Binder et al., 2003; Chouinard & Rouleau, 1997; Greiffenstein et al., 1994; King, Gfeller, & Davis, 1998; Meyers, Morrison, & Miller, 2001; Sherman, Boone, Lu, & Razani, 2002). However, the recognition memory measure exhibits a high degree of specificity for motivation to perform poorly but only modest sensitivity. For example, Binder et al. (2003) recently reported that 92% of patients with moderate-to-severe head injuries obtained scores of more than 5 correct, whereas only 38% of poorly motivated patients (classed according to performance on a SVT, the Portland Digit Recognition Test) obtained such scores.

Abnormal serial position effects (absence of primacy effects in recall) have also been explored. Bernard (1991) found that individuals attempting to fake injury tend to do so by suppressing recall of words from the first third of the list (absence of primacy but not recency effect), behaving like patients with severe amnesia. However, subsequent studies have yielded contradictory results. Thus, Suhr (2002) reported that simulators (including those who had been warned about the possibility of detection) showed a suppressed primacy effect during learning trials, while normal subjects and moderate to severely head-injured patients tended to have normal serial position curves. She noted that a flattened primacy index is not commonly seen in head-injured individuals; however, a minority of simulators show such a pattern (her primacy index correctly identified only 13% of malingerers, with only a 3% false-positive rate). That is, a suppressed primacy effect appears relatively specific, but not particularly sensitive, to malingering. Further, others have found that indices based on serial position effects fail to reliably distinguish between simulators and controls (Bernard, Houston, & Natoli, 1993; Sullivan et al., 2002). Other indicators (e.g., discrepancies in recall-recognition scores; failure to recognize words recalled at least three times on the learning trials) are of some utility but are not very effective in identifying deliberate attempts to perform poorly on the RAVT (Suhr & Gunstad, 2000; Sullivan et al., 2002).

The addition of a second delayed recall and recognition trial at 60 min (referred to as the expanded AVLT or AVLTX) may enhance diagnostic accuracy. Barrash et al. (2004) constructed an exaggeration index (EI) based on the notion that malingerers would have difficulty estimating their 30-min performance, keeping track of the words that they reported and those that they feigned forgetting. The EI is a composite index reflecting the extent to which memory performance is characterized by inconsistencies that are atypical of brain-damaged individuals. It comprises seven aspects of improbable performance: exceedingly poor learning, lack of primacy effect, worsening recall, worsening recognition, failure to recognize learned words, recalled words not recognized, and exceedingly poor recognition. The EI demonstrated good sensitivity, identifying two thirds of the probable malingerers as such, and positive predictive accuracy (PPA) was 0.84 (with a base rate of malingering of 30%). In comparison to the EI, the Recognition Memory Test (Warrington, 1984) demonstrated a higher level of sensitivity but lower PPA (0.67).

Measures derived from the RAVLT (e.g., recognition trial score, delayed recall score) show modest/moderate relations with other indices of motivational status (e.g., Warrington Recognition Memory Test, Rey 15-Item), although the amount of shared variance is less than 50% (Nelson, Boone, Dueck, Wagener, Lu, & Grills, 2003). The implication is that the RAVLT provides nonredundant information and can serve as a relatively independent source of information regarding the validity of neuropsychological test performance.

Summary

The value of indices of SOP developed from conventional tests is that it allows them to do "double duty," providing evidence regarding performance as well as validity of results (see also Meyers & Volbrecht, 2003). One can argue that such measures should be investigated for all existing tests that are widely used, and that all new conventional measures or revisions of existing measures should be constructed with "built-in" indices of SOP that are evaluated as part of the norming process. In addition to being cost-efficient, use of these indicators is important for other reasons.

First, because individuals may have variable or inconsistent motivation across the course of an assessment, these indicators compliment SVTs serving as useful additional validity checks. Second, the literature suggests that these indicators, while somewhat correlated with one another, may provide relatively independent information regarding performance validity. This is probably due in part to inter-individual variability; some may feign or exaggerate a memory problem, whereas others may exaggerate cognitive slowing or reading difficulties. These different SOP profiles may be better detected by techniques specific to various conventional neuropsychological measures than by standard SVTs, which, with few exceptions, are presented as tests of memory. In addition, analog studies have demonstrated that SVTs do not have perfect sensitivity, and so will always miss some malingerers. Further, given the easy availability of the neuropsychological literature to the general public (as well as to lawyers), claimants may recognize standard forced-choice procedures and evade detection. Finally, as Bernard et al. (1993) have pointed out, developing validity checks in neuropsychological instruments allows the clinician to make inferences about the vulnerability of the other tests used in the examination. Considering these issues, whenever an examination is in the context of incentive to malinger or underperformance is otherwise suspected, clinicians should make use of all well-validated indices of SOP derived from the conventional measures that they employ. Given the amount of research activity in this area, clinicians are advised to keep abreast of current developments in the field.

It is important to bear in mind, however, that these indicators have typically been developed for use with young adults and to assess the performance of individuals who suffered TBIs. Their use with persons outside this age range (e.g., the very young or very old) or with those complaining of other conditions (e.g., chronic pain, depression, and stress-related disorders) has received relatively less study and should be undertaken with due caution. More generally, all psychometric measures of SOP are inherently limited in that while they may reliably detect underperformance, they cannot be used in isolation to diagnose malingering. Such a diagnosis requires integration of multiple types of information and full consideration of exclusionary conditions or factors (Slick, Sherman, & Iverson, 1999).

Acknowledgment

This work was supported in part by an NSERC grant to E. Strauss.

References

Ashendorf, L., O'Bryant, S. E., & McCaffrey, R. J. (2003). Specificity of malingering detection strategies in older adults using the CVLT and WCST. *The Clinical Neuropsychologist*, *17*, 255–262.

Barrash, J., Suhr, J., & Manzel, K. (2004). Detecting poor effort and malingering with an expanded version of the Auditory Verbal Learning Test (AVLTX): Validation with clinical samples. *Journal of Clinical and Experimental Neuropsychology*, *26*, 125–140.

Bernard, L. C. (1991). The detection of faked deficits on the Rey Auditory Verbal Learning Test. *Archives of Clinical Neuropsychology*, *6*, 81–88.

Bernard, L. C., Houston, W., & Natoli, L. (1993). Malingering on neuropsychological memory tests: Potential objective indicators. *Journal of Clinical Psychology*, *49*, 45–53.

Bernard, L. C., McGrath, M. J., & Houston, W. (1996). The differential effects of simulating malingering, closed head injury, and other CNS pathology on the Wisconsin Card Sorting Test: Support for the "pattern of performance" hypothesis. *Archives of Clinical Neuropsychology*, *11*, 231–245.

Bianchini, K. J., Mathias, C. W., & Greve, K. (2001). Symptom validity testing: A critical review. *The Clinical Neuropsychologist*, *15*, 19–45.

Binder, L. M., Kelly, M. P., Villanueva, M. R., & Winslow, M. M. (2003). Motivation and neuropsychological test performance following mild head injury. *Journal of Clinical and Experimental Neuropsychology*, *25*, 420–430.

Binder, L. M., Villanueva, M. R., Howieson, D., & Moore, R. T. (1993). The Rey AVLT recognition memory task measures motivational impairment after mild head trauma. *Archives of Clinical Neuropsychology*, *8*, 137–147.

Boake, C. (2000). Edouard Claparède and the Auditory Verbal Learning Test. *Journal of Clinical and Experimental Neuropsychology*, *22*, 286–292.

Bolter, J. F., Picano, J. J., & Zych, K. (1985). *Item error frequencies for the Halstead Category Test: An index of performance validity*. Paper presented at the annual meeting of the National Academy of Neuropsychology, Philadelphia, PA.

Camara, W. J., Nathan, J. S., & Puente, A. E. (2000). Psychological test usage: Implications in professional psychology. *Professional Psychology: Research and Practice*, *31*, 141–154.

Chouinard, M.-J., & Rouleau, I. (1997). The 48-Pictures Test: A two-alternative forced-choice recognition test for the detection of malingering. *Journal of the International Neuropsychological Society*, *3*, 545–552.

DiCarlo, M. A., Gfeller, J. D., & Oliveri, M. V. (2000). Effects of coaching on detecting feigned cognitive impairment with the Category Test. *Archives of Clinical Neuropsychology*, *15*, 399–413.

Donders, J. (2001). Clinical utility of the Category Test as a multidimensional instrument. *Psychological Assessment*, *13*, 592–594.

Glassmire, D. M., Bierley, R. A., Wieniewski, A. M., Greene, R. L., Kennedy, J. E., & Date, E. (2003). Using the WMS-III Faces subtest to detect malingered memory impairment. *Journal of Clinical and Experimental Neuropsychology*, *25*, 465–481.

Greiffenstein, M. F., Baker, W. J., & Gola, T. (1994). Validation of malingered amnesia measures with a large clinical sample. *Psychological Assessment*, *6*, 218–224.

Greve, K. W., Bianchini, K. J., Mathias, C. W., Houston, R. J., & Crouch, J. A. (2002b). Detecting malingered performance with the Wisconsin Card Sorting Test: A preliminary investigation in traumatic brain injury. *The Clinical Neuropsychologist*, *16*(2), 179–191.

Heaton, R. K., Smith, H. H. Jr., Lehman, R. A. W., & Vogt, A. T. (1978). Prospects for faking believable deficits on neuropsychological testing. *Journal of Consulting and Clinical Psychology*, *46*, 892–900.

Iverson, G. L., & Franzen, M. D. (1994). The Recognition Memory Test, Digit Span, and Knox Cube Test as markers of malingered memory impairment. *Assessment*, *4*, 323–334.

Iverson, G. L., & Tulsky, D. S. (2003). Detecting malingering on the WAIS-III: Unusual Digit Span performance patterns in the normal population and in clinical groups. *Archives of Clinical Neuropsychology*, *18*, 1–9.

Johnstone, B., Holland, D., & Hewett, J. E. (1997). The construct validity of the Category Test: Is it a measure of reasoning or intelligence? *Psychological Assessment*, *9*, 28–33.

Killgore, W. D. S., & DellaPietra, L. (2000). Using the WMS-III to detect malingering: Empirical validation of the Rarely Missed Index (RMI). *Journal of Clinical and Experimental Neuropsychology*, *22*, 761–771.

King, J. H., Gfeller, J. D., & Davis, H. P. (1998). Detecting simulated memory impairment with the Rey Auditory Verbal Learning Test: Implications of base rates and study generalizability. *Journal of Clinical and Experimental Neuropsychology*, *20*, 603–612.

King, J. H., Sweet, J. J., Sherer, M., Curtiss, G., & Vanderploeg, R. D. (2002). Validity indices within the Wisconsin Card Sorting Test: Application of new and previously researched multivariate procedures in multiple traumatic brain injury samples. *The Clinical Neuropsychologist*, *16*, 506–523.

Langeluddecke, P. M., & Lucas, S. K. (2003). Wechsler Adult Intelligence Scale—third edition findings in relation to severity of brain injury in litigants. *The Clinical Neuropsychologist*, *17*, 273–284.

Lindeboom, J. (1989). Who needs cutting points? *Journal of Clinical Psychology*, *45*, 679–683.

Mathias, C. W., Greve, K. W., Bianchini, K. J. (2002). Detecting malingered neurocognitive dysfunction using the Reliable Digit Span in traumatic brain injury. *Assessment*, *9*, 254–269.

Meyers, J. E., Morrison, A. L., & Miller, J. C. (2001). How low is too low, revisited: Sentence repetition and AVLT-recognition in the detection of malingering. *Applied Neuropsychology*, *4*, 234–241.

Meyers, J. E., & Volbrecht, M. E. (2003). A validation of multiple malingering detection methods in a large clinical sample. *Archives of Clinical Neuropsychology*, *18*, 261–276.

Millis, S. R., Ross, S. R., & Ricker, J. H. (1998). Detection of incomplete effort on the Wechsler Adult Intelligence Scale—Revised: A cross validation. *Journal of Clinical and Experimental Neuropsychology*, *20*, 167–173.

Millis, S. R., & Volinsky, C. T. (2001). Assessment of response bias in mild head injury: Beyond malingering tests. *Journal of Clinical and Experimental Neuropsychology*, *23*, 809–828.

Mittenberg, W., Azrin, R., Millsaps, C., & Heilbronner, R. (1993). Identification of malingered head injury on the Wechsler Memory Scale-Revised. *Psychological Assessment*, *5*, 34–40.

Mittenberg, W., Patton, C., Canyock, E. M., & Condit, D. C. (2002). Base rates of malingering and symptom exaggeration. *Journal of Clinical and Experimental Neuropsychology*, *24*, 1094–1102.

Mittenberg, W., Theroux-Fichera, S., Heilbronner, R. L., & Zielinshi, R. E. (1995). Identification of malingered head injury on the Wechsler Intelligence Scale-Revised. *Professional Psychology: Research and Practice*, *26*, 491–498.

Mossman, D. (2003). Daubert, cognitive malingering, and test accuracy. *Law and Human Behaviour*, *27*, 229–249.

Nelson, N. W., Boone, K., Dueck, A., Wagener, L., Lu, P., & Grills, C. (2003). Relationships between eight measures of suspect effort. *The Clinical Neuropsychologist*, *17*, 263–272.

Poreh, A. M. (2000). The Quantified Process Approach: An emerging methodology to neuropsychological assessment. *The Clinical Neuropsychologist*, *14*, 212–222.

Reitan, R. M., & Wolfson, D. (1996). The question of validity of neuropsychological test scores among head-injured litigants: Development of a Dissimulation Index. *Archives of Clinical Neuropsychology*, *11*, 573–580.

Sherman, D. S., Boone, K. B., Lu, P., & Razani, J. (2002). Re-examination of a Rey Auditory Verbal Learning Test/Rey Complex Figure discriminant function to detect suspect effort. *The Clinical Neuropsychologist*, *16*, 242–250.

Simmel, M. S., & Counts, S. (1957). Some stable determinants of perception, thinking, and learning: A study based on the analysis of a single test. *Genetic Psychology Monographs*, *56*, 3–157.

Slick, D. J., Sherman, E. M. S., & Iverson, G. L. (1999). Diagnostic criteria for malingered neurocognitive dysfunction: Proposed standards for clinical practice and research. *The Clinical Neuropsychologist*, *13*, 545–561.

Strauss, E., Hultsch, D. F., Hunter, M., Slick, D. J., Patry, B., & Levy-Bencheton, J. (2000). Using intraindividual variability to detect malingering in cognitive performance. *The Clinical Neuropsychologist*, *14*, 420–432.

Strauss, E., Slick, D. J., Levy-Bencheton, J., Hunter, M., Macdonald, S. W. S., & Hultsch, D. F. (2002). Interindividual variability as an indicator of malingering in head injury. *Archives of Clinical Neuropsychology*, *17*, 423–444.

Suhr, J. A. (2002). Malingering, coaching, and the serial position effect. *Archives of Clinical Neuropsychology*, *17*, 69–78.

Suhr, J. A., & Boyer, D. (1999). Use of the Wisconsin Card Sorting Test in the detection of malingering in student simulator and patient sample. *Journal of Clinical and Experimental Neuropsychology*, *4*, 500–514.

Suhr, J. A., & Gunstad, J. (2000). The effects of coaching on the sensitivity and specificity of malingering measures. *Archives of Clinical Neuropsychology*, *15*, 415–424.

Sullivan, K., Deffenti, C., & Keane, B. (2002). Malingering on the RAVLT Part II. Detection strategies. *Archives of Clinical Neuropsychology*, *17*, 223–233.

Sullivan, K., Keane, B., & Deffenti, C. (2001). Malingering on the RAVLT Part I. Deterrence strategies. *Archives of Clinical Neuropsychology*, *16*, 627–641.

Sweet, J. J., & King, J. H. (2002). Category test validity indicators: Overview and practice recommendations. *Journal of Forensic Neuropsychology*, *3*, 241–274.

Tenhula, W. N., & Sweet, J. J. (1996). Double cross validation of the Booklet Category Test in detecting malingered traumatic brain injury. *The Clinical Neuropsychologist*, *10*, 104–116.

Trueblood, W. (1994). Qualitative and quantitative characteristics of malingered and other invalid WAIS-R and clinical memory data. *Journal of Clinical and Experimental Neuropsychology*, *16*, 597–607.

Trueblood, W., & Schmidt, M. (1993). Malingering and other validity considerations in the neuropsychological evaluation of mild head injury. *Journal of Clinical and Experimental Neuropsychology*, *15*, 578–590.

Warrington, E. K. (1984). *Recognition Memory Test manual.* Windsor, England: NFER Nelson.

Wechsler, D. (1955). *Wechsler Adult Intelligence Scale—Revised.* New York: The Psychological Corporation.

Wechsler, D. (1981). *Wechsler Adult Intelligence Scale—Revised.* New York: The Psychological Corporation.

Wechsler, D. (1997). *Wechsler Adult Intelligence Scale—third edition: Administration and scoring manual.* San Antonio, TX: The Psychological Corporation.

Afterword: Future advances of the Quantified Process Approach

Amir M. Poreh

It is widely accepted that the success of any scientific discipline in the 21st century, as that of almost any enterprise, is affected by its ability to rapidly and continuously assimilate and correctly utilize the powerful tools and concepts created by the information revolution. Just as the invention of the printing press in the 15th century led to the demise of the handwritten manuscript and the emergence of the industrial revolution, so did the invention of the modern computer lead to the demise of manual data collection and the emergence of the information revolution. Industries that refuse to embrace new technologies are at risk of becoming obsolete.

Clinical neuropsychology has been reluctant to assimilate innovative information technology (IT) toward the advancement of one-on-one psychological and cognitive tests. Clinicians continue to record test performance using pencil and paper. Consequently, they can only rely on sum scores and tabulated norms to make clinical decisions. This method has been the standard practice since the 1930s despite the growing discontent with the resolution of the data that it generates, namely, the attainment of the sum score on any particular test may result from the use of different cognitive skills which may be reflected by various solution paths. Armengol de la Miyar, Moes, and Kaplan (2003, p. 76) recognized the limitations of the current standard practice and wrote: "One of the potential advantages of computerized approaches to assessment is the ability to capture sequential qualitative aspects of performance, although this potential remains largely unfulfilled at this time."

The slow assimilation of IT by practicing neuropsychologists may be due to the complexity of developing and validating new computerized tests, and the difficulty of incorporating the qualitative observations clinicians make, as recommended by proponents of the Boston Process Approach. Thus, it is not surprising that some clinical neuropsychologists have opted to move toward the use of functional neuroimaging to study cognition. Although this method of inquiry may provide new insights into brain–behavior relationships, it will take considerable time before such studies produce practical assessment tools and even if such tools become available, few consumers will have the resources to pay for such studies.

Against this backdrop, the emergence of the Quantified Process Approach to neuropsychological assessment reflects a refreshing, fundamental paradigm shift. This shift is driven, in part, by what Kohn (1963) termed "agents of change" that are outside the mainstream of our profession, such as the changing role of neuropsychologists in rehabilitation and forensic settings. In these settings there is a growing need for cost-effective and higher-resolution tests that adhere to quantitative and rigorous scientific methodology. The collection of studies in this book provides a blueprint for the future of this emerging paradigm.

Naturally, in this case too, one wonders whether practicing clinical neuropsychologists will be able to carry out the cumbersome data collection of quantitative processes in their daily practice. Will a clinician manually calculate the clustering and switching indexes on verbal fluency tasks as described by Angela K. Troyer and Morris Moscovitch in Chapter 9? Will clinicians use their resources to calculate the multiple indexes of the Auditory Verbal Learning Test as described by John L. Woodard in Chapter 8?

The solution to this problem needs to be guided by several maxims. First, one cannot expect this stage to arrive before we clearly delineate what process-related information needs to be collected. Next, the proposed solution must maintain the one-on-one format of traditional tests. Computerized tests that require the examinee to sit in front of a monitor and respond using a keyboard or a response box to series of stimuli are useful, but are not practical for the assessment of distractible or moderately impaired patients. Moreover, many tasks, particularly those that require the manual manipulation of objects and use of a pencil and paper (such as the Trail Making Test), are not amenable to this format.

To overcome this hurdle, a novel method for collecting and analyzing process-related data has been developed and patented. According to this method, the examiner, not the examinee, is placed in front of the computer. A graphical representation of the task (i.e., a pegboard) is displayed on the monitor in the form of a series of buttons. Each time an examinee places a peg or completes a predetermined portion of a task, the examiner clicks on the corresponding button, which is displayed on the monitor. Using this method, the sequence of clicks reproduces the examinee's solution pass. Once these data are collected, they are analyzed using algorithms that are based on either data- or theory-driven models (see Chapter 4). The resulting data make it easy to calculate complex indexes in real time, using either the Composition or Decomposition Paradigms. This method also allows for real-time statistical analyses as well as the use of multivariable normative regression equations instead of tabulated norms. We hope that by using this method, practicing clinicians will be able to enhance the resolution of traditional measures and discern the role of various neurocognitive mechanisms that underlie these tests. In some cases, the use of this method may improve the detection of examinees employing suboptimal effort strategies, as is discussed by Daniel J. Slick and Esther Strauss in Chapter 17.

What I have discussed up to now is the use of IT to streamline what neuropsychologists have done all along—administer tests and collect data. However, as noted by the renowned American economist Peter Drucker (1998), the next information revolution is well underway. "It is not a revolution in technology, machinery, techniques, software, or speed. It is a revolution in concepts. The next information revolution asks what is the meaning of information, and what is its purpose? And this is leading rapidly to redefining the tasks to be done with the help of information, and with it, to redefining the institutions that do these tasks." Thus, borrowing from Drucker's outlook about the future of economics, the next information revolution in neuropsychology might emerge in the form of the development of indexes for existing measures that would not only allow neuropsychologists to describe the present neurocognitive functioning of examinees but would also provide quantifiable, predictive, decision-useful information.

To sum up, the diverse individual contributions collected in this book confirm the existence of a multifaceted effort to explore the information embedded in traditional cognitive tests, and outlines a way to strengthen the field of neuropsychological assessment. This effort ensures that cognitive assessment will continue to play a role in both clinical and research settings and provides the impetus for incorporating modern IT into the mainstream neurocognitive assessment, allowing practitioners to integrate their test findings with our current understanding of modern neuroscience. Such a feat requires the collaboration of neuropsychologists in the formation of large databases as well as the embracement of modern data collection methods. In doing so, the field of neuropsychology will continue to thrive by contributing unique information to neuroscience.

References

Armengol de la Miyar, C., Moes, E. J., & Kaplan, E. (2003). In R. Fernández-Ballesteros (Ed.), *Encyclopedia of psychological assessment*. Thousand Oaks, CA: Sage.

Drucker, P. (1998). Next information revolution. *Forbes*, August, 47–58.

Author Index

Subject Index